The Three Battles of Wanat

Also by Mark Bowden

Doctor Dealer

Bringing the Heat

Black Hawk Down

Killing Pablo

Finders Keepers

Road Work

Guests of the Ayatollah

The Best Game Ever

Worm

The Finish

The Three Battles of Wanat

and Other True Stories

Mark Bowden

Atlantic Monthly Press
New York

Published simultaneously in Canada
Printed in the United States of America

FIRST EDITION

ISBN 978-0-8021-2411-1
eISBN 978-0-8021-9066-6

Atlantic Monthly Press
an imprint of Grove Atlantic
154 West 14th Street
New York, NY 10011

Distributed by Publishers Group West

groveatlantic.com

16 17 18 19 20   10 9 8 7 6 5 4 3 2 1

For John Hersey

Contents

SPORTS

ESSAYS

Introduction

I am particularly grateful to *Vanity Fair* and the *Atlantic* for supporting not just me, but so many other journalists intent on treating ideas and stories in depth. In my early work as a newspaper reporter I often felt that my finished stories had just scratched the surface. Like many reporters, I was in a running battle with my editors for more time and more space. Fortunately, I have had very sympathetic editors. Deeper investment usually resulted in a richer story.

Take, for example, Wanat, the title story of this collection. When my editor at *Vanity Fair*, Cullen Murphy, first suggested it to me in August 2010, I envisioned it as a detailed account of a tragic 2008 battle in Afghanistan that had left nine American soldiers killed and twenty-seven wounded. I had not written a story about combat since *Black Hawk Down* ten years earlier. This new one concerned a mountain combat outpost under construction that had been attacked by a large Taliban force and nearly overrun. When I began I imagined a story much like the one I told in that book.

But true stories are never alike. The more you stir, the thicker the stew. I was surprised to discover, when I started reporting, that there had been not one but several detailed investigations of what had happened at Wanat. The one that had received the greatest attention was a preliminary draft of a study by the U.S. Army Combat Studies Institute. Written by Douglas Cubbison, a contract military historian, it was sharply critical of the army units involved, placing blame for inadequate defenses at Wanat on poor command decisions.

Cubbison's draft had inspired detailed stories by the *Washington Post*, by NBC News, and by the noted military affairs blogger Tom Ricks. It was indeed rare for a study from that source to be controversial, and especially for it to be so sharply critical of officers still serving. One of the things that made Cubbison's take on Wanat so attractive to reporters was the poignant human story behind it. The institute's study had been instigated by Dave Brostrom, the father of Jonathan Brostrom, a young lieutenant who had been killed in the fight. Dave Brostrom, a retired army colonel, had examined detailed reports about the incident, and had become convinced that the death of his son and the others at Wanat had resulted from incompetent or reckless leadership. When I spoke with Cubbison it became clear that Dave Brostrom not only had requested the report but had played an important role in shaping it. The story of a career army officer determined to hold his peers accountable was irresistible.

But after meeting Dave Brostrom; Lieutenant Colonel Bill Ostlund, the officer who bore the brunt of his criticism; and others involved up and down the command chain, I found a story far more complex than that. It involved a grieving father troubled not only by command decisions in Afghanistan but also by his own role in placing his son at that vulnerable combat outpost. It involved commanders struggling to fulfill a difficult mission with limited men and resources at a time when the primary

American military focus had shifted to Iraq. The string of reports and findings ended, ironically, by faulting, of all people, Jonathan Brostrom. *Vanity Fair* published my account in December 2011, nearly a year and a half after Cullen first suggested it to me. Without the time and editorial support to fully explore all of these branches of the story, and to travel and meet personally with those directly involved, I would never have been able to arrive at my own fuller understanding of what happened.

However my own use of the opportunity is judged, magazines (now also websites) that encourage long-form reporting and writing are carrying on one of the great traditions in American journalism. From the work of abolitionists who recorded the brutal practices of slave owners; Nellie Bly's famous trip to a madhouse for the *New York World*; Ida Wells's courageous documentation of lynching; the powerful exposés of Lincoln Steffens, Ida Tarbell, Upton Sinclair, and the other great contributors to *McClure's* in the early twentieth century; and the work of John Hersey, Gay Talese, and Truman Capote to the flamboyant New Journalists of *Rolling Stone*, *Ramparts*, *Harper's*, and *Esquire* who so inspired me as a college student, journalists free to explore every branch of a complex story have produced a body of work every bit as important to the canon of American literature as that of novelists, poets, playwrights, and screenwriters.

I see more of it today than ever, even as print publications dwindle. The Internet affords, if anything, a superior platform for every kind of journalism, and I have no doubt that long-form narratives will remain essential. Prose is the most subtle and precise form of communication: the language of thought itself. No other medium is capable of so deeply exploring and explaining human experience. At the same time that headlines and images flash around the world on cell phones instantaneously, time and again we learn that our initial take on a story is incomplete and often wrong. Whether it's social media prominently fingering an innocent man in the days after the Boston Marathon bombing, or early reports of a "trench coat Mafia" from the scene of the Columbine High School shootings, until an independent reporter is turned loose to dig deeper and write longer, we don't understand what really happened. This is true of the stories we think we know, and also of those we would never hear if journalists were not encouraged to follow their own noses. We would never, for instance, have heard the story of Henrietta Lacks, whose fatal tumor was used to create the cell line for cancer research worldwide, or of a quirky investor like Steve Eisman, who famously foresaw the clay feet of Wall Street's collateralized debt obligations, and cashed in when the stock market crashed in 2007. In both of these cases, it was the professional curiosity and unique talents of Rebecca Skloot and Michael Lewis that uncovered stories essential to our understanding of the modern world.

And I don't buy for a moment the notion that people don't read these stories. My own experience directly contradicts it. I regard as entirely bogus the popular theory that young people, in particular, have a declining attention span or are unwilling to read anything longer than a sound bite. My children, my students, and my readers are better informed at a young age than I ever was, and are every bit as receptive as I am to a story that grabs them and won't let them go. I also think that writers have a responsibility not to bore people. If the story is long, it had damn well better be fun to read.

I have in some cases restored these stories to the form I gave them prior to editing for publication. The demands of fitting them into magazines sometimes required making cuts I would rather not have made. I have also made corrections suggested by helpful readers, some kindly, others less so, but I am always happy to get things right.

WAR

The Three Battles of Wanat

Published as "Echoes from a Distant Battlefield,"
Vanity Fair, December 2011

1. The Lieutenant's Battle

One man on the rocky slope overhead was probably just a shepherd. Two men were suspicious, but might have been two shepherds. Three men were trouble. When Second Platoon spotted four, then five, the soldiers prepared to shoot.

Dark blue had just begun to streak the sky over the black peaks that towered on all sides of their position. The day was July 13, 2008. Captain Matthew Myer stood at the driver's-side door of a Humvee parked near the center of a flat, open expanse about the length of a football field where the platoon was building a new combat outpost, known as a COP. The vehicle was parked on a ramp carved in the rocky soil by the engineering squad's single Bobcat, with its front wheels high so that its TOW* missiles could be more easily aimed up at the sheer slopes to the west.

* Tube-launched, optically tracked, wire-guided.

The new outpost was hard by the tiny Afghan village of Wanat, at the bottom of a stark natural bowl; and the forty-nine American soldiers who had arrived just days earlier felt dangerously exposed.

Myer gave the order for an immediate coordinated attack with the platoon's two heaviest weapons—the TOW system and a 120-millimeter mortar—which sat in a small dugout a few paces west of the ramp surrounded by HESCO barriers, canvas and wire frames that are filled with dirt and stone to create temporary walls. The captain was walking back to his command post about fifty yards north when the attack started.

It was twenty minutes past four in the morning. Myer and Second Platoon, one of three platoons under his command scattered in these mountains, were at war in a place as distant from America's consciousness as it was simply far away. Wanat was legendarily remote, high in the Hindu Kush, at the southern edge of Konar Province in Afghanistan's rugged northeast. It shared a long border with the equally forbidding territories of north Pakistan. Here was the landscape where Rudyard Kipling in 1888 had set his cautionary tale, *The Man Who Would Be King*, about British soldiers with ill-fated dreams of power and conquest. Little had changed. It is one of the most mountainous regions of the world, with steep gray-brown peaks reaching as high as twenty-five thousand feet. Its jagged mountains towered over V-shaped valleys that angled sharply down to winding rivers. Wanat was at the confluence of the Waygul River and a small tributary. It was home to about fifty families, who carved out a spare existence on a series of green irrigated terraces that rose like graceful stairsteps to the foot of the stony eastern slopes. A single partly paved road wound south toward Camp Blessing, the headquarters for Task Force Rock—Second Battalion, 503rd Infantry Regiment, 173rd Airborne Brigade. This battalion HQ was just five miles away in the fish-eye lens of a high-flying drone, but on the ground it was a perilous journey of almost an hour—perilous because improvised explosives and ambushes were common. In Wanat it was easy to feel that you were hunkered down on the far edge of nowhere fighting the only people in the world who seemed to badly want the place. You needed something like a graduate degree in geopolitics and strategy to have any idea why it was worth dying for.

Yet killing and dying—mostly killing—were what Task Force Rock was doing here on the front lines of America's forgotten war. In army parlance, Afghanistan had become an "economy of force" action, which meant, in so many words, "Make do." The hopeful infrastructure and cultural development projects that had arrived with the first wave of Americans seven years earlier had dried to a trickle. Ever since President Bush had followed up rapid military success in Afghanistan with a massive invasion of Iraq in 2003, the nation's attention had been riveted there. But the war against the Taliban, Al Qaeda, and like-minded local militias had never ended in these mountains. Small units of American soldiers were dug into scores of isolated tiny combat posts, perched high on promontories, crouched behind HESCO walls and barriers of concrete and sand, ostensibly projecting the largely theoretical Afghan central government into far-flung valleys and villages where politics and loyalties had been stubbornly local and tribal since long before Kipling.

Second Platoon was part of Myer's Chosen Company, the "Chosen Few," who wore patches on their uniforms displaying a stylized skull fashioned after the insignia of the Marvel comic book character "Punisher." Twenty-first-century America had staked its claim to this patch of ground, punctiliously negotiating its purchase from village landlords. The platoon had occupied it in darkness, in a driving rain, just three days earlier.

Myer had arrived only the day before. He had sketched out a basic plan for the outpost, and then left supervision of the construction to First Lieutenant Jonathan Brostrom, a cocky, muscular, popular twenty-four-year-old platoon leader from Hawaii. Brostrom had a long, slender face, and dark brown hair worn, like the other soldiers', in a buzz cut, high and tight. His body had been sculptured by daily weight lifting over the fourteen months of this deployment. After consultations with Myer and the battalion commander, Lieutenant Colonel Bill Ostlund, the lieutenant had drawn up detailed maps of the new outpost on whatever scraps of paper he could find, so that he could show his men sectors of fire for all of the vehicles, placement of the Claymore mines, fighting positions, latrine, and everything else. A small force of Afghan engineers with heavy equipment were to handle most of the construction, but they had been delayed at Camp Blessing, awaiting the completion of a road-clearing mission that would enable them to make the trip safely. In the interim, the platoon itself had begun digging out and building the outpost's preliminary defenses, toiling through hundred-degree-plus days with limited water and resources, hacking away at the baked, stubborn soil with picks and shovels, building sandbag walls, stringing razor wire, and filling the HESCOs as well as they could—the Bobcat could not reach high enough to dump earth into the frames, so they had been cut down to just four feet.

The men of the platoon had felt particularly vulnerable in these first days, expecting to be attacked. It was particularly unsettling because they had nearly completed their hazardous tour. They were just two weeks away from heading home. Platoon Sergeant David Dzwik had rallied them as best he could to complete this dangerous assignment before leaving, pointing out that they had signed on to fight for the whole fifteen-month tour, and how they were better equipped to handle the danger than the inexperienced troops who would replace them. But down deep Dzwik shared their misgivings. He hated both the task and the location.

It wasn't just that the outpost sat at the bottom of a giant bowl. There were dead zones all around it where you couldn't see. The ground dipped down just outside the perimeter, down to the creek, which ran to the west, and to the road that ran bordered it to the southeast. The battalion could not provide them with steady, overhead visual surveillance because of weather and limited availability of drones. So they lacked a clear eye on the terrain. Where the land sloped uphill to the northeast there were the bazaar and the mosque and other buildings. It was as though the Afghan village—and Dzwik was a long way from trusting even the Afghans whom he knew—were staring right down at them. There were just too many places for the enemy to hide. In the preceding weeks, he had heard reports of Taliban by the hundreds gathering for an attack on Bella, the outpost they had evacuated to move here. They had managed to clear out before that attack came, but Bella was only four or five miles north. And even though the terrain was formidable, the enemy was skilled at moving rapidly and silently through it. Worse, everybody in the Waygul Valley knew exactly where the Americans had purchased property and planned to resettle.

Dzwik was a puckish, solid, career soldier from Michigan who enlisted after starring on the gridiron in high school and realizing that he would never be able to sit still long enough to finish college. He was fit and full of youthful energy, and after a boyhood spent hunting, fishing, and camping he took readily to the rigors of military life. He had been in the army now for thirteen years and planned to stay until retirement, even though the job meant spending precious little time at home with the wife and three kids. This was his second tour in Afghanistan. He had inherited the position of platoon sergeant when his predecessor, the man for whom this COP was named, Sergeant First Class Matthew Kahler, had been killed by a shot fired by a "friendly" Afghan soldier. The army had ruled it an accident, but Dzwik, like many in the platoon, wasn't convinced. They considered the tragedy of Matt Kahler's death somehow emblematic of the whole Afghan conflict.

Despite the precarious position they now occupied, Dzwik had been forced to slow construction of defenses because of the extreme heat and limited water supplies. Gradually, as the stunted

HESCOs were filled and as shallow excavations were chipped out, their position improved, and Dzwik found himself hating it a little less. When Myer arrived on the fourth day, the captain was impressed by all that had been accomplished, but he could see that the COP was still far from secure.

All of the fighting positions were makeshift. The command post was a sunken space about two feet deep, no larger than a big conference table, framed by Dzwik's Humvee, a line of HESCOs, and the outer mud wall of a structure built to house the village's bazaar. Southward down the gentle sloping ground were the TOW Humvee, parked on the ramp; two mortar positions similarly excavated and surrounded by HESCO walls; and, farther south toward the road, two more positions, the closer one marked by a Humvee, and beyond it an Afghan army position, placed there to man the outer checkpoint on the road. There were several more dugout fighting positions to the north, and two larger positions toward the northern edge manned by the Afghan troops, with two Humvees armed with M-19 grenade launchers. The Bobcat was already at work that morning digging a trench around one of the mortar positions to drain off water that had pooled in it the day before.

The biggest problem was obvious: the platoon did not control the high ground. Every outpost on this frontier had observation posts high in the hills to spot approaching enemy troops, and sent out regular foot patrols to make contact with the locals and to discourage hostile approaches. Lacking enough men for both construction and patrolling, Brostrom had chosen to concentrate on construction. He had sent several perfunctory patrols just to scout the immediate vicinity, but that was it. And the platoon had yet to establish a useful observation post.

It was a pressing priority. As Myer was giving the order to fire that morning, Brostrom was busy assembling a thirteen-man patrol to look for a suitable location in the hills to the south. As was the daily practice, the entire platoon had all been up for almost an hour, all the men dressed in full battle gear and "standing-to" their small fighting positions.

They did have one elevated position, which they called Topside, and it was visible to the northeast over the rooftops of the bazaar. The nine men there had two machine guns and a grenade launcher in three fighting positions behind a maze of low sandbag walls and a loose perimeter of unstaked razor wire. Topside was midway up the lazy terrace steps, and was set against three large boulders. Myer was not happy with it. It was not high enough to be very useful, and the men there were dangerously isolated from the main force. But he could understand Brostrom's thinking. Any farther away, Topside would have been impossible to quickly reinforce. Until the promised engineering group arrived and freed up more men to patrol, it was about as far away as the platoon dared to put it. As it was, it would be hard to defend if it came under attack.

Which it did, suddenly, on this morning. Two long bursts of machine-gun fire were followed immediately by a crashing wave of rocket-propelled grenades, or RPGs. It felt and sounded as if a thousand came at them at once, deafening blasts and fiery explosions on all sides, from close range and continuing without letup. Myer judged that the first had come from behind the homes looking down on them from Wanat, but soon enough they were zeroing in from everywhere. The TOW and mortar teams had not yet fired; they had still been checking grid numbers when the onslaught began.

Myer ran the rest of the way to the command post, ducking behind cover and standing in the open door of his Humvee beside his radio operator Sergeant John Hayes, who had two FM radios, one tuned to the platoon's internal net and the other to the battalion headquarters at Camp Blessing.

"Whatever you can give me, I'm going to need," Myer told headquarters calmly, the sound of intense gunfire and explosions in the background lending all the emphasis his words needed. "This is a Ranch House–style attack," he said, referring to the worst single assault his men had experienced months earlier at an outpost by that name farther north.

No one at Wanat expected this level of intensity to continue for long. Often a single big show of force—an artillery volley or a bomb dropped from an aircraft—would be enough to end things. The enemy would typically scatter. But Wanat was too remote to get help fast. The closest air assets were at the Forward Operating Base Fenty in Jalalabad, and it would be nearly an hour before planes or choppers would arrive. Reinforcements by road would take at least forty-five minutes. The big guns at Blessing had to be pointed nearly straight up to lob shells over the mountains; this diminished their effectiveness, especially when the enemy was so close to the outpost. Some Taliban were shooting from the newly dug latrine, right on the western perimeter.

Myer directed artillery to fire on the riverbed that ran near the latrine ditch along the western edge of the village. It might not hit anyone, but the blast alone might make the enemy think twice.

"Hey, shoot these three targets," he said; "then we can adjust them as needed."

Before he had time to finish that order, the main source of enemy fire had shifted to the northeast, toward Topside, which was getting hammered. Grenade explosions could be heard.

"We have to do something," said Brostrom. The men were too pinned down to assemble a large group, but the lieutenant knew Topside was outgunned. "We have to get up there," he said.

"OK, go," said Myer.

It was like the lieutenant to insist on joining the firing line. It had been an issue between him and the captain. Myer was six years older than Brostrom, with five long years of experience in warfare in Iraq and Afghanistan. He saw in Brostrom

a tendency shared by many talented young officers; they became too chummy with their men. Brostrom was always hanging around with them, lifting weights, joking; he had joined
the army out of ROTC at the University of Hawaii, and, with
his every-present Oakley shades and his surfer nonchalance,
he wore the burdens of command lightly. He had once signed
an e-mail to Myer, "Jon-Boy," and that struck Myer—a West
Point grad—as characteristically off-key. Of a piece, as Myer
saw it, was Brostrom's inclination to wade forward into a fight
alongside his men. Much as that endeared him to the platoon,
it was sometimes unwise. There were times Myer had needed
him at the command post in a fight and couldn't find him. The
captain would be juggling urgent requests for artillery and air
support, and calculating grids, while Brostrom, who might have
helped him, was instead off shooting a rifle.

"That's not what your role is," the captain had explained
later. "You need to be able to bring more than an M-4 to the
fight. You have all these other assets that you bring, which is more
firepower than the rest of the platoon combined."

Brostrom had acknowledged it, and was working on it, but
this situation was different. The need was dire, and both officers
knew it.

The lieutenant ran to the fighting position of the platoon's
second squad. After a short consultation there, he took off with
Specialist Jason Hovater and the platoon's medic, Private William Hewitt. No sooner did they emerge from cover than Hewitt
was hit by a round that blew a hole as big as a beer can out of
the back of his arm. He crawled back toward cover and began
bandaging himself. Brostrom and Hovater, the fastest runner in
the platoon, continued up toward Topside.

It was not immediately obvious—too much was happening at
once—but the enemy's attack was cunning and well orchestrated.
The Taliban were primarily targeting the platoon's crew-served

weapons. The Humvee with the TOW missile system had been hit hard right at the outset—it hadn't gotten off a shot. Two RPGs hit the driver's side, one setting the engine ablaze and the other exploding against the driver's-side rear. A third RPG exploded against the rear of the passenger side. The engine was destroyed, and the vehicle caught fire. The three-man TOW team fled to take cover in the command post, leaving nine unfired missiles trapped in the inferno.

Dzwik had been walking over to the horseshoe-shaped 120-millimeter mortar pit when the shooting started. He was at the entrance when he heard the first shots, and in front of him Specialist Sergio Abad was hit by a round that clipped the back side of his body armor and entered his chest. He was still talking and breathing, but the wound was severe, and would prove mortal. As Dzwik dived for cover, he dropped his radio mike into the pool of water inside the pit. That effectively removed him from the command loop. He was just another rifleman now. Attackers were firing into the pit from the roofs of village dwellings and from a clump of trees just beyond the perimeter wire.

The platoon was used to exchanging fire with the enemy, but for many this was the first time they could actually see who they were shooting at—and who was shooting at them. Some of the enemy fighters wore masks. They were dressed in various combinations of combat fatigues and traditional Afghan flowing garments. Dzwik watched one enemy fighter, high in the trees with a grenade launcher, who had a perfect bead down on their flooded pit. But every time the shooter launched a grenade, its fins would clip leaves and branches and spin off wildly. Others were firing from the rooftops of the village dwellings, from behind the bazaar, and from the cover afforded by the terrain on all sides. This was clearly a well-planned, well-supplied, coordinated assault.

The mortar crew fought back with grenades and small arms, with the engineering squad feeding them ammo. They managed to fire off four mortars before machine-gun rounds began pinging off the tube. One RPG flew right through an opening in the HESCO wall, passing between Staff Sergeant Ryan Phillips, the crew leader, and Private Scott Stenowski, then on across the outpost to explode against the bazaar wall, setting it on fire. When an RPG exploded inside the pit, injuring two more soldiers and sending sparks from the store of mortar rounds, Phillips ordered everyone out. Carrying Abad, they ran to the now jammed command post.

Dzwik felt as if he were moving in slow motion, rounds crackling across the empty space and kicking up dust at his feet.

It was hard to believe the enemy had so many grenades to shoot. Everyone kept waiting for a lull, but it didn't come. The village had clearly been in on the attack, stealthily stockpiling RPGs for days, if not weeks. There had been clues: unoccupied young men just sitting and watching the post under construction over the last few days, as if measuring distances, observing routines, counting men and weapons. The men of the platoon had sensed that they were being sized up, but what could they do? They couldn't shoot people for just standing and watching. There had been a few warnings that an attack was coming, one just the night before, but they believed on the basis of long experience that they had time. Ordinarily the enemy would work up to a big attack, preceding it with a small unit assault on one position, a lobbed grenade, or a few mortars from the distance. This is what experience had taught them to expect. Not a massive attack completely out of the blue.

Inside the crowded command post, Myer worked the radio furiously, trying to guide Camp Blessing's artillery crews. Communications were spotty, because the destruction of the TOW Humvee had taken out the platoon's satellite antenna. He was working up grids for aircraft and artillery, trying to figure out exactly what was going on, and hoping to land a few big rounds to end this thing. He was struggling to stay calm and think methodically. He knew Lieutenant Colonel Ostlund would have already dispatched a reaction force, and would be steering in air support—bombers and Apache gunships. Myer took stock of his remaining assets, and where the enemy was concentrated. He guessed that the Taliban leaders believed they were too close to the perimeter for artillery rounds to be used effectively. If he could just drop a few shells close enough to disabuse them of this notion, maybe they would break off.

At that point the captain was relying on his men to do what they had been trained to do. He left cover briefly to check in at the two closest firing positions, moving with rounds snapping nearby and the chilling sight of RPGs homing in—he could actually see them approaching, arcing in eerily from the distance. He was back inside the command post when the burning TOW Humvee exploded, throwing missiles in all directions. Two landed inside the command post, one with its motor still running. Phillips grabbed one, using empty sandbags to protect his hands from the hot shell, and carried it out of the crowded command post under heavy fire, depositing it a safe distance away and then returning miraculously unharmed. Myer grabbed the other one and hurled it up and over the sandbag wall. A flap of fabric from the HESCO wall began to smolder, filling the crowded space with black smoke.

At the same time, six minutes into the fight, the howitzer shells began to fall, beginning with four big blasts on the southern and western sides of the outpost. Ostlund had delayed firing until he was able to confirm, with Myer, the location of every member of the platoon. He had the crews perform a mandatory recheck before each 155-millimeter shell was fired. Out of concern, again, for their own comrades, the howitzer battery had armed the shells with delay fuses, which gave those on the ground a chance to dive for cover, an advantage that also helped the enemy. Nevertheless, the barrage became a steady, slow, loud drumbeat. It did little to check the assault.

All of the fighting positions at the post were heavily and continually engaged at this point. The Afghan contingent, with their three U.S. Marine trainers, were firing from their bunkers to the eleven o'clock and five o'clock positions with small arms and M-240 machine guns. The two Humvees with M-19 grenade launchers were unable to use them because the enemy was within the weapon's minimum arming distance. The last of the platoon's Humvees, at the lower position, had its fifty-cal taken out early on. Specialist Adam Hamby had been pouring rounds at a spot where he had seen an RPG launched. Amazingly, fire *increased* from that spot. As he ducked down to reload, the inside of his turret exploded from the impact of bullets, one of which hit the weapon's feed tray cover, which he had raised to reload. The hit had disabled the weapon.

So, minutes into the fight, the platoon was left to defend the main outpost with small arms, shoulder-fired rockets, hand-thrown grenades, the fifty-cal machine gun mounted on Myer's Humvee at the command post, and the M-240s. The weapons systems that Ostlund had freed up to give the platoon some additional firepower, the mortars and TOW system, were destroyed. Much of the incoming fire now was concentrated on the command post and its big machine gun. The Humvee was taking a pounding. Moving from point to point on the outpost was dangerous, but there were now occasional lulls, which enabled Myer and Dzwik to maneuver men along the perimeter as the fight shifted. Mostly the besieged platoon remained hunkered into its fighting positions, returning fire ferociously, and waiting for help or for the enemy to back off.

"Where is my PO [platoon officer]?" shouted Dzwik. "Where's Lieutenant Brostrom?"

The veteran platoon sergeant and the laid-back lieutenant from Hawaii had been inseparable for months. Theirs was a familiar army relationship, the older, experienced sergeant charged with mentoring a younger, college-educated newbie who outranked him, and it was rarely frictionless. But Dzwik and Brostrom had clicked. They got along like brothers, with the platoon sergeant feeling both a personal and a professional responsibility for his lieutenant. Sometimes he felt he was keeping Brostrom on a leash. When Myer had chewed out the lieutenant for leaving the radio in a firefight to shoot his weapon, Dzwik had been chewed out at the same time by the company's first sergeant.

"Why the hell are you letting the PO get away from the radio?" the first sergeant asked. "You need to stop him from doing stupid stuff like that."

But Brostrom was fun, and brought out Dzwik's playful streak, whether it was by means of video games or lifting weights or watching movies. Dzwik had taken him on as a friend and as a project. He was alarmed now to find him absent from the command post, and relieved to hear that he was absent this time with the captain's permission.

"He went up to the OP," said Myer.

Bad as things were on the main outpost, they were much worse at the observation post. After the battle, the battalion intel officer would surmise that the assault had been designed to wipe out the smaller force at Topside. The heavy fire would pin down the bulk of the platoon and disable its big weapons while the smaller position was overrun. Brostrom had intuited this weakness quickly, and had raced to help his men.

They were in big trouble. All nine men had been either killed or wounded. Specialist Tyler Stafford was blown backward by the blast, losing his helmet. Bits of hot shrapnel cut into his legs and belly, and at first, because of the burning sensation, he thought he was on fire. He rolled and screamed before he realized that there was no fire, just pain. He pulled his helmet on again and called for help to his buddy, Specialist Gunnar Zwilling, who looked stunned. Then Zwilling disappeared in a second blast that blew Stafford down to the bottom terrace.

Specialist Matthew Phillips, the platoon's marksman, was on his knees below a wall of sandbags nearby.

"Hey, Phillips, man, I'm hit!" shouted Stafford. "I'm hit! I need help!"

Phillips smiled over at him, as if to say he would be there in a moment. He then stood to throw a grenade just as another RPG exploded. Stafford ducked and felt something smack hard against the top of his helmet, denting it. When the dust settled he looked up. Phillips was still on his knees, only slumped over forward, arms akimbo.

"Phillips! Phillips!" shouted Stafford, but his buddy did not stir. He was dead.

Stafford crawled back up to Topside's southernmost fighting position, where he found Staff Sergeant Ryan Pitts, the platoon's forward observer, severely wounded in the arms and legs. Alongside, Specialist Jason Bogar and Corporal Jonathan Ayers were putting up a heroic fight. Bogar had his Squad Automatic Weapon (SAW) on cyclic, just loading and spraying, loading and spraying, until it jammed. The barrel was white-hot. Ayers was working an M240 machine gun from the terrace overhead until he ran out of ammo. He and Specialist Chris McKaig were also struggling to put out a fire inside their small fighting position. When Ayers's machine-gun ammo was gone, they fought back with their M-4s, popping up at intervals to shoot short bursts until Ayers was shot and killed. McKaig's weapon overheated, so he picked up Ayers's, only to find that it had been disabled by the shot that killed him.

The remaining men at Topside fought back with small arms, throwing grenades, and detonating the Claymore mines they had laid around the perimeter. Bogar tied a tourniquet around Pitts's bleeding leg.

Meanwhile, under heavy fire, Brostrom and Hovater raced uphill along one wall at the lower portion of the bazaar, and then to the outer wall of a small hotel before scrambling up the first terrace. The lieutenant stood there, partly shielded by a big rock, and called up to the wounded Pitts, telling him to hand down the machine gun that Ayers had been using.

Stafford could not see Brostom and Hovater, but he heard the lieutenant shouting back and forth with a third soldier who had joined them there, Specialist Pruitt Rainey. Then he heard one of them shout, "They're inside the wire!"

There was a crescendo of gunfire and shouting. It was surmised later that Brostrom and Rainey had been trying to set up the machine gun, with Hovater providing covering fire, when they were surprised by Taliban fighters who emerged from behind the big rock, inside the perimeter. All three were shot from the front, and killed.

The lieutenant's battle was over. He died fully engaged. His bravery had little impact on the course of the fight. He could not rescue most of the men on Topside, and those who survived may have done so without the terrible sacrifice he and Hovater made. As it is with all soldiers who die heroically in battle, his final act would define him emphatically, completely, and forever. In those loud and terrifying minutes he had chosen to leave a place of relative safety, braving intense fire, and had run and scrambled uphill toward the most perilous point of the fight. A man does such a thing out of loyalty so consuming that it entirely crowds out consideration of self. In essence, Jon Brostrom had cast off his own life the instant he started running uphill, and only fate would determine if it he would be given it back when the shooting stopped. He died in the full heat of that effort, living fully his best idea of himself.

The remaining wounded soldiers at Topside fought on. Eventually all but one, Staff Sergeant Pitts, managed to tumble and crawl their way back downhill to the platoon's easternmost fighting position. Although wounded so severely in the legs and arms that he could not shoot his machine gun, Pitts managed to hurl grenade after grenade into the dead space alongside the perimeter, and stayed in radio contact with the command post (he would receive the Medal of Honor) until reinforcements finally came.

There was still an eternity of minutes for the living members of the platoon, fighting off a determined enemy until air support arrived, but the worst for them was over when a B-1 dropped heavy bombs to the north, and then, not long afterward, Apache gunships began raining fire on the attackers. At roughly the same time the quick reaction force arrived from Camp Blessing, having blazed up the dangerous and still uncleared road north in record time. The fight would rage on for hours, but the attackers bore the brunt of it now, as the reinforced outpost and choppers flushed them out and chased them down, exacting a heavy toll. Later inquiries would estimate that at least a third of the attacking force of two hundred to three hundred had been either killed or wounded. With the sun still behind the peaks above them to the east, Sergeant Dzwik organized nine men to follow him up to Topside.

They were still under fire as they retraced the path taken by Brostrom and Hovater. As Dzwik crested the terrace he saw bodies. For a few minutes, the shooting stopped. The scene was eerily calm. As the others fanned out to reman the observation post defenses and tend to the wounded, Dzwik took grim inventory. Eight of the day's toll of nine killed lay here. Seven were dead. Another was mortally wounded; the sergeant's men were busy working on him. There was a dead Taliban fighter hanging from the razor wire, and there were other bodies farther out.

Brostrom and Hovater were by the boulder. Dzwik noted that Brostrom's mouth was open. It was a habit, one the platoon sergeant had nagged him about, telling him it made him look juvenile, or stupid. Brostrom had a comical way of carrying himself, sometimes deliberately presenting himself as the strong but dim ranger. He made people laugh. He and Dwzik were often together during briefings or meetings, and they got into trouble because the lieutenant would make him laugh and then the two of them would be giggling like high school kids in the back of the classroom. Dzwik enjoyed his role as mentor and scold. Whenever he would catch Brostrom openmouthed he was on him.

"Why is your mouth open?" he would ask. "You look retarded."

"Shut up, man, that's just how I am," the lieutenant would say.

"Well, sir, I'm here to help you with that."

Dzwik now reached down and closed the lieutenant's mouth for him.

"I got your back, sir," he told him.

And when the enemy fire kicked up again, Dzwik made a point of holding his ground over his fallen friend, even when an RPG exploded in the tree right above him. A piece of shrapnel tore a hole through his arm. He looked down at it, telling himself, *It's not too bad*; but when a stream of blood shot out of it, he screamed.

Later, when he had been patched up, he said to his wounded comrades, "Man, I screamed like a bitch, didn't I?"

The sun was just sliding over the surrounding peaks as word of what had happened in this isolated valley raced around the world. Nine Americans killed, thirty-one wounded (twenty-seven Americans and four allied Afghans). The Battle of Wanat was at that point the army's worst single day in the seven-year Afghan conflict, and it would cause waves of anger and recrimination that would last for years. For nine American families in particular, the pain would last a lifetime.

The sad tidings were reported on the radio by one of the returning Apache pilots.

"I have a total of nine KIA," he said, then added, "*Godamn it!*"

2. The Father's Battle

It was a Sunday morning in Aiea, Hawaii, so Mary Jo and Dave Brostrom went to Mass. Their home is perched high on a green hillside, and in the back the ground plunges into a verdant valley of palm branches and you can gaze down on the flight of brightly colored birds. When a sudden storm sweeps through like a blue-gray shade, it will often leave behind rainbows that arch over the distant teal inlet of Pearl Harbor.

White monuments far below mark this as a military neighborhood, past and present. Camp HM Smith, headquarters for the U.S. Pacific Command, is just down the hill. The Brostroms are a military family. Dave is a retired colonel, an army aviator, who served nearly thirty years with helicopter units. Their two sons, Jonathan and Blake, had gone the same way. Jonathan was a first lieutenant and Blake was in college with the ROTC program. So when Mary Jo, a petite woman with dark brown hair and hazel eyes, saw a military van parked on Aiealani Place, their narrow residential street, she thought that somebody was misusing a government vehicle—the vans were not authorized for private use, and, on Sunday, would ordinarily have been parked on the base. They drove past it, turned down their steep driveway, and entered the house.

Dave answered the knock on the front door minutes later. There were two soldiers in full uniform.

"What's up?" she heard him ask.

Then, "Mary Jo, you need to come here."

She knew immediately why they had come, and she collapsed on the spot.

Dave Brostrom is a very tall, sandy-haired man with a long, lean face, a slightly crooked smile, and small deep-set blue eyes under a shock of blond eyebrows. When he talks about Jonathan, sadness seems etched in the lines around those small eyes. He moves with an athletic slouch, and his fair skin is weathered from years of island sun. In his flip-flops, flowery silk shirt, sunglasses, and worn blue jeans he doesn't look like a military man, but the army has defined his life. He works today for Boeing, helping to sell helicopters to the units he once served.

Jonathan used to tease him about having been an aviator. There was a spirited competition between father and son, whether on surfboards—Dave had taught his sons on a tandem board—or the golf course. Jonathan was competitive by nature. He was a good golfer and an early stickler for the course rules. If Mary Jo moved a ball a few inches from behind a tree, he would announce, "One," noting the penalty point. She didn't like to play with him. He had golfed once, as a teenager, with his father and a general, and complained when the general tried to improve his lie.

"Sir, you can't do that," Jonathan said. "It's a stroke."

"Just go along," counseled the veteran colonel.

"No," Jonathan insisted. "Either he plays right or he doesn't play at all!"

When Jonathan decided in his junior year of high school to join the army, the goal was not just to imitate his father, but to surpass him. He was determined to prove himself more of a soldier, to accumulate more badges, more decorations. He would qualify as a paratrooper, something his father had not done, and then complete air assault training. Then came Ranger school and dive school—two more elite achievements. Apart from its overt hierarchy of rank, the army has an elaborate hierarchy of status, the pinnacle of which is "special operator," the super soldiers of its covert counterterror units. The surest path there was through an elite infantry unit. That was where Jonathan aimed. He viewed his father's career in aviation dismissively, as a less manly pursuit than foot-soldiering. He volunteered to enlist for two extra years in order to guarantee that path. Ordinarily, ROTC officers in training will opt for the extended commitment in order to avoid the infantry, where the work is dirty and hard and the hazards are immediate, in order to steer themselves into a cushier specialty . . . like, say, aviation.

"You volunteered to spend two extra years in the army to go into *infantry?*" his incredulous father had asked. "That's stupid!"

"No, it's not," said Jon. "I don't want to be a wimp like you. Damn aviator."

Dave enjoyed this kind of banter with Jonathan, but in this case the stakes were higher. He cautioned his son. It was one thing to want to show up your old man and prove you were not a wimp, but frontline infantry in wartime was not a step to be taken lightly.

"You have to understand you are going to be at the point of the spear," said Dave. "There's a war on."

But Jonathan was driven. The danger was the point. His parents worried about it, but they would support their son's ambition. Dave did more than that. He helped land his son an immediate berth with the elite airborne unit. He called his old friend Colonel Charles "Chip" Preysler, commander of the 173rd Airborne Brigade, one of the regular army's frontline fighting units, and collected a favor. This was in 2007, just as Jonathan was completing Ranger school . . . on his third try. He had been assigned to the First Cavalry Division out of Fort Hood, a heavy armored unit that was slated for another tour in Iraq. Dave saw that the 173rd had recently been assigned a second tour in Afghanistan. So the maneuver actually satisfied both of the father's objectives: he had helped move his son closer to his goal and also swing him away from Iraq, then the more treacherous of the army's two theaters of war. After a two-week stint at the 173rd's home base in Vicenza, Italy, Jonathan joined the deployed brigade in Afghanistan. His first assignment was as an assistant at Camp Blessing on the staff of Lieutenant Colonel Ostlund's Second Battalion, Task Force Rock. Within months he was a platoon leader, commanding the outpost at Bella, and exchanging fire with the enemy. He called home excitedly after he was awarded a combat infantry badge, the army's official recognition that a soldier has been personally engaged in ground combat.

"Is Dad home?" he asked his mother.

"No, he's not here right now," she said.

"Well, I need to talk to him. When will he be home? I got my combat infantry badge."

Just then Dave walked in the door. Mary Jo handed him the phone.

"Jonathan needs to talk to you," she said.

"I got mine!" he told his father. "I got mine!" Rubbing it in. In all his decades of service, Dave had never been in combat. Jonathan would from then on take every opportunity to remind his father of it, and Dave was happy and proud of him for it.

But the father felt another emotion. He worried about what his son had gotten himself into . . . what he had *helped* get his son into. There are subtleties to the ideal of courage that occur more readily to older men than young ones, more readily especially to fathers than sons. The two great errors of youth were to trust too little, and to trust too much. A man did what he had to do if necessary. To do less was cowardice. But to rush headlong toward danger? Wisdom whispered: *Better than passing the test is not being put to the test.* A wise man avoids the *occasion* of danger, as capable as he might be of meeting it. He does not risk all for too little. To the extent that he trusted in his mission and his leadership, what Jonathan was doing in seeking combat was not foolish. Danger was part of the job. The U.S. Army was in the business of managing risk and was good at it. In the modern age, it brought the men, equipment, tactics, and training to a fight with such authority that it all but guaranteed mission success, and mission success, especially in America in the modern age, meant, at least in part . . . no casualties. Well, *zero* casualties would be unrealistic. Death and injury were part of the job—that's what made Jonathan's combat infantry badge a coveted decoration. But *minimal* casualties. In modern war, compared with previous eras, earlier wars, death and severe injury had become blessedly rare. At the very least a soldier trusted that his commanders would not treat his existence lightly. Dave Brostrom, as much as he believed in the army, as much as he loved his country, was not so ready as his son to believe that whatever prize was to be had in a godforsaken combat outpost in the Hindu Kush was worth one's very life. A combat ribbon lent critical authenticity to any infantry officer's career, but what career would there be if a Taliban bullet found his boy?

A bullet had found Jonathan's platoon sergeant and friend Matt Kahler in January, not long after he took over Second Platoon. The death of a platoon sergeant is not just a personal tragedy; it's an organizational blow. It had shaken everyone in the brigade, up and down the ranks. The Brostroms got a phone call first from the wife of Colonel Preysler in Germany. She told them that Jonathan would be calling home, and when he had called, hours later, it was clear to Mary Jo that he had been crying. He said he had to prepare a eulogy, and she wondered, *How does a twenty-four-year-old prepare a eulogy?*

When Dave spoke to his friend Preysler, he asked if Preysler had been to the outpost to talk with Jonathan and the other men. Preysler said he had been unable to get there. Dave knew enough about informal army protocol to know that when someone as senior as a platoon sergeant went down, the commanders came calling to reassure the troops. Preysler hadn't gone to the outpost, not because he didn't care, but because his brigade was stretched too thin. He was being pulled in too many directions at once.

It cast an ominous shadow. Jonathan would call them by satellite phone every two or three weeks. The conversations were short, usually coming early in the morning. He would assure them he was all right, and then tell them he had to go. It was clear he and his men were under a lot of pressure, and were taking regular casualties. Dave and Mary Jo found it hard to picture where exactly Jonathan was, and what he was doing.

The picture came into clearer focus, along with his parents' misgivings, after Jon surprised them by showing up at home for a Mother's Day party. He appeared at the door that day in May with a bouquet of flowers for Mary Jo, and was bubbling with enthusiasm for his command at Bella. He steered his parents straight to his laptop and called up pictures of his guys, and some video clips from *Vanity Fair*'s website, which had featured a series months earlier by writer Sebastian Junger and the late photographer Tim Hetherington, "Into the Valley of Death," about soldiers in a sister company manning outposts in the same region. Jonathan was excited. "Here's where I work," he said. It was all new and very cool to him. Dave looked at the videos and had a completely different reaction. He thought, *This is some bad shit.*

He saw young soldiers squatting in makeshift forts in distant mountains, risking their lives for reasons he could not fathom. The military side of him came out. He knew all about COIN, the army's counterinsurgency doctrine, which had been employed to such marked effect in the previous year by General David Petraeus in Iraq. It centered on protecting and winning over a population, turning people against the violent extremists in their midst, and it called for soldiers to leave the comfort and safety of large bases to mingle with the people where they lived. It was the only rationale Dave Brostrom could see for the risks Jonathan and his platoon were taking.

"How often do you relate to the population?" he asked. "What kind of humanitarian assistance do you give them?"

"Nope, we don't do that anymore," said Jonathan. "We just try to kill them before they kill us. When we go outside, it's serious business. We're on a kill mission patrol."

It scared Dave. There was one picture Jonathan showed them, proudly, which drove it home. It showed him attending a *shura*, a conference of elders, with local villagers. The Afghan men around him were old and wizened, with long gray beards and leathery skin. They were survivors, men who had carved out a life for half a century or more in those austere mountains. Through famine, pestilence, and war. And here, apparently presiding, was his Jonathan, twenty-four years old, fresh out of army ROTC at the University of Hawaii, the little boy he had taught to surf not too long ago, with his high-and-tight haircut, a wad of tobacco stuffed in his cheek, wearing his cool sunglasses, trying to look tough. He knew that Jonathan's transition to Afghanistan, partly because of his own intervention, had meant he had missed any kind of specialized training for the Afghan mission. He was there just weeks out of Ranger school! He didn't speak the language. He knew nothing of Afghan history or culture. He knew bubkes about the loyalties or motivations of those tough old men around him, members of tribes isolated in those Hindu Kush valleys for centuries. Dave could readily imagine how they saw his boy. To Dave the picture showed Jonathan out of his element, and not realizing it.

"You have got to get the hell out of there," said Dave. "You know, this is stupid. You are spread too thin. Why are you doing this? These guys are just taking potshots at you every day."

Jonathan explained that they would soon move from Bella. Task Force Rock had inherited the outposts when it arrived in country, and Ostlund had recognized that some of the distant ones made little sense. They would be moving closer to Camp Blessing, to a new outpost that could be supplied and reinforced by ground as well as air. So it at least sounded to Dave as though the men in charge shared his concerns. But Jonathan also told him that the enemy at Bella would surely follow them south to the new place, called Wanat.

"They're going to come after me," he said. "They've threatened me."

Jonathan was in Hawaii for two great weeks in May. Dave spent a lot of time with his son. They surfed. The Sunday before Jonathan left, the priest at their church blessed him before the congregation.

Six weeks later he was back in the same church in a coffin. Some of the grieving father's worries about the mission came out in an interview with a local reporter, but he had nothing but praise for his son's commanders. He told a local reporter: "His leadership at the brigade and below were probably the best you will ever find, the best in the world. But they were put in a situation where they were underresourced."

Along with the families of the other soldiers killed, as a courtesy the Brostroms got a copy of the "15-6" investigation of the incident. Army Regulation 15, Section 6 is the standard for official inquiries. It included a detailed account of the fight and the events that had led up to it. It emphasized the correctness of the decision to relocate the outpost to Wanat, and the heroism of the men who fought, but also noted the decision to vacate the unfinished outpost three days later. It noted the likely complicity of the village in the attack, and recommended that the Afghan district governor and chief of police be dismissed, "if not arrested and tried." It recommended that plans to purchase or lease land for future outposts be streamlined, and that the road north from Camp Blessing be repaired.

"I would not characterize this as anything more than the standard fighting that happens in this area in good weather that the summer provides," wrote Dave's friend Colonel Preysler.

And that, apparently, as far as the army was concerned, was that. The brave soldiers of Second Platoon, along with their Afghan counterparts and marine advisers, had tenaciously defended the outpost from hundreds of attackers. They had prevented it from being overrun. First Lieutenant Jonathan Brostrom was posthumously awarded a Silver Star for valor, along with eight others who were decorated for their actions that day, among them Captain Myer, Sergeant First Class Dzwik, and Staff Sergeant Pitts.

The battlefield honor, which he knew his son would have cherished, did nothing to ease Dave Brostrom's anguish. Beyond the grief, he felt a heart-crushing mix of anger, guilt, and betrayal. The anger was unfocused, but it was rooted in his earlier suspicion that his son's platoon had been inadequately supported and directed. The guilt was more insidious and ran deep. He felt terrible about how the lifetime of macho competition between him and Jonathan had fed his son's ambition to follow in his footsteps, and then upped the game to odds that had proved fatal. He felt guilty about having pulled strings to get Jonathan into the 173rd, even though, at the time, he believed steering him away from the First Cavalry and its Iraq mission was sending him to a safer place. That was where the sense of betrayal was rooted. Dave had done his homework before approaching Preysler. In 2007, all of the official reports from Afghanistan had been rosy. The fighting there was all but over, the assessments read; the work was all humanitarian projects and nation-building. Brostrom now saw that as propaganda, and was furious that he had fallen for it.

His anger crystallized after a careful reading of the 15-6 report. Preysler gave his old friend a redacted version, along with hundreds of pages of documentation. The deeper Brostrom dug into the source material, the more convinced he became that report was a whitewash. All of his ill-formed misgivings about his son's mission were tragically affirmed, and here in the interviews and documents of the inquiry was the machinery of a true fiasco. The new outpost had been located in a natural kill zone. The engineers who were tasked with building its defenses never showed up. In the first days water ran low; the HESCOs had to be cut in half to accommodate the limited reach of the single Bobcat; the platoon was stretched so thin it could not conduct essential security patrols. The day before the attack, the drones were pulled. There had been direct warnings of a surprise attack. And yet his son had been left out there to run the show. Where was his company commander? Where was the battalion commander? What priorities would have kept them away? Yet there was no hint of mistake in the report itself.

His overall distress was distilled into something personal. Dave no longer saw the officers who had led his son to his death as "the best in the world." They were directly responsible and they had not been paying attention. The mission to Wanat had gone off the rails well before Second Platoon was attacked. Studying what he saw as the mismatch between the documentation and findings in the 15-6, he grew convinced that the army, left to its own devices, wasn't even going to learn anything from its mistakes, or from his son's sacrifice. Colonel Preysler, Lieutenant Colonel Ostund, Captain Myer, and the rest of the command chain were going to skate away unscathed. Their careers would continue to prosper, leading them to higher commands where they would have more power over young men's lives.

Anger and second-guessing are common among the families and friends of fallen soldiers. After the flag-draped burial ceremony, after the initial shock wears off, many grief-stricken parents and spouses find themselves left with anger and disbelief, and come to blame the army itself for their tragedy. But Dave

Brostrom was a special case. His rage, his pain and that of Mary Jo and their family, was not destined to remain a private torment. The retired colonel was formidable. He was smart, passionate, angry, and driven. Because of his long military career, he knew exactly what questions to ask, and where to ask them. He knew how to move in the army's intimidating bureaucracy. He had accumulated a lifetime of friends and valued colleagues, in and out of the army, and in the summer of 2008 he began working those levers with a will that would leave no one associated with Wanat untouched.

When Dave's old friend General Bill Caldwell called to offer condolences, and asked, as a friend, if there was anything he could do, Brostrom had a request ready. He asked Caldwell to look into the matter further. Jonathan had cut Caldwell's lawn when his father had served with him at Fort Drum years earlier. The general was now leading the Combined Arms Center, at Fort Leavenworth, which includes the Command and General Staff College, the military's graduate school; and the Combat Studies Institute (CSI), which collects and publishes contemporary historical studies.

"Write about this," Brostrom urged him. "It's the worst battle in Afghanistan. Nothing makes sense here."

Caldwell honored his old friend's request. He invited Brostrom to visit Fort Leavenworth to brief the officers at CSI, who were given the redacted 15-6 report along with audio and video recordings made by the Apache gunships when they arrived on-site, an hour into the battle. Brostrom shared his misgivings with Douglas Cubbison, a military historian who was assigned to write a report of the incident. The two consulted throughout the months of research, and Cubbison showed Brostrom an early draft. This report was not going to be, as Cubbison would later put it to me, "the nice safe hero story" the institute might have imagined at the outset.

When Cubbison's meticulously researched draft—not yet
the official CSI report—was leaked early in 2009, it caused a stir.
The institute is known for its attention to tactical and strategic
theory, the kind of stuff that keeps military graduate students
up all night drinking strong coffee, but is rarely of interest to
outsiders. Here was a highly critical study of ongoing operations,
dramatically written, scathingly critical of the decisions made by
officers currently serving in frontline command positions. Any
questions about the propriety of Cubbison's tone were trumped
by General Caldwell's strong endorsement.

It was a genuine in-house army scandal. The draft report
made a formidable case for Brostrom's take on the battle. It implicated the elite brigade's entire chain of command in what was
characterized as a boondoggle. Second Platoon was portrayed as
a victim not just of the Taliban, but of its own leadership. It had
been pushed into a precarious outpost without proper supervision, defensive precautions, or logistical support, as part of a badly
botched and underresourced counterinsurgency effort that had
succeeded only in antagonizing the local population. The report
portrayed the platoon as sitting ducks. The ten-month negotiation for the land at Wanat had given enemy forces throughout
the Waygul Valley ample time to plan a coordinated assault. Cubbison's interviews with the survivors and their families and friends
showed that the men themselves suspected they were likely to be
hit hard at the site, just as Jonathan had told his father. Lack of
overhead surveillance; an inadequate force; delays in construction
crews, equipment, and water supplies; absence of community
outreach; the fact that Captain Myer had been too busy to take
direct command of the operation until the day before the attack . . . all of it suggested distracted and complacent leadership.
Even the mission's basic goal was miscalculated: "A single platoon
in the open field near the bazaar lacked the capability of holding
Wanat," the draft report concluded.

That line would be quoted by Tom Ricks, the influential military journalist, who got a copy of Cubbison's draft and wrote a series of blogs based on it in early 2009. This rekindled critical attention on the incident. Drawn into the emerging story by sources familiar with Brostrom's campaign, Ricks had already written critically of the 15-6 inquiry, which he saw as the worst kind of self-congratulatory claptrap. He was bothered by what he would term the "fuck-you-edness" of it. He characterized it to me as dismissive, a "thank-you-very-much-for-your-interest-in-national-defense" kind of report, "unusually poor." He would eventually post Cubbison's entire draft, which, as we shall see, was not the CSI's final word on the subject.

The draft report and Ricks's pointed critique meant that Brostrom's complaints could no longer be dismissed as the isolated ravings of a bereaved father. Dave now filed a formal complaint with the Department of Defense, with the inspector general's office, accusing the 173rd's entire chain of command, including his old friend Chip Preysler, of dereliction of duty. He enlisted the help of Robert "Skip" Orr, the president of Boeing Japan, who had met Jonathan on his last visit home. Orr helped put Brostrom in touch with Senator Jim Webb of Virginia, a decorated marine veteran. The senator remarked that the incident reminded him of the scandalous cover-up of events surrounding the death of Pat Tillman, the NFL star who gave up his football career to fight in Afghanistan, only to be killed, as the story eventually emerged, by friendly fire. Webb took the questions about Wanat directly to the chairman of the Joint Chiefs, Admiral Mike Mullen. The savvy senator also advised Brostrom to take his story to the press, which he did to great effect.

It made a wrenching and powerful story—the furious father of a martyred American hero, a retired colonel taking on the army, turning on his former colleagues—and it attracted a lot of attention. Reporters cannot resist a story about military incompetence. There was a complete airing in the *Washington Post* by reporter Greg Jaffe, and the newspaper built a state-of-the-art multimedia presentation of the story online, complete with excerpts from the Apache gunship video of the battle. From there the story aired on CBS, and then NBC's *Dateline* came calling. It would eventually air a powerful, award-winning, hour-long presentation of Brostrom's take on Wanat, narrated by Richard Engel, called "A Father's Mission."

In this episode, the grieving family members talked about the young men lost, and accused the officers who led them of "pure recklessness" and of using their loved ones as "cannon fodder."

"Nothing made sense here," Brostrom told NBC. "Even if you look at the terrain, they were trying to establish a combat outpost in a natural kill zone."

No one in the TV report spoke for the officers who stood accused. The train of research, publicity, and pressure eventually drove the army, in September 2009, to order an official reassessment of the battle, under the auspices of General David Petraeus, then CENTCOM commander. A retired Marine Corps lieutenant general, Richard Natonski, was asked to lead the investigation. Four months later Natonski dropped a bomb.

He affirmed most of the findings of Cubbison's report. He recommended that Colonel Ostlund and Captain Myer be cited for dereliction of duty—which would mean citing Myer for both valor and incompetence in the same engagement. General Petraeus went further in signing off on the recommendations. He personally amended the findings to include Preysler among those to receive reprimands.

If the reprimands stood, then the careers of Preysler, Ostlund, and Myer were effectively over. Since the battle, Ostlund and Myer had been promoted, to colonel and to major, respectively. Those promotions were now to be reconsidered. Preysler,

Brostrom's old friend who had done him a favor by getting Jonathan assigned to his brigade, would resign before the reprimands were issued. General Jeffrey J. Schloesser, who had commanded all U.S. forces in eastern Afghanistan, and who was officially cleared of wrongdoing in the report, would resign as well, choosing to share responsibility with his subordinates.

The howl of pain from the slain lieutenant's father threatened to topple the entire command structure of the 173rd. The last step was to forward the findings and recommendations for final disposition to General Charles C. "Hondo" Campbell, the soon-to-retire head of the U.S. Army Forces Command.

Before that final step was taken, Brostrom remembers attending an event in Hawaii in February 2010, an interment ceremony for a former army chief of staff. He ran into General George W. Casey, who then held that position. As Brostrom remembers it, the conversation went like this:

"Listen, I'm so sorry for your family's loss," said Casey.

"I'm sorry about all this stuff," he told Casey.

The general stiffened.

"Whatever makes you happy," he said.

"It doesn't make me happy," Brostrom protested.

As Brostrom remembered it, the army chief of staff then leaned in closer, pointed a finger at his chest, and confided cryptically, "Hondo Campbell is going to fix all of this."

Casey remembers the meeting, but says he never heard Brostrom apologize for his role in scrutinizing and assigning blame for the losses at Wanat.

"I would not have expected him to apologize," Casey told me. "I really felt for him. I saw him standing there—he's a striking guy, tall, sandy hair—and I recognized him from some of the reporting I had seen about the incident. I walked up to him to express my sorrow over his loss. I could certainly understand his desire to better understand what happened."

Casey said he would "never" have said, "Whatever makes you happy," because he took no umbrage at the ongoing investigation. He had agreed with the decision to order it, and had called Petraeus himself to ask that CENTCOM place the official probe with Natonski, a marine, to ensure its independence, and to avoid the appearance of the army investigating itself. He said he has no memory of mentioning Campbell, who had just taken up Natanski's findings and would soon issue letters of reprimand to Ostlund and Myer. If he had said anything like what Brostrom remembered regarding Campbell, he would have meant only to reassure a grieving father that "Hondo was going to get to the bottom of it."

3. The Colonel's Battle

The letter of reprimand Colonel Bill Ostlund received on March 5, 2010, was a hard slap in the face.

"As battalion commander, you failed in several major respects," General Campbell's memo began.

He went on to itemize four specific and damning findings from the Natonski report. (1) A failure of planning and execution: "You did not not provide your soldiers with the guidance, support, and supervision to which they were entitled." (2) Permitting the company commander, Captain Myer, to remain at Camp Blessing for the first four days of the Wanat construction, in order to participate in a 15-6 investigation "in which he was only a witness." (3) Not inspecting Wanat himself during those days, but instead attending a *shura* (a council of Afghan elders), visiting a community center, and preparing a lessons learned document—a long memo to General Petraeus outlining the battalion's experiences over the previous fourteen months. (4) Inadequately assessing the risk at Wanat.

Ostlund considered the findings false, from first to last. For an ambitious career army officer, the memo's conclusion was brutal: "You are reprimanded. Your actions fell below the high standard expected of an experienced, senior officer commanding an infantry battalion in the unforgiving combat environment of Afghanistan. They raise legitimate questions about your judgment, professionalism, leadership, and tactical competence. In a word, they were unacceptable."

His promotion to full colonel would be withdrawn. He would most likely never lead men into combat again. Campbell noted that he would consider any matters that Ostlund chose to submit "before filing a final decision." The colonel had fourteen days to respond.

It seemed futile to resist. The resignations of Schloesser and Preysler suggested that after three separate reviews the final word on the battle had been pronounced. The chain of command had been found wanting and was bowing to that harsh verdict— Schloesser without having been reprimanded. It seemed time for good soldiers to go away quietly.

But Ostlund was not about to go quietly. He regarded the finding as not just a slur on his reputation, but a slur on Chosen Company, which had served so valiantly and at such cost. His company commander, Matt Myer, who had also been reprimanded and reduced in rank, faced the end of his career and a lifelong stain on his judgment and character. The verdict would be felt not just by Ostlund, but by his wife and three sons. It was one thing to retire as a general or a full colonel; most careers were finished then anyway. Ostlund was still in his early forties. His career was in full and rapid stride. He was not about to fall on his sword.

Dave Brostrom had picked a fight with a fighter—a professional fighter. Ostlund is from Nebraska, is partly of Cherokee descent, and joined the army in a delayed-entry enlistment program when he was still a junior in high school. It is all he ever wanted to do. He served four years as an enlisted soldier and two more as a National Guard soldier as he set his sights on becoming an officer. He took advantage of an ROTC program to attend the University of Omaha, determined to earn a degree faster and with a higher GPA than anyone else ever did. He loved the army. As an enlisted man he had observed leaders in uniform who inspired him like no other, and he wanted to be one of them. The speed and excellence with which he "rangered" through college caught the eye of Petraeus, who worked to spot and nurture ambitious officers who shared his scholarly bent. He was selected, on Petraeus's recommendation, to join the faculty at West Point, which included attendance at the Fletcher School at Tufts University, where he earned a master's degree in international security studies. The young officer from Omaha seemed destined for the army's highest ranks.

Part of his path included combat command. He helped lead the 101st Airborne Brigade into Iraq in 1991, served there again with the 173rd after the 2003 invasion, and eventually took command of Task Force Rock in Afghanistan. Ostlund was highly regarded, indefatigable, with a reputation for pushing himself as hard as his men, for being a "fighting" commander, and for tackling the toughest missions. He appeared to be on a smooth trajectory toward general officer when he was blindsided by Wanat. Now, reprimanded and defrocked, he did not seem bitter, angry, or even frustrated. He seemed focused. The energy, intelligence, and experience he had brought to his career and to the fight against the Taliban were turned toward defending himself and his men. He filled an enormous footlocker with thick binders stuffed with thousands of pages of documentation—maps, interviews, memos, articles, passages from pertinent army manuals concerning doctrine and practice—as though marshaling data for a doctoral thesis. He regarded the effort as "an obligation."

Early on, when word of Brostrom's campaign had first reached him, Ostlund had sought advice from a longtime mentor.

"Bill, all your life, you've clung to facts and truth, and that's kind of been your mantra, your drumbeat," his friend said. "But this battle's not about truth and facts. It's about politics and perception. And when you realize that, you'll be more effective in the fight. So, beating your head against the wall about truth and facts at the wrong time is going to send the wrong perception and wrong message to those involved."

So he had held his fire. How do you fight back against the grieving father of a soldier killed under your command? Ostlund put his faith in the institution, in the army, believing that in the end his fellow officers would not accept Brostrom's take on what happened. He calmly collected copies of the insulting comments about him that showed up in the various critical news stories and programs. He did not answer them. He did not consent to be interviewed. He reassured Captain Myer that the truth would win out in the end. But once Campbell's memo arrived, with its invitation to respond, the footlocker came out. He showed up with it for all the interviews demanded by the various investigating teams, and repeated his version of events again and again. He could not compete with Brostrom's grief in the court of public opinion, but inside the army he believed he would prevail "with the facts and the truth."

Ostlund is a portrait in contained, channeled energy. He is an extremely fit man with short, curly black hair; pale blue eyes; and a square, tightly muscled jaw. His manner is ferociously serious . . . contents under pressure. You want to open a window in case there is an explosion. Lieutenant Jonathan Brostrom was one of twenty-six men he lost commanding Task Force Rock in Afghanistan. He says he feels every day the loss of each soldier. It's an emotional issue with him, he says, a reminder of the unbearably high price war exacts, but the colonel shows little emotion

about it. It is, he will tell you bluntly—and one senses a conviction here that runs deeper than sorrow—"a fact of combat."
Those who have been there understand, he says. Those who have
not . . . cannot.

Downrange he shaves his head. He has commanded troops
in three wars, and he prides himself on doing it well. Task Force
Rock under his command was the most decorated unit to serve in
the Afghan war. He had over a thousand men scattered in fifteen
combat outposts in the Hindu Kush, spread over an area the size
of Connecticut. Its high mountains and deep valleys made transportation a nightmare, by ground or air. It was the most difficult
terrain and the most violent sector of the war. There were four
or five attacks every day in his area of command, often attacks
that required battalion assistance—artillery, airpower, reinforcements—which in turn required Ostlund's active participation.
Among his outposts was Restrepo, famous because of a documen-
tary film of the same name made by Junger and Hetherington, in
which Ostlund appears briefly (as a tough, eloquent, passionate,
smart commander). Junger, in a book he subsequently wrote
about the fifteen-month deployment, called *War*, had this to
say of Ostlund: "He had such full-on enthusiasm about what
he was doing that sometimes when I was around him I caught
myself feeling bad that there wasn't an endeavor of equivalent
magnitude in my own life." Junger wrote that Ostlund seemed
to work eighteen-hour days for the entire time. The film and the
book helped define that period of the Afghan war experience
for most Americans as a bloody, grueling, and lonely campaign.
These accounts showed that the men of Task Force Rock were
not just fighting occasionally; they were living combat, day after
day, week after week, month after month, in a way few American
soldiers have done in generations. The lieutenant colonel moved
constantly in helicopters and Humvees through the mountains
from outpost to outpost. His master sergeant told me that he

would hand preset firing grids to the choppers' gunners on those trips, because they grew so used to taking fire from the same places—"The enemy is a creature of habit," he growled, with professional scorn.

Even as Ostlund was leading his men, he was constantly meeting with village elders throughout his territory, negotiating, listening, settling disputes, organizing humanitarian aid programs, building goodwill, arguing America's case, and pleading for their support. Attending each local *shura* was not just a polite gesture, but a major priority. The army, for instance, had adopted regulations that barred its troops from simply seizing land for outposts. Land must be purchased. In the case of Wanat, it had taken months of negotiations. If Afghans were regarded as partners in the war, as allies, and if under the COIN doctrine maintaining that relationship was considered *the key* to winning the war, then attending the *shura* was an obligation critical to mission success. Sometimes this was a pressing priority, as when an Apache helicopter attack on two fleeing pickup trucks just weeks before the Battle of Wanat killed a local doctor and workers from a medical clinic. The task force had taken mortar fire from the fleeing group, who may have been taken hostage by Taliban fighters, but the fallout from that event had turned many in the Waygul Valley against the entire American effort. Such disputes cut to the core of Ostlund's mission.

Since Afghanistan in 2008 was an "economy of force" effort, Task Force Rock faced constant shortages of engineers, aircraft, humanitarian dollars—everything. Iraq was still draining the nation's military resources. For Ostlund, this affected his entire command. He was shorthanded. Some of his outposts were manned by half platoons, commanded by a sergeant, because the platoon leader, a lieutenant, could be in only one place at a time. Ostlund was constantly shuffling things between outposts—TOW firing platforms, mortars, artillery, surveillance drones—moving them to be where they were most needed, trying to anticipate where the enemy, a cunning and mostly invisible force, would next strike. His intelligence staff carefully plotted the daily attacks, noting the size of the enemy force, the kinds of weapons and tactics used. The staff had developed templates—like the command sergeant's preset firing grids—of enemy movements and tactics. But the enemy was smart, too. When Ostlund arrived in country in the spring of 2007, one of his first decisions was to pull back and consolidate. He collapsed Ranch House and Bella to Wanat, a move designed to close two of the farthest-flung outposts, which could be reached only by helicopter and were, as Jonathan Brostrom had told his father, too vulnerable and understaffed to conduct community outreach. Wanat was chosen because it was a district center and because it was close enough to Camp Blessing to be reinforced by road. These advantages were judged to outweigh the danger of residing in the bottom of the bowl.

This calculation took into account the fact that Wanat, and the entire Waygul Valley, was one of the least violent sectors in Ostlund's battle theater. Over the entire deployment, the task force experienced only forty-four clashes with the enemy there. It had over five hundred in the Korengal. The same parcel of ground where COP Kahler was to be built had been occupied earlier in the war by an American engineering unit that encountered little or no hostility. The engineering unit had completed a bridge that was considered a boon to the village, and while there had provided a small boom in employment and commerce. There was reason to believe that this new outpost would enjoy a similar experience. Planning for the outpost had included detailed maps and construction schedules, including predetermined fields of fire and potential locations for observation posts on the high ground. After purchasing the land, Ostlund, Myer, and Brostrom had visited Wanat in April for a *shura* with the village elders. None expressed objections to the outpost. The American officers had together walked the grounds. Two days before the move from Bella, Ostlund had met with Brostrom to further discuss the move. He said he found the lieutenant eager to proceed.

Intelligence reports predicted that COP Kahler would be particularly vulnerable in the first few days, before effective defensive measures were established. So Ostlund took steps to beef up Brostrom's platoon, reallocating the TOW missile vehicle, the 120-millimeter mortars, and multiple surveillance systems from other outposts. These weapons added five vehicles to the fighting position, which included two fifty-cal machine guns, forty-nine U.S. soldiers, and two dozen Afghan soldiers. According to intelligence estimates and aerial surveillance reports, a series of light probing Taliban attacks would be likely, and the force deployed was more than capable of defending itself. This may have figured into Lieutenant Brostrom's calculations when he was willing to sacrifice some situational awareness in the first days by using his men to build instead of patrol.

On the day of the move from Bella—a complicated effort, which had to be orchestrated on land and in the air—two of Ostlund's other outposts were attacked. Aerial surveillance was withdrawn from Wanat, *over the task force's objections*, because there was judged to be more pressing need elsewhere.

The day before the platoon rolled into Wanat, a Task Force Rock soldier was killed in the Chowkay Valley. That day, Ostlund attended a *shura* with district leaders where the incident occurred, and visited the men at the outpost that suffered the loss. When the arrival of combat engineers and supplies was delayed because of threats along the road from Camp Blessing, arrangements were made to deliver additional supplies to Brostrom by air. Two or more attacks on Task Force Rock outposts came in each of the following days. At the same time Ostlund was supervising from afar the move to Wanat, he was

coordinating a visit to his area of operations by Admiral Mike
Mullen, the chairman of the Joint Chiefs. The lieutenant colonel
was present with Mullen when an outpost they were visiting was
attacked. Scheduled to visit Wanat in the days before the battle,
he was prevented from doing so because the road from Camp
Blessing had not been cleared—the same problem stranding the
engineers—and the chopper he ordinarily had at his disposal was
grounded. Nevertheless, reports from Brostrom indicated that
the work was proceeding as planned, despite the setbacks. Myer
arrived on the afternoon of the twelfth day to assume direct
command, and his reports confirmed that all was quiet. In the
larger context of his command, Ostlund was working overtime
to manage his battle space with limited resources. There was
no reason to judge that the troops at Wanat were in imminent
danger of a large-scale attack. In the larger picture, the move
to Wanat might have been the battalion's "main priority," but
clearly there were urgent demands elsewhere.

The attack that began on the morning of July 13, and that
ended so tragically, came as a surprise and constituted a betrayal.
Later investigations showed that the same villagers who had received Ostlund, Myer, and Brostrom in a friendly way just weeks
earlier had helped Taliban fighters gather the weapons, ammunition, and men to sustain the assault. Ostlund argued consistently
that it is a commander's duty to prepare for *likely* threats. An all-
out coordinated attack like the one at Wanat had happened only
once before during his command, at Ranch House, and had been
repelled by the half platoon based there. The ability of the enemy
to enlist village support, amass stockpiles of weapons and ammunition, and gather hundreds of fighters for such a concentrated
and sustained assault was highly *unlikely*, which is why the forces
attacking Wanat had achieved surprise and were able to inflict such
damage. In other words, the enemy was a capable force. It had
the sense to occasionally act unpredictably . . . a fact American

forces had encountered often in the seven-year conflict. In war, defeat and death also come to those who do everything right.

To respond to Campbell's letter of reprimand, Ostlund dug back into the same trunk of facts he had presented to Natonski's investigators, only this time he carefully marshaled that evidence to address, point by point, the report's findings. In retrospect, Ostlund said, he believes that the sheer volume of information may have detracted from the CENTCOM investigators' understanding of Wanat. He presented little to Campbell that he had not presented earlier, but he delivered it more effectively. He believed that anyone who weighed the evidence fairly could reach only one conclusion: that he and his fellow officers had been wrongly chastised. "Either the decision would be made on the basis of the facts, or it would be politically driven," he said. He met with Campbell for an hour and a half on April 14, 2010. The general also heard from Preysler and Myer. And two months later, Campbell *completely* reversed himself.

Ostlund's reprimand was revoked, utterly, as were Preysler's and Myer's. The second memo to Ostlund from the general is a study in throwing a speeding train violently into reverse.

"I withdraw, cancel, and annul the reprimand because it does not reflect the totality of the facts as now known," he wrote. Campbell found that the earlier probe had focused too narrowly on the events of the battle itself, and had failed to adequately consider the context of Ostlund's command. He found, "My review led me to believe that you, Captain Myer, and Colonel Preysler . . . [exercised] a degree of care that a reasonably prudent person would have exercised under the same or similar set of circumstances. To criminalize command decisions in a theater of complex combat operations is a grave step indeed. It is also unnecessary, particularly in this case."

Campbell's was the last word on the investigation. Probably the best that the reprimanded officers could hope from him was leniency, that he would weigh the errors of Wanat against the entirety of their careers and decide that the charge of dereliction was too harsh. But Campbell went way past that. He erased and debunked every single criticism of Preysler, Ostlund, and Myer.

Citing the complete evidence and testimony offered by the officers, and particularly by Ostlund—all of which had been made available to earlier investigators—Campbell wrote, "You can say that my interpretation of your decisions and actions evolved. . . . There is no such thing as a perfect decision in war, where complexity, friction, uncertainty, the interlocking effects of the actions of independent individuals, and the enemy all affect the outcome of events." He went on, "That U.S. casualties occurred at Wanat is true. However, they did not occur as a result of deficient decisions, planning, and actions of the entire chain of command. . . . In battle, casualties are inevitable. Regrettably, they are often the price of victory."

4. Aftermath

Major Matt Myer didn't do much to defend himself. When he saw the extraordinary effort Ostlund was making, he put his faith in his commander . . . and in the army.

Myer has a taciturn self-assurance that struck some of his inquisitors as smug, but he is the son of an infantry officer, and in the last decade he has seen far more combat than most of the officers judging him. He is inclined to let his conduct speak for itself. He was not ashamed of his actions at Wanat. His heroism in the fight itself had been officially recognized. If the army was going to fault him for things outside his control . . . well, that said more about the institution than it said about him.

He had personally supervised Second Platoon's hazardous move from Bella, and had been the last man to leave. Instead of immediately joining Brostrom and the men at Wanat, he had flown on to Camp Blessing, where he had been directed to answer the questions of army investigators looking into the Apache attacks of July 4 that had caused such a stir. Myer was not just a "witness" to that incident, as the original reprimand had pointedly stated—he was its central figure. He had cleared the targets for attack. The deaths had colored perceptions of the American effort throughout the Waygul, so getting the facts out was an urgent battalion priority—indeed, later critiques of the Battle of Wanat pointed to the July 4 Apache attacks as a possible cause of the local hostility that apparently aided the Taliban attackers. When he had finished testifying, he left for Wanat on the first available transport, bringing water and supplies with him. He had arrived the afternoon before the battle. He had been, in the words of Sergeant Dzwik, "Exactly where he was supposed to be when he was supposed to be there."

He told General Campbell in their one-on-one interview, "This is very humbling. I'm not just conversing with you to try to get out of something. I looked at this very critically, and here are the reasons why I was doing what I was doing, which I think are well within the scope of my duties."

He didn't say much more.

In June 2010, at about the same time that Ostlund, Myer, and Preysler were receiving their letters from Campbell—the letters that withdrew the reprimands—family members of the men killed in the battle gathered at Fort McPherson in Georgia to be briefed by both Natonski and Campbell about the CENT-COM investigation. The families knew nothing of Campbell's about-face. They were expecting something grimly ceremonial—expecting to hear a detailed account of the mistakes the CENT-COM investigation had documented, and then to have, as it were, the heads of the three officers most directly responsible for the deaths of their sons and husbands handed to them on a plate. The event was heavy with grief, but electric with anger and indignation.

Natonski went first, and did not disappoint. He walked the families through the details of the battle and the supposed failings of its commanders. He noted the good intentions of everyone involved, but pronounced his detailed, damning judgments of Preysler, Ostlund, and Myer. It was as though the U.S. Army, through this retired Marine general, was humbling itself before them, admitting that its leadership errors had contributed to their losses . . . in a sense, apologizing. It went on for more than two hours, and the family members found it cathartic.

Brostrom felt as though he and the others had finally achieved some "closure," although Natonski's pronouncements seemed to stimulate in him and some of the others a desire for still more official mortification. There was talk immediately afterward about possibly bringing criminal charges. The effort had felled the chain of command from brigade down to company level. At one point, Brostrom remarked, "The division got off scot-free," suggesting that blame for the episode now ought to reach even higher up.

Then, after a short break, Campbell appeared. He told the audience that this was going to be yet another a "difficult day" for them, and then stunned them with his verdict, overturning every finding Natonski had just presented. The audience sat in silence as he explained the authority he had been given by the secretary of the army to pronounce judgment, walked them through the procedure he followed, and explained his decision.

"The officers listed in the report exercised due care in the performance of their duties," he said. "These officers did not kill your sons. The Taliban did."

The silence lasted for a few moments more. Then Brostrom erupted. He made an effort to control his anger, but his voice rose to a shout, "Nine soldiers dead and twenty-seven wounded!" He repeated the findings in the report that had just been officially presented—lack of resources, of manpower, of equipment, of supervision—and when things had started to go wrong, "No risk mitigation!" he shouted. "You tell me what the battalion commander did to mitigate those risks! . . . If he was too busy taking care of thirteen other outposts, then why in the hell did they go to [Wanat] in the first place?"

He was interrupted by applause from other family members.

"It's because nobody had the balls to say don't do it!" said Brostrom. ". . . There is no excuse. Things were going wrong. Nobody took any action. . . . They left those kids out there to be slaughtered!"

"I can absolutely understand your emotion," said Campbell.

"You can't," answered Brostrom. "You didn't lose a son."

Campbell held his ground. General Casey had advised him when he took the assignment to make sure before deciding that he was firmly convinced, "because however you decide you are going to piss somebody off." The session devolved further. Brostrom remarked to one of the other shocked family members, "This is a nightmare." He went on to accuse Campbell, who had in fact bucked the findings of the entire chain of command with his opinion, of acting as a toady for the army.

"You were told to soften this for the U.S. Army, and that's exactly what happened here," he said. "You went out and did your own investigation and came up with totally 180-degree-out findings. . . . I didn't send my son to Afghanistan to be executed!"

His wrath toward Ostlund boiled over. Beneath his polished and very savvy campaign to expose leadership failures, beneath all of the charges of inadequate supplies and support, there was a simple desire to hurt those who had put his son and the other dead in jeopardy. His hatred was now in the open. Brostrom's opinion of the battalion commander, once glowing, was now dark. Colonel Ostlund not only had led their sons "to slaughter," but had set back the American effort in that part of Afghanistan "two or three years." Ostlund was a "narcissist," a war-lover, and a coward, who stayed safely behind the defenses of his command post while pushing his men to take unnecessary risks in order to win his unit medals and glory—indeed, Chosen Company had recently received a Presidential Unit Citation. He accused Ostlund of inappropriately using white phosphorus, an incendiary weapon that burns so fiercely that it can destroy enemy munitions, and that has been linked to war crimes.

Campbell countered that the record showed just the opposite, that Task Force Rock had been superbly led. He cited several indicators of efficiency, noted his own thirty years of experience in command, and said he had rarely seen a battalion so well led.

"*I know this guy* and he is going to do it again," said Brostrom.

In fact, the two men have never met. They spoke on the phone several times soon after his son's death, after Ostlund offered to answer any questions about the episode, and during that same period they had exchanged several e-mails. But the contacts had ended when Brostrom had begun his campaign.

The Battle of Wanat became the most exhaustively examined incident of Afghan war. Whatever lessons can be learned from it have been learned. Ostlund has been fully reinstated, and recently returned from a second tour in Afghanistan as commander of the Joint Special Operations unit responsible for covert raids on the Taliban and Al Qaeda leaders. It was a central leadership post at a very high level in the Afghan campaign, serving directly with Petraeus, so the Wanat episode has not hobbled his standing in the army. In the long run it probably will. Any ambition Ostlund may have had for general officer is gone. There are scores of eligible colonels for every such slot, and the cloud raised by Brostrom's charges will linger despite the official vindication. Ostlund is currently completing a fellowship at Tufts University, and has hopes of rejoining the special operations command.

"I will continue to serve until the army tells me to go home," he told me, "as it very nearly did two years ago!"

He is disappointed, he said, that the fallout from Wanat will continue to distort perceptions of Task Force Rock's service in Afghanisan.

"No one had even come close to replicating our success," he said wistfully, "and yet that tour's actions are continually being called into question, and will be forever."

Matt Myer was inspired by this whole bruising experience to stay in the army, despite whatever shadow it casts over his reputation.

"Look, the army could've flicked me away easily," he said. "Nobody would have even said anything. They would've been like, 'Yeah, who was that guy again? I don't know.' Because the army's just this huge machine. I would be replaced handily. Yet hours and hours of time were put into [evaluating the charges against] Captain Myer and Colonel Ostlund, because I think leaders cared about us. Their values point to doing what is right, not just what is easy." He aspires to that himself, he said, and if someone like him gets discouraged and leaves, disenchanted by the difficulty of the process, then "that's one less person who is going to do things the right way."

For Brostrom, the story got worse. When the CSI released the final version of its history of the battle, it substantially rewrote Cubbison's first draft. Gone were the criticisms of the command decisions to locate and resource the outpost at Wanat, and gone were suggestions that the brigade command had botched the operation. If any American officer had made fatal mistakes at Wanat, the final version now concluded, it was Lieutenant Jonathan Brostrom. In the final CSI study, instigated by his father, Jon Brostrom is faulted, always indirectly—the report uses the term "platoon leadership"—for the placement of Topside, and for failing to utilize the Afghan soldiers at the outpost to conduct patrols. It noted the sour opinion Second Platoon had of its Afghan allies, based on experience—Afghan troops had fled during the Ranch

House attack, and the outpost under construction was named for a beloved comrade killed by "friendly" Afghan fire. In this battle, all the studies found that the Afghan soldiers at Wanat performed well, held their ground, and contributed critical fire in the base's defense. Using them to patrol might have alerted the platoon to massing enemy forces. Senior officers who pored over details of the battle believe the lieutenant's most serious mistake may have been not complaining about Second Platoon's vulnerability. He did not, as an infantry officer would say, "shoot up the red star cluster," demanding more help from his company commander when things had started to go wrong. Lieutenant Brostrom had chosen to work with the men and equipment he had and make the best of it, an understandable and even commendable decision, but in retrospect one that proved fatally wrong.

So the train Dave Brostrom set in motion has ended by tarnishing the memory of his son's leadership. Brostrom is now battling the CSI to again amend its report. And he has not given up his pursuit of Bill Ostlund. This summer he filed a motion seeking the colonel's personal correspondence from the period in question. Ostlund has refused to provide it.

No one has been left unsullied by the protracted and painful effort to dissect what happened at Wanat. Who, apart from a determined enemy, is to blame for the nine American soldiers dead and twenty-seven wounded? Do we blame the lieutenant who, working with limited resources, opted to build defenses instead of mounting patrols? Do we blame the captain who obeyed orders to answer questions in an important investigation instead of hurrying to supervise work at the new outpost? Do we blame the lieutenant colonel who was forced to constantly shuffle men and mortars and missile systems and observation drones among fifteen widely scattered outposts in an ever-changing landscape of threat? Do we blame the generals who accepted this seemingly impossible mission and tried to achieve it with forces and resources stretched thin? Or do we blame the Bush administration for trying to do too many things at the same time? Do we blame an ever-hopeful America for its historic tendency to overreach?

Brostrom, for one, feels strongly where the blame should go. He is convinced that Campbell's about-face was a cover-up, pure and simple, an instance of the army closing ranks around its own. "The fix was in," he says, referring back to the comments General Casey made to him at the ceremony in Hawaii, the conversation Casey remembers differently. The Brostroms' anger and suspicion continue, even as their second son, Blake, serves as an army helicopter pilot. Casey, who retired in April, remains troubled by Wanat. He said that he has been asked several times at speaking engagements to name something that he regrets from his service as chief of staff. Each time he has mentioned Wanat. He feels the army bungled its responsibility to the families of those killed after the battle, and "lost" some of them. He says "some," but he is thinking particularly of Dave Brostrom.

There is one thing that about the Battle of Wanat that will remain forever beyond reproach. At the worst of the fight, Lieutenant Jonathan Brostrom ran to the point of greatest danger and died to help his men.

The Ploy

Atlantic, May 2007

1. The Body

It was a macabre moment of triumph. At a closed compound within Balad Air Base in Iraq, behind Jersey barriers thirty feet high, the men and women of the interrogation mill crowded around a stark display: two freshly dead men, bare and supine on the floor.

The audience members were expert interrogators, most of them young, some of them military, others civilian contract workers. They called themselves "gators," and they were the intelligence arm of Task Force 145, the clandestine unit of Delta Force operators and Navy SEALs who hunt down terrorists on America's most-wanted list. For years, their primary target had been Abu Musab al-Zarqawi, the Jordanian leader of the grandly named Al Qaeda in Mesopotamia, the gloating, murderous author of assassinations, roadside bombings, and suicide attacks. Together, living and working inside this "battlefield interrogation facility," the gators had produced leads for the Task Force to chase. They had put in thousands of hours probing, threatening, flattering, browbeating, wheedling, conning, and questioning, doing what Major General William B. Caldwell IV, in his press conference the next day, would call "painstaking intelligence gathering from local sources and from within Zarqawi's network." It was, as Caldwell would put it, "the slow, deliberate exploitation of leads and opportunities, person to person," all striving to answer just one critical question: Where is Zarqawi *right now?*

This day, June 7, 2006, had finally produced the answer.

And so here he was, stretched out on the floor, stiff, pale, gray, and swollen in death, his "spiritual adviser," Shcikh al-Rahman, lying alongside him. The men had been killed, along with two women and two small children, when an American F-16 had steered first one and then another five-hundred-pound bomb into the house they occupied in a palm grove in the village of Hibhib. Task Force operators had recovered the men's bodies and carried them as trophies to Balad. Both now had swaths of white cloth draped across their midsections, but were otherwise naked. Zarqawi's face—wide, round, and bearded; his big eyes closed; a lurid smear of blood across his left cheek—was unmistakable from his frequent videotaped boasts and pronouncements. He had been more sought-after than Osama bin Laden, and in recent years was considered the greater threat.

No more. The mood was one of subdued celebration. President Bush would call that day to congratulate the Task Force's boss, the Joint Special Operations Commander Lieutenant General Stanley McChrystal. For many, the satisfaction was tempered by photos of the dead children. They were hard to look at.

The unit's female J2, or chief intelligence officer, embraced a young woman in a T-shirt and khaki cargo pants who was part of the two-person gator team that had produced what is known in the trade as "lethal information."

"I am so glad I chose you for this," she said.

McChrystal himself came by. A tall, slender, very soldierly looking man, he was an army briefer during the Persian Gulf war, but has been infrequently seen or photographed in recent years because of his clandestine post. He and his top commanders stared down at Zarqawi with evident satisfaction. Everyone leaned in to listen.

"Yep," said one of the colonels, "that's one dead son of a bitch."

Early the next morning, the terrorist's demise was revealed to the rest of the world at the Combined Press Information Center, in Baghdad.

"Today is a great day in Iraq," said General Caldwell, the spokesman for the Multi-National Force in Iraq. "Abu Musab al-Zarqawi is dead, no longer able to terrorize innocent Iraqi civilians. . . . Today, Iraq takes a giant step forward—closer to peace within, closer to unity throughout, and closer to a world without terror."

Perhaps. Like so much else about the Iraq war, it was a feel-good moment that amounted to little more than a bump on the road to further mayhem. Today, Iraq seems no closer to peace, unity, and a terror-free existence than it did last June. If anything, the brutal attacks on civilian targets that Zarqawi pioneered have worsened.

Still, the hit was without question a clear success in an effort that has produced few. Since so much of the "war on terror" consists of hunting down men like Zarqawi, the process is instructive. In the official version of how it happened, which is classified, the woman embraced by McChrystal's J2, and her two male interrogation partners, received primary credit for the breakthrough. All three were duly decorated. But like the whole war in Iraq, the real story is more complicated, and more interesting.

The truth is known to those interrogators involved, to their immediate chain of command, to a military historian who

interviewed the principals, and to a small circle of officials who
have been briefed about it. There are detailed accounts of the
interrogation sessions that describe the tactics and motivations
of the gators. So there are those who know the story well who
were not directly involved in it. In deference to the secret nature
of the work, I have used, not the real names of the interrogators
involved, but the aliases they assumed in Iraq. Their story affords
a unique glimpse of the kinds of people employed in this secret
effort and how they work, and it limns the hidden culture of
interrogation that has grown up in the last six years.

2. "The Customer"

Most of the gators directly involved in this breakthrough were
recruited in 2005. They were young men and women who had
accumulated valuable experience conducting hostile interrogation.
Some were on active duty, a good number from military police
units. Some were veterans of Afghanistan and Iraq, where they had
so distinguished themselves that the Special Operations Command
had sought them out. Some were working for private contractors
such as L-3 Communications; some were civilian employees of the
Defense Intelligence Agency. Some had experience in civilian law
enforcement or criminal law, and had volunteered to do such work
for the military. Some were lawyers. Some had advanced degrees.
Some called themselves "reserve bums," because they signed on
for tours of duty in various parts of the world for six months to a
year, and then took long, exotic vacations before accepting another
job. One raced cars when between jobs; another was an avid surfer
who between assignments lived on the best beaches in the world;
another had earned a law degree while working as a city cop in
Arlington, Texas; another worked as an investigator for the U.S.
attorney's office in Montgomery, Alabama. They all loved the work
and accepted the most dangerous and important assignments.

This one had come with an irresistible job description that included phrases like *high priority*, *top secret*, and *for an unidentified military client*. Enlistees were sent to the army's interrogation school at Fort Huachuca, in southeastern Arizona, for a few weeks of brushup training. They all received a dazzling two-hour Power-Point presentation about Iraqi history and culture. They had all surmised right away that the job meant working with "special operators"—the military's elite, secret soldiers, who handle only top-priority jobs—but they did not know for sure until after the training, when they were flown from Arizona to Fort Bragg, in North Carolina, headquarters for the Special Operations Command. At Bragg, no one speaks directly of Task Force 145, but it was abundantly clear that this was the outfit they would be working with. They were told, "There is no such thing as rank where you are going; everyone is focused on the mission. No one will get any credit for anything that happens."

Before being sent to Iraq, the gators underwent a final interview designed to weed out anyone emotionally ill-suited for the work. During the interview, the eager recruit would usually be insulted. "You must be kidding," the questioner would say. "You don't have anywhere near enough experience to do a job like this." Any recruits who got angry, flustered, or upset—and some did—were sent home. Those selected to proceed were instructed to adopt aliases by which they would be known "in theater."

Only then were they told that the "customer" would be Zarqawi.

3. The Team

Balad Air Base is a sun-blasted fifteen-square-mile expanse of concrete, crushed stone, and sand about an hour's drive north of Baghdad. It is one of the largest and busiest bases in Iraq, complete with a Green Beans coffee shop, Pizza Hut, and Burger

King open around the clock. It is also known as Camp Anaconda, or, informally, as "Mortaritaville," for the frequency of mortar attacks on the twenty-five thousand personnel stationed there. Few of that number ever set foot behind the towering concrete barriers in the far north corner, known to one and all as "the Compound," home to the estimated one thousand American and British special-operations soldiers of Task Force 145, and to the most urgent special-ops campaign in the world.

Because of the exigency of the fight in Iraq, according to groundbreaking reports by Sean Naylor of *Army Times*, Zarqawi had been assigned a higher priority than even Osama bin Laden or Osama's second in command, Ayman al-Zawahiri. The Task Force's elite soldiers, its "shooters," include Delta operators, SEALs, members of the air force's Twenty-Fourth Special Tactics Squadron, and selected soldiers from the army's Seventy-Fifth Ranger Regiment. Transportation is provided by helicopter crews and pilots from the Nightstalkers, the army's 160th Special Operations Aviation Regiment. The tempo is rapid; the unit conducts an average of a mission a day, with four strike forces stationed around Iraq. The intel operation that guides the Task Force hums around the clock, seven days a week. Its mission is to unravel Al Qaeda in Mesopotamia and other insurgent groups from the inside out, by squeezing each new arrest for details about the chain of command. Newly arrested detainees are continually delivered to the facility, blindfolded, bound, wearing blue jumpsuits.

Inside the Compound are a number of small buildings that have been recently erected as well as two large ones left over from when Saddam Hussein's air force owned Balad—one a dome-shaped airplane hangar, the other a flat-roofed structure of about the same size. Both were painted tan to blend with the desert landscape. The flat-roofed building houses the holding cells, each of which has stone walls, a concrete slab, a pillow, and a blanket. Detainees are kept one to a cell. The interior of the hangar is

divided into ten interrogation rooms, separated by plywood walls
and usually furnished with white plastic chairs and a small table.
Each room has a video camera so that a senior interrogator in a
separate control room with two rows of TV monitors can observe
the questioning.

During the hunt for Zarqawi, interrogations took place in
two shifts, morning and night, with interpreters, or "terps," providing translation. The gators wore civilian clothes for their sessions, and were allowed to grow out their hair or beards. The less
the detainees knew about the gators' rank or role in the military,
the better. There was virtually no downtime. When the gators
were not questioning detainees, they were writing up reports
or conferring with one another and their commanders, brain-
storming strategy, eating, or sleeping in their air-conditioned
"hooches," small metal rectangular containers flown in by contractors. Alcohol was forbidden. Their rec center had a gym, a
television set that got the Armed Forces Network, and a small
Internet café. But recreation was not especially encouraged. One
gator described the atmosphere as "spare and intense, in a good
way." They were doing their country's most vital work.

The hunt for Zarqawi had begun shortly after the invasion
of Iraq, in the summer of 2003, when the U.S. military took two
Special Forces units (one was in Iraq looking for Saddam Hussein; the second had been in Afghanistan hunting for Osama bin
Laden and other Al Qaeda leaders) and joined them into what
was then called Task Force 6-26. The Special Forces had come
maddeningly close to getting Zarqawi on several occasions. In
late 2004, Iraqi security forces actually captured Zarqawi near
Falluja but, supposedly ignorant of his identity, released him. In
February 2005, Task Force members had learned that he would
be traveling on a stretch of road along the Tigris River, but their
timing was off, and after the elusive terrorist crashed through
their roadblock, he was gone.

The interrogation methods employed by the Task Force were initially notorious. When the hunt started, in 2003, the unit was based at Camp Nama, at Baghdad International Airport, where abuse of detainees quickly became common. According to later press reports in the *New York Times*, the *Washington Post*, and other news outlets, tactics at Nama ranged from cruel and unusual to simply juvenile—one account described Task Force soldiers shooting detainees with paintballs. In early 2004, both the CIA and the FBI complained to military authorities about such practices. The CIA then banned its personnel from working at Camp Nama. Interrogators at the facility were reportedly stripping prisoners naked and hosing them down in the cold, beating them, employing "stress positions," and keeping them awake for long hours. But after the abuse of prisoners at Abu Ghraib came to light in April 2004 and developed into a scandal, the military cracked down on such practices. By March of last year, thirty-four Task Force members had been disciplined, and eleven were removed from the unit for mistreating detainees. Later last year, five army Rangers working at the facility were convicted of punching and kicking prisoners.

The unit was renamed Task Force 145 in the summer of 2004 and was moved to Balad, where the new batch of gators began arriving the following year. According to those interviewed for this story, harsh treatment of detainees had ended. Physical abuse was outlawed, as were sensory deprivation and the withholding or altering of food as punishment. The backlash from Abu Ghraib had produced so many restrictions that gators were no longer permitted to work even a standard good cop–bad cop routine. The interrogation-room cameras were faithfully monitored, and gators who crossed the line would be interrupted in mid-session.

The quest for fresh intel came to rely on subtler methods. Gators worked with the battery of techniques outlined in an army manual and taught at Fort Huachuca, such as "ego up," which involved flattery; "ego down," which meant denigrating a detainee; and various simple con games—tricking a detainee into believing you already knew something you did not, feeding him misinformation about friends or family members, and so forth. Deciding how to approach a detainee was more art than science. Talented gators wrote their own scripts for questioning, adopting whatever roles seemed most appropriate and adjusting on the fly. They carefully avoided making offers they could not fulfill, but often dangled "promises" that were subtly incomplete—instead of offering to move a prisoner to a better cell, for instance, a gator might promise to "see the boss" about doing so. Sometimes the promise was kept. Fear, the most useful interrogation tool, was always present. The well-publicized abuses at Abu Ghraib and elsewhere put all detainees on edge, and assurances that the U.S. command had cracked down were not readily believed. The prospect of being shipped to the larger prison—notorious during the American occupation, and even more so during the Saddam era—was enough to persuade many subjects to talk. This was, perhaps, the only constructive thing to result from the Abu Ghraib scandal, which otherwise remains one of the biggest setbacks of the war.

It was an exciting, challenging job, filled with a sense of urgent purpose. Most of the gators had a military background, and they found the lack of protocol liberating. As the gators had been told, rank inside the Compound was eschewed entirely. People referred to each other by their nicknames. The key players in the final push for Zarqawi were known as follows:

- "Mary." The young woman congratulated by the J2, Mary was a stocky woman in her early twenties, with Asian features and straight dark hair; her intelligence and tenacity had earned her the reputation of being the most skilled interrogator in the unit.

- "Lenny." A navy reservist from the Philadelphia area, Lenny had a background in the computer industry and had done a previous tour at Guantánamo Bay's Camp X-Ray. A wiry man in his mid-thirties, he smoked a lot, shaved his head, and wore a goatee. He had a tough-guy, street-kid manner and was usually teamed with Mary.
- "Dr. Matthew," aka "Doc." A tightly wound, precise man in his thirties, with short, thin blond hair, Doc had worked as a military police investigator before becoming a reservist. A senior interrogator at Balad, he was considered an intellectual, though "Dr." was an exaggeration: he had earned two master's degrees, one in international relations and another in management. Between jobs, he surfed.
- "Matt." A slender, dark-haired active-duty air force technical sergeant in his early thirties, Matt liked to present himself as a simple country boy, but was not one. He was from the Midwest and liked to race cars.
- "Mike." A commercial pilot from Nebraska in his early thirties, he had joined the army because he wanted to be involved in the war effort. Mike had less experience than most of his colleagues, but was extremely energetic and gung-ho, and was quickly regarded as a natural.
- "Nathan." Tall, wiry, and dark-haired, Nathan was one of the few gators who could speak some Arabic. A civilian contractor, he once got into trouble with the unit commander for stretching even the Task Force's loose apparel standards by wearing a bright Hawaiian print shirt to the mess area.
- "Tom." A veteran of Bosnia in his late forties, Tom was unlike most of the others in that he was married and had children. He was short and round and balding, and was always slightly unkempt.

This was the team that would locate Zarqawi.

4. The Interrogation Begins

The first major clue on the trail that led to Zarqawi came in February 2006, from a detainee Mike was questioning. The man had admitted his association with the "Anger Brigades," a Sunni group loosely aligned with Al Qaeda. In a series of intense sessions that the other gators regarded as brilliant, Mike learned of residences in Yusufiya that the insurgent leadership sometimes used as safe houses. These were placed under heavy surveillance, and through a mid-April series of raids during which a number of suicide bombers were killed, a new crop of suspected mid-level Al Qaeda operatives was captured and delivered to Balad. It was on one of these raids that Task Force operatives found a videotape with outtakes from a recent press release by Zarqawi, the one showing him wearing a black do-rag, a black shirt, and a suicide belt, and carrying an automatic rifle. The outtakes showed this fearsome terrorist fumbling awkwardly with the weapon and being instructed in its use by another man. The military released the new images in hopes of diminishing Zarqawi's stature. What the Task Force members didn't realize when they discovered the tape was that Zarqawi himself was only one block away.

Five of the men captured during these raids were assigned to teams of interrogators at Balad. Two of them would prove to be the most valuable. The first, whom we will call Abu Raja, was assigned to Matt and Nathan. The second, an older and more imposing figure, we will call Abu Haydr. He was assigned to Mary and Lenny.

Abu Raja was a sophisticated man in his mid-thirties, a professional who spoke fluent English. Round, soft, and balding, he wore the regulation Saddam-era Sunni mustache. He came from a family that had been well connected during the tyrant's reign; before the American invasion, he'd had a thriving business. A relative of his had been killed in the long war Iraq fought with

Iran in the 1980s, and Abu Raja hated all Iranians. He saw the American invasion as a conspiracy between the Iranian mullahs and the United States to wipe out Iraq's minority Sunni. Though Abu Raja was initially defiant, Matt and Nathan sized him up as a timid man, neither ideologically committed nor loyal. They battered him with rapid-fire questions, never giving him time to think, and they broke him—or so they thought—in two days. He agreed to talk about anyone in Al Qaeda who outranked him, but not about those who held less important positions. Since the Task Force's method was to work its way up the chain, this suited the gators perfectly.

Abu Haydr was more difficult. He was a big, genial man who nearly buckled the white plastic chairs in the interrogation rooms. He was forty-three years old, with a wide, big-featured face, big ears, a well-trimmed beard, and fair skin. He was married and had four children. He also spoke fluent English. Before the American invasion, he'd had an important government job and had made a good living. He had hated Saddam, he said, but when the tyrant fell, he had lost everything. He looked tough and boasted that he had a black belt in karate, but his manner was gentle and his hands were smooth and delicate. He spoke in a deliberate, professorial way. He had studied the Koran and, while not overtly pious, knew a great deal about his faith. He admitted his sympathy for the insurgency. He had been arrested once before and had served time in Abu Ghraib, he said, and did not wish to return. He said Abu Raja had asked him to attend the meeting where they had both been captured, and that he was there only because the people at the house needed him to operate a video camera. This was the same story told by Abu Raja.

"I don't even know why we were there," he told Mary and Lenny.

For three weeks, from mid-April to early May, Abu Haydr was questioned twice daily, and gave up nothing. Three weeks are a long time for interrogators to hold on to someone. Mary was forceful and thorough. Lenny's approach was consistent; he tended to hammer at the man relentlessly, taking him over the same ground again and again, trying to shake his confidence or just wear him out. It wasn't sophisticated, but it often got results, especially when combined with Lenny's imposing tough-guy demeanor. Abu Haydr took it all in stride, stubbornly unruffled. Before every response, he would lean his bulk back in the groaning chair, fold his graceful hands, and meditate like a scholar.

Doc, who was observing both interrogations in his role as a supervisor, saw that Mary and Lenny were getting nowhere, so he asked the army captain supervising the process to replace them. This was not an unusual request from a senior gator; detainees were often placed with different teams when someone felt that an alternative approach might work, and Doc had asked to shift detainees before. But this request was denied. Given the circumstances of Abu Haydr's arrest—and his age and sophistication—the Task Force was highly suspicious of him, and there were those high up the chain, Doc was told, who wanted Mary on his case.

It was easy to dismiss Doc's concern, for several reasons. He was known to be overbearing, and some of the gators felt he supervised their work a little *too* closely. That may have been particularly galling to Mary, who had been at Balad longer than Doc and was regarded as the best in the Task Force. Their colleagues knew that there was something of an ego clash between those two. Doc was older and more experienced, and could not always disguise his resentment at the organization's higher regard for his younger colleague. To orient him when he first arrived at Balad, Task Force officers had assigned Doc to observe Mary. After a few days, he had told his commander that he was unimpressed and had asked to be placed with someone else. When he was assigned the supervisory role, he reprimanded

Mary directly and complained to others that she seemed to spend an inordinate amount of time on the Internet chatting with her boyfriend, who was also serving in Iraq. She sometimes skipped staff meetings, and while some of the gators were doing three and four interrogation sessions a day, she stuck resolutely to two. Doc argued that she seemed inexcusably out of step with the fervid pace. Others had also expressed concern about the way she dressed. Mary usually wore khaki cargo pants and two layers of T-shirts, which they suggested were cut too low at the top, exposing cleavage, or too high at the bottom, showing her midriff—displays offensive to religious Muslim detainees. But neither Mary's status nor her habits had changed in response to Doc's complaints. The tension between them was observed by all. For whatever combination of reasons, Doc's attempt to move her aside failed.

Abu Raja, meanwhile, was a wreck. After weeks of grilling, he had given up all that he could give, he complained, but the gators kept after him day and night. One day, Doc sat in on his questioning. Watching an earlier interrogation, he had noticed that Abu Raja had slipped. Going over a story he had told many times before, Abu Raja mentioned for the first time that Abu Haydr had sometimes met alone with Abu Raja's boss.

This was different, and odd. Why, Doc now asked, would Abu Haydr, Abu Raja's subordinate, a man who had been called in just to operate a video camera, be meeting separately with Abu Raja's boss? The detainee had no convincing explanation for it, and it left Doc with a hunch: What if Abu Raja had been lying about the other man's status all along? Why would he do that? Was he frightened of Abu Haydr? Protecting him? It forced a fresh look at the older prisoner, who was more impressive than Abu Raja anyway. What if he had been Abu Raja's superior in the organization? That would mean Abu Haydr was even more important than they had suspected. The problem was that Mary and Lenny were stymied, and the team had all but given up on getting information from Abu Haydr. He had made a final statement, had been issued new clothes, and was on the list for transport back to Abu Ghraib.

With Abu Haydr just hours away from being shipped out, Doc asked for and received permission to speak to him one more time. He knew Abu Haydr dreaded going back to Abu Ghraib, and he had an idea for how to get him talking.

5. Breaking Abu Haydr

The two men—the big Iraqi and the intense blond gator—talked for five hours in the interrogation room; because Doc was a supervisor himself, their conversation was not monitored. They talked about children and football and wrestling.

"I was a great wrestler," Abu Haydr announced.

"You look like one," Doc told him.

In his weeks of watching, the American had noted Abu Haydr's habitual braggadocio. The Iraqi constantly trumpeted his skills—the black belt in karate, advanced knowledge of the Koran, expertise in logic and persuasion— like a man determined to prove his importance and worth. He spoke little about his family: his wife and children. He seemed completely preoccupied with himself, and he presented his frequent opinions forcefully, as the simple truth. The two men discussed the historical basis of the rift between the Sunni and the Shia, something Doc had studied. And when the Iraqi lectured him on child rearing, Doc nodded with appreciation. When Abu Haydr again proclaimed his talents in the arts of logic and persuasion, Doc announced himself out-argued and persuaded.

Their conversation turned to politics. Like many other detainees, Abu Haydr was fond of conspiracy theories. He complained that the United States was making a big mistake allowing the Shia, the majority in Iraq, to share power with the Sunni. He lectured Doc on the history of his region, and pointed out that the Iraqi Sunni and the United States shared a very dangerous enemy: Iran. He saw his Shia countrymen not just as natural allies with Iran but as more loyal to Iranian mullahs than to any idea of a greater Iraq. As he saw it—and he presented it as simple fact—the ongoing struggle would determine whether Iraq would survive as a Sunni state or simply become part of a greater Shia Iran. America, Abu Haydr said, would eventually need help from the Sunni to keep this Shia dynasty from dominating the region.

Doc had heard all this before, but he now said that it was a penetrating insight, that Abu Haydr had come remarkably close to divining America's true purpose in Iraq. The real reason for the U.S. presence in the region, the gator explained, was to get American forces into position for an attack on Iran. They were building air bases and massing troops. In the coming war, the Sunni and the Americans would be allies. Only those capable of looking past the obvious could see it. The detainee warmed to this. All men enjoy having their genius recognized.

"The others are ignorant," Abu Haydr said, referring to Mary and Lenny. "They know nothing of Iraq or the Koran. I have never felt comfortable talking with them."

It was not a surprising comment. Detainees often tried to play one team of gators off another. But Doc saw it as an opening, and hit on a ploy. He said that he now understood the prisoner's full importance. He said he was not surprised that Abu Haydr had been able to lead his questioners around by their noses. Then he took a more mendacious leap. He told Abu Haydr that he, Doc, wasn't just another gator; that he was, in fact, in charge of the Compound's entire interrogation mill. He was the boss; that was why he had waited until the last minute to step in.

"I believe you are a very important man," he told Abu Haydr.
"I think you have a position of power in the insurgency, and I
think I am in a position to help you."

Abu Haydr was listening with interest.

"We both know what I want," Doc said. "You have information you could trade. It is your only source of leverage right
now. You don't want to go to Abu Ghraib, and I can help you,
but you have to give me something in trade. A guy as smart as
you—you are the type of Sunni we can use to shape the future of
Iraq." If Abu Haydr would betray his organization, Doc implied,
the Americans would make him a very big man indeed.

There was no sign that the detainee knew he was being played.
He nodded sagely. This was the kind of moment gators live for.
Interrogation, at its most artful, is a contest of wits. The gator has
the upper hand, of course. In a situation like the one at Balad, the
Task Force had tremendous leverage over any detainee, including
his reasonable fear of beating, torture, lengthy imprisonment,
or death. While gators at that point were not permitted even to
threaten such things, the powerless are slow to surrender suspicion. Still, a prisoner generally has compelling reasons to resist. He
might be deeply committed to his cause, or fear the consequences
of cooperation if word of it were to reach his violent comrades.

The gator's job is to somehow find a way through this tangle
of conflicting emotions by intimidation or bluff. The height of
the art is to completely turn the detainee, to con him into being
helpful to the very cause he has fought against. There comes a
moment in every successful interrogation when the detainee's
defenses begin to give way. Doc had come to that moment with
Abu Haydr. He had worked at the detainee's ego as if it were a
loose screw. All of his ruses dovetailed. If Doc was an important,
powerful man—better still, if he was secretly in charge—his respect for Abu Haydr meant all the more. After all, wouldn't it

take the most capable of the Americans, the man in charge, to fully comprehend and appreciate Abu Haydr's significance?

Doc pressed his advantage.

"You and I know the name of a person in your organization who you are very close to," Doc said. "I need you to tell me that name so that I know I can trust you. Then we can begin negotiating." In fact, the American had no particular person in mind. His best hope was that Abu Haydr might name a heretofore unknown mid-level insurrectionist.

Ever circumspect, Abu Haydr pondered his response even longer than usual.

At last he said, "Abu Ayyub al-Masri."

Doc was flabbergasted. Masri was the senior adviser to the second in command of Al Qaeda in Mesopotamia, Zarqawi. The gator hid his surprise and excitement. He thanked the prisoner, pretending that this was the name he had expected.

"Now we can begin negotiating, but I have to leave now."

"I only will talk to you," said Abu Haydr.

"I can't promise you that," the American said. "You should talk and be friendly to whoever comes in to question you. I will be watching."

He promised—avoiding the usual hedge—to get Abu Haydr an extra blanket and extra food, and did. And he got the detainee off the list for transport to Abu Ghraib.

6. The Feud That Felled Zarqawi

"Why did he decide to talk?" asked Doc's commander.

The gator explained that he had promised Abu Haydr "an important role in the future of Iraq." He also reported that he had represented himself to the detainee as the man in charge. That infuriated Lenny, who was already annoyed that Doc had been questioning "his" prisoner behind his back. Lenny complained that the lie undermined his position in future interrogations.

"He was scheduled to leave," Doc reminded him.

Despite Abu Haydr's insistence that he speak only to "Dr. Matthew," his interrogation resumed with the regular team of gators. Lenny promptly told him that their colleague had lied when he said he was in charge.

Doc was infuriated, and he took his outrage to his commander. Lenny was more concerned about protecting his turf than the mission, Doc complained, and demanded that Lenny be reassigned, but this request, too, was denied. Concerned that his breakthrough would be squandered, Doc decided to go behind his commander's back. He paid the first of many unauthorized visits to Abu Haydr's cell in the holding block, away from the cameras monitoring the interrogation rooms. He told Abu Haydr that his colleagues were not allowed to reveal that he was in charge.

"I'm still around, and I'm still watching," Doc told him. "Talk to them as if you were talking to me."

Abu Haydr asked how much information he would have to give to earn Doc's assistance.

"Right now, you are at about 40 percent," he was told, "but you must never mention our deal to anyone." Doc swore him to secrecy about their informal talks.

And, curiously, the feud between the gators began to help the interrogation. Abu Haydr seemed to enjoy the subterfuge. Doc's visits with him were unauthorized; if his fellow gators found out about them, they would be furious, as would his commander. So Doc, unable to deliver the captive's information himself, had to persuade Abu Haydr to talk, not to him but to Mary and Lenny. He stayed vague about what information he wanted and kept using the percentage scale to push the detainee. Sure enough, Abu Haydr responded. In his sessions with the others, he confirmed that his status was above Abu Raja's and began talking about significant figures in Al Qaeda. He was still cagey. He wanted to buy himself Doc's help, but he didn't want to pay any more for it than necessary.

Doc would regularly slip into Abu Haydr's cell to grade his progress.

"What percent am I at now?" the detainee would ask.

"Fifty percent," Doc would say.

This went on for three weeks, and soon the Task Force was mapping Zarqawi's organization with greater and greater detail. During a series of raids on May 13 and 14, shooters killed one of Zarqawi's lieutenants, Abu Mustafa, and fifteen others in his network. Eight suspects were detained. Intel gleaned from them sent the shooters back out to arrest more men, who delivered still more information. The eventual result was what the Task Force called an "unblinking eye" over the network. On May 17, two of Zarqawi's associates were killed, one of them his manager of foreign fighters. Punishing raids went on throughout that month.

Still, even though he clearly relished his "secret" sessions with Doc, Abu Haydr protected the men at the very top of the organization. The ploy played on his belief that he was operating in a multilayered reality, and at a deeper level than those around him; the secrecy just reinforced the ruse that Doc was a high-level connection. In the middle of this process, Mary started questioning Abu Haydr with the older gator they called Tom, and Lenny continued on in separate shifts by himself.

In early June, after Doc told the prisoner he was at "90 percent," Abu Haydr promised to give up a vital piece of information at his next session. And he did.

"My friend is Sheikh al-Rahman," he told Mary and Tom.

He explained that Rahman, a figure well-known to the Task Force, met regularly with Zarqawi. He said that whenever they met, Rahman observed a security ritual that involved changing cars a number of times. Only when he got into a small blue car, Abu Haydr said, would he be taken directly to Zarqawi.

Days later, with the Task Force watching from a drone high over Baghdad, Rahman got into a small blue car, but the surveillance team promptly lost him in traffic. There was tremendous disappointment and frustration at the Compound. Another precious chance had been lost. But after just a few more days, late in the afternoon of June 7, Rahman got into the blue car again. This time the Task Force observed him all the way to the little concrete house in the palm grove at Hibhib. Electronic intercepts may have helped confirm that Rahman was meeting with Zarqawi in the house (the terrorist leader never used cell phones, which are relatively easy to track, but he did use satellite phones, which are harder to pinpoint, but not—as he apparently assumed—impossible). Convinced they had their man, the Task Force leaders decided not to wait for their shooters to get into position. Waiting seemed ill-advised, and besides, storming the house would be likely to result in a firefight; in the confusion, Zarqawi might find another chance to slip away. A faster, more certain, and more deadly strike was ordered.

High over Iraq, the U.S. Air Force maintains a constant patrol of strike aircraft that can be called on immediately. The mission was assigned to two F-16 pilots, who had spent the day looking for roadside bombs from the sky. The pilots were told only that the target was "high value." At 6:12 p.m., one of the jets dropped the first laser-guided bomb; minutes later, it dropped the second. Both hit their target, reducing the house to rubble. Villagers said the earth shook with each blast.

According to General Caldwell, Iraqi forces were on the scene first, having heard the explosion from nearby. They found Zarqawi badly wounded but still alive, the only one to survive the strike. About half an hour after the second bomb hit, he was being carried out on a stretcher when the first American soldiers arrived, an eleven-man military training team embedded with a local Iraqi army unit. The Americans took Zarqawi from the Iraqis, and a medic began treating him, securing his airway. Zarqawi spat blood and drifted into and out of consciousness. Caldwell said that the terrorist tried to get off the stretcher, but the soldiers resecured him. His breathing was labored, and his lungs soon failed him. Then his pulse gave out. It was pleasing to his pursuers that Zarqawi's last sight was of an American soldier.

Caldwell initially said that a child was killed in the bombing, but altered his statement the next day to say that no children had been killed. In the Compound, pictures from the blast site showed two dead children, both under age five.

7. The Fight Goes On

A tape of the air strike was played at Caldwell's press conference. A black-and-white video shot from one of the bomber jets shows the long shadows of late afternoon on a dense patch of palm trees, and a large house before a narrow road. The first blast sends dark billows of gray smoke in four directions, in the shape of a cross. About two minutes later, when the smoke has blown off, the second blast produces a smaller, more contained plume of white smoke. Those inside would have had no warning. They would not have heard the jets, nor the bombs hurtling toward them.

Four of the gators involved were decorated for their service. Mary, Lenny, Tom, and Doc were called to the general's office. Doc and Lenny, the navy reservist, were awarded Bronze Stars; Mary and Tom received civilian medals. Two other civilian analysts were also recognized.

Several of those who had worked on the case for months felt the recognition was appropriate but somewhat misallocated. Mike, after all, had developed the information that had led to the arrests of Abu Raja and Abu Haydr; Matt and Nathan had broken Abu Raja; and Doc had invented the ploy that ultimately enabled the killing blow. His deep knowledge of Iraqi history and religion, and of Abu Haydr's distinctly Arab outlook, went well beyond the two-hour PowerPoint lecture on Iraqi culture the gators got at Fort Huachuca.

In the long run, the successful hunt for Zarqawi may not amount to much, but it offers lessons in how to use American power in subtler and more effective ways.

"The elimination of Zarwaqi is neither the beginning nor is it the end, but it is a stride in the direction of law and order, to an Iraq that is primed for the future, by a government that respects the rights of all Iraqi citizens," said General Caldwell at his triumphant press conference. He later added, "For the first time in three years, the Iraqi people really do have a chance here."

Some of the members of Task Force 145 were less sanguine. "Zarqawi's death was an achievement, but it was only symbolic," said one of them. "Zarqawi had hoped to incite a sectarian war, according to his letters, and he accomplished that. His strategy worked: target the Shia so they will retaliate. When we killed Zarqawi, there were ten just like him to take his place. As I see it, there is no incentive right now for the Sunni *not* to join the insurgency. We haven't offered them anything—no economic, ideological, or personal incentives. We tell them, 'You will have a voice in the government,' but they know that will not happen. They don't believe the Shia will give them a say. They hate the United States for creating this nightmare that destroyed their lives, and which clouds their future, but they need us as a buffer. I've talked to a lot of Sunni, and most are not motivated by religion or ideology. They are just trying to make it."

"This is the story of the whole war," said another. "'Kill this one guy, and it will make things all better.' I still don't understand where this notion comes from. It's like we are still fighting a conventional war. This one doesn't work that way."

Seventeen other raids were conducted in and around Baghdad soon after Zarqawi's death. The shooters found suicide vests, passports, Iraqi army uniforms, and license plates hidden under floorboards. Another twenty-five Iraqis were issued blue jumpsuits and led to the interrogation rooms. Task Force 145's primary focus shifted to Zarqawi's successor, Abu Ayyub al-Masri. The insurgents' bombings continued. The fight went on.

As for Abu Raja and Abu Haydr, they were processed and shipped out. "Probably to Camp Cropper," said one of the gators, referring to a detention facility near Baghdad International Airport.

Mary and Lenny felt that Abu Haydr deserved a reward of some kind, but they were reminded that he had been an important mid-level figure in the deadly insurgency, a man who had on his hands, at least indirectly, the blood of many civilians and American soldiers. The idea of a reward was quickly dropped.

And what of Doc's pledge to Abu Haydr?

"Doc promised him an important role in the future of Iraq," said one gator. "And, by God, Abu Haydr got it. He was the man who led us to Zarqawi."

The Last Ace

Atlantic, March 2009

The Doorstep of Oblivion

Over Cesar Rodriguez's desk hangs a macabre souvenir of his decades as a fighter pilot. It is a large framed picture, a panoramic cockpit view of open sky and desert. A small F-15 Eagle is visible in the distance; but larger and more immediate, filling the center of the shot, staring right at the viewer, is an incoming missile.

It is a startling picture, memorializing a moment of air-to-air combat from January 19, 1991, over Iraq. Air-to-air combat has become exceedingly rare. Even when it happens, modern fighter pilots are rarely close enough to actually see the person they are shooting at. This image recalls a kill registered during the Gulf war by Rodriguez, who goes by Rico; and his wingman, Craig Underhill, known as Mole.

A special-operations team combed the Iraqi MiG's crash site, and this was one of the items salvaged, the last millisecond of incoming data from the doomed Iraqi pilot's head-up display, or HUD. It was the final splash of light on his retinas, probably arriving too late for his brain to process before being vaporized with the rest of his corporeal frame. Pilots like Rodriguez don't romanticize such exploits. These are strictly matter-of-fact men from a world where war is work, and life and death hang on a rapidly and precisely calibrated reality, an attitude captured by the flat caption mounted on the frame: "This is an AIM-7 air-to-air missile shot from an F-15 Eagle detonating on an Iraqi MiG-29 fulcrum during Operation Desert Storm."

A snapshot from the doorstep of oblivion, the photo is a reminder that the game of single combat played by Rico and Mole, and by fighter pilots ever since World War I, is the ultimate one. It may have come to resemble a video game, but it is one with no reset button, no next level. It is played for keeps.

When Rodriguez retired from the air force two years ago, as a colonel, his three air-to-air kills (two over Iraq in 1991 and one over Kosovo) were the most of any American fighter pilot on active duty. That number may seem paltry alongside the twenty-six enemy planes downed by Eddie Rickenbacker in World War I, or the forty notched by Richard Bong in World War II, or the thirty-four by Francis Gabreski in World War II and Korea. Rodriguez's total was two shy of the threshold number for the honorific *ace*, yet his three made him the closest thing to an ace in the modern U.S. Air Force.

This says more, of course, about the nature of American airpower than it does about the skills of our pilots. It's hard to call what happens in the sky over a battlefield today "single combat." More than ever, an air war is a group effort involving skilled professionals and technological marvels, from the ground to Earth orbit. But within the world of military aviation there remains a hierarchy of cool, and fighter jocks still own the highest rung. The word *ace* denotes singularity, the number *one*, he who stands alone at the top. Its mystique still attracts ambitious young aviators, even if nowadays the greatest danger most of them face is simply flying the aircraft at supersonic speed.

American pilots haven't shot down many enemy jets in modern times because few nations have dared rise to the challenge of trying to fight them. The F-15, the backbone of America's airpower for more than a quarter century, may just be the most successful weapon in history. It is certainly the most successful fighter jet. In combat, its kill ratio over more than thirty years is 107 to zero. Zero. In three decades of flying, no F-15—not even any F-15 flown by an air force other than America's—has ever been shot down by an enemy plane. Rival fighters rarely test those odds. Many of Saddam Hussein's MiGs fled into Iran when the United States attacked during the Gulf war. Of those who did fight the F-15, like the unfortunate pilot whose cockpit view is framed on Rodriguez's wall, every last one was shot down. The lesson was remembered. When the United States invaded Iraq in 2003, Saddam didn't just ground his air force; he *buried* it.

That complete dominance is eroding. Some foreign-built fighters can now match or best the F-15 in aerial combat, and given the changing nature of the threats our country is facing and the dizzying costs of maintaining our advantage, America is choosing to give up some of the edge we've long enjoyed, rather than pay the price to preserve it. The next great fighter, the F-22 Raptor, is every bit as much a marvel today as the F-15 was twenty-five years ago, and if we produced the F-22 in sufficient numbers we could move the goalposts out of reach again. But we are building fewer than a third of the number needed to replace the older fighters in service. After losing hope of upgrading the whole F-15 fleet, the air force requested 381 F-22s, the minimum number that independent analysts said it needs to retain its current edge. Congress is buying 183, and has authorized the manufacture of parts for twenty more at the front end of the production line, enough to at least keep it working until President

Obama decides whether or not to continue building F-22s. Like so many presidential choices, it's Scylla and Charybdis: a decision to save money and not build more would deliver a severe blow to a sprawling and vital U.S. industry at a time when the nation is mired in recession. And once the production line for the F-22 begins to shut down, restarting it, even in reaction to a new threat, will not be easy or cheap. Each plane consists of about a thousand parts, manufactured in forty-four states, and because of the elaborate network of highly specialized subcontractors needed to fashion its unique airframe and avionics, assembling one F-22 can take as long as three years. Modern aerial wars are usually over in days, if not hours. Once those 183 to 203 new Raptors are built, they will have to do. Our end of the fight will still be borne primarily by the current fleet of aged F-15s.

When Obama unveiled his national security team in December, he remarked that he intended "to maintain the strongest military on the planet." That goal will continue to require the biggest bill in the world, but the portion that bought aerial dominance for so long may have become too dear. (The team's lone holdover from the Bush administration, Secretary of Defense Robert Gates, has not been an advocate for the F-22.) If Obama opts to shut down production on the aircraft, it will certainly be a defensible decision. After all, our impressive arsenals did not stop one of the most damaging attacks in our history seven years ago, mounted by men armed with box cutters. There are various ways of computing the cost of a fighter, from "unit flyaway cost," which is the price tag as the plane rolls off the line, to "program acquisition unit cost," which adds in the cost of the research, development, and testing. The former for the F-22 is about $178 million, and the latter about $350 million. Either way, the F-22 is the most expensive fighter ever built.

But even reasonable decisions can have harsh consequences. Without a full complement of Raptors, America's aging fighters are more vulnerable, and hence more likely to be challenged. Complaints from the air force tend to be dismissed as the laments of spoiled fighter jocks denied the newest, hottest toy. But the picture on Rodriguez's wall reminds us of the stakes for the men and women in the cockpit. Countries such as Russia, China, Iran, and North Korea will be more likely to take on the U.S. Air Force if their pilots stand a fighting chance. This could well mean more air battles, more old-style aces—and more downed American pilots. Not only aviators will feel the impact. Owning the sky is the first prerequisite of the way we fight wars today. Air supremacy is what enables us to send an elaborate fleet of machinery caterwauling over a targeted nation, such as Afghanistan or Iraq: the orchestrating AWACS (Airborne Warning and Control System, the flying surveillance-and-command center); precision bombers; attack planes, helicopters, and drones; ground support; rescue choppers; and the great flying tankers that keep them all fueled. This aerial juggernaut enables modern ground-fighting tactics that rely on the rapid movement of relatively small units, because lightly armed, fast-moving forces can quickly summon devastating air support if they encounter a heavy threat. Wounded soldiers can count on speedy evacuation and sophisticated emergency medical care. Accomplishing all this with anything like the efficiency American forces have enjoyed since the Vietnam war depends on owning the sky, which means having air-to-air hunter-killers that can shoot down enemy planes and destroy surface-to-air missile (SAM) sites before the rest of the fleet takes to the sky. Superior fighters are the linchpin of our modern war tactics. Having owned the high ground for so long, we tend to forget that it is not a birthright. Unless the twenty-first century is the first in human history to somehow transcend geopolitical strife, our military will face severe tests in the coming years. The United States will be expected to take the lead in any showdown against a sophisticated air force. So it is worth examining the nature of air-to-air combat today, and the possible consequences of not building a full fleet of F-22s. At the center of this question is that most romantic of modern warriors, the ace.

Going Acro

The skills that make a fighter pilot great have, like aircraft, evolved. Japan's celebrated World War II ace, Saburo Sakai, who shot down more than sixty planes in aerial combat, described in his memoir—*Samurai!*—the extensive acrobatic training he and his fellow recruits received in pilot school to improve their strength and balance even before they flew. They worked on reducing their reaction time and perfecting their hand-eye coordination by swiping flies out of the air. Balance, coordination, reaction time, a feel for the airplane, gunnery, the ability to calmly perform complex aerobatic maneuvers while under fire, a talent for thinking and acting quickly even while upside down or tumbling or out of control—these were all vitally important. But the paramount skill, Sakai recalled, was something the recruits had at the start: exceptional vision.

All of the young pilots had been selected for their perfect eyesight, but even more important was how broadly they could see, how wide a horizon they commanded, and how quickly they could focus on even the faintest off-center visual cue. They competed to locate stars in daylight. Sakai wrote:

> Gradually, and with much more practice, we became quite adept at our star-hunting. Then we went further. When we had sighted and fixed the position of a particular star, we jerked our eyes away ninety degrees, and snapped back again to see if we could locate the star immediately. Of such things are fighter pilots made.

> I personally cannot too highly commend this particular activity, inane as it may seem to those unfamiliar with the split-second, life-or-death movements of aerial warfare. I know that during my 200 air engagements with enemy planes, except for two minor errors I was never caught in a surprise attack. . . .

Surprise attack—seeing the enemy before he sees you—is still the killing edge; that is why Antoine de Saint-Exupéry, the fighter pilot and author, described dogfighting as less combat than "murder." Getting the jump on an enemy, hitting him before he sees you, is the best-case scenario, or the worst, depending on where you sit. As the air war over Japan became one-sided, in 1945, Sakai's eyes kept him alive; only two other pilots in his unit survived.

Today, of course, electronic systems extend a fighter's vision well beyond the range of the most acute eyeball. Aerial combat is no longer a matter of fixing your sights on a dodging enemy. Most of the maneuvering in air-to-air combat today takes place beyond visual range, or BVR. The modern fighter pilot flies strapped into the center of a moving electronic cocoon. His speeding jet emits a field of photons that can find, identify, and target an enemy long before he will ever see it. At the same time, his electromagnetic aura defends him by thwarting the enemy's radar. American pilots strive to find and shoot down enemy aircraft from outside what they call the "weapons engagement zone," or WEZ, which means safely beyond range of the enemy's missiles. Traveling faster than sound, the fighter pilot is part of a network that can spot an enemy over the horizon, sometimes before the enemy even leaves the ground; that can attack multiple targets simultaneously; and that in an emergency can react to an incoming threat before the pilot is even aware of it. Today's jet is a machine so powerful, so smart, and so fast that the fighter jock's biggest challenge is to safely fly and land it.

Combat in this arena has become virtual in every way except in its consequences. Tactics in a world of dueling electrons can be best understood in the abstract. Pilots speak of the need to extend their "timeline."

"When cavemen fought they had their fists, first of all," F-15 pilot Colonel Terrence "Skins" Fornof explained to me last year in Alaska. "Then someone came up with the sling, which meant he could attack before his enemy could get close enough to take a swing. The history of warfare technology has all boiled down to increasing the distance between you and your enemy's fist. Distance means time, and you gain the advantage by extending that timeline. Our goal is the same as it ever was: to kill the enemy before he even has a chance to employ his weapon. War is not fair. You don't want him to even get close enough to fight."

The best flier in the world stands little chance against a superior aircraft, but that doesn't mean just anyone can be a good fighter pilot. The skills required today are related to those of the early aces, but different. Perhaps the best way to explain is to take a closer look at Rodriguez. A lifelong military man, he is of average height with a bullish torso, a round face, brown eyes, and thinning gray hair. The house in Tucson where the picture hangs has been his home for two years—longer than any other place he has ever lived. He exudes brisk, straightforward confidence, without pretense or misgiving. Asked to name his single most important flying skill, the modern equivalent of Sakai's peripheral vision, Rodriguez struggles for an answer. It is something harder to grasp. It boils down to a talent for processing multiple information streams simultaneously.

"A World War II pilot would look at all of the things going on in the cockpit today, and his first reaction would be, 'You guys have too many things going on here at once.' You know, it is sensory overload," he said when we talked at his home. "When you put one of those old pilots in a modern simulator, he can fly the airplane. The airplane is as easy to fly today as it was back then, maybe actually easier, because now it has aerodynamic features that make it more forgiving from the standpoint of taking off and landing. But the old pilot will very quickly say, 'I can't keep up with all the sensors that are buzzing into my brain right now.' And every sensor that talks to you has a different frequency, a different tone, a different format, and with some of them you are only picking up audio, with others it's a visual, with some a combination of the two."

Rodriguez began pilot training in 1981, after graduating from the Citadel. He knew going in that, of the class of seventy pilot trainees, only about five would qualify to fly fighters. Most would graduate and play vital roles in the great air-war machine, but only the cream would win coveted fighter seats. The first wave of washouts came during simple maneuvers on the training jets. According to Rodriguez, "You start maneuvering and they'd get violently airsick. That was the biggest cut."

In the group that reached the next level, the academic workload sorted out the players who were most intense from the wannabes. Rodriguez was used to the cloistered atmosphere and grinding academic pace of a military school, so he excelled in that area, too. Those who excelled with him faced a new test: going acro.

"Suddenly acro was not just a cool thing you'd watch at the air show anymore," Rodriguez says. "*You* were acro. You were part of it and you had to be able to think on your back, on your head, at zero g and then at high g's, depending on the maneuver." Avoiding "gravity-induced loss of consciousness," G-LOC, during aggressive acrobatics is a physical struggle. As the force of gravity intensifies, blood drains rapidly from the brain unless the pilot fights back. The pressurized suit helps, tightening on the extremities and lower body, but the pilot learns to flex his legs, buttocks, and stomach muscles and to control his breath.

He emerges from such maneuvers wrung out and drenched with sweat.

It is a literal gut check. Rodriguez was lucky. He had the constitution for it. The only time he ever got airsick was one morning when the flying conditions looked unpromising and, assuming that his flight would be scrapped, he "proceeded to power down on two big, huge breakfast burritos." Then he had to fly after all.

"I was told we were going to go up and actually do some advanced handling, which was a fairly physically challenging event because it was putting the airplane to the extreme aerodynamic limits . . . falling down and getting into spins and stuff like that, so it was one of those things where I go, 'OK, stand by one.' I reached down and grabbed my barf bag, filled it up, put it back in my G suit, and said, 'OK, let's keep going.'"

Complex exercises required rapid mental calculations: if you entered a loop ten knots slower than anticipated, that meant your airspeed would be too slow to complete the entire maneuver, so you would have to make an adjustment, quite literally, on the fly.

"These were the kind of things that you could do sitting on your chair in your room, but when you have an airplane strapped to your back and you're sweating and you're pulling g's, then it's another matter," he said. "You had to do the math in your head." Needless to say, some people were better at this than others. Some pilots seemed to be able to do it intuitively, by the seat of their pants. Rodriguez was not one of them. But patient instructors and long hours in simulators, combined with a kind of desperation to succeed, eventually earned him a chance to fly the air force's hottest jets.

Only then did his real training begin, in Tucson and at Holloman Air Force Base, in New Mexico, and finally at the air force's "top gun" school, Nellis Air Force Base, in Nevada, where he flew training missions against a faux enemy, a dedicated force of experienced pilots trying hard to shoot him down. Technology is only part of what gives American pilots their advantage. As hugely expensive as it is to design, produce, fly, and maintain vanguard fighters, it takes far more effort and money to hone pilots' skills, to keep squadrons of pilots like Rodriguez constantly flying, practicing, and getting better. Even if other nations had the know-how, few could afford to build a fleet of advanced modern fighters, and fewer still could afford to sustain an up-tempo environment for the men and women who fly and maintain it.

Being the best means learning to fully inhabit that screaming node, high above the slow curve of the Earth, strapped down in a bubble where the only real things are the sound of your own breathing and the feel of sweat rolling down the center of your back. You are alone but not alone. You cope with constant, multiple streams of data, everything from basic flight information—airspeed, altitude, attitude, fuel levels—to incoming radar images displayed on small, glowing green screens stacked in rows before you and to both sides. In your helmet are three or four radio links: with the AWACS, with the ground, with your wingman, and with your flight leader. It is a little bit like trying to navigate at high speed with four or five different people talking to you at once, each with a slightly different set of directions. It is not for amateurs. By the time Rodriguez first flew into combat, he had hundreds of hours of training behind him, and being in the jet was second nature. With him were his wingman, his formation, and the superhuman reach of America's technological eyes and ears.

Hurling a few dozen jets into the sky against this, as Saddam did in 1991, was most unwise.

"Fox!"

Rodriguez and his wingman, Craig "Mole" Underhill, confronted their first Iraqi MiG-29s early on the third morning of the war that took back Kuwait from Saddam Hussein. They were leading a helicopter assault on Saddam's early warning radar sites on the border with Saudi Arabia, clearing the way for devastating bombing runs on Iraqi airfields.

The air battle in this conflict was brief, decisive, and more intense than most Americans realized. By the time the Pentagon began showing off publicity videos of "smart bombs" pulverizing Iraqi targets, America and its allies owned the sky, but in getting there, thirty-eight allied aircraft were destroyed. On this early sortie, Rodriguez and Underhill were flying out of Tabuk, an air base in northwestern Saudi Arabia, near the border with Jordan. As often happened in this fast-moving arena, they were initially tasked with one objective and then reassigned when they were airborne. They moved out at the head of a thirty-six-aircraft strike force bearing down on a target forty miles southwest of Baghdad. As they approached, several MiG-29s came up to challenge them.

The MiG-29, like the F-15, is considered a "fourth-generation" fighter. (Since the first jet fighters started flying, there have been four great evolutionary advances, each representing a significant leap in technology.) The Soviet Union began deploying the MiG-29 about nine years after the F-15s went on line, and the plane itself is comparable to its American counterpart. But given all the other advantages enjoyed by the allied pilots, the brave, outnumbered Iraqi pilots launching themselves at the approaching juggernaut might as well have been committing suicide. "From western eyes, it's a suicide mission," Rodriguez told me. "From the eyes of the guy being invaded, he's protecting the homeland."

Even greatly disadvantaged, the Iraqi fighters were dangerous, and as it happened the large American force made a potentially fatal mistake that Saturday morning. The incoming MiGs were spotted, of course, but in the confusion of the moment either tactical errors were made by the strikers, or the Iraqi pilots exploited a seam in the American defenses. The AWACS command had spotted the MiGs immediately when they took off, and had handed them on to a navy formation of F-14s, which failed to intercept them. When Rodriguez and Underhill were alerted to the approaching threat, it came as a jolting surprise. The MiGs were just thirteen miles out and closing at a speed of more than a thousand knots. Both pilots immediately began evasive maneuvers.

Rodriguez dived steeply, getting below the lead MiG, where he would be harder to find on its radar—pointing down, the radar's signal can get confused by all the signals bouncing back up from the ground. Then Rodriguez began flying in a low arc, keeping the MiG on his wing line, making himself "skinny," presenting as small a radar target as possible. Within minutes the two fighters would be in a visual turning fight, a situation familiar to many experienced pilots from earlier wars, but one that is not supposed to happen in modern air warfare. The biggest difference between this fight and the old ones was speed. It would unfold not in minutes but in seconds. Rodriguez's posture was strictly defensive: he could not target and shoot at the Iraqi plane, but it could shoot at him.

A cockpit alarm warned him when the MiG's radar locked on him. The threat was still just a blip on his screen; he hadn't actually seen it yet. He was frightened and thinking furiously when in his headset he heard Underhill shout, "Fox!"—the code word for *I have just fired a missile.*

Rodriguez looked back over his shoulder, following the smoke trail of Underhill's missile, and then, looking out ahead of it, caught his first and only glimpse of the MiG. This is the precise instant captured from the Iraqi pilot's perspective in the photo on Rodriguez's wall. It turns out that the picture preserves—not a moment of personal triumph for him, as I had originally supposed—but a moment of intense fear and vulnerability. Rodriguez's little F-15 in the distance was not predator but prey, trapped and awaiting a kill shot that would never come, because in the next instant the MiG became a huge fireball in the sky. The whole encounter lasted a little more than ten seconds.

"Mole saves my bacon because he kills this guy before he can take a shot at me," Rodriguez said as we sat in his office.

There was no time to celebrate, because the destroyed MiG's wingman was now closing in on them, just seven miles out. Underhill and Rodriguez split their planes wide apart and assumed different altitudes. That way, the incoming MiG might spot one of them, but probably not both, and they improved their chances of eyeballing it. Before shooting at it, they had to make sure it was Iraqi—many planes were in the air that morning—but they wouldn't have time to run the normal electronic matrix used to distinguish friend from foe.

They both saw the MiG at the same time. It had an Iraqi flag painted on it. Rodriguez passed the enemy fighter about three hundred feet off its wing.

"He notices that I am there," Rodriguez said. "He also notices that Mole's about twenty thousand feet above us. But at no point do I think he correlates the two of us as a formation."

If the MiG pilot went for Underhill, then Rodriguez could shoot him down; if he came for Rodriguez, "then Mole eats him up." Confused, the angling MiG started up, and then down; this gave Rodriguez time to fly inside the MiG's turning circle, putting himself into roughly the same attack position the earlier MiG had had on him.

The Iraqi pilot, no doubt hearing an alarm telling him that an F-15 had locked him in its radar, attempted a classic split S maneuver, which is the quickest way to reverse direction in the air. Flying parallel to the ground, he flipped his aircraft upside down and then attempted to fly a half circle, diving down, pulling up, and leveling off to head in the opposite direction. It was the right escape maneuver for an altitude of at least five thousand feet, but the pilot, in his alarm and haste, neglected to compute one vital bit of data: he was only six hundred feet up. He flew his jet straight into the desert floor.

"He had lost his situational awareness," Rodriguez explained. "He was trying to perform a maneuver that he can do comfortably at five thousand or ten thousand feet, and doesn't realize that the fight, which started at eight thousand feet, had degraded and degraded closer to the desert floor. It's a lack of training, a lack of experience, but given the situation he was in against two F-15s, my argument is that no one would have done much better. He's already seen his flight lead explode. He might not have hit the desert floor, but he was going to die anyway."

These air kills were among the first by American pilots since Vietnam. An entire generation of fighters had come and gone without encountering an enemy in the sky. Three dozen Iraqi jets were shot down in the war, and Rodriguez was one of six pilots in his squadron who got two.

The second of his aerial kills was what he called "more routine," more typical of modern aerial combat. A week after the first episode, he was flying in what the air force calls a "wall of Eagles," a formation of four F-15s spread out in the sky over roughly five to eight miles at thirty-three thousand feet to maximize their visibility and radar range. Beneath them was thick undercast, a carpet of clouds opaque to their eyes but transparent to electronic surveillance systems. At that point, the remaining Iraqi air force was so vulnerable that the AWACS plane assisting the F-15s picked up the enemy jets the minute they started their engines, while they were still on the ground. Rodriguez and the other pilots watched three radar blips form on their screens as the MiGs took off and climbed. Rodriguez assumed that the planes were, like the rest of Saddam's air force, escaping into Iran.

"They were basically running scared," he says. "Extremely scared."

It took a few moments to identify the jets as MiG-23s, and then the wall of Eagles began preparing to launch missiles at them.

"We think we're going to have to stay above the clouds and we're never going to see the missiles do their job, and all of a sudden there's a big sucker hole, an opening in the clouds below," he says. "The F-15s dived to about thirteen thousand feet. The fleeing MiGs were hugging the terrain, flying just three hundred to four hundred feet above the ground, when we started launching AIM-7 missiles at them.

"And, sure enough, the missiles did their job."

The Iraqi flight leader took the first hit. An American missile sliced through his plane, taking out the engine but leaving the shell of the plane intact. With the plane trailing a thick cloud of smoke, the pilot began turning to the north, apparently trying to return to his base. Rodriguez's flight leader fired a Sidewinder, a heat-seeking missile that lit up the sky when it hit, turning the unfortunate Iraqi pilot and his plane into an enormous fireball.

Rodriguez's missile ripped straight through his target. The MiG apparently flew right into it. There was no large explosion. The missile just tore the jet to pieces, turning it into what Rodriguez called "a ground-level sparkler," scattering debris across a wide swath of desert.

Rodriguez's third and last kill came eight years later, on March 24, 1999, when he flew his F-15 as part of the NATO force attacking Serbian positions during the Kosovo campaign. Rodriguez's squadron was assigned to lead an attack on a Serbian SAM site in Montenegro. On the way they would pass over an airfield in Pristina, Kosovo, where the Serbs had carved out hangars for their fighters inside a mountain. No one was sure what kinds of planes, if any, were hidden there.

Rodriguez took off from Cervia, Italy, on a clear night. As he ascended, he could see the Italian coast to the west, lit up like a throbbing discotheque. He was pointed east, toward what was then still called Yugoslavia.

"It was pitch-black," he recalls. "You know, here's a region of the world that has been at war, and where every light at night is a potential target. So everything below was just pitch-black. You go, 'Man, it's two different worlds here.'"

The plan was for the multinational formation to fly lights-out, but the different levels of training and experience began to tell. American pilots fly black all the time, so when the order came to turn off lights, it was just another night's work. But for some of the Dutch, German, British, Italian, Spanish, and Turkish pilots, this wasn't so easy.

"The first time we tried it, as I looked, I could see a train of fighters spread out over a hundred miles behind me, and when the 'lights-out' order came, they all went black," said Rodriguez. "Then, sure enough, the comfort factor for some of these guys started to go. They started getting a little antsy and then, all of a sudden, *pooh, pooh, pooh,* the lights started coming back on. And we go, 'OK, guys, we really need to do this completely lights-out. If we don't do this, we're not going to be ready.' But we got everybody into the train."

A measure of confusion persisted, however. When the target was reached, the squadron commenced an air assault that would have taken an all-American unit five to eight minutes. This one took nearly an hour. Feeling increasingly vulnerable to attack by ground or air threats, Rodriguez circled and waited, trying to make his flight pattern unpredictable. As Rodriguez and his wingman, Bill Denham, turned back toward Italy, they picked up an aircraft coming up from the airfield in Pristina. At first it bore north, away from them, but then it turned.

The American planes began to conduct the standard series of checks to identify the plane. The F-15 is equipped with a full range of instruments to, in effect, interrogate an unidentified plane in the air. They were coordinating with an AWACS, working through some language difficulties (the controllers spoke accented English). A process that would normally take twenty seconds took three times as long, which is a huge difference when you're traveling hundreds of miles per hour. Rodriguez and his wingman were rapidly approaching the weapons engagement zone, where they would lose the advantage of their longer-range missiles.

They were on the edge of the WEZ as the ID was completed, and Rodriguez launched an "advanced medium-range air-to-air missile," or AMRAAM, a new element of his arsenal added after the Gulf war. In the air force, they call it the Slammer. One advantage it affords is a "fire and forget" feature; because the missile has its own homing and guidance system, the pilot need not stay pointed at the target. He is free to turn and evade the incoming jet in case his shot for some reason misses. Rodriguez stayed with his missile for as long as he could.

"It all went into slow motion, and I felt like the missile and I were kind of flying in formation for a while," he recalls. "It just seemed to stay there for a couple of seconds and then, whoosh! It disappears. You see that glow [the missile's exhaust], and that becomes just a little ember, and then it's gone. And of course at night you can't follow it anymore. The smoke trail goes away. But I could see it start to curve, and I go, 'OK, it looks like it's doing the right lead-pursuit tracking.' And the missile did everything it was advertised to do. We have a little counter display inside the cockpit that ticks down the time to intercept, and when the counter said zero, I looked outside through my canopy to the general vicinity of where I knew the target was going to be. I mean, that fireball was huge."

Rodriguez said it was as though three or four giant sports stadiums had turned on all their lights at the same time.

"The reason it was so magnificent," he said, "was that everything was covered in snow. So the fireball reflected off the snow, causing an even bigger illumination of the sky and everything around it."

It was the first air kill of the Kosovo campaign, and the last of Rodriguez's career. He gave little thought to the person he had just incinerated.

"I'm sure he had been a Yugoslav air force pilot, which was a good air force for what they have," he said. "I don't personalize the war. He was doing what I was doing for my country."

"Eye-Watering"

Manufactured by McDonnell Douglas starting in the early 1970s, the twin-engine, supersonic F-15 was the first aircraft built with the understanding that a plane's avionics, or electronic guts, were as important as its aeronautics, its flying capabilities. It was designed and built around an enormous radar disk.

"When it came on line thirty years ago, it had the best radar, the best weapons-employment displays ever, and the best maneuverability of any aircraft out there," Brigadier General Thomas "Pugs" Tinsley told me when I visited him in Alaska last spring, a few weeks before his death. At the time, Tinsley commanded the air force's Third Wing out of Elmendorf Air Force Base, in Anchorage. "The F-15's thrust-to-weight ratio was way ahead of anything else, and its flight-control system was much smarter and more stable. It could go out there and just fly circles around the F-4 [the Phantom, its immediate predecessor] and have its way with MiG-23s [the Soviets' best fighter], just eat them up."

For more than a quarter century, the speed and sound of a formation of F-15s or F-16s have made a commanding statement about American power, as anyone who has ever stood under such a formation can attest. You feel its approach before you can hear or see it, a low vibration that starts in your toes and rises until the gray jets flick past overhead. Only then comes the roar. They are gone before your eyes focus on them, leaving behind the orange glow of their afterburners and a wash of energy that hammers your ears and rattles your spine. As a patriotic display it is impressive, something to stir pride and admiration—but imagine being on the receiving end of such power, to have it shooting at you. It is one of the most convincing arguments ever made for surrender.

Despite the romantic legend of the fighter pilot in his leather helmet and silk scarf, aerial combat has always been more about engineering than flying. When we consider that the Wright brothers' first tentative flight at Kitty Hawk took place just over a century ago, the evolution of aerial combat has been astonishing. Within forty years, from World War I to the Korean conflict, pilots went from shooting at each other with pistols from propeller-driven biplanes to dueling with cannons and missiles in jet aircraft moving faster than sound. At the start of World War II, American fighter and bomber pilots were adapting their tactics to cope with superior German and Japanese fighters, and by the end they had aircraft that could fly so high, so fast, and for so long that few enemy fighters could even get close enough to shoot at them. Saburo Sakai noted, sadly, that the B-29 Superfortress was simply "insuperable." By the time of the conflict in Korea, "air breathers," or jets, had replaced the finely crafted propeller-driven fighters of lore, and aerial duels between American F-86 Sabres and Soviet-built MiG-15s were fleeting visual encounters where the biggest challenge was to get close enough to fire.

Today the fight has moved beyond visual range, into the realm of electromagnetic waves, and involves what fighter pilots call "look-down, shoot-down" capability. The air war is a contest between radar systems, countermeasures, and missiles. American pilots have long enjoyed the advantages of seeing an enemy first and of having missiles with the range and speed to hit the enemy from beyond the WEZ. But those advantages have gradually eroded. A fighter jet's theoretical "kill ratio" is based on projections of how many enemy fighters it could shoot down before getting shot down itself when faced with an unlimited number of attackers at once. The F-15's eight-to-one kill ratio—which is what it enjoyed throughout most of its history and which reflected more than anything else the finite capability to carry munitions—is now closer to three to one. "If the enemy has radar-guided missiles, now we're shooting at each other," Lieutenant Colonel Chuck "Corky" Corcoran told me last year at Elmendorf. Corcoran is a former F-15 pilot who now commands the 525th Fighter Squadron, the Bulldogs, one of the three F-22 squadrons just now getting planes. "If those enemy weapons have similar capabilities to ours, I've got to employ some sort of tactic to gain an advantage, whether it's getting higher and faster so I can shoot first, or checking away [shifting slightly off course] to increase his missile's time of flight."

Drawing out that time, even by a split second, can mean everything, because it allows your missile to strike first. Once the enemy's plane is destroyed, its radar can no longer steer his missile.

"His missile is looking for reflected radar energy that he's pointing at you, so if your missile gets to him and blows him up and kills his radar before his missile gets to you, then you are going to live," Corcoran explained.

An AMRAAM missile like the one Rodriguez used over Kosovo was a major step forward because it frees the attacking plane from having to keep its radar pointed at the target. The American plane can launch a missile from outside the WEZ, turn, and kick on its afterburners before the target has a chance to even shoot.

These tools rely, of course, on radar, which can be jammed.

"If you can't match your enemy's technology, you can always subtract from it," says Wayne Waller, a Virginia contractor who designs radar systems for the F-15. "You may invent something that gives you an advantage, but you can't hang on to it for very long. Our radar used to be difficult to jam, but the capability to do that has improved geometrically. That knowledge is out there. And the jamming advances cost a lot less than improving the radar."

Countries that cannot afford to build fleets of the most advanced supersonic fighters can afford to build pods with clever software to mount on older airframes. This was brought home dramatically in Cope India 2004, a large aerial-combat training exercise that pitted F-15 pilots from Elmendorf against India's air force, which is made up of the MiG-21 and MiG-29, and the newer Mirage 2000 and Russian-built Su-30. The exercises were conducted high over north-central India, near the city of Gwalior.

"We came rolling in, like, '*Beep-beep*, superpower coming through,'" Colonel Fornof told me. "And we had our eyes opened. We learned a lot. By the third week, we were facing a threat that we weren't prepared to face, because we had underestimated them. They had figured out how to take Russian-built equipment and improve on it."

A small country can buy a MiG-21 on the world weapons market for about $100,000, put in a better engine, add radar and jamming systems that are more sophisticated, improve the cockpit design, and outfit it with "launch and leave" missiles comparable to the AMRAAM. These hybrid threats are more dangerous than any rival fighters America has seen in generations, and they cost much less than building a competitive fourth-generation fighter from scratch. The lower expense enables rival air forces to put more of them in the air, and because the F-15 can carry only so many munitions, American pilots found themselves overwhelmed by both technology and sheer numbers during the exercises over India.

Today the average age of the F-15s in use is twenty-four years, which in the world of modern electronics means they were born several geological ages ago. When the F-15 started flying missions, Jimmy Carter was president and the Cold War was shaping geopolitics. Most Americans didn't own a home computer. People were still buying music on vinyl albums and cassette tapes. The first F-15s had roughly the computer capability of the video game Pong. If anything, the pace of innovation is even faster in the military than in the civilian world, and as better look-down, shoot-down capabilities have come on line, they have been systematically layered and squeezed into the aging airframe of the F-15. This has led to the dizzying complexity of the fighter's cockpit. But no matter how many gizmos the wizards can squeeze into the F-15, it remains an old fighter.

"If you take a Pinto and put really nice tires on it, it's still a Pinto," Colonel Corcoran says. His choice of the unlovely, pedestrian Ford sedan as a metaphor is telling: pilots like Corcoran see the F-22 as a Formula One racer by comparison. "You can put a bigger engine in the Pinto, but the frame is not built to handle the higher speeds," he said. "To build a fifth-generation fighter, you have to start from the ground up."

Some of the pilots I spoke to described the F-22 as such a huge leap in capability that it ought to be considered not a fifth-generation fighter, one step up from the F-15, but sixth-generation.

"It is really two big steps ahead of anything else out there," Corcoran told me. "All of the data from all the different sensors in the aircraft are fused. The F-22 has one big display in the middle of the cockpit, so you are kind of sitting in the middle of that display, and all of the sensors run on their own. And tracks show up all around you, 360 degrees, and all of it in color. So the red guys are bad, the green guys are good, and the yellow guys—we don't know who the yellow guys are yet. So without the pilot doing anything, you have this 360-degree picture of the battle space around you. With the F-15, after a couple of years of training, you might be able to achieve that level of awareness."

Major Derek Routt and Lieutenant Colonel Murray Nance have a unique perspective on the new fighter. They both fly for the air force's Sixty-Fifth Aggressor Squadron, mimicking the tactics and capabilities of enemy air forces in war games. I met them last summer at Elmendorf, where they were in the middle of Red Flag exercises—realistic war games carried out every few years—featuring "battling" F-15s and F-22s.

"I saw a Raptor just yesterday," Routt said. "It was way above me. I was just being called dead at the time. You usually don't see it until it's done with you, flying overhead, rocking its wings, saying, 'Thanks for playing, fellows.'

"I flew in a comparison test with both the F-15 and the F-22," he continued. "You flew against the F-22 one day, and the next day we took the same profile and flew against the F-15. I fought both of those, and there was absolutely no comparison. This is not a paid advertisement for the F-22. You talk to any aviators in the world, ask what they would like to fly, and if they don't say the F-22, then they are lying. I would kill to fly it."

"It is hard to kill what you can't see," Nance said. "It's eye-watering, the kind of turning it can do."

"Eye-watering?" I asked.

"Makes you cry. I mean, you realize, 'How did he just do that?'"

Last summer at Elmendorf, Corcoran sat me down in the cockpits of both an F-15 and an F-22 to show me just how different they are. As the F-22 is to a modern point-and-click laptop—user-friendly—the F-15 is to the first clunky personal computers, the ones where you had to type instructions in basic computer language to perform the simplest of tasks. All of the avionics on the F-22 were designed from the ground up, and are fully integrated. The big central screen makes situational awareness intuitive. Better still, it is linked with all the other Raptors in its formation, and with the AWACS command. There is now only one page, and everyone is on it.

"It's all there in front of you," General Tinsley explained. "Where am I? Where are you? Who is out there? Who is locking on to me? It gives you a God's-eye view that is simply a thing of beauty. I have sensors in the F-22 that don't just look out the front of the airplane; they are spread all over the aircraft. I can see somebody anywhere. It is easier on the pilot, which makes him a more efficient killing machine."

The improvement is so great that some of the older F-15 pilots tend to look down their noses at the youngsters flying the F-22.

"To be good in the F-15, you have to work at it," Corcoran told me. "It's easier to separate the men from the boys and identify the real talent. But the way I see it, the less time my F-22 pilots have to spend sorting out all the data, the more time they have to think tactically and react to what is happening around them. That means our entire force, from top to bottom, is more effective."

The F-22's most remarkable quality is that it is "combat-coated," which means it is painted with material that absorbs rather than deflects the signals beamed out by the enemy's defense systems, making it virtually invisible to radar. Talking about it, Tinsley grew gruffly animated.

"Now I have stealth!" he said. "The F-15 is a big airplane; you can see that thing outside of ten nautical miles. The F-16 is a little bit better in a dogfight, visually, because it's a smaller aircraft. I might not be able to see it turning until about seven or eight nautical miles. The F-22, the bad guys can't even see me on their radar, and even in visual range the Raptor is small. My missiles hit them before they even know I am there. And I'm not just talking about air-to-air; I'm talking about air-to-ground."

The biggest threat to American fighters during the first wave of an assault is from surface-to-air missiles. They are much cheaper to build and maintain than a fleet of supersonic fighters, so smaller countries such as Iran have invested heavily in them. Attacking SAM sites in an F 15 is risky work. But with the F-22, pilots are back to shooting fish in a barrel. "The F 22 avionics allow me to be a better battle-space manager and efficient killer," Tinsley explained. "I have stealth, so I have the surprise piece. And then on top of all that, I can do it at supercruise. I can climb higher than other fighters, I can go faster with lower fuel consumption, so I can cover a larger space. And no one can see me. Now we're getting that eight-to-one kill ratio I need to maintain superiority."

The Return of the Fair Fight

The air force fears that the dominance of U.S. airpower has been so complete for so long that it is taken for granted. The ability of the United States to own the skies over any battlefield has transformed the way we fight. The last American soldier killed on the ground by an enemy air attack died in Korea, on April 15, 1953.

Russia, China, Iran, India, North Korea, Pakistan, and others are now flying fourth-generation fighters with avionics that match or exceed the F-15's. Ideally, from the standpoint of the U.S. Air Force, the F-22 would gradually replace most of the F-15s in the U.S. fleet over the next fifteen years, and two or three more generations of American pilots, soldiers, and marines would fight without worrying about attacks from the sky. But that isn't going to happen.

"It means a step down from air dominance," said Richard Aboulafia, an air-warfare analyst for the Teal Group, which conducts assessments for the defense industry. "The decision not to replace the F-15 fleet with the F-22 ultimately means that we will accept air casualties. We will lose more pilots. We will still achieve air superiority, but we will get hurt achieving it." General Tinsley suggested that there will be a deeper consequence: other countries will be more tempted to challenge us in the air. The dominance of the F-15 had already begun to erode before the Soviet Union collapsed, in 1991. The last fighter the Soviets produced, the MiG-29, had similar aeronautic capabilities, and its radar and weapons systems gave it look-down, shoot-down tools on a par with the F-15's. Today, Russia is equipping its air force with Su-35s, and has offered them for sale. Hugo Chávez's Venezuela is a customer of the plane's close cousin, the Su-30. These fighters are every bit the match of the F-15. Combine that with the hybrid threat posed by revamped older fighters, and the fight in the air begins to look fair for the first time in a half century.

It was fashionable in the years after the collapse of the Soviet Union to argue that the threat of conventional warfare was no longer relevant, because no other nation could compete with the United States on conventional terms. The attacks of September 11, 2001, underlined that argument; the new threat was "asymmetrical"—small cells of sophisticated terrorists against whom our huge arsenals were useless.

Conventional weaponry may be useless against terrorists, but that doesn't mean the old threats have disappeared. Russia's incursion into Georgia and threatening gestures against the Baltic states; Iran's persistence in pursuing nuclear weapons and ballistic missiles; North Korea's decision to ignore its agreement to cease building nuclear weapons—all are reminders that the threat posed by belligerent nation-states is still real. If Georgia is admitted to NATO, the United States and other member nations will be obliged by treaty to defend it from Russia. China continues to rapidly expand its air force. Conflict with these nations isn't inevitable or even necessarily probable, but as we become more vulnerable in the air, it may well become more likely.

"What happens when we no longer own that advantage in the air?" Tinsley asked me. "Are our enemies going to feel a little froggy and push the limits? Why haven't we fought that many wars? If America hadn't built the F-15, would it have been the same story? How much did our fleet of F-15s keep other countries at bay? If we had been stuck with the F-4 and someone had come along with a MiG-29, would he have stepped out and done some damage? We have to replace *all* the F-15s with F-22s."

This is the position you would expect from an air force general, whose job was to make sure America continues its unquestioned ownership of the sky. One might just as easily argue that lack of such complete superiority will act as a healthy restraint on American military aggression. After all, the latest big war, in Iraq, was one we started. If we are more likely to bleed, perhaps we will be slower to fight.

But fights will come. The squadron Colonel Corcoran is pulling together at Elmendorf will consist of an elite few. The 525th Bulldogs have a tradition reaching back to World War II, when their pilots flew P-51 Mustangs and P-47 Thunderbolts over Europe. Such squadrons are small, close-knit clubs and, especially when based in such remote outposts as Elmendorf, define their pilots' personal, social, and professional lives. Their members sit at the pinnacle of their profession, every bit as much an elite as (perhaps more so than) professional athletes, though without the athletes' pay or celebrity. Photos of the Bulldogs' exploits and decorated heroes line the walls of the squadron's bar—or, as one happy pilot told me with a shot glass in one hand and a beer in the other, "Not a bar, a 'Heritage Room'!"—where pilots gather for ritualized bouts of drinking, roasting, and storytelling. There are already two operational F-22 squadrons at Langley Air Force Base, in Virginia, and eventually Corcoran's will be one of two in Alaska. If and when a conflict arises, they will be stretched wide and far.

The good news is that the air force has had some success integrating the newer fighter with its older ones. Part of its argument for the F-22s was that they were too sophisticated to be teamed with older, lesser planes. But early results in Red Flag competitions suggest otherwise. "When the F-15s are up doing their tactics, we're kind of back behind them a little bit and helping them out if they have trouble," Colonel Jim Hecker, the operations group commander at Elmendorf, told me. "If an F-15 is having some trouble dealing with electronic counter-measures where he can't shoot, that's when we'll go in and get rid of that guy for him. I think the synergistic effect of having a couple of F-22s in with those fourth-generation fighters is great. Based on the buy, I think we're going to have to do that if we stay at the same number of F-22s. We simply don't have enough, so we have to find ways to integrate like this to opti-mize our capability."

So America's fighter fleet is likely to remain F-15–based, backed up by the F-22 and F-35, a fifth-generation fighter that resembles the Raptor but without the same maneuverability and speed. It means that the days when the air force's leading "ace" has only three kills may be coming to an end. If more vulner-ability means more challenges—and it usually does—then more fighters will be seeing action. If the cost of air supremacy is not paid in dollars, it may be paid in blood.

*   *   *

After twenty-six years of flying, Rodriguez is no longer in the fight. Pushing fifty, he now works for Raytheon. One of his responsibilities is to sell the AMRAAM, an assignment that puts to good use the story of his killer sortie over Pristina, when he lit up the snowy night with that MiG. He hasn't flown an airplane since 2004. After all his years of going acro in the F-15, it's hard for him to get a thrill in the cockpit of anything else.

"I've relinquished myself to business class," he said.

He's passed the baton. But no matter how different the demands on a fighter pilot have become, Rodriguez is convinced that the job itself hasn't changed that much.

"It's the same person," he said. "He's just introduced to technology. I mean, when you think about it, today kids are growing up exposed to multitasking, multisensory inputs when they play a video game. So that person is going to evolve into someone technically friendly with everything new that comes up. Back in World War I, World War II, the concept of flying itself was a leap, you know, a leap of faith in some cases. And that's the same one that we want flying fighters today, the one willing to take the leap."

The Killing Machines

How to Think About Drones

Atlantic, September 2013

1. Unfairness

Consider David. The shepherd lad steps up to face in single combat the Philistine giant Goliath. Armed with only a slender staff and a sling, he confronts a fearsome warrior clad in brass and mail from head to toe, wielding a spear with a head as heavy as a sledge and a staff "like a weaver's beam," nearly three inches thick and about seven feet long. Goliath scorns the approaching youth: "Am I a dog, that thou comest to me with staves?" (I Samuel, 17:43).

David then famously slays the boastful giant with a single smooth stone from his sling.

A story to gladden the hearts of underdogs everywhere, its biblical moral is, *Best to have God on your side*—but subtract the theological context and what you have is a parable about technology. The sling, a small, lightweight weapon that applies simple physics to launch a missile with lethal force from a distance, was an innovation that made all of the giant's advantages irrelevant. It ignored the spirit of the contest. David's weapon was, like all significant advances in warfare, essentially unfair.

As anyone who has ever been in combat will tell you, the last thing you want is a fair fight. Technology has been tilting the balance of battles since Goliath fell. I was born into the age of push-button war. Ivy Mike, the first thermonuclear bomb, capable of vaporizing an entire modern metropolis, of killing millions of people at once, was detonated over the Pacific before my second birthday. When I was growing up, the concept of global annihilation wasn't just science fiction. We held civil defense drills to practice for it.

Within my lifetime, that evolution has taken a surprising turn. Today we find ourselves tangled in legal and moral knots over the drone, a weapon that can find and strike a single target, often a single individual, by remote control.

Unlike nuclear weapons, the drone did not emerge from some multibillion-dollar crash program on the cutting edge of science. It isn't even completely new. The first Predator drone was a snowmobile engine mounted on a radio-controlled glider. When linked via satellite to a distant control center, the slow-moving aircraft exploits telecommunications methods perfected years earlier by TV networks—in fact, the air force has gone to ESPN for advice. But when you pull together this disparate technology, what you have is a weapon capable of finding and killing someone just about anywhere in the world.

Drone strikes are a far cry from the atomic vaporizing of whole cities, but the horror of war doesn't seem to diminish when it is reduced in scale. If anything, the act of willfully pinpointing a human being and summarily executing him from afar distills war to a single ghastly act.

Fast-forward two millennia, to January 2013. A small patrol of marines in southern Afghanistan was working its way at dusk down a dirt road not far from Kandahar, staying to either side to avoid planted bombs, when it unexpectedly came under fire. The men scattered for cover. A battered pickup truck was closing on them and popping off rounds from what sounded like a big gun.

Continents away, in a different time zone, a slender nineteen-year-old American marine lance corporal sat at a desk before a large color monitor watching this action unfold in startlingly high definition. He had never been near a battlefield. He had graduated from boot camp straight out of high school, and was one of a select few recruits invited to train and fly Predators. This was his first time at the controls, essentially a joystick and the monitor. The drone he was flying was roughly fifteen thousand feet above the besieged patrol; each member was marked clearly in monochrome on his monitor by an infrared uniform patch. He had been instructed to watch over the patrol, and to "stay frosty," meaning, *Whatever happens, don't panic*. No one had expected anything to happen. Now something was happening.

The young marine zoomed in tight on the approaching truck. He saw in its bed a fifty-caliber machine gun, a weapon that could do more damage to an army than a platoon of Goliaths.

A colonel, watching over his shoulder, said, "They're pinned down pretty good. They're gonna be screwed if you don't do something."

He told the pilot to fix on the truck. A button on the joystick pulled up a computer-generated reticle, a grid displaying exact ground coordinates, distance, direction, range, etc. Once the computer locked on the pickup, it kept the moving target precisely zeroed.

"Are you ready to help your fellow marines?" the colonel asked.

An overlay on the grid showed the anticipated blast radius of an AGM Hellfire missile—the drone carried two. The colonel

THE KILLING MACHINES   111

instructed the men on the ground to back off, then gave them a few seconds to do so.

The pilot scrutinized the vehicle. Those who have seen unclassified clips of aerial attacks have only a dim appreciation of the optics available to the military and the CIA. The young marine describes his view as "perfect," and "cinematic."

"I could see exactly what kind of gun it was in back," he told me later. "I could see two men in the front [the cab]; their faces were covered. One was in the passenger seat and one was in the driver's seat, and then one was on the gun and I think there was another sitting in the bed of the truck, but he was kind of obscured from my angle."

On the radio, they could hear the marines on the ground shouting for help.

"Fire one," said the colonel.

The Hellfire is a hundred-pound antitank missile, designed to destroy an armored vehicle. When the blast of smoke cleared there was only a smoking crater on the dirt road.

"I was kind of freaked out," the pilot said. "My whole body was shaking. It was something that was really different. The first time doing it, it feels bad almost. It's not easy to take another human being's life. It's tough to think about. A lot of guys were congratulating me, telling me, 'You protected them; you did your job; that's what you are trained to do, supposed to do,' so that was good reinforcement, but it's still tough."

One of the things that nagged at the lance corporal, and that was still bugging him months later, was that he had delivered this deathblow without having been in any danger himself. The men he killed, and the marines on the ground, were at war. They were risking their hides, whereas he was working his scheduled shift in a comfortable office building, on a sprawling base, in a peaceful country. It seemed unfair. He had been inspired to enlist by his grandfather's manly stories of battle in the Korean war. He had wanted to prove something to himself and to his family, to make them as proud of him as they had been of his Pop-pop.

"But this was a weird feeling," he said. "You feel bad. You don't feel worthy. I'm sitting there safe and sound, and those guys down there are in the thick of it, and I can have more impact than they can. It's almost like I don't feel like I deserve to be safe."

After slaying Goliath, David was made commander of the Israelite armies and given the hand of King Saul's daughter. When the Pentagon announced earlier this year a new medal for drone pilots and cyberwarriors, it provoked such outrage from veterans that production of the new decoration was halted and the secretary of defense sentenced it to a review and then killed it. Members of Congress introduced legislation to ensure that any such award be ranked beneath the Purple Heart, the medal given to every wounded soldier. How can someone who has never physically been in combat receive a combat decoration?

The question hints at something more important than war medals, getting at the core of our uneasiness about the drone. Like the sling, the drone fundamentally alters the nature of combat. While the young Predator pilot has overcome his unease—his was a clearly justifiable kill shot fired in conventional combat, and his fellow marines on the ground conveyed their sincere gratitude—the sense of unfairness lingers.

If the soldier who pulls the trigger in safety feels this, imagine the emotions of those on the receiving end, left to pick up the body parts of their husbands, fathers, brothers, or friends. Where do they direct their anger? When the wrong person is targeted, or an innocent bystander is killed, imagine the sense of impotence and rage. How do those who remain strike back? No army is arrayed against them; no airfield is nearby to be attacked. If they manage to shoot down a drone, what have they done but disable a small machine? No matter how justified a strike seems to us, no matter how carefully weighed and skillfully applied, to those on the receiving end it is profoundly arrogant, the act of an enemy so distant and superior that he is untouchable.

"The political message [of drone strikes] emphasizes the disparity in power between the parties and reinforces popular support for the terrorists, who are seen as David fighting Goliath," Gabriella Blum and Philip B. Heymann, both law professors at Harvard, wrote in their 2010 book *Laws, Outlaws, and Terrorists: Lessons from the War on Terrorism*. "Moreover, by resorting to military force rather than law enforcement, targeted killings might strengthen the sense of legitimacy of terrorist operations, which are sometimes viewed as the only viable option for the weak to fight against a powerful empire."

Is it any wonder that the enemy seizes on opportune targets —a crowded café, a passenger jet, the finish line of a marathon? There is no moral justification for deliberately targeting civilians, but one can understand why it is done. Arguably the strongest force driving lone-wolf terror attacks in recent months throughout the western world has been anger over drone strikes.

The drone is effective. Its extraordinary precision makes it an advance in humanitarian warfare. In theory, when used with principled restraint, it is the perfect counterterrorism weapon. It targets indiscriminate killers with exquisite discrimination. But because its aim can never be perfect, can be only as good as the intelligence that guides it, it sometimes kills the wrong people—and even when it doesn't, its cold efficiency is literally inhuman.

So how should we feel about drones?

2. Gorgon Stare

The Department of Defense has a secret state-of-the-art control center in Dubai with an IMAX-sized screen at the front of the main room that can project video feed from dozens of drones at once. The air force has been directed to maintain capability for sixty-five simultaneous Combat Air Patrols, or CAPs, as they are called. Each of these involves multiple drones; the CAP maintains a persistent eye over a potential target. The Dubai center, according to one who has seen it, resembles the control center at NASA, with hundreds of pilots and analysts arrayed in rows before monitors.

This is a long way from the first known drone strike, on November 4, 2002, when a Hellfire launched from a Predator over Yemen blew up a car carrying Abu al-Harithi, the Al Qaeda leader responsible for the bombing of the USS *Cole* in 2000. Killed with him in the car were five others, including an American citizen, Kamal Derwish, who was suspected of leading a terror cell based near Buffalo, New York. The drone used that day had only recently been reconfigured as a weapon. During testing, its designers had worried that the missile's backblast would shatter the lightweight craft. It didn't. Since that day drones have killed thousands of people.

John Yoo, the law professor who, as a legal counselor to President George W. Bush, got caught up in tremendous controversy over harsh interrogation practices, was surprised that drone strikes have provoked so little hand-wringing.

"I would think if you are a civil libertarian, you ought to be much more upset about the drone than Guantánamo and interrogations," he told me when I interviewed him recently. "Because I think the ultimate deprivation of liberty would be the government taking away someone's life. But with drone killings you do not see anything, not as a member of the public. You read reports perhaps of people who are being killed by drones, but it happens three thousand miles away and there are no pictures, there are no remains, there is no debris that anyone in the United States ever sees. It's kind of antiseptic. So it is like a video game; it's like Call of Duty."

As illustrated by the dimensions of the hub in Dubai, one of many, the drone war has gone global. After 2014, when American combat forces leave Afghanistan, the drone will be the primary weapon we have in the fight.

The least remarkable thing about the system is the drone itself. The air force bristles at the very word—*drones* conjures autonomous flying robots, reinforcing the notion that human beings are not piloting them. The air force prefers that they be called "remotely piloted aircraft." But this linguistic battle has already been lost: my *New Oxford American Dictionary* now defines *drone* as—in addition to a male bee and monotonous speech—"a remote controlled pilotless aircraft or missile." Even though drones now come in sizes that range from the handheld Ravens thrown into the air by infantry units so they can see over the next hill to the Global Hawk, which looks more like a Boeing 737, the craft itself is just an airplane. Most drones are propeller driven and slow moving—early-twentieth-century technology.

In December 2012, when Iran cobbled together a reha-bilitated version of a ScanEagle that had crashed there, the catapult-launched weaponless navy drone was presented on Iranian national television as a major intelligence coup.

"They could have gone to Radio Shack and captured the same 'secret' technology," Vice Admiral Mark I. Fox, the navy's deputy chief for operations, plans, and strategy told the *New York Times*. The vehicle had less computing power than a smartphone.

Even when, the year before, Iran managed to recover a downed RQ-170 Sentinel, a stealthy, weaponless, unmanned ve-hicle flown primarily by the CIA, one of the most sophisticated drones in the fleet, it had little more than a nifty flying model. Anything sensitive inside had been remotely destroyed before the Sentinel was seized.

James Poss, a retired air force general who helped oversee the Predator's development, says he has grown so weary of fascination with the vehicle itself that he's adopted the slogan, "It's the data link, stupid." The craft is essentially a conduit, an eye in the sky. Cut off from its back end—from its satellite links and its data processors, its intelligence analysts and its controller—the drone is as useless as an eyeball disconnected from the brain. What makes the system remarkable is everything downrange—what the air force, in its defiantly tin-eared way, calls "Processing, Exploitation, and Dissemination," PED. Despite all the focus on missiles, what gives a drone its singular value is its ability to provide perpetual, relatively low-cost surveillance, watching a target continuously for hours, days, weeks, even months. Missiles were mounted on Predators only because too much time was lost when a fire mission had to be handed off to more conventional weapons platforms—a manned aircraft or a ground-based or ship-based missile launcher. That delay reduced or erased the key advantage afforded by the drone. With steady, real-time surveillance, a controller could strike with the target in his sights. He can, for instance, choose a moment when his victim is isolated, or traveling in a car, reducing the chance of harming anyone else.

I recently spoke with an air force pilot who asked to be identified only as "Major Dan." He has logged six hundred combat hours in the B-1 bomber and, in the past six years, well over two thousand hours flying Reapers—larger, more heavily armed versions of the Predator. He describes the Reaper as a significantly better war-fighting tool for this mission than the B-1, by every measure. The only thing you lose when you go from a B-1 to a Reaper, he says, is "the thrill of lighting four afterburners" on a runway.

From a pilot's perspective, drones have several critical advantages. First, mission duration can be vastly extended, with rotating crews. No more trying to stay awake for long missions, nor enduring the physical and mental stresses of flying. ("After you've been sitting in an ejection seat for twenty hours, you are very tired and sore," Dan says.) In addition, drones provide far greater awareness of what's happening on the ground. They routinely watch targets for prolonged periods—sometimes for months—before a decision is made to launch a missile. Once a B-1 is in flight, the capacity for ground observation is far more limited than what is available to a drone pilot at a ground station during this final, attack stage of the mission. From his control station at the Pentagon, not only is Dan watching the target in real time; he has immediate access to every source of information about it, including a chat line with soldiers on the ground. Dan calls his station an "information node."

Dan was so enthusiastic about these and other advantages of drones that, until I prodded him, he didn't even mention the benefit of being home with his family and sleeping in his own bed. Dan is thirty-eight years old, married, with two small children. In the years since he graduated from the U.S. Air Force Academy, he deployed several times to far off bases for months-long stretches. Now he is regularly home for dinner.

The dazzling clarity of the drone's optics does have a downside. As a B-1 pilot, Dan wouldn't learn details about the effects of his weapons until a post-mission briefing. But flying a drone, he sees the carnage close-up, in real time—the blood and severed body parts, the arrival of emergency responders, the anguish of friends and family. Often he's been watching the people he kills for a long time before pulling the trigger. Drone pilots become familiar with their victims. They see them in the ordinary rhythms of their lives—with their wives and friends, with their children. War by remote control turns out to be intimate and disturbing. Pilots are sometimes shaken.

"There is a very visceral connection to operations on the ground," Dan says, "when you see combat, when you hear the guy you are supporting who is under fire. You hear the stress in his voice, you hear the emotions being passed over the radio, you see the tracers and the rounds being fired, and when you are called on to either fire a missile or drop a bomb, you witness the effects of that firepower." He witnesses it in a far more immediate way than in the past, and he disdains the notion that he and his fellow drone pilots are like video gamers, detached from the reality of their actions. If anything, they are far more attached. At the same time, he dismisses the idea that the carnage he now sees close-up is emotionally crippling.

"In my mind, as far as understanding what I did, I wouldn't say that one was significantly different from the other," he says.

Drones collect three primary packages of data: straight visual; infrared (via a heat-sensing camera that can see through darkness and clouds); and what is called SIGINT (Signals Intelligence), gathered via electronic eavesdropping devices and other sensors. One such device, known as LDAR (a combination of the words *light* and *radar*), can map large areas in 3-D. The optical sensors are so good, and the pixel array is so dense, that the device can zoom in clearly on objects only inches wide from well over fifteen thousand feet above. With computer enhancement to eliminate distortion and to calm motion, facial recognition software is very close to being able to pick individuals out of crowds. Operators do not even have to know exactly where to look.

"We put in the theatre [in 2011] a system called 'Gorgon Stare,'" Lieutenant General Larry James, the air force's deputy chief of staff for intelligence, surveillance, and reconnaissance, told me. "Instead of one soda-sized-straw view of the world with the camera, we put essentially ten cameras ganged together, and it gives you a very wide area of view of about four kilometers by four kilometers—about the size of the city of Fairfax [Virginia]—that you can watch continuously. Not as much fidelity in terms of what the camera can see, but I can see movement of cars and people—those sorts of things. Now, instead of staring at a small space, which may be like a villa or compound, I can look at a whole city continuously for as long as I am flying that particular system."

Surveillance technology allows more than just looking: computers store these moving images so that analysts can dial back to a particular time and place and zero in, or they can mark certain individuals and vehicles and instruct the machine to track these over time. A suspected terror cell leader or bomb maker, say, can be watched for months. The computer can then instantly draw maps showing patterns of movement, where the target went, when there were visitors or deliveries to his home. If you were watched in this way over a period of time, the data could not only draw a portrait of your daily routine but identify everyone with whom you associate. Add to this cell phone, text, and e mail intercepts, and you begin to see how special-ops units in Iraq and Afghanistan can, after a single nighttime arrest, round up entire networks before dawn.

All of this requires what James says is the most difficult technical challenge involved: the collection and manipulation of huge amounts of data.

"Getting our arms around what we call the big data problem is something we're absolutely invested in," he says. "We are part of a big data IPT [Internet Processing Technology], if you will. . . . And so we are marching down that path pretty hard and in fact the secretary [of defense] has given us a task to really develop a road map for those tools. Take video, for example: ESPN has all kinds of tools where it can go back and find Eli Manning in every video that was shot over the last year and can probably do so in twenty minutes. So how do we bring those types of tools [to intelligence work]? *OK, I want to find this red 1976 Chevy pickup truck in every piece of video that I have shot in this area for the last three months.* We have a pretty hard push to really work with the air force research lab, and the commercial community, to understand what tools can I bring in to help make sense of all the data."

To be used effectively, a drone must be able to stay over a potential target for long periods. A typical Predator can stay aloft for about twenty hours; flown in relays, Predators can maintain a continuous CAP. Surveillance satellites pass over only once each Earth orbit. The longest the U2, the most successful spy plane in history, can stay over a target is about ten hours, because of the need to spell its pilot and refuel. The Predator gives military and intelligence agencies a surveillance option that is both significantly less expensive and more useful, because it flies unmanned, low, and slow.

Precisely because drones fly so low and slow, and have such a "noisy" electronic signature, operating them anywhere but in controlled airspace is impractical. The U.S. Air Force completely controls the sky over active war zones like Afghanistan and Iraq— and has little to fear over countries like Yemen, Somalia, and Mali. Over the rugged regions of northwestern Pakistan, where most drone strikes have taken place, the United States operates with the tacit approval of the Pakistan government. Without such permission, or without a robust protection capability, the drone presents an easy target. Its data link can be disrupted, jammed, or hijacked. It's only slightly harder to shoot down than a hot-air balloon.

So there's little danger of enemy drone attacks in America anytime soon. As a weapons-delivery platform, drones are vastly inferior to manned aircraft. A fighter or bomber with a pilot or crew is, in essence, a self-contained system. It is able to carry more and different kinds of weapons; in addition, its brains are on board. A manned bomber is fully functional even when its communications links are shut down, which enables stealth. Any foreign power contemplating an air attack on the U.S. home-land or military bases overseas would be better off launching a missile or attacking with a squadron of jet fighters than launch-ing a drone. And anyone interested in detonating a bomb in an American city, as the Boston Marathon bombers demonstrated, can more easily deliver it by backpack than by drone.

Drone technology has applications that go way beyond military uses, of course—to everything from domestic law enforcement to archeological surveys to environmental studies. As they become smaller and cheaper, drones will become commonplace. Does this mean the government might someday begin hurling thunderbolts at undesirables on city sidewalks? Unlikely. Our entire legal system would have to collapse first. If the police wanted to just shoot people on the street from a distance, they already can—they've had that capability going back to the invention of the Kentucky long rifle and, before that, the crossbow. I helped cover the one known instance of a local government dropping a bomb on its own city, in 1985, when a stubborn back-to-nature cult called MOVE was in an armed standoff with the Philadelphia police. Wilson Goode, who was then the mayor, authorized dropping a satchel packed with explosives from a hovering helicopter on a West Philadelphia row house in order to set fire to a rooftop bunker. The bomb ignited a conflagration that consumed an entire city block. The incident will live long in the annals of municipal stupidity. The capability to do the same from a drone will not make choosing to do so any smarter, or any more likely. And as for Big Brother's eye in the sky, authorities have been monitoring public spaces from overhead cameras, helicopters, and planes for decades. Many people think it's a good idea.

The drone is new only in the sense that it combines known technology in an original way—aircraft, global telecommunications links, optics, digital sensors, supercomputers, etc. It greatly lowers the cost of persistent surveillance. When armed, it becomes a remarkable but highly specialized tool: *a weapon that employs simple physics to launch a missile with lethal force from a distance*, a first step into a world where going to war does not necessarily mean fielding an army, or putting any of your own soldiers, sailors, or pilots at risk.

3. The Kill List

It is the most exclusive list in the world, and you would not want
to be on it.

The procedure may have changed, but several years back,
at the height of the drone war, President Obama held weekly
counterterrorism meetings at which he was presented with a list of
potential targets—mostly Al Qaeda or Taliban figures—complete
with photos and brief bios laid out like "a high school yearbook,"
according to a report in the *New York Times.*

The list is the product of a rigorous vetting process that the
administration has kept secret. Campaigning for the presidency
in 2008, Obama made it clear (although few of his supporters
were listening closely) that he would embrace drones to go after
what he considered the appropriate post-9/11 American military
target—"core Al Qaeda." When he took office, he inherited a
drone war that was already expanding. There were fifty-three
known strikes inside Pakistan in 2009 (according to numbers
assembled from press reports by the *Long War Journal*), up from
thirty-five in 2008, and just five the year before that. In 2010,
the annual total more than doubled, to 117. The onslaught was
effective, at least by some measures. Letters seized in the raid that
killed Osama bin Laden in 2011 showed his consternation over
the rain of death by drone.

As U.S. intelligence analysis improved, the number of targets
proliferated. The definition of a legitimate target and the methods
employed to track such a target were increasingly suspect. Relying on other countries' intelligence agencies for help, the United
States was sometimes manipulated into striking people who it
believed were terrorist leaders, but who may not have been; or it
was implicated in practices that violate American values.

Reporters and academics at work in zones where Predator
strikes had become common warned of a large backlash. Gregory

Johnsen, a scholar of Near Eastern studies at Princeton University, documented the phenomenon in a 2012 book about Yemen, *The Last Refuge*. He showed that drone attacks there appeared to have the opposite of their intended effect, particularly when people other than extremists were killed or hurt. Drones hadn't whittled Al Qaeda down, Johnsen argued; the organization had grown threefold there. "U.S. strikes and particularly those that kill civilians—be they men or women—are sowing the seeds of future generations of terrorists," he wrote on his blog in 2012.

Michael Morrell, who was deputy director of the CIA until June, was among those in the U.S. government who argued for more restraint. During meetings with John Brennan, who was Obama's counterterrorism adviser until taking over as CIA director last spring, Morrell said he worried that the prevailing goal seemed to be using the drone as artillery, striking anyone who could be squeezed into the definition of terrorist—an approach derisively called "Whack-a-Mole." Morrell insisted that if the purpose of the drone program was to diminish Al Qaeda and to protect the United States from terror attacks, then indiscriminate strikes were counterproductive. Drones might be helping us to win the battle, Morrell argued, at the cost of losing the war.

Brennan launched an effort to select targets more carefully. Formalizing a series of ad hoc meetings that had begun in the fall of 2009, Brennan in 2010 instituted weekly conclaves—in effect, death penalty deliberations—where the fate of would-be successors to Osama bin Laden and Khalid Sheikh Mohammed was selected for execution, for the "kill list" presented to Obama. Brennan demanded clear definitions. There were "High-Value Targets," which consisted of important Al Qaeda and Taliban figures; "Imminent Threats," such as a load of roadside bombs bound for the Afghan border; and, most controversial, "Signature Strikes," which were aimed at characters engaged in suspicious activity in known enemy zones. In these principals' meetings, which

Brennan chaired from the Situation Room in the basement of the
White House, deliberations were divided into two parts—law and
policy. The usual participants included representatives from the
Pentagon, CIA, Department of State, National Counterterrorism Center, and, initially, the Department of Justice—although
after a while the lawyers stopped coming. In the first part of the
meetings, questions of legality were considered: Was the prospect
a lawful target? Was he a high-level target? Could he rightly be
considered to pose an "imminent" threat? Was arrest a feasible
alternative? Only when these criteria were met did the discussion
shift toward policy. Was it smart to kill this person? What sort of
impact might the killing have on local authorities, or on relations
with the governments of Pakistan or Yemen? What effect would
killing him have on his own organization? Would it make things
better or worse?

Brennan himself was often the toughest questioner. Two
regular participants in these meetings described him to me as
thoughtful and concerned, with a demeanor one described as
"almost priestly." Another routinely skeptical and cautious par-
ticipant was James Steinberg, the deputy secretary of state for
the first two and a half years of Obama's first term, who adhered
to a strict list of acceptable legal criteria drawn up by the State
Department's counsel, Harold Koh. These criteria stipulated
that any drone target would have to be a "senior member" of
Al Qaeda who was "externally focused"—that is, actively plotting imminent attacks on the United States or on its citizens
or armed forces. Koh was confident that even if his criteria did
not meet all of the broader concerns of human rights activists,
they would, under international law, support a claim of self-
defense—and for that reason he thought the administration
ought to make the criteria public. Throughout Obama's first
term, members of the administration argued about how much of
the deliberations process to reveal. During these debates Koh's

position on complete disclosure was dismissively termed "the full Harold." He was its only advocate.

Many of the sessions gave rise to contention. The military and the CIA pushed back hard against Koh's strict criteria. Special Forces commanders, in particular, abhorred what they saw as excessive efforts to "litigate" their war. The price of every target the White House rejected, military commanders said, was paid in American lives. Their arguments, coming from the war's front line, carried significant weight.

Cameron Munter, a veteran diplomat who was U.S. ambassador in Pakistan from 2010 to 2012, felt that weight firsthand when he tried to push back. Munter saw American influence declining with nearly every strike. While there were factions in the Pakistani military and Inter-Services Intelligence (ISI) who believed in the value of strikes, the Pakistani public was increasingly outraged, and elected officials were increasingly hostile. Munter's job was to contain the crisis, a task complicated by the secrecy of the drone program. It prevented him from explaining and defending America's actions.

Matters came to a head in the summer of 2011 during a meeting to which Munter was linked digitally. The dynamics of such meetings—where officials turned to policy discussions after legal determination had been made—placed a premium on unified support of policy goals. Most participants wanted to focus on the success of the drone program in the battle against America's enemies, not on its corrosive side effects in foreign policy.

At the decision meetings, it was hard for someone like Munter to say no. He would appear digitally on the screen in the Situation Room, gazing out at the vice president, the secretary of defense, and other principals, and they would present him with the targeting decision they were prepared to make. It was hard to object when so many people who titularly outranked him already seemed set.

By June 2011, however, two events in Pakistan—first the arrest and subsequent release of the CIA contractor Raymond Davis, who had been charged with murdering two Pakistanis who accosted him on the street in Lahore; and then the raid at Abbottabad that killed Osama bin Laden—had brought the U.S.-Pakistani partnership to a new low. Concerned about balancing the short-term benefits of strikes (removing potential enemies from the battlefield) and their long-term costs (creating lasting mistrust and resentment that undercut the policy goal of stability and peace in the region), Munter decided to test what he believed was his authority to halt a strike. As he recalled it later, the move played out as follows.

Asked whether he was on board with a particular strike, he said no.

Leon Panetta, the CIA director, said the ambassador had no veto power; these were intelligence decisions.

Munter proceeded to explain that under Title 22 of the U.S. Code of Federal Regulations, the president gives the authority to carry out U.S. policy in a foreign country to his ambassador, delegated through the secretary of state. That means no American policy should be carried out in any country without the ambassador's approval.

Taken aback, Panetta replied, "Well, I do not work for you, buddy."

"I don't work for you," Munter told him.

Then Secretary of State Hillary Clinton stepped in: "Leon, you are wrong."

Panetta said, flatly, "Hillary, *you're* wrong."

At that point, the discussion moved on. When the secretary of state and the CIA director clash, the decision gets made upstairs.

Panetta won. A week later, James Steinberg called Munter to inform him that he did not have the authority to veto a drone strike. Steinberg explained that the ambassador would be allowed to express an objection to a strike, and that a mechanism would be put in place to make sure his objection was registered—but the decision to approve or reject a strike would be made higher up the chain. It was a clear victory for the CIA.

Later that summer, General David Petraeus was named to take over the intelligence agency from Panetta. Before assuming the job, Petraeus flew from Kabul, where he was still the military commander, to Islamabad, to meet with the ambassador. At dinner that night, Petraeus poked his finger into Munter's chest.

"You know what happened in that meeting?" the general asked. (Petraeus had observed the clash via a secure link from his command post in Afghanistan.) "That's never going to happen again."

Munter's heart sank. He thought the new CIA director, whom he liked and admired, was about to threaten him. Instead, Petraeus said: "I'm never going to put you in the position where you feel compelled to veto a strike. If you have a long-term concern, if you have a contextual problem, a timing problem, an ethical problem, I want to know about it earlier. We can work together to avoid these kinds of conflicts far in advance."

Petraeus kept his word. Munter never had to challenge a drone strike in a principals' meeting again during his tenure as ambassador. He left Islamabad in the summer of 2012.

By then, Brennan's efforts to make the process more judicious had begun to show results. The number of drone strikes in Pakistan and Yemen fell to eighty-eight in 2012, and it has dropped off even more dramatically since.

The decline partly reflects the toll that the drone war has taken on Al Qaeda. "There are fewer Al Qaeda leadership targets to hit," a senior White House official who is working on the administration's evolving approach to drone strikes told me. The reduction in strikes is "something that the president directed. We don't need a top-twenty list. We don't need to find twenty if there are only ten. We've gotten out of the business of maintaining a number as an end in itself, so therefore that number has gone down."

Any history of how the United States destroyed Osama bin Laden's organization will feature the drone. Whatever questions it has raised, however uncomfortable it has made us feel, the drone has been an extraordinarily effective weapon for the job. The United States faced a stateless, well-funded, highly organized terrorist operation that was sophisticated enough to carry out unprecedented acts of mass murder. Today, while local Al Qaeda franchises remain a threat throughout the Middle East, the organization that planned and carried out 9/11 has been crushed. When Osama bin Laden himself was killed, Americans danced in the streets.

"Our actions are effective," President Obama said in a speech on counterterrorism at the National Defense University in May. "Don't take my word for it. In the intelligence gathered at bin Laden's compound, we found that he wrote, 'We could lose the reserves to enemy's air strikes. We cannot fight air strikes with explosives.' Other communications from Al Qaeda operatives confirm this as well. Dozens of highly skilled Al Qaeda commanders, trainers, bomb makers, and operatives have been taken off the battlefield. Plots have been disrupted that would have targeted international aviation, U.S. transit systems, European cities, and our troops in Afghanistan. Simply put, these strikes have saved lives."

So why the steady drumbeat of complaint?

4. Drones Don't Kill People.
People Kill People.

The most ardent case against drone strikes is that they kill innocents. Brennan has argued that claims of collateral carnage are exaggerated. In June 2011, he famously declared that there had not been "a single collateral death" due to a drone strike in the previous twelve months.

Almost no one believes this. Brennan himself later amended his statement, saying that in the previous twelve months, the United States had found no "credible evidence" that any civilians had been killed in drone strikes outside Afghanistan and Iraq. (I am using the word *civilians* here to mean "noncombatants.") A fair interpretation is that drones unfailingly hit their targets, and so long as the U.S. government believes its targets are all legitimate, the collateral damage is zero. But drones are only as accurate as the intelligence that guides them. Even if the machine is perfect, it's a stretch to assume perfection in those who aim it.

For one thing, our military and intelligence agencies generously define *combatant* to include any military-age male in the strike zone. And local press accounts from many of the blast sites have reported dead women and children. Some of this may be propaganda, but it's unlikely that all of it is. No matter how precisely placed, when a five-hundred-pound bomb or a Hellfire missile explodes, there are sometimes going to be unintended victims in the vicinity.

How many? Estimates of body counts range so widely and are so politicized that none of them is completely credible. At one extreme, anti-American propagandists regularly publish estimates that make the drone war sound borderline genocidal. These high numbers help drive the anti-drone narrative, which equates actions of the U.S. government with acts of terror. In two of the most recent Islamist terror attacks as of this writing—the Boston Marathon bombing and the beheading of a soldier in London— the perpetrators justified their killings as payback for the deaths of innocent Muslims. At the other extreme, there is Brennan's zero. The true numbers are unknowable.

Secrecy is a big part of the problem. The government doesn't even acknowledge most attacks, much less release details of their aftermath. The Bureau of Investigative Journalism, a left-wing organization based in London, has made a strenuous effort, using news sources, to count bodies after CIA drone strikes. It estimates that from 2004 through the first half of 2013, 371 drone strikes in Pakistan killed between 2,564 and 3,567 people (the range covers the minimum to the maximum credible reported deaths). Of those killed, the group says, somewhere between 411 and 890—somewhere between 12 percent and 35 percent of the total—were civilians. The disparity in these figures is telling. But if we assume the worst case, and take the largest estimates of combatant and civilian fatalities, then one quarter of those killed in drone strikes in Pakistan have been civilians.

Everyone agrees that the amount of collateral damage has dropped steeply over the past two years. The Bureau of Investigative Journalism estimates that civilian deaths from drone strikes in Pakistan fell to 12 percent of total deaths in 2011 and to less than 3 percent in 2012.

No civilian death is acceptable, of course. Each one is tragic. But any assessment of civilian deaths from drone strikes needs to be compared with the potential damage from alternative tactics. Unless we are to forgo the pursuit of Al Qaeda terrorists entirely, U.S. forces must confront them either from the air or on the ground, in some of the remotest places on Earth. As aerial attacks go, drones are far more precise than manned bombers or missiles. That narrows the choice to drone strikes or ground assaults.

Sometimes ground assaults go smoothly. Take the one that killed Osama bin Laden. It was executed by the best-trained, most experienced soldiers in the world. Killed were Osama; his adult son Khalid; his primary protectors, the brothers Abu Ahmed al-Kuwaiti and Abrar al-Kuwaiti; and Abrar's wife, Bushra. Assuming Bushra qualifies as a civilian, even though she was helping to shelter the world's most notorious terrorist, civilian deaths in the raid amounted to 20 percent of the casualties. In other words, even a near-perfect special-ops raid produced only a slight improvement over the worst estimates of those counting drone casualties. Many assaults are not that clean.

In fact, ground combat almost always kills more civilians than drone strikes do. Avery Plaw, a political scientist at the University of Massachusetts, estimates that in the Pakistanis' ground offensives against extremists in their country's tribal areas, 46 percent of those killed were civilians. Plaw says that proportions of civilian deaths from conventional military conflicts over the past twenty years range from 33 percent to more than 80 percent. "A fair-minded evaluation of the best data we have available suggests that the drone program compares favorably with similar operations and contemporary armed conflict more generally," he told the *New York Times*.

When you consider the alternatives—even, and perhaps especially, if you are deeply concerned with sparing civilians—you are led, as Obama was, to the logic of the drone.

But don't drone strikes violate the prohibition on assassination, Executive Order 12333? That order, signed by Ronald Reagan in 1981, grew out of revelations that the CIA had tried to kill Fidel Castro and other left-leaning political figures in the 1960s and 1970s. It was clearly aimed at halting political assassinations; in fact, the original order, signed in 1976 by Gerald Ford, refers specifically to such acts. Attempting to prevent a dangerous international organization from committing mass murder may stretch the legal definition of armed conflict, but it is not the same as political assassination. Besides, executive orders are not statutes; they can be superseded by subsequent presidents. In the case of President Bush, after the attacks of September 11, Congress specifically authorized the use of lethal operations against Al Qaeda.

When Bush called our effort against Al Qaeda "war," he effectively established legal protection for targeted killing. The tactic is long-established in the context of war. According to international treaties, soldiers can be killed simply for belonging to an enemy army—whether they are actively engaged in an attack or only preparing for one, whether they are commanders or office clerks. During World War II, the United States discovered and shot down the plane carrying Admiral Isoroku Yamamoto, the commander in chief of the Japanese navy, who had been the architect of the attack on Pearl Harbor. The order to attack the plane was given by President Franklin Roosevelt.

But beyond what international treaties call "armed conflict" is "law enforcement," and here, there are problems. The 1990 United Nations Congress on the Prevention of Crime and the Treatment of Offenders laid out basic principles for the use of force in law enforcement operations. (The rules, although non-binding, elaborate on what is meant by Article 6 of the International Covenant on Civil and Political Rights, to which the United States has agreed.) The pertinent passage—written more than a decade before weaponized drones—reads as follows:

> Law enforcement officials shall not use firearms against persons except in self-defense or defense of others against the imminent threat of death or serious injury, to prevent the perpetration of a particularly serious crime involving grave threat to life, to arrest a person presenting such a danger and resisting their authority, or to prevent his or her escape, and only when less extreme means are insufficient to achieve these objectives. In any event, intentional lethal use of firearms may only be made when strictly unavoidable to protect life.

Once the "war" on Al Qaeda ends, the justification for targeted killing will become tenuous. Some experts on international law say it will become simply illegal. Indeed, one basis for condemning the drone war has been that the pursuit of Al Qaeda was never a real war in the first place.

Sir Christopher Greenwood, the British judge at the International Court of Justice, has written: "In the language of international law there is no basis for speaking of a war on al-Qaeda or any other terrorist group, for such a group cannot be a belligerent, it is merely a band of criminals, and to treat it as anything else risks distorting the law while giving that group a status which to some implies a degree of legitimacy." Greenwood rightly observes that America's declaration of war against Al Qaeda bolstered the group's status worldwide. But history will not quarrel with Bush's decision, which was unavoidable, given the national mood. Democracy reflects the will of the people. Two American presidents from different parties and with vastly different ideological outlooks have, with strong congressional support, fully embraced the notion that America is at war. In his speech at the National Defense University in May, Obama reaffirmed this approach. "America's actions are legal," he said. "Under domestic law and international law, the United States is at war with Al Qaeda, the Taliban, and their associated forces." He noted that during his presidency, he has briefed congressional overseers about every drone strike. "Every strike," he said.

Osama bin Laden himself certainly wasn't confused about the matter; he held a press conference in Afghanistan in 1998 to declare jihad on the United States. Certainly the scale of Al Qaeda's attacks went well beyond anything previously defined as criminal. But what are the boundaries of that war? Different critics draw the lines in different places. Mary Ellen O'Connell, a law professor at the University of Notre Dame, is a determined and eloquent critic of drone strikes. She believes that while strikes in well-defined battle spaces like Iraq and Afghanistan are justified, and can limit civilian deaths, strikes in Pakistan, Yemen, Somalia, and other places amount to "extrajudicial killing," no matter who the targets are. Such killings are outside the boundary of armed conflict, she says, and hence violate international law.

Philip Alston, a former United Nations special rapporteur on extrajudicial, summary, or arbitrary executions, concedes that Al Qaeda's scope and menace transcend criminality, but nevertheless faults the U.S. drone program for lacking due process and transparency. He told *Harper's* magazine:

> [International] laws do not prohibit an intelligence agency like the CIA from carrying out targeted killings, provided it complies with the relevant international rules. Those rules require, not surprisingly when it's a matter of being able to kill someone in a foreign country, that all such killings be legally justified, that we know the justification, and that there are effective mechanisms for investigation, prosecution, and punishment if laws are violated. The CIA's response to these obligations has been very revealing. On the one hand, its spokespersons have confirmed the total secrecy and thus unaccountability of the program by insisting that they can neither confirm nor deny that it even exists. On the other hand, they have gone to great lengths to issue unattributable assurances, widely quoted in the media, both that there is extensive domestic accountability and that civilian casualties have been minimal. In essence, it's a "you can trust us" response, from an agency with a less than stellar track record in such matters.

President Obama has taken steps in recent months to address Alston's concerns. He has begun transferring authority for drone strikes from the CIA to the Pentagon, which will open them up to greater congressional and public scrutiny. He has sharply limited "signature strikes," those based on patterns of behavior rather than strict knowledge of who is being targeted. (Because most signature strikes have been used to protect American troops in Afghanistan, this category of drone attack is likely to further diminish once those forces are withdrawn.) In his May speech, he came close to embracing "the full Harold," publicly outlining in general terms the targeting constraints drafted by Koh. He also made clear that the war on Al Qaeda will eventually end—though he stopped short of saying when. American combat troops will be gone from Afghanistan by the end of next year, but the war effort against "core Al Qaeda" will almost certainly continue at least until Ayman al-Zawahiri, the fugitive Egyptian doctor who now presides over the remnants of the organization, is captured or killed.

Then what?

"Outside of the context of armed conflict, the use of drones for targeted killing is almost never likely to be legal," Alston wrote in 2010. Mary Ellen O'Connell agrees. "Outside of a combat zone or a battlefield, the use of military force is not lawful," she told me.

Yet this is where we seem to be headed. Obama has run his last presidential campaign, and one senses that he might cherish a legacy of ending three wars on his watch.

"Our commitment to constitutional principles has weathered every war, and every war has come to an end," he said in his May speech. "We must define the nature and scope of this struggle, or else it will define us. We have to be mindful of James Madison's warning that 'no nation could preserve its freedom in the midst of continual warfare.'"

The changes outlined by the president do not mean we will suddenly stop going after Al Qaeda. If the war on terror is declared over, and the 2001 Authorization for Use of Military Force (AUMF) is withdrawn, then some other legal justification for targeting Al Qaeda terrorists with drones would be necessary, and would probably be sought.

"We believe we have a domestic and international legal basis for our current efforts," Ben Rhodes, who is Obama's deputy national security adviser for strategic communications, told me. "If you project into the future, there are different scenarios, you know, so they are kind of hypothetical, but one is that you might have a narrower AUMF that is a more targeted piece of legislation. A hypothetical: the Taliban is part of the AUMF now, but we could find ourselves not in hostilities with the Taliban after 2014." In that case, the military authority to attack Taliban targets, which account for many drone strikes and most signature strikes, would be gone. Another scenario Rhodes sketched out was one in which a local terrorist group "rose to the level where we thought we needed to take direct action. You might have to go back to Congress to get a separate authorization. If we need to get authority against a new terrorist group that is emerging somewhere else in the world, we should go back to Congress and get that authorization."

You can't know in advance "the circumstances of taking direct action," Rhodes said. "You may be acting to prevent an imminent attack on the United States or you may be acting in response to an attack, each of which carries its own legal basis. But you have to be accountable for whatever direct action you are taking," rather than relying on some blanket authority to strike whomever and whenever the president chooses. "You would have to specifically define, domestically and internationally, what the basis for your action is in each instance—and by each instance, I don't mean every strike, per se, but rather the terrorist group or the country where you are acting."

Seeking such authorization would help draw the debate over continued drone strikes out of the shadows. Paradoxically, as the war on terror winds down, and as the number of drone strikes falls, the controversy over them may rise.

5. Come Out with Your Hands Up!

Once the pursuit of Al Qaeda is defined as "law enforcement," ground assaults may be the only acceptable tactic under international law. A criminal must be given the opportunity to surrender, and if he refuses, efforts must be made to arrest him. Mary Ellen O'Connell believes the raid at Abbottabad was an example of how things should work.

"It came as close to what we are permitted to do under international law as you can get," she said. "John Brennan came out right after the killing and said the SEALs were under orders to attempt to capture bin Laden, and if he resisted or if their own lives were endangered, then they could use the force that was necessary. They did not use a drone. They did not drop a bomb. They did not fire a missile."

Force in such operations is justified only if the suspect resists arrest—and even then, his escape is preferable to harming innocent bystanders. These are the rules that govern police, as opposed to warriors. Yet the enemies we face will not change if the war on terror ends. The worst of them—the ones we most need to stop—are determined suicidal killers and hardened fighters. Since there is no such thing as global police, any force employed would probably still come from, in most cases, American special-ops units. They are very good at what they do—but under law enforcement rules, a lot more people, both soldiers and civilians, are likely to be killed.

It would be wise to consider how bloody such operations can be. When President Obama chose the riskiest available option for getting Osama bin Laden in Abbottabad—a special-ops raid—he did so not out of a desire to conform to international law but because that option allowed the possibility of taking bin Laden alive and, probably more important, because if he was killed in a ground assault, his death could be proved. The raid went well. But what if the SEAL raiding party had tripped Pakistan's air defenses, or if it had been confronted by police or army units on the ground? American troops and planes stood ready in Afghanistan to respond if that happened. Such a clash would have been likely to kill many Pakistanis and Americans, and to leave the countries at loggerheads, if not literally at war.

There's another example of a law enforcement–style raid conforming to the model that O'Connell and other critics of drones prefer: the October 1993 Delta Force raid in Mogadishu, which I wrote about in the book *Black Hawk Down*. The objective, which was achieved, was to swoop in and arrest Omar Salad and Mohamed Hassan Awale, two top lieutenants of the outlaw clan leader Mohammed Farrah Aidid. As the arrests were being made, the raiding party of Delta Force operators and U.S. Army Rangers came under heavy fire from local supporters of the clan leader. Two Black Hawk helicopters were shot down and crashed into the city. We were not officially at war with Somalia, but the ensuing firefight left eighteen Americans dead and killed an estimated five hundred to one thousand Somalis—numbers comparable to the total civilian deaths from all drone strikes in Pakistan from 2004 through the first half of 2013, according to the Bureau of Investigative Journalists.

Somalia is an extreme example. But the battle that erupted in Mogadishu strikes me as a fair reminder of what can happen to even a very skillful raiding party. Few of the terrorists we target will go quietly. Knowing they are targets, they will surely seek out terrain hostile to an American or a UN force. Choosing police action over drone strikes may feel like taking the moral high ground. But if a raid is likely to provoke a firefight, then choosing a drone shot not only might pass muster as legal (UN rules allow lethal force "when strictly unavoidable in order to protect life") but also might be the more moral choice.

The White House knows this, but it is unlikely to announce a formal end to the war against Al Qaeda anytime soon. Obama's evolving model for counterterrorism will surely include both raids and drone strikes—and the legality of using such strikes outside the context of war remains murky.

Ben Rhodes and others on Obama's national security team have been thinking hard about these questions. Rhodes told me that the "threat picture" the administration is mainly concerned with has increasingly shifted from global terrorism, with Al Qaeda at its center, to "more traditional terrorism, which is localized groups with their own agendas." Such groups "may be Islamic extremists, but they are not necessarily signing on to global jihad. A local agenda may raise the threat to embassies and diplomatic facilities and things like [the BP facility that was attacked in Algeria early this year], but it diminishes the likelihood of a complex 9/11-style attack on the homeland."

If terrorism becomes more localized, Rhodes continued, "we have to have a legal basis and a counterterrorism policy that fits that model, rather than this massive post-9/11 edifice that we built." This means, he said, that post-2014 counterterrorism will "take a more traditional form, with a law enforcement lead. But this will be amplified by a U.S. capability to take direct action as necessary in a very narrowly defined set of circumstances." What U.S. policy will be aiming for, Rhodes said, is "traditional [law enforcement–style] counterterrorism plus a limited deployment of our drone and special-forces capabilities when it is absolutely necessary."

To accommodate the long-term need for drone strikes, Obama is weighing a formal process for external review of the target list. This might mean appointing a military-justice panel, or a civilian review court modeled on the Foreign Intelligence Surveillance Court, which oversees requests to monitor suspected foreign spies and terrorists in the United States. But this raises

thorny constitutional questions about the separation of powers—
and presidents are reluctant to surrender their authority to make
the final call.

How should we feel about drones? Like any wartime innovation, going back to the sling, drones can be used badly or well. They
are remarkable tools, an exceedingly clever combination of existing
technologies that has vastly improved our ability to observe and
to fight. They represent how America has responded to the challenge of organized, high-level, stateless terrorism—not timidly, as
Osama bin Laden famously predicted, but with courage, tenacity,
and ruthless ingenuity. Improving technologies are making drones
capable not just of broader and more persistent surveillance, but
of greater strike precision. Mary Ellen O'Connell says, half jokingly, that there is a "sunset" on her objection to them, because
drones may eventually offer more options. She said she can imagine
one capable of delivering a warning—"Come out with your hands
up!"—and then landing to make an arrest using handcuffs.

Obama's efforts to mitigate the use of drones have already
made a big difference in reducing the number of strikes—though
critics like O'Connell say the reduction has come only grudgingly,
in response to "a rising level of worldwide condemnation." Still,
Obama certainly deserves credit: it is good that drones are being
used more judiciously. I told Ben Rhodes that if the president
succeeds in establishing clear and careful guidelines for their use,
he will make a lot of people happy, but a lot of other people mad.

"Well, no," Rhodes said. "It's worse than that. We will make
a lot of people mad and we will not quite make people happy."

No American president will ever pay a political price for
choosing national security over world opinion, but the only right
way to proceed is to make targeting decisions and strike outcomes
fully public, even if only after the fact. In the long run, careful
adherence to the law matters more than eliminating another bad
actor. Greater prudence and transparency are not only morally

and legally essential; they are in our long-term interest, because the strikes themselves feed the anti-drone narrative, and inspire the kind of random, small-scale terror attacks that are Osama bin Laden's despicable legacy.

"Weak laws . . . favor the states of terror," wrote Philip Bobbitt in his seminal study of twenty-first-century wars, "Terror and Consent." He defines the modern struggle as one between "states of consent," democratic nations where the rule of law is paramount; and "states of terror," which are ruled by fear and by force alone. Because rule by law and by consent is inherently more attractive to most people, terrorists seek to frighten lawful states into forsaking their principles. The contest is reduced then simply to force versus force. Bobbitt wrote, "Rendering persons too frightened to act lawfully on their basic values is both a means and an end, for such a situation of terror, of terrified people in a terrified society too fearful to freely choose their actions (and thus manifest their values) is an end roughly equivalent to the total destruction of western values."

In our struggle against terrorist networks like Al Qaeda, the distinction between armed conflict and law enforcement matters a great deal. Terrorism embraces lawlessness. It seeks to disrupt. It targets civilians deliberately. So why restrain our response? Why subject ourselves to the rule of law? Because abiding by the law is the point—especially with a weapon like the drone. No act is more final than killing. Drones distill war to its essence. Abiding carefully by the law—man's law, not God's—making judgments carefully, making them transparent and subject to review, is the only way to invest them with moral authority, and the only way to clearly define the terrorist as an enemy of civilization.

Jihadists in Paradise

Atlantic, March 2007

1. The Ringleader

The Sulu Sea is a dazzling and distinct maritime domain, a roughly rectangular patch of Pacific Ocean defined by two chains of small islands—the peaks of volcanic ridges—that parallel each other at a distance of about three hundred miles, reaching northeast from the coastline of Borneo to the main body of the Philippine Islands. Tracing a line along the northwestern end is a long, thin island called Palawan. The southeastern boundary is more punctuated, a chain of nearly a thousand small islands called the Sulu Archipelago. The enclosure creates a kind of oceanic lake, sheltered on all sides from strong currents. Its waters are generally calm and stunningly clear. The conditions are ideal for the formation of reefs, which attract scuba divers from all over the world.

But long before there were such things as recreational diving and vacations in paradise, the Sulu Sea was outlaw territory, a haven for pirates variously called Malay, Sulu, or Moro—pirates so fierce that for centuries even western warships gave the area a wide berth. The most infamous of these pirates came from the Sulu Archipelago, which is home to the Sama people, notable for seagoing and for their embrace, centuries ago, of Islam. Officially part of the Philippines, the provinces in this region have long been at odds with the nation's larger, primarily Christian collection of islands to the northeast, and for generations guerrilla forces have roamed the triple-canopied jungles of its island interiors. In the latter part of the twentieth century, the guerrilla movement was dominated by the Moro National Liberation Front, a group with a socialist flavor. In 1996 this group reached an accommodation with the Philippine government and became politically legitimate. But the instinct for rebellion runs deep in these islands, and insurrectionists remain; some style themselves not socialists or communists but jihadists.

It was from one of the area's rebel bastions, the island of Basilan, that twenty-one gunmen in military fatigues and long-sleeved black shirts boarded a flat wooden speedboat and embarked on a daring overnight run across three hundred miles of the Sulu Sea. The date was May 27, 2001. With three huge outboard motors, the thirty-foot craft was built for velocity, not comfort, bounding at high speed from crest to crest, its flat bottom occasionally slapping down hard in the troughs. The men were all members of a relatively new Islamist faction called Abu Sayyaf, which roughly translates as "Bearer of the Sword." They carried machine guns and bolos—the traditional long, single-edged machetes. The larger world was as yet ignorant of their cause—Mohammed Atta was still polishing his flight skills in Florida, three months before 9/11—but these Filipino guerrillas were already veteran jihadists.

Historically, the dispute in Sulu was local, but among the men on this hurtling boat was one with a larger vision. He was Aldam Tilao, a stocky and gregarious man with a round face, smooth brown skin, and a receding hairline that he disguised somewhat by shaving his head and topping it with a beret or wrapping it in a black do-rag like an American hip-hop artist. With his single hoop earring and Oakley sunglasses, he affected the look of a Hollywood pirate.

He was not the group's official leader—that was Khadaffy Janjalani, a younger brother of the group's founder (who had been killed by local police in a firefight in 1998). But the younger brother had been eclipsed by Tilao, the group's most flamboyant recruit. Tilao was a criminal, and to him Islam was just the latest cover for a lifetime of increasingly violent thuggery. Years earlier he had been linked by local police to Moro guerrillas, and he was thrown out of Zamboanga College, in Mindanao, where he had studied criminology. If one of his fellow insurrectionists is to be believed, he was even tossed out of an Al Qaeda training camp during the years he spent in the Middle East, in the 1990s. It was during those years in Saudi Arabia and Libya that he began to worship jihadist superstars like Ramzi Yousef and Khalid Sheikh Mohammed, who both had briefly set up shop in Manila after Yousef's failed first attempt, in 1993, to destroy the World Trade Center.

Tilao returned to his home islands a middle-aged man. Taking the name Abu Sabaya ("Bearer of Captives"), he began a campaign of kidnapping, rape, and murder, and emerged as the spokesman and most visible face of the Abu Sayyaf movement. Tilao became a frequent voice on the radio in Mindanao, and he apparently so enjoyed this public persona that he nicknamed himself "DJ," embroidering the initials on his backpack. His brazen insouciance and sense of style tapped a universal juvenile vein of rebellion, which gave the group, despite its shocking cruelty, a hip, antiestablishment feel. Tilao's ambition was nothing less than to become the premier southern franchise of global jihad.

His target that spring morning was Amanpulo, the most expensive diving resort on the southern coast of Palawan, where he and the others hoped to harvest a crop of wealthy foreign hostages. They would extort large ransom payments from the victims' families and employers, and shatter the friendly calm vital to the Philippine tourism industry. Palawan was considered completely safe. The trouble in recent years had been confined for the most part to the southern islands. This thrust across the Sulu Sea was a bold move by Abu Sayyaf, and something of a stretch. Indeed, when Tilao and his men arrived in the unfamiliar waters off Palawan, in the predawn darkness, they got lost. The plan called for them to strike before sunrise and set off on the long return trip while it was still dark. But with dawn rapidly approaching, they grabbed several local night fishermen off their boats and pressed them into service as guides. Abandoning their primary goal, the raiders settled for a resort called Dos Palmas. It was built on a tiny island just off the coast, where visitors could stay in the bay area in little white cottages on stilts above the water.

Among the nearly twenty guests asleep in the bay cottages that morning were three Americans: Guillermo Sobero, a naturalized citizen from Peru who ran a waterproofing business in Corona, California; and a Baptist missionary couple, Martin and Gracia Burnham, who worked for the New Tribes Mission, a global evangelical group. Martin Burnham was a pilot, and his wife worked as his ground support. They were celebrating their eighteenth wedding anniversary, having left their three children with friends in Manila. Sobero's wife (whom he was divorcing) and his four children were in the United States. He had told them he was celebrating his fortieth birthday with relatives at a resort in Arizona. Instead, he was halfway around the world, sharing a cottage with his young Filipino girlfriend, Fe.

The guerrillas raided the resort before dawn, first capturing the two guards and then moving from cottage to cottage, banging

on doors and kicking them in if they were not answered quickly
enough. Martin Burnham put on a pair of khaki cargo shorts and
opened the door to his room. Gunmen seized him and took him
away. Gracia managed to pull on shorts and a T-shirt and grab flip-
flops for herself and her husband before being dragged out behind
him, as other gunmen raided the minibar for food. All told, the
kidnappers took away twenty people, including the guards and a
cook. The vacationers turned out to be mostly Chinese Filipinos,
and when the raiders learned that two of their three American
hostages were missionaries, they were deeply disappointed. The
missions were generally poor, savvy, and fatalistic, notoriously
unwilling to pay ransom. With their captives huddled on the
boat under a tarp against the blazing midday sun, the kidnappers
headed southeast toward Basilan.

They would need five days and four nights to complete
the return voyage. They miscalculated their fuel, and when
they ran low on gasoline they hijacked a fishing vessel and set
their flat wooden boat adrift; the Philippine marines eventually recovered it. As Gracia Burnham recounts in her memoir,
In the Presence of My Enemies, the hostages sang Disney tunes
and Beatles songs to maintain morale, in between their captors'
harangues about Islam. Despite their frightening situation, they
marveled at the beauty of the sea around them. Dolphins raced
alongside the boat, dodging under its outriggers and occasionally leaping high out of the clear blue water. A tarp-enclosed
platform was erected off one side of the boat for the women to
use as a bathroom. Martin Burnham, handy with tools, made
himself useful to his captors, even showing them how to strap
together D batteries to recharge their satellite phone, which
seemed particularly important to Tilao. He had the captives use
it to call family and friends and implore them to pay ransom,
and he used it himself to call a radio station in Mindanao and
proudly announce his crime.

"The government only listens when we take people," he said. "Well, I'll admit we took those hostages. If [the government] wants to negotiate, it's up to them." He also warned the station, "Now that we have three Americans, you should not take us for granted." He then put Martin Burnham on the line:

"Hi, my name is Mr. Martin Burnham. I am a United States citizen. I am a missionary. . . . I along with my wife, Gracia, are in the custody of the Abu Sayyaf, Khadaffy Janjalani's group. We are safe; we are unharmed. Our needs are being met. . . . We are appealing for a safe negotiation. They are treating us well."

Tilao had wanted Burnham to also identify his kidnappers as "the Osama bin Laden Group," but Burnham was unfamiliar with that name and stuck with the more familiar local appellation.

The president of the Philippines, Gloria Macapagal-Arroyo, who had been in office for only a few months, quickly dashed any hopes that she would adopt a conciliatory approach toward Abu Sayyaf. "I will finish what you started," she pledged. "Force against force. Arms against arms. This is what the challenge you hurled against me calls for. I will oblige you."

On the fifth night, the kidnappers and their captives slipped off the boat into the warm, chest-high water off Basilan and walked ashore through the lazy lapping of the tide. Behind them, the spotlights of fishing vessels dotted the horizon. Islanders lived along the shore, but like these guerrillas, they knew how to move inland along narrow trails that pushed uphill into the black jungle. By straying just ten feet, a person could vanish into the dense vegetation.

2. The Colonel

Over the next year and a half, Aldam Tilao would in fact be hunted down and cornered, in a Philippine military operation that involved the CIA and the American military. Eliminating him was a small, early success in what the Bush administration calls the "global war on terror"; but in the shadow of efforts like the invasions of Afghanistan and Iraq, it went largely unnoticed. As a model for the long-term fight against militant Islam, however, the hunt for Tilao is better than either of those larger engagements. Because the enemy consists of small cells operating independently all over the globe, success depends on local intelligence and American assistance subtle enough to avoid charges of imperialism or meddling, charges that often provoke a backlash and feed the movement.

The United States would play a crucial but almost invisible role in finding and killing Tilao, enlisting the remarkable skills of the Philippine marine corps for the most important groundwork, and supplying money, equipment, and just enough quiet technological help to close in for the last act. Such an approach does present problems; the Philippine operation exposed some of the legal, logistic, and moral challenges of this kind of work. For one thing, the Americans worked hand in hand with Philippine forces who almost certainly murdered people standing in the way of their intelligence operation.

At the time of the Dos Palmas raid, Colonel Juancho Sabban, the deputy commander of southern operations for the Philippine marine corps, was in Hawaii beginning an advanced officer training course offered by the U.S. Department of Defense. On the first day of classes, the attendees from military forces around the Pacific took turns introducing themselves. Sabban—a thickset brown-skinned man in his forties with short-cropped black hair, full lips, big teeth, and a bull neck—spoke at some length. He dwelled particularly on Palawan, where he had been based for part of his career, and which he considered to be heaven on earth. So when he received a first report of the kidnapping, he expressed disbelief: Palawan was much too far away from Abu Sayyaf's territory; the movement lacked the means to strike at the far side of the Sulu Sea. When the details were confirmed, he was embarrassed, but he was also impressed by what the guerrillas had pulled off.

Meanwhile, Abu Sayyaf was tying the Philippine armed forces in knots. The army conducted raids all over Basilan but was always one step behind. The island's five hundred square miles are mostly jungle, and its people have a long tradition of supporting rebels. Abu Sayyaf found moving and evading relatively easy. Tilao paused now and then to give cocky, even cheerful, radio interviews. From the midst of one firefight, with gunfire popping in the background, he fielded questions from the Radio Mindanao Network.

Where are the hostages? he was asked.

"I don't know," he said. "I'm not with the captives. I'm a hundred meters away from them. . . . We have thirty hostages now. We abducted ten fishermen when we left Palawan. . . . So we can't be blamed now if we make good what we said earlier, that we will execute the hostages one by one. It's up to you."

There was a burst of gunfire.

"Perhaps Gloria [President Macapagal-Arroyo] thinks we can be frightened," he said. "We'll keep adding hostages, even if they reach a thousand."

Tilao went on to say that trigger-happy government forces were killing off the hostages faster than he and his men were. "The military thought that the hostages were our comrades, so two of them were killed. But I can't tell you their nationalities nor identities. What we will do now, perhaps today, we will [have] executions, but we cannot tell how many and at what time."

The Philippine army did seem more intent on killing guerrillas than on rescuing hostages. The captives were dragged from hidden camp to hidden camp all over the island that summer, as the rebels engaged in frequent shoot-outs with their pursuers. Martin Burnham and Guillermo Sobero had both been wounded in one such clash; Burnham had taken a stinging spray of shrapnel in his back; and Sobero was hit in the foot, so that it became increasingly difficult for him to keep up. To distract and throw off government forces, Abu Sayyaf operatives conducted numerous raids, including one at a coconut plantation called Golden Harvest; they took about fifteen people captive there and later used bolos to hack the heads off two men. The number of hostages waxed and waned as some were ransomed and released, new ones were taken, and others were killed.

One victim, in early June, was Sobero. He had irritated his captors from the beginning, partly because of his disregard for their show of Islamic piety. He would, for instance, remove his shirt in the oppressive heat, exposing his arms and torso in a way they considered "un-Islamic." They also coveted his young girlfriend. One day several of the guerrillas marched him off into the jungle after telling him, "Someone wants to see you." Sobero had tossed his shirt to Gracia Burnham and asked her to keep an eye on his backpack until he returned. He never did.

Tilao turned the American's execution into a joke. In another of his frequent radio interviews, he announced, "As a gift to the country on its Independence Day, we have released unconditionally Guillermo Sobero." Then he paused, and added: "But we have released him without his head. It's up to you to find Sobero's head . . . but the dogs may beat you to it."

Trudging behind their captors, the missionary couple endured. They focused on staying alive, attending to basic bodily needs—eating, sleeping, staying clean. No strangers to religious conviction, the Burnhams gently engaged their captors in theological discussion and found these jihadists to be shallow, even adolescent, in their faith. Unfamiliar with the Koran, the outlaws had only a sketchy notion of Islam, which they saw as a set of behavioral rules, to be violated when it suited them. Kidnapping, murder, and theft were justified by their special status as "holy warriors." One by one they sexually appropriated several of the women captives, claiming them as "wives."

Despite Sobero's murder and the Burnhams' continuing ordeal, the American government and the American public were largely indifferent. In this pre-9/11 era, the matter was regarded as a typical third-world outrage, the kind of nightmare often faced by missionaries in dangerous places. The official U.S. response was limited to occasional comments from the embassy in Manila, condemning the crime and demanding the hostages' release. Despite a policy of refusing to negotiate with terrorists, the FBI would eventually be involved in a futile attempt to ransom the Burnhams, losing $300,000 in the process. The money is believed to have been stolen by elements within the Philippine police.

After 9/11, everything changed. No longer was Abu Sayyaf just an obscure group of kidnappers; it was now a regional arm of the international Islamist menace. The fate of Sobero and the Burnhams was suddenly on the lips of powerful people in Washington. During a White House meeting with President Macapagal-Arroyo, President Bush said the United States was prepared to help "in any way she suggests." Given the hamhanded efforts of the Philippine army to that point, she was clearly in the market for new tactics. Tilao continued to taunt Philippine authorities in frequent radio interviews from his satellite phone.

In the fall of 2001, Colonel Sabban returned from his training course and was put in charge of the Philippine marine intelligence operation targeting Abu Sayyaf. Sabban is a charismatic man, popular, tough, and highly regarded within the marine corps, an elite group so cohesive that at times its members have seemed more faithful to one another than to the government. As a young officer in 1989, Sabban himself had been arrested and imprisoned for following his leaders in a failed coup against

Corazon Aquino, who was then the president. Many of the officers caught up in that plot were absolved and reinstated years later; their involvement was seen as motivated less by politics than by unit loyalty. The colonel's career hadn't suffered. If anything, his rebel past added to his luster as a man to be reckoned with. He knew the southern islands well, and he had what he called "assets in place."

The marines ran an old-fashioned intelligence operation. They did not have a budget to rival the army's, and they had none of the technological wizardry of the Americans, who were deploying to the Philippines that summer for joint military exercises; but they had smart, trustworthy corpsmen who spoke the local languages without an accent and were plugged into the islands' families and clans.

Early on, the colonel made Tilao the primary target, and noted two obvious weaknesses. The first was Tilao's love of attention, his need to boast of his exploits on the airwaves; there had to be a way to take advantage of that. The second was his local roots. He had been born in Malamawi, a little island just off Basilan, where he still had friends and extended family. It was a small, small world, and Tilao had become a very big fish. He had been outgoing, and an attention seeker, all his life, so he had left a larger circle of connections than most others in his shadowy organization, a circle stretching from Malamawi to Basilan and beyond. Sabban's undercover agents began mapping Tilao's connections, identifying family members, old friends, teachers, schoolmates. Then they fanned out, acting as undercover "spotters" to make informal contact. They would strike up conversations with targets, pretending to vaguely remember Tilao from school, or perhaps just to have read about him in the newspaper or heard his voice on the radio. They began to learn things; Tilao had been less guarded than he should have been. People had received letters, some with requests for supplies. The spotters were able to discover who had delivered them. The couriers were then followed, and fresh letters were intercepted and copied. Sabban's men were careful not to disturb this web; they were content to patiently gather information.

One thing the colonel learned was that a prominent tennis pro on Basilan sometimes played with a man who claimed to have been Tilao's closest childhood friend. The friend's name was Alvin Siglos, and there was something very important about him beyond his lifelong connection with Tilao, something that the guerrilla himself did not know.

Being a terrorist often means killing strangers to make a political point, and in terrorists' eyes, such deaths have no meaning beyond the political one. But in Abu Sayyaf's brutal attack on the Golden Harvest plantation, four of the plantation workers the terrorists had marched off into the jungle were cousins of Alvin Siglos. And one of the two men killed was his uncle.

Sabban had his ticket to Tilao.

3. The Informer

Squat, dark, and powerful, Alvin Siglos had been the leader of a rambunctious gang at Basilan High School three decades earlier. The boys hung out together constantly, playing sports during the day and gathering to raise hell at night. Siglos was the soccer team's captain and best player, and Tilao was a pugnacious defenseman. Reckless and fun-loving, Tilao seemed as far from serious thought about politics or religion as a young man could be. He skipped classes and got into trouble for fighting. His father was an honorable, pious Muslim, but Tilao was not. He and the other boys liked girls, and they liked to drink, gamble, and fight.

Siglos had not strayed far from home or from his youthful pursuits. Sabban found him living in the city of Zamboanga, a sprawling metropolis just a short boat ride from Basilan at

the southwestern end of the large island of Mindanao. He was
a cheerful, garrulous man with pockmarked skin, thick black
hair, and a wide face with narrow dark eyes set wide apart. He
didn't look like an athlete, but he was a star in the local softball
leagues and was considered one of the city's best tennis players.
He had little education and no interest in religion or politics.
He worked only when the need was strong and a suitable opportunity presented itself; he was the kind of man who lived off
hustle and charm. He was also an enthusiastic gambler, wagering heavily on the hugely popular Zamboanga cockfights. He
knew that his old high school friend had moved to Saudi Arabia
years earlier, and he'd learned only by accident that Tilao was
back in the Philippines: one day in 2000 he heard someone who
sounded like Tilao boasting on the radio, though the voice had
been identified as belonging to someone named "Abu Sabaya."
He was curious enough to ask one of Tilao's cousins, and was
told that his old soccer buddy was now the most notorious jihadist in the Philippines. Siglos began boasting that he was the
outlaw's "best friend."

Months later, word apparently reached Tilao that his old
friend had been talking up their relationship, and out of the blue
the terrorist leader surprised Siglos with a phone call.

"Are there lots of millionaires there in Zamboanga City to
kidnap?" he asked.

"No," Siglos told him. "We are all poor."

After the kidnapping at Dos Palmas, another surprise call
came, and this time Tilao wanted help. He asked if Siglos had
a bank account. He was looking for someone he could trust,
someone outside known Abu Sayyaf circles, to collect and hold
ransom money. Siglos said he had never had enough money to
need a bank.

"I will call you again," Tilao promised.

These furtive contacts with his friend on the run were thrilling for Siglos, and at first he didn't waste much time thinking about the nature of Abu Sayyaf's crimes, or about its victims. Their childhood friendship transcended such abstract considerations, and he was inclined to help Tilao if he could. Then came the kidnapping at Golden Harvest. What Tilao was doing no longer seemed so abstract.

It was at this moment that Siglos was first contacted by an operative of Colonel Sabban's. The marine asked if Siglos wanted to work as an "action agent." Apart from the pay he would receive, the Philippine government was offering a $100,000 reward for information leading to Tilao's capture or death. (The Americans would later put up a reward of $5 million. Tilao scoffed at the local reward, which he considered too small, but was proud of the Americans' offer.) At some level Siglos still loved his old friend; and he would later see that Tilao still trusted him. But as Siglos figured it, not even their friends could fault him for informing on the outlaw. Nor could they accuse him of selling Tilao out for money: blood was thicker than friendship. Revenge weighed heavily on the scale. Siglos was so eager to cooperate that the marine intelligence unit was at first taken aback.

Captain Gieram Aragones was unimpressed after the initial interview. He didn't trust Siglos. A wiry man with pale skin, Asian eyes, and the nickname "Bong," Aragones was obsessed with getting Tilao. It was the most important job he had been given, and apart from his ambition and professional pride, he personally found Abu Sayyaf offensive, and Tilao particularly so. Aragones—who was the son of a marine chaplain and had graduated from the Philippine naval academy—was a convert to Islam. He had taken well to undercover intelligence work, immersing himself in the culture and languages of Sulu Province. To him, Abu Sayyaf was an illegitimate political movement and a bogus religious one. Tilao and the other jihadists gave his adopted religion a bad name. As a symbol of his determination, Aragones announced to his men that he would neither cut his hair nor shave until Tilao was either in custody or dead.

Siglos was a potentially important avenue to Tilao, but Aragones judged that anyone who talked so much and displayed such transparent lust for reward money was dangerous. The would-be informer boasted that he had worked many times as an undercover agent for the Philippine organized-crime task force, but his claims didn't check out. Aragones saw him as a blowhard and an opportunist. Before putting Siglos on the payroll as an action agent, Aragones recommended to Colonel Sabban that the recruit be put to a test.

4. The Reporter

Colonel Sabban, as it happened, had exactly the same thing in mind. He'd been looking for a way to exploit Tilao's vanity and obsession with publicity, and he had a friend who would be perfect for the job: a remarkable and daring young journalist, Arlyn dela Cruz.

Arlyn dela Cruz was a well-known TV personality, short and slender with long dark hair, big eyes, and full lips; very articulate and very ambitious. Her success as a journalist had been so sensational that it had brought personal and professional problems. In 1993, as a rookie reporter, she had been assigned, much to her surprise, to try to interview members of Abu Sayyaf, after they kidnapped Father Bernardo Blanco, a Spanish missionary. Not only did dela Cruz get an exclusive interview with the group's leaders; at least one of them, Khadaffy Janjalani, took a shine to her. Over the next few years she repeatedly visited jungle hideouts, bringing back scoop after scoop—videotapes and notes of exclusive interviews with Abu Sayyaf's notorious leaders. Tilao was among those leaders, and he had greeted her in the jungle camp like an old acquaintance, a fellow celebrity. This struck her as so odd that she had asked Janjalani about him. He explained that Tilao had essentially appointed himself the group's spokesman: "He likes to talk."

Intelligence agents disappointed by her unwillingness to share information spread false rumors about dela Cruz—that she was having an affair with Janjalani; that her husband was somehow related to the rebel leader. On one occasion, while working as an independent journalist, she sold the videotape of an interview to a TV station for broadcast, and her rivals denounced her as mercenary. The backbiting took such a toll on her personally and professionally that she resolved to stop covering Abu Sayyaf altogether. So when Tilao began calling, offering an interview after the kidnappings at Dos Palmas, she turned him down.

She continued to refuse interview opportunities until Bob Meisel, the head of the New Tribes Mission office in Manila, personally implored her to get involved. He explained that official efforts had not borne fruit, and that after all these months the Burnhams' family and friends were eager for any contact at all. Moved by Meisel's pleas, dela Cruz began looking for a way to arrange a visit with Tilao and the captive missionaries. In November she flew to Zamboanga City.

Colonel Sabban's men had been watching dela Cruz for weeks. When she arrived in Zamboanga, they tailed her. Much to their surprise, within days she led them to Alvin Siglos. The colonel called her. "We know what you're up to," he said. Dela Cruz was not surprised; she was used to playing games with the various government intelligence units. Sometimes they used her, and sometimes she used them. Often her goals and theirs coincided. Sabban did not inform her at this point that his own team had been talking to Siglos. "Go ahead and keep on doing what you're doing," he told her. He said that if she and the informer went into the Basilan jungle, he would make sure they would not be delayed at any of the military checkpoints along the way.

The venture would provide exactly the test of Siglos the marines wanted. If he could take the reporter to meet with Tilao and bring her back safely, it would demonstrate that he had the access he claimed to have. Debriefing him later would give them a better fix on where, how numerous, and how well armed the guerrillas were. It might even allow the marines to set up an ambush immediately afterward. Further, a videotaped interview might provide "proof of life," showing that the Burnhams were indeed alive and giving some indication of their condition.

The trip into the jungle took two days. The reporter and the informer sailed through the military checkpoints, as the colonel had promised, and set off on foot into the jungle. They walked for about two hours, guided by a villager. Dela Cruz wore a blue sweatshirt and khaki pants, and carried a small digital video camera. She and Siglos were eventually met by about a dozen guerrilla fighters in a little clearing. Leading them was Tilao, looking thinner than usual after his months on the run, but still wearing his trademark sunglasses and black head wrap, dressed in a long-sleeved black shirt and army fatigue pants, with a rifle over one shoulder and a pistol strapped to his hip.

Tilao and Siglos embraced, laughing and crying, delighted to see each other again. "Auntie and Uncle will meet you tomorrow," Tilao told dela Cruz, referring to the American captives. Then he and Siglos walked off together to talk. Sitting that evening with Tilao's men, dela Cruz could hear the two friends talking animatedly well into the night, sometimes laughing boisterously, sometimes talking quietly for long periods. They spoke to each other in a local dialect that she didn't understand. When dela Cruz awakened the next morning, the two were still talking, and she lay on the ground listening to them telling stories and laughing.

Later that day, Tilao produced the Burnhams. Both of them looked emaciated. Martin's beard had come in thick and red, redder than the thin, sandy hair on the sides of his head. His cheeks and eye sockets were hollow, and his neck appeared long and very thin. His worn clothing hung on him. Gracia was similarly wan; her face was lined and her eyes were puffy. She smiled warmly and then quietly wept when she was introduced to dela Cruz and Siglos. Gracia was amazed that a reporter had found them in the jungle—but why a reporter and not a rescue force?

They spoke for more than an hour; the meeting was recorded on videotape. Martin seemed matter-of-fact about their predicament, even resigned to it. He was poised, in firm control of his emotions. He talked about his determination to return home to his children. Gracia's pain was closer to the surface, as was her anger. She spoke of her fear of being executed, her expectation of death. Most of Gracia's anger was directed at the Philippine government.

They parted later that day. Dela Cruz hugged Gracia and Martin, promising to carry their message to their children, to their friends, and to the world. Tilao and Siglos choked up on parting. Dela Cruz and Siglos were then led away, and after a surprisingly short walk down the mountain, they arrived at a military outpost. Soon after dela Cruz's return to Manila, her interview aired all over the Philippines and around the world.

Sabban and Aragones were heartened: Siglos had delivered exactly what he had promised. After debriefing him and dela Cruz, and watching the videos, the two marines determined approximately where Tilao and his men must be living on the island. But the Philippine army refused to allow the marines to conduct a rapid raid in pursuit. Sabban's efficiency had embarrassed the army, and it wasn't about to let the marines close out the mission. Instead, the army decided to pluck Tilao all by itself. Philippine army troops descended in force on Tilao's hideout, and found no one.

Tilao and the captives had vanished.

5. The Special Agent

Outside the small world of military intelligence, Colonel Sabban's success was perceived as failure: a mere journalist had walked into the Basilan jungle and scored an interview with a man the Philippine armed forces somehow couldn't find. But within intelligence circles it was a different matter. Sabban's small unit had accomplished more than all the rest of the Philippine military: it had not only found Tilao but also secured, in Alvin Siglos, a direct line to the guerrilla leader.

Other military and police intel units began vying for the services of this new action agent, and Sabban had to use all his clout to fend them off. In secret reports about the operation in Manila, the marine intelligence group was identified only as "MC-2." When American embassy officials began inquiring about MC-2, they were told at first that no such group existed. This was apparently an honest mistake, because no one at the highest levels of the Philippine government had ever heard of it. But contact was finally made, and Colonel Sabban was suddenly awash in offers of help, from both the CIA and U.S. military intelligence.

In short order he was dealing with the complexities of America's military intelligence bureaucracy, and being amazed by how strictly the Americans followed their rules. He discovered, for instance, that there were things that one agency could deliver but another could not. For military equipment and ammunition, it was best to ask the military intelligence folks, who were also permitted by the U.S. government to share "lethal information"—intelligence that might lead to a target's death. For technology and money, he learned, it was best to approach the CIA. Unlike military intel, the CIA had deep pockets. The agency was barred, however, from directly sharing lethal information.

Sabban's primary American contact was a bald, trig dynamo: Kent Clizbee, a CIA officer who showed up in Zamboanga City raring to go. The term *gung-ho* was inadequate to describe this big, pale, muscular American. He was nothing like the conventional image of the retiring, blend-into-the-background spy. Looming over his new Filipino collaborators, dressed in a T-shirt, shorts, and hiking boots, he looked like an American tourist who had taken a wrong turn. But Clizbee was an expert in Southeast Asian languages and cultures. When Sabban invited him along on a strenuous uphill hike for some exercise one afternoon, Clizbee, a U.S. Special Forces vet, earned any marine's deepest measure of respect by easily keeping pace. He was the perfect ally. He wanted no credit. He didn't want to plan or run the operation. He was a good listener.

"What do you need?" he asked Sabban. One of the first things the CIA provided was money to buy a new satellite phone—for Tilao. The guerrilla had asked Siglos to get one for him; his own had either broken down or been lost, and he'd been using his cell phone to make calls out of the jungle. There were several cell phone towers on Basilan, but service was poor. The colonel wanted Tilao to have a satellite phone, because it facilitated the kidnapper's vital link to Siglos; and with the help of the CIA, it potentially meant being able to pinpoint his location. Siglos bought the phone at a store in Zamboanga; the marines recorded its serial number, and then Siglos passed it along to the couriers who would take it into the jungle with the groceries Tilao had requested—also purchased with money from the CIA. Tilao later called Siglos on the satellite phone and confirmed that he had received the goods, and he even put his captives on the phone— "Uncle and Auntie want to talk to you," he said. Siglos recorded the call, as instructed, and collected $500 for his work.

Other units and agencies, Philippine and American, with an interest in pursuing Tilao were suspicious of Siglos. The FBI, which regarded all Philippine efforts as untrustworthy, wanted to pick him up as a suspected member of Abu Sayyaf.

But the truth was that Siglos was fully committed to taking Tilao down. The knowledge that he was betraying his friend pained him from time to time, but once he started along that road he never seriously considered turning back. The way he saw it, Tilao would be arrested and sent to jail, the hostages would be set free, and he would collect the reward money. He would avenge the murder of his uncle and get rich, which seemed a fair outcome to him.

With the Tilao-Siglos connection authenticated, the marines set about making it exclusive. They had been intercepting the terrorist's letters and phone calls for months, and knew that he had other connections in Zamboanga who served the same purpose as Siglos, sending groceries and supplies. These other contacts began meeting with unfortunate accidents. They were eliminated one by one, until, by early 2002, Tilao had only one avenue for his requests.

And Siglos was a bountiful provider. The CIA arranged things to look as if he was getting money secretly from local political figures sympathetic to the guerrillas, and virtually everything Tilao asked for was promptly delivered. His steady stream of requests included many from Martin and Gracia Burnham, who saw the sudden bounty as an answer to Gracia's prayers. At times in the previous months, Martin had hoarded cookie and candy wrappers so that he could simply smell them to ease his hunger pangs. Gracia had prayed for such items as sanitary napkins, a Scrabble game, Nestea, Bisquick, peanut butter, and even hamburgers; and the CIA began seeing to it that these very specific prayers were answered. When Tilao asked for a backpack, the CIA had one prepared with a tracking device sewn into the fabric. Its signals were of no use at first, however, because the agency had to wait for the war in Afghanistan to end before it could get aircraft—manned and unmanned—to track them.

For most of early 2002, thanks to the CIA, the marines had at least a periodic fix on the meandering guerrilla band. When Tilao boasted in radio interviews—saying, for instance, "It's really an embarrassment [to the authorities], because the superpower can't do anything to us"—he was doing so on a CIA-funded satellite phone, which gave away his position as he spoke.

The only hitch was that the CIA was not allowed to relay the precise coordinates—in part to cloak the capabilities of its own equipment, in part because it had not been given a "lethal finding"—permission to pass along potentially lethal information. When its agents on the ground pressed, their request triggered an argument in Washington. The Pentagon wanted the precise coordinates turned over to Philippine forces, but the CIA refused, instructing its agents to give Sabban and his men only a five-mile radius.

The marines had other troubles. Every time Colonel Sabban requested permission to send a small force of his men under Captain Aragones into the jungle to find the Burnhams and deal with Tilao, the lumbering Philippine army insisted on doing the work itself, sometimes sending whole battalions after the nimble guerrillas. Although it had only general coordinates, the army did come close several times. Abu Sayyaf lost men in these skirmishes. Tilao and his group were feeling enough heat that in early April they slipped off Basilan in a small boat. By now, all of the hostages had been ransomed or abandoned but three: the Burnhams and a Filipino nurse. They made their way across the short passage to the Zamboanga peninsula, stopped briefly at a small island, and then moved to a fishing village just north of Zamboanga City.

In the days afterward, the guerrillas seemed to have vanished, but then, just as suddenly, they reappeared. Tilao began calling Siglos from his cell phone—service was reliable in Zamboanga

City, so he did not need to use the satellite phone. The U.S. and Philippine intelligence agents could not get the same precise fix on his position that they had gotten from the satellite phone, but by now they had something even better: aircraft.

6. The Rescue

In moments of despair, Gracia Burnham told her husband she would rather be dead than continue running with their kidnappers. Martin reminded her of their children: "What do you think the kids would say if you could pick up the phone and call them?" Gracia was haunted by their vow to grow old together—it was happening; they were both so haggard that they seemed to have aged forty years. Martin's weight loss was aggravated by such intense diarrhea that when he was chained to a tree each night, he tied rags between his legs to catch the flow. His ribs were showing through his T-shirts.

After a short stay in the fishing village, the band moved off into the jungle north of the city. Here the guerrillas, no longer on familiar or friendly ground, had to be concerned about being seen, even by villagers. They could not let the Burnhams be seen, so the couple were no longer allowed to bathe in rivers. Tilao seemed increasingly beleaguered, and it was apparent that he was tired of living on the run. In May, during an interview with Radio Mindanao Network, he warned, "If we see our situation becoming difficult, maybe we will just bid good-bye to these two." It was clear which "two" he was talking about.

From a base in Zamboanga City, the marines had reestablished their Siglos supply line. The action agent delivered supplies to a courier named Hamja, who took them to the guerrillas. From a house on stilts in the fishing village, he would steer his boat up the coast and leave the goods at a drop point on the beach; Tilao's men would pick them up and carry them into the jungle.

At about that time, in early spring, the CIA agents finally got their aircraft: a Predator, an unarmed, unmanned surveillance drone, which flew so high in the sky that it could not be seen or heard from the ground. It was equipped with high-resolution video cameras, one of them infrared.

As long as the guerrillas stayed close to the city, food—even fast food—was plentiful. When Gracia told Tilao she had prayed for a hamburger and pizza, he told Siglos, "I would like my goats to eat hamburger and pizza." Pizza was purchased, along with burgers from Jolli-bee's, a local fast-food chain. The food was still hot when it was delivered, its glow registering brightly on the Predator's infrared. Reprovisioned, the guerrillas pushed farther north into the hills of Zamboanga del Norte.

Clizbee and a fellow agent tracked the fugitives, working in their "office," a blue shipping container installed under the reviewing stand at the marine base in Zamboanga City. They studied monitors displaying data from a variety of tracking and surveillance systems. To make up for the CIA's refusal to provide exact coordinates, Colonel Sabban sent Aragones and an eleven man team into the jungle to keep visual tabs on their targets. Aragones, whose hair now hung to his shoulders and whose wispy mustache and beard blew in the wind, found them easily, guided by the tracking devices. The marine captain and his men blended silently into the jungle, and waited and watched. Tilao had nineteen men with him, and the three hostages. Aragones felt that if he and his men could choose the moment, they could easily rescue the hostages and either kill or arrest the kidnappers.

But once again competition arose over who would attempt the rescue. The American command, with forces again in the Philippines for the annual joint exercises, wanted to conduct the raid, using one of its SEAL teams. The Filipinos balked at this, and squabbled among themselves. Colonel Sabban argued that since his unit had found Tilao, and since his men were already in position, and since they counted only twenty armed men guarding the Burnhams, the marines not only deserved to conduct the mission but were best positioned and best suited for it. He did not prevail. Army commanders were determined to prove themselves.

The raid took place on the afternoon of June 7, 2002, in the rain. The guerrillas had stopped to camp atop a small mountain, the ground descending steeply before them to a stream. As the Philippine army troops encircled the camp and prepared to assault it, the Burnhams were quietly stringing up the small shelter they used on rainy days and hanging their hammock. They had just closed their eyes for a nap when the army struck and gunfire erupted. Martin Burnham was killed in one of the first volleys, shot through the chest. The Filipino nurse was also killed, as were some of Tilao's men. Eight of the attacking soldiers were injured. Lying beside her mortally wounded husband, herself shot in the leg, Gracia played dead, resisting the urge to cry out in pain and terror. When the shooting stopped, she raised a hand slowly, trying to draw attention without drawing fire. The raiding party at first tried to reassure her that her husband was still alive, but more than a year on the run in the jungle had turned Gracia into a hard-eyed realist.

"Martin is dead," she told them curtly.

The attempt to rescue the three hostages ended up killing two of them. It was a failure in yet another way: Tilao himself had escaped. The army found his backpack—the one with the hidden beacon—but the rebel leader and a small group of men had once again slipped the noose.

Gracia Burnham arrived back in civilization to a storm of media attention. Doctors in Zamboanga City attended to her wounded leg, and by phone she both celebrated and grieved with her family. Just before leaving the Philippines for the United States, three days after her rescue, she was wheeled out to microphones at the airport in Manila, her leg propped up in front of her. She was still gaunt, but she looked clean, rested, and enormously relieved. She seemed suddenly ten years younger. The raid had been characterized by many in the press as a debacle, but Gracia lived up to her name. She thanked the Philippine people for their prayers, and she thanked the government for her rescue. She talked about how much her husband had loved the country. She expressed no sympathy for the riddled, fleeing band of kidnappers, or for their "holy war."

7. The Endgame

Colonel Sabban was furious about the raid. He believed there would have been a better chance of keeping the three hostages alive and of capturing all the guerrillas if Aragones and his reconnaissance team had been allowed to go in. Sabban was determined that the next move would be by his own men. He expected that Tilao's plan would be to flee the peninsula for his home islands, and for that he would need a boat. This presented an opportunity: If the guerrillas could be confronted on the water, the marines had clear jurisdiction. Sabban also knew that the peninsula was unfamiliar ground for the kidnappers, so they would probably seek to leave it from the place where they had entered. And since they had few friends or allies on the peninsula, they would be likely to summon the same courier and the same vessel that had been serving them so well. Sabban ordered his men to quietly pick up Hamja. If they were going to lure Tilao out onto the water, they would need the courier's help.

Hamja had painted his boat with an image of a crouching Spider-Man and called it the *Kingfisher*, emblazoning the name on the side in the sweeping script of graffiti artists everywhere. For months he had been piloting the *Kingfisher* without knowing that he was being watched, or that both the boat and the supplies it carried had come from the Philippine marines and the CIA. But he would soon learn.

Hamja was snatched by Aragones and his men off a street in Zamboanga City, and immediately and wisely agreed to cooperate—the marines had a deservedly fierce reputation. Now it was just a matter of waiting for Tilao to summon the boat. The call came sooner than Colonel Sabban had anticipated, on the afternoon of June 20. The guerrilla leader wanted to be picked up between three and four in the morning, at a spot that was a four- to five-hour boat ride north. That meant the marines had to be ready to leave before midnight. Colonel Sabban was on a flight to Manila, so Aragones had to wait for more than an hour until he landed. The captain knew that the other branches of the military would be angry if the marines did this themselves, so he was reluctant to go ahead without the colonel's direct authorization. When Sabban called right after landing, he told Aragones he would fly back to Zamboanga immediately.

"But you go ahead," the colonel instructed him. "And just keep on calling me if you need any advice."

Aragones was daunted by the responsibility, but he had so much to do that he didn't have time to dwell on it. He had to coordinate the mission on the water with the Americans, so they could get their surveillance plane and backup boats ready. The *Kingfisher* was still tied up under the safe house in the fishing village, and sending Hamja back to retrieve it was out of the question. The marines didn't trust him enough to let him go to the house, and sending anyone else to retrieve the boat might sound an alarm. So Aragones and his men waited until dark, then slipped into the water, swam in under the house, cut the ropes tethering the boat to the stilts, and gently and silently eased it out and away. When they were far enough from the shore they climbed aboard, started the engines, and steered it to the navy pier, where the SEALs affixed infrared beacons called "fireflies" to the bow and stern.

Hamja would be piloting his boat, but to keep an eye on him, Aragones recruited a trusted Basilan man, Gardo, who had worked as an agent for him in the past. Hamja phoned Tilao to tell him that all was ready, and that his "cousin" would be coming along because he was more accustomed to navigating between the peninsula and the island. Aragones told Hamja that this was to be just a reconnaissance mission, that he and Gardo were going to be watched from above as they ferried the guerrillas back to the island. But Gardo knew that once they had steered the *Kingfisher* about a mile offshore, the marines would confront them. The approach would be made far enough from land that none of the guerrillas could swim back. Gardo was instructed that if gunfire erupted, he was to dive off the *Kingfisher* and break a Chemlight he was wearing as a necklace so that he could be easily seen in the water. Hamja, who had earned neither the trust nor the affection of the marines, was not so fortunate. He was not told that his boat would be attacked; and once it was, he would be on his own in the water.

The *Kingfisher* was outfitted with several large plastic jugs of what appeared to be gasoline. They were about four-fifths full of water, and the rest was gasoline—the fuel is lighter than water and doesn't mix, so anyone uncapping a jug would smell pure gasoline. The ruse ensured that if somehow Tilao was able to evade the ambush, he would quickly run out of fuel.

Late on the evening of June 20, just thirteen days after the botched rescue, four boats slipped away from berths at the navy pier in Zamboanga City and steered north along the coast. Two were U.S. Navy vessels, each carrying a SEAL team. Another was the same flat, open, gray wooden speedboat used by Abu Sayyaf in the kidnapping at Dos Palmas, now carrying Captain Aragones and fifteen men armed with assault rifles, and bearing two M-60 guns mounted at the bow. Moving well in front of these three was the long, sleek boat that Hamja, its young owner, had for months been using to supply Tilao.

On the monitor inside the CIA's container back at the base in Zamboanga City, the four vessels showed as gray shadows on a field of black, tracked from above by two CIA pilots in a high-flying RG-8 Schweitzer aircraft. The agents on the ground monitored the vessels' slow progress for hours.

Sabban was still at the Manila airport when the boats set off. High overhead, the CIA plane executed wide, silent sweeps, moving over the jungle and then back out over the water, keeping its cameras trained on the boats. In the speedboat, Aragones slept. His long hair and wispy beard made him the scruffiest military officer in the Philippines. He could not imagine Tilao slipping out of this trap, and didn't expect him to go down without a fight. The guerrilla had often boasted of his eagerness to be martyred for his cause. With luck, he would get his wish.

The CIA officers watching the monitors in their office in the container could see everything. The deserted beach registered bright white against the dark gray of the sea, and just in from the water's edge were the splayed gray silhouettes of palm trees as seen from high above. As the other boats waited just over the horizon, the *Kingfisher* touched sand. The two men appeared on the CIA monitor as black shadows. Hamja stepped out on the beach, slowly approached the tree line, and then stood and waited.

The aircraft cameras slowly panned up and down the beach, and back into the jungle. After long minutes of waiting, one black figure emerged from the foliage. He and Hamja stood together. They looked as if they were talking; the second man could be seen gesturing with his hands. Then, from a point farther up the beach, a group of figures emerged—it was hard to tell how many. They were moving close together, and on the screen they blended into a black blob. A bird flew above them. As they moved down the beach, they spread out into separate shadows, so distinct that the CIA monitor in Zamboanga City showed their legs moving as they walked toward the boat.

While Hamja was on the beach with the others, Gardo had activated the fireflies as instructed, by pushing a button on the bottom of each. The signals, silent and invisible to the naked eye, appeared as bright, blinking beacons to the aircraft's infrared camera. Once the *Kingfisher* had moved offshore, the beacons would allow the pursuers to spot it with night-vision binoculars.

The boat shoved off. When it had steered somewhat more than half a mile offshore, it turned south. The marines followed the vessel's progress for a time, waiting for it to come farther out to sea, but it seemed to have set its course, and was staying at about its original distance from shore. This was a problem. What if the guerrillas decided to make a run for it? The *Kingfisher* was fast and maneuverable, and Tilao might be able to get close enough to the shore for him and his men to swim to land. So the marines changed plans: they would ram it. Their boat was much larger than the *Kingfisher*, so ramming would most likely break and sink the smaller craft. The men aboard would be dumped into the water.

On the CIA's screen, the white speck of the *Kingfisher* could be seen plowing steadily on, leaving its long black wake. When the Schweitzer passed directly overhead, the officers could see the forms of nine men on board, most of them toward the stern.

Then the marine speedboat, moving much faster, jumped onto the screen from the bottom, cut rapidly across the smaller vessel's wake, and then turned hard right, aiming straight for the *Kingfisher*'s port side.

Aboard the speedboat, Aragones and his men leaned forward expectantly. Their three motors were quieter than the *Kingfisher*'s, so Aragones's strike force would be seen before being heard.

"Five hundred yards," announced one of the men in the bow, peering ahead through his night-vision goggles.

"Two hundred yards."

"Get ready!" Aragones shouted, and the men braced themselves and raised their weapons; someone switched on the speedboat's searchlights.

Seconds before the collision, puffs of white appeared on the CIA screen, just off the *Kingfisher*'s starboard side. Tilao and the other men aboard, including Hamja and Gardo, had seen what was coming and hurled themselves overboard; the puffs were heat from the guns of two guerrilla fighters who opened fire on the speedboat as soon as they hit the water. Onscreen, the speedboat came to a sudden stop, halted by the force of the collision. It then appeared to plow straight through the smaller boat; actually, it was pushing under it and tearing it in two.

Just before impact, the faces of the men in the waves were clearly visible in the speedboat's searchlights, and their weapons flashed when they fired. As the speedboat swung around after the collision, the marines unleashed a torrent of fire from their starboard side. Aragones felt the burn of the guns beside him and inhaled the smell of gunpowder. He knew the shooting from the men bobbing in the waves would be inaccurate—they were treading water as they fired—so he chose his own shots with care. Mixed with the smoke came the distinct coppery smell of blood.

Then the firing stopped. For a few moments there were just the sounds of men shouting and the lapping of the water. The marines unleashed another furious cascade from the starboard side. Then Aragones heard again the *pop-pop-pop* of an automatic weapon from the waves. One of the guerrillas was shooting up at the vessel from the port side. Aragones raced to join his men on that side and, as the other men cut loose with their weapons, he squeezed off the last ten rounds in his magazine. The body of the man in the water was cut in half, and vanished under the waves.

Cries came from terrified men in the water. Gardo had activated his Chemlight. Hamja had swum under the marine speedboat and was clinging to it. Hauled aboard with the others—four of Tilao's men survived—Hamja told Aragones that he had ducked underwater and swum to the port side after the shooting started. Tilao, he said, had done the same. Hamja had grabbed onto the boat, but Tilao had swum out farther, shouted, and opened fire. The man whose body was cut in half had been Tilao.

Captain Aragones phoned Clizbee and announced, "We just killed the motherfucker."

8. The Aftermath

Tilao's body was never found; this fed rumors that he had somehow escaped yet again. But interrogation of the four captured Abu Sayyaf men—one of whom died during questioning—confirmed Hamja's story. Tilao was the final victim of his bloody kidnapping spree.

He had failed to ignite jihad. In the four and a half years since his death, Abu Sayyaf has faltered. Although it survives as a stubborn regional insurrection, it has mounted no spectacular attacks or kidnappings. This past December, police discovered what was believed to be the body of Khadaffy Janjalani. Abu Sayyaf continues to battle marines and to set off bombs on contested islands like Jolo, but shows no sign of resurrecting itself into the charismatic movement it became in the time of "Abu Sabaya." His removal by Philippine forces did not inspire the larger Islamist struggle he had hoped for; the invisibility of the United States' role reduced the effort to a local police action. In a world where any visible U.S. military intervention prompts a dangerous backlash, Aldam Tilao slipped quietly and permanently under the waves.

"His death significantly downgraded the leadership and strength of the group," said Sabban in an interview last year. "He was spokesperson and operations officer. Janjalani is just a figurehead. It was Sabaya who made all the real decisions. Even after the kidnappings in 2001, the others all drifted away. It was Sabaya who kept the most valuable hostages. That right there shows you who the most important figure was."

Alvin Siglos has yet to receive any reward from the U.S. government. Why? The reasons are unclear.

Sabban is now a brigadier general, based in two small rooms off a corrugated shed at the Philippine marine base on Jolo. Captain Aragones is now a major, and clean-shaven, but since he still does undercover work, he wears his hair longer than most marines. Arlyn dela Cruz was kidnapped herself not long after her successful interview with Tilao and the Burnhams, and underwent her own ordeal in the jungle before being released through the intercession of her "friend" Khadaffy Janjalani. She writes a column for the *Philippines Daily Inquirer*, and reports for Net-25 TV, a UHF TV network in the Philippines.

Gracia Burnham visited President Bush at the White House a month after her return to the United States. Her leg had healed, and she moved confidently in a long, flowery skirt and a lacy white blouse. She spoke about her husband's unfailing kindness toward their kidnappers, even as they handcuffed him to a tree every night. And she added: "Even though Martin was kind to them, we never forgot who the good guys were and who the bad guys were. The men who abducted us and held us—who murdered some and mistreated others, who kept us running and starving in the jungle—are criminals, and they deserve to be punished."

Alvin Siglos collected the $100,000 in Philippine reward money and reportedly blew it quickly, gambling on cockfights and throwing big parties. Sabban and Aragones urged him to keep a low profile, pointing out that the terrorist group might target him for revenge, but he seemed unafraid. He has never collected a penny of the $5 million American reward. When speaking of his role in the mission during an interview last year, he broke down crying several times as he recalled his stark betrayal of his childhood friend, and he even defended Tilao. He said the jihadist had been planning to release the Burnhams unharmed. The marines had never told him, Siglos complained, that they intended to kill his friend. "Still, he killed my uncle," he said through his tears. "He was the blood of my mother."

He still thinks he is owed the American reward, and it would seem he is right.

PROFILES

Just Joe

Published as "The Salesman,"
Atlantic, October 2010

"Shermanesquely, No"

In January 1973, not long after he was sworn in to the Senate seat he would hold for more than three decades, Joe Biden attended a dinner party in the upscale Washington suburb of McLean, Virginia. The event, thrown by Biden's fellow freshman, Senator Bennett Johnson Jr. of Louisiana, offered the newcomers a chance to mingle with some of the Senate's old guard.

Political analyst Charlie Cook, then a freshman at Georgetown University working as a congressional intern, remembers well both the evening and the presence of Biden, then a thirty-year-old unknown from Delaware. "A bunch of us kids had been wangled into wearing white jackets and serving drinks and helping out in the kitchen," he said. "All of us were floored by how young Biden was! He was more one of us than one of the senators. And, sure enough, when the grown-ups retreated to the dining room, Biden drifted back to the kitchen to hang out

with us twentysomethings. . . . It was hard for us to believe that
someone our age, give or take a few years, was already a United
States senator."

Elected when he was just twenty-nine, Biden was the youngest member of the upper chamber in modern times, and the sixth-
youngest in American history. Inexperienced and unheralded,
he'd nonetheless ousted a veteran incumbent, J. Caleb Boggs,
who had enjoyed the full backing of President Richard Nixon
and the national Republican Party. Biden arrived in Washington
with the luster of unlimited promise. Back home they called him
the "Delaware Kennedy," a parallel he would consciously exploit.
He was a man for whom the White House seemed not merely a
possibility but a likelihood. In a notoriously revealing 1974 profile Kitty Kelley wrote for the *Washingtonian*, Biden talked about
becoming "a good senator" *and* "a good president." Biden's
sister Valerie, who had managed his surprise victory, told Kelley,
"Joey is going to be president someday. He was made to be in
the White House. . . . Just you wait and see."

Fast-forward to 2007, and the presidential campaign fields
of Iowa. Biden's once slender facial features had thickened somewhat, giving him the look of an elder statesman from central
casting. What little remained of his modishly long hair had long
since gone white; at the front of his otherwise bald dome, a
patient hair plug regimen had replanted a thin copse of strands,
which he combed back, so that when the lighting and angle were
just right it afforded the semblance of a silver mane. And not
only did he look the part. He was one of the most recognized
and influential members of Congress. Scarred by intense personal tragedy, a close brush with his own mortality, and his share
of embarrassing missteps, Biden at age sixty-four was a survivor,
in life and in politics. Though the luster of the wunderkind was
long gone, the talents he had displayed at the outset of his career
had matured. Yet here he was, six months away from the first

contest of the 2008 presidential campaign, badly trailing a pack of less seasoned Democratic hopefuls, mired in the low single digits in every poll, and struggling to raise enough money just to keep going.

It was a mystery. Back home in Delaware, Biden had a bond with voters that transcended issues and party politics, a stature that bordered on reverence. "I remember being in a cheesesteak shop in Claymont, just outside Wilmington, just eating dinner by myself one night years ago, when Joe came in to order something," said Cris Barrish, now a senior reporter for the *Wilmington News Journal*. "It was like royalty or Jesus Christ himself had walked in. He didn't know a reporter was watching, so none of this was for my benefit, but he charmed everybody in that place for a full five minutes. He knew the names of all the women behind the counter. Everyone seemed to want a piece of him, to touch him. That was the first time I fully appreciated the appeal he enjoys in this state."

But that unfailing local electricity, which had propelled him back to the Senate with ease in five consecutive elections, stubbornly refused to travel. His first run for the presidency, in 1987, had sputtered out of the gate, when Biden was discovered passing off as his own passages from a speech by a British Labour politician. Now, twenty years later, he was on his way to another early fizzle. In those months before the Iowa caucuses—where Biden would ultimately finish with less than 1 percent of the vote—it was fair to wonder why he even bothered. Might he be seeking something else? Might he be angling to become secretary of state in the next Democratic administration, or even vice president?

On August 16, riding with Biden as he raced from one Iowa event to another, the *News Journal*'s Nicole Guardino asked him exactly this question. Biden crushed the suggestion with such flourish and finality that Guardino couldn't fit the whole denial into her story the next day. She reported it in full in a blog:

"Absolutely, positively, unequivocally, Shermanesquely, no," Biden declared. "No. No. I would not be anybody's secretary of state in any circumstance I could think of and I absolutely can say with certainty I would not be anybody's vice president. Period. End of story. Guaranteed. Will not do it."

Today, Vice President Biden's sunny, spacious office sits just off the main lobby in the West Wing, at the hub of American power. The other guy on the ticket may have gotten the oval-shaped room overlooking the Rose Garden—Biden's windows face west toward the Eisenhower Executive Office Building—but it is only a few quick strides away. Sitting across from the vice president this summer on facing colonial-vintage sofas, I reminded him of his comment in Iowa, emphasizing the word *Shermanesque*.

He leaned back, folding his big hands before him, and shrugged.

"And that was absolutely positively true when I said it. I swear to God. Ask anybody. I never, never, never, never aspired to be vice president. It had nothing to do with who the hell the president was."

Certain allowances need to be made, of course, for campaign rhetoric. But I believe him. Both quotes—the one from the campaign trail and the one from the White House—are so quintessentially Biden: direct, earnest, forceful, earthy, overstated—note the triple "no" in the first and the quadruple "never" in the second—and ultimately, as it turns out, negotiable.

Biden is a salesman, a high-level one, but a salesman at heart. His father sold cars back in Wilmington, and the son has all the same moves. He is a virtuoso talker. That fluency is not a gift but an accomplishment: attaining it meant defeating a severe boyhood stutter, a feat in which he still takes pride. His prodigious loquacity is not about vanity, as his critics claim—although

Biden is as vain as the next successful man. It's about selling. It's about the deal. In fact, that's one of his favorite expressions: *Here's the deal.*

In *What It Takes*, the monumental chronicle of the 1988 presidential campaign, author Richard Ben Cramer had this to say about Biden, then in his first formal run for the presidency:

> Joe can literally talk fast. It's like the stutter left it all pent up, and when he starts talking deal, he goes at a gallop. . . . He'll talk that deal until it is shimmering before your eyes in God's holy light . . . like the Taj Mahal.

For most of his adult life, Biden has been selling himself. In 2008, he began selling Barack Obama. The vice presidency is a perfectly respectable office, to be sure, but historically it has more often been a ticket to obscurity than to distinction. It has few official duties or responsibilities that rise above the ceremonial. It was most famously described by Franklin Delano Roosevelt's two-term VP John Nance Garner as being worth less than "a bucket of warm piss." For a man of Biden's abiding energy and early promise, it is a comedown. But midway through the administration's first term, he seems to be making it work.

"I was talking to the president about this just the other day," said David Axelrod, Obama's chief of staff. "He was saying that choosing Joe was really the first presidential decision he made, and that as time goes on, he's more and more convinced he made a good one. From his perspective, it could not have worked out better."

The relationship with Biden was by no means a given. Axelrod noted that not long before being asked to take the second position on the ticket, Biden had been competing hard against Obama, and had seen himself as better qualified for the top job. Lashing together two such big egos was risky. "It's a little like a shotgun wedding," Axelrod told me. "Sometimes they take and sometimes they don't."

Declaring his determination "not to be a pain in the ass" to the president, Biden has carved out a dynamic role, one of the most involved of any vice president's. He is close to the president on a professional level, but seems content to remain on the outer fringe of Obama's trusted core. The idea, he says, is to be "value-added."

Walter Mondale is widely considered the first truly modern vice president, in that he was not simply a replacement in the wings, but an important player in the administration in his own right. With the exception of Dan Quayle, every VP since has done the same—none more so than the man Biden would succeed, Dick Cheney, who some believed was on certain issues actually steering the ship. And while that was an exaggeration, there is no doubt that Cheney built himself a kind of shadow national security staff during President George W. Bush's two terms. One of the first things Biden did when taking office was to hand back many of those positions: "I mean, Cheney had, like, thirty, or whatever the hell it was," he told me. "I said, 'Mr. President, you can't have two national security staffs.' So I went to [national security adviser] Jim Jones, whom I recommended for the job. And I said, 'Jim, here's the deal. I don't want any of these staff.' And he was like, 'Holy God, you're kidding.' I said, 'Under one condition: I get to help pick these guys, and I can individually task them. I'll let you know who I'm tasking, but that's it.' We only need one National Security Council. There used to be two. Literally, not figuratively. I mean, literally."

No one believes Obama would want, need, or tolerate a Rasputin across the lobby. But whether it has been managing the tricky drawdown of American involvement in Iraq, or implementing the $787 billion Recovery Act—"Lousy job," says Biden—or soothing worries in eastern Europe over Obama's revised missile defense strategy, or helping select two Supreme Court nominees, Biden seems the opposite of a pain in the ass. He has made himself indispensable.

During the nine-month deliberations over Afghanistan, Biden was the harshest skeptic at the table. Encouraged by Obama, he vetted the military's plans so insistently that to some in the chain of command he became the enemy. These evidently included the man in charge of the war effort, General Stanley McChrystal, who was captured in a *Rolling Stone* article joking with his inner staff as they derided the vice president. After the president accepted McChrystal's resignation, the general apologized to Biden, who says the gesture wasn't necessary. "To be very blunt with you, I was flattered," Biden told me. "I mean, it was clear that I was the only guy they worried about."

Like most modern vice presidents, Biden has been subjected to the constant ridicule and caricature that seem to accompany the office. And he is, by his own admission, prone to verbal blunders. But Biden's stock has risen steadily in the West Wing, and as the Democrats appear poised to lose much of their leverage in Congress in the upcoming midterm elections, his long experience as a legislator, his warm relationships with his former Senate colleagues, and his relentless salesmanship are likely to become even more important to the president. Even his occasional well-publicized gaffes have served to humanize a leadership team that all too often seems aloof, cerebral, and elitist.

And here's the curious thing. By stepping back, by sublimating his own considerable ego and ambition, by settling for second place, Joe Biden may finally have found a way to transplant that Delaware magic. In making his own political fortunes secondary, he has advanced them further than he ever could have on his own.

Getting "Bidened"

Joe Biden doesn't just meet people; he engulfs them. There's immediate, direct contact with his blue eyes, the firm handshake while his other hand grasps your arm, a flash of those famously perfect white teeth, and an immediate frontal assault on your personal space. He shoulders right through the aura of fame and high office. Forget the Secret Service, the ever-present battery of aides and advisers, the photographers clicking away: the vice president of the United States moves in like an old pal with something urgent to tell you, just you. If he's in a chair, he'll scoot it closer; when the furniture's not portable, he'll lean forward, planting his elbows on his knees, gesturing with both hands while he speaks, occasionally reaching over to touch your arm or leg for emphasis.

Aboard Air Force Two, when Biden wanders back to the cheap seats to greet the reporters in his entourage, he isn't content to simply stand in the aisle and banter. He leans, he reaches, and before you know it he's lowering himself to the cabin floor.

"Mr. Vice President," a reporter protests politely, "take my seat."

"No, no, no," says Biden, cheerfully dismissing the gesture. And then the second-highest officeholder in the free world is seated on the aisle floor, legs stretched out on worn blue carpet, elbows propped on the aisle-side armrests, so he can resume his monologue at eye level, close in.

Biden is well known for commuting to and from Washington from Wilmington aboard Amtrak, a habit he started decades ago when he was a widower with two small boys. Sitting alone in one of those cramped, four-seat Acela booths around a table, Biden would often recognize passengers and wave them over to join him. I had the pleasure myself once years ago, riding the train from Washington to Philadelphia. The space was knee-to-knee intimate—perfect for his purposes—and Biden held forth animatedly for the entire eighty-minute trip. When he stepped off at Wilmington station, the sudden silence in the car seemed like a physical presence, the swift descent of a vacuum. When I described the experience to a friend who'd taken the same ride more than once, he nodded knowingly and said, "We call it getting *Bidened*."

Biden is famous, of course, for talking too much. Indeed, it is exceedingly rare to find anyone in a prominent position who does so much of his thinking out loud. It has led not only to a propensity for straying off message—a tendency which has bedeviled generations of his political handlers—but also to an outsize reputation for oratory. The vice president is a confident and skillful public speaker, to be sure, but he is best at rousing the converted, rather than at the higher art of persuading the skeptical and undecided. His thousands of turns behind public lecterns have yielded not a single indelible speech. The one for which he is most famous is the one he'd most like to forget: the disastrous campaign trail appearance at the 1987 Iowa State Fair in which he borrowed freely, and without attribution, from British Labour politician Neil Kinnock.

Biden's special talent is not speaking, but *talking*. The former is a public act, a practiced performance. The latter is personal and improvisational. All good salesmen know that the key to closing the deal is trust. You need to hold your customers' attention and convince them that you are *just like them*. Biden is eager to share his own experiences, because trustworthy men have nothing to hide. He takes you immediately into his confidence—this is often what gets him into trouble with reporters—so that you will offer him your own. His language is instructive. He interjects, *Look*, to make sure you are listening closely. If he feels his pitch straying into abstraction, he'll stop in mid-sentence to say, *Let me break this down for you*. He'll dispel complexity with a personal story—*My Dad, he used to say to me, "Joey," he'd say.* . . . His syntax is confiding, earthy, real, and peppered with mild profanity. He repeats himself for effect—no, no, no; never, never, never. Despite his patrician appearance, he is proudly, stubbornly blue collar—*Call me Joe.*

Biden always has facts and figures handy, but he seeks your support less with logic than with bonhomie. His own emotions are so close to the surface that when he is excited you feel it; when he is disappointed or sad or angry, he chokes up and his eyes moisten, and you feel that, too. The depth of his belief is, as Cramer put it, "like a strong hand" on your back.

Biden admits his weakness for revealing too much on occasion, but he sees it as a strength, a part of his "brand": his gaffes reflect his determination to remain just Joe, to tell it like it is. In truth, his problem runs deeper. Biden has the limber storyteller's propensity to stretch. Though hardly a hanging offense—which of us hasn't burnished a tale now and then?—it's a dangerous tendency on the national political stage. In addition to the plagiarism scandal, in which he embellished his family's humble origins, Biden has in the past exaggerated his scholastic résumé. And for many years, he described the driver of the truck that struck and killed his first wife and daughter in December 1972 as "drunk," which the driver apparently was not. The tale could hardly be more tragic; why add a baseless charge?

More recently, Biden has told a story of privately upbraiding President George W. Bush over the Iraq war. Challenging Bush's assertion that he was a "leader," Biden claims to have told him, "Mr. President, look over your shoulder. No one is following." The former president's chief of staff, Karl Rove, insists the exchange never took place, calling the vice president "a blowhard and a liar." And though Biden sticks to his story, his past brushes with embroidering the truth continue to haunt him.

Though plenty smart, Biden is not an intellectual. He makes few references to books and learned influences in his speeches and autobiography, and he displays little interest in theory. An indifferent student at the University of Delaware and Syracuse University College of Law—he describes the latter as "a bore"—Biden got by with prodigious cramming sessions. Today, by contrast, he is described by Tony Blinken, who advises him on national security issues, as a compulsive studier who likes to be "overbriefed."

"He likes to tell the story of the time he got up on the Senate floor to deliver a speech on a bill concerning stripper wells"—i.e., oil wells nearing the end of their productive lives—said Blinken. "When he finished, an opponent, Senator Russell Long from Louisiana, got up and asked, 'Senator Biden, have you ever seen a stripper well?' He had not. Long proceeded to demonstrate such an intimate knowledge of wells and oil extraction that the import of Biden's own argument was just overwhelmed. Now he demands that his briefings go fifty feet deep even if the discussion is only expected to go five feet deep."

When he was a senator, his proudest legislative accomplishment was the Violence Against Women Act of 1994, which broadened law enforcement tools to protect women from abusive partners, and which the National Organization for Women called "the greatest breakthrough in civil rights for women in nearly two decades." Biden's congressional voting record was generally left of center, but not dramatically so. He was inspired as a young man by the civil rights movement, he is a strong civil libertarian, and he clearly sees an active role for government in American life. But at the same time, the national Chamber of Commerce has sometimes rated him highly for a liberal lawmaker—as high as 62 percent in 2004. In his personal life, Biden could hardly be more traditional. In the scruffy 1960s, when so many young men of his generation went unkempt as a social and political statement, Biden attended college classes wearing a suit and tie. He says his first wife, Neilia, described him as "the most socially conservative man I have ever known."

Though Biden prides himself on his fluency in foreign policy, he's been all over the map on national security issues. Author Tom Ricks likes to point out that Biden voted against the first Persian Gulf war in 1991 (a quick triumph); voted in favor of the invasion of Iraq in 2003 (a prolonged disaster); and voted against the "surge" in troops to Iraq in 2007 (a remarkable success). Though Biden has tended to oppose military action, during the Bosnian war his was the loudest voice in Congress in favor of arming the Muslim minority and encouraging NATO's air strikes against the Serbs.

On the global stage, as in Delaware, the guideposts in Biden's political landscape are often not ideas, but people. Many of the world leaders with whom the United States has business are men and women he has known for years, even decades. In the fall of 2009, for example, after Obama had decided to dismantle land-based missile defenses in eastern Europe—a move interpreted as a concession to Moscow—the White House sent Biden on a three-day swing through Poland, Romania, and the Czech Republic to reassure the leaders of those countries that their security would not be compromised. Biden had mastered the details of the issue—the virtues of sea-based versus land-based antimissile technology, and so on—but his most important asset was that he knew many of the leaders personally.

Barry Pavel, senior director for defense policy on the National Security Council, was along on that trip. He describes how, in high-level meetings, Biden would wave his hand and reduce the expert advisers accompanying him to decorative furniture. "It's a thing he does," Pavel said, referring specifically to discussions Biden held in Warsaw with President Lech Kaczynski. "We're across the long tables with the coffee and the water and stuff in these formal meetings, and he'll say, 'Now, these guys are going to tell you all the statistics and these are the brainiacs, but I'm here to tell you this is much better for Polish security. I'm here to tell you this is in your interest.' He connects in a very street-wise way. . . . And that's something I couldn't do, and there are few people in the government who could play the role, I think."

And once he's connected, once he's leaned in close and has your undivided attention ... well, watch your wallet.

Here's the deal.

Rags to Riches

In his 2005 book, *The Seven Basic Plots*, British author Christopher Booker distills what he considers the archetypal human narratives. The second of these (after "Overcoming the Monster") is "Rags to Riches," which he defines thus:

> We see an ordinary, insignificant person, dismissed by everyone as of little account, who suddenly steps to the center of the stage, revealed to be someone quite exceptional.

This is, in effect, the story that Biden tells in his 2007 campaign autobiography, *Promises to Keep*.

We begin with little Joey Biden, growing up in Scranton, Pennsylvania, crippled by a stutter so dreadful that he is dubbed "Joey Bye-Bye" or "Joe Impedimenta" by classmates and teachers alike. He overcomes the disability through diligent practice and eventually delivers the valedictory speech at his high school graduation.

Like many of the heroes in rags-to-riches tales, Biden is a lost child of privilege, a prince among paupers. His father had grown up close to a wealthy maternal cousin, with whom he shared a posh life of country estates, sailing, and partying. But a series of business ventures gone sour sent the senior Joe Biden crashing back down to the blue-collar streets of Scranton, where he was reduced to moving his family in with his in-laws and taking a job as a car salesman. "He was the most elegantly dressed, perfectly manicured, perfectly tailored car sales manager Wilmington, Delaware had ever seen," Biden wrote. "He was a great dancer. He loved to sing, and he had a thoroughgoing grace; I never saw him flustered in a social setting."

In little Joey's eyes, the family had been exiled from wealth and social standing; regaining this lost patrimony has been one of the central themes of Biden's life. As a boy he set his heart on Archmere Academy, a Catholic prep school on a leafy campus across the road from the house his family moved to in Claymont, Delaware, when Joey was ten. His parents couldn't afford the full tuition, but Joey eventually won a work/scholarship, and labored on the school's grounds crew in order to attend classes with the elite. He was a handsome boy and a good athlete, and he worked hard at fitting in, at looking and sounding the part, and like many of those who do so, would surpass most of those born to privilege. Biden's fascination with the trappings of wealth is evident in his description of his first visit to the upstate New York home of his eventual first wife, Neilia Hunter:

> The first time I pulled up to Neilia's house on the lake, I realized that the Hunters were different than the Bidens. Her dad had done well in the restaurant business. Even in the dark I could see the outlines of the house, and it was huge by my standards.

Biden would later marry Neilia, finish law school, and set out to build for them the same kind of lavish life. He had the taste and style of an affluent young man, and what he lacked in money he made up for in drive. Cramer vividly records the newly married Biden's pursuit of a suburban mansion equal to his ambitions, an estate that had once belonged to Delaware's native gentry, the Du

Ponts. It was a home far beyond his means, but Biden pursued it with an enthusiasm bordering on obsession, exhibiting the kind of optimism and deal-making that would distinguish his whole adult life. He got the house, and has since moved several times over the years to ones newer or better appointed, assiduously maintaining the affluent lifestyle he grew up admiring.

Biden's rise was so rapid that his future prospects seemed limitless. Before he was thirty, he had an enviable suburban home-stead with a beautiful wife and three children, and had somehow managed to win election to the U.S. Senate. But it all crashed down in an instant on December 18, 1972. Just weeks after the election, before Biden had been sworn in, Neilia accidentally steered her car into the path of a hay truck in rural Pennsylvania. The collision killed her and their baby daughter, Naomi. Their two young sons, Beau and Hunter, were severely injured. Overcome with grief, Biden questioned his faith, contemplated suicide, and was so filled with rage that he walked the streets of Wilmington at night, half-looking for a fight.

One of his first decisions was to abandon his hard-won Senate seat. He began making plans to move with his boys to Vermont, to start over where no one knew them. He memorably told reporters, "We can find another senator; my boys cannot find another father." Ironically, it was this heartfelt statement that may have permanently secured Delaware's passion for its young senator. He was eventually persuaded to change his mind, as he tells it, by the kindness and stubbornness of Mike Mansfield—who was then the majority leader—and other prominent senators. He took his seat in 1973, long after the other members of his incoming class had been sworn in. It was arranged for him to take his oath of office beside the hospital bed where his son Hunter was recovering from his injuries.

Biden's ferocious love of and loyalty to his sons was a testimony to his character that endured through decades of commuting home every night to Wilmington. Who could fail to be moved by it? If such a thing happened today—a promising junior senator, stricken with tragedy, soldiering through his grief, gathering close his wounded boys—it would play out breathlessly on cable TV and the Internet before the entire world. In 1972, it was primarily a local story, and this made its impact at home all the more intense. It touched hearts in every corner of Delaware, and voters there have never forgotten. It explains the deep connection Barrish witnessed at the Claymont steak shop all those years ago.

He and his boys gradually recovered and, over time, the young senator emerged as the most eligible bachelor in Washington. In 1974, he was interviewed for the *Washingtonian* by Kitty Kelley, a pioneer in the art of the embarrassing celebrity profile. A pert blonde—a type that tended to catch Biden's eye—Kelley clearly charmed the young senator, who foolishly (and typically) took her into his confidence, speaking openly of his grief, and in startlingly intimate terms about his relationship with Neilia. Biden described her as, "my very best friend, my greatest ally, my sensuous lover." The two of them had enjoyed the "perfect" marriage, sharing everything "from sex to sports." He spoke of his ability to "satisfy" her in bed and, showing Kelley a picture of Neilia in a bikini, said that she "had the best body of any woman I ever saw. She looks better than a *Playboy* bunny, doesn't she?" He spoke openly, needily of his desire to meet the right woman and remarry: "I want to find a woman to adore me again."

It was painful to read, especially for Biden. In his autobiography he wrote, "It was devastating. I had been very wary of the press until then. Now I began to actively hate it." But he had done this to himself. For all its prurience, the story captured Biden exactly: the frank emotionalism, the recklessly unguarded nature, the penchant for drama, the ambition, the shameless romanticism.

Romance would return not long afterward, when Biden spotted Jill Jacobs—another gorgeous blonde—in posters advertising Delaware's New Castle County Park System. He sought out her name and an introduction, and swept her off her feet. She married Biden in 1977, adopted Beau and Hunter, and gave birth to the couple's daughter Ashley in 1981. Together, they restored the perfect picture, and set Joey's rags-to-riches journey back on the rails. Biden had a bad scare in 1988, when a brain aneurysm came near enough to killing him that a priest administered the last rites. But he recovered from this, too. (When he speaks of it, Biden often credits his humiliating plagiarism stumble in the prior year's presidential campaign with saving his life; had he stayed in the race, he says, he would probably have pushed through the warning signs that sent him to the doctor.)

Though Biden is consistently ranked as among the least wealthy U.S. senators, his family has enjoyed a distinctly affluent lifestyle. All three children attended Ivy League schools. His son Beau is now the attorney general of Delaware. But if appearances are one thing, the Biden "brand" is another. Despite the suburban estate, the well-tailored suits, the superb golf game—Obama reportedly invited the vice president to the links only once; Biden shot seventy-seven and has not been invited back—in private Biden is still the kid on the grounds crew, the kid with something to prove, Joey Bye-Bye from the streets of Scranton.

Anything You Want

According to Biden, it went like this: It was spring 2008. He was out of the race for president. He had known his campaign was dead when he finished fifth in Iowa—"We got our asses kicked," is how he puts it—behind Obama, John Edwards, Hillary Clinton, and even New Mexico's governor Bill Richardson. "It was no problem," he told me. "I ran my race. I have no regrets. Went out and did what I thought. Said what I said."

Obama and Clinton were slugging it out in the remaining primaries, and Biden was back to being the senior senator from Delaware, still commuting most days in his familiar spot on the Acela. It was there, in fact, in June, that he fielded the first call from Obama about the vice presidency.

During the campaign, he had variously mocked the freshman senator from Illinois for parroting his own more seasoned views on complex issues; had notoriously patronized him as "the first mainstream African American who is articulate and bright and clean and a nice-looking guy"; and had repeatedly characterized Obama as too inexperienced for the job . . . but that was all part of the game. They liked each other, and Biden respected Obama's political skills. Still, it would have been hard for Biden not to see this forty-six-year-old first-term colleague as a parvenu, as someone cutting in line. Such is the unfair nature of political stardom in America. Biden's early role model, Jack Kennedy, had been even younger when he ran for president.

"Joe," Obama asked, "I'd like your permission to vet you."

For someone in Biden's position, this was not a surprise. After dropping out of the race months earlier, he had declined to endorse either Clinton or Obama, and he had offered both candidates advice. On a trip to the Virgin Islands after he dropped out of the race, he and his wife, Jill, had talked through the option of accepting a job in a new Democratic administration—Biden thought Clinton was more likely than Obama to ask him—and they had decided he would not accept, regardless of who won the nomination. But one remote possibility remained. It had come up in a conversation with John Marttila, one of his senior advisers, and a final meeting of his campaign staff five months earlier.

Marttila told him, "You really ought to be vice president."

"John, I do not want to be vice president," Biden replied. "Do not talk up vice president for me, OK?"

"Well, Senator, you ran for public office because of civil rights," said Mike Donilon, a campaign consultant. "You mean to tell me if an African American tells you that he needs you on the ticket in order to win, you'll say no?"

The question was left hanging. There was no certainty at this point that Obama would be the nominee. Months later, when the call on the train came, that prospect was more certain. But Biden doubted that Obama would end up choosing him. There had been some friction between the two during the campaign, when Biden had mocked Obama's inexperience and—another gaffe—patronized him as "articulate." But more than that, Biden was leery of becoming a vice presidential also-ran, whose name was floated and then discarded. He had seen presidential front-runners "drag that bloody rag" through the Senate, he said, giving everyone the scent.

He told Obama: "No, no, no. Look, I told you I'd help you. I'll do anything you want."

So, said Obama, why the hesitation?

"Yeah, but that didn't include vice president," said Biden.

Obama said he thought "anything" should mean *anything*, adding, "I need an answer now."

"If you need an answer now, the answer's no," said Biden.

"Well, how much time do you need?" Obama asked.

"I don't need any more time."

Obama told Biden to think about it more anyway. So Biden called a family meeting. Present were Jill, their children, his sister, Valerie, and longtime aide Ted Kaufman, who has since been appointed to Biden's Senate seat.

"I don't want to do this," Biden told them. But Jill's reaction surprised him, given the decision they had made on vacation.

"You really ought to do it," she said.

Jill, whom Biden describes as "fiercely" partisan, was alarmed by the possibility of continued Republican governance, of John McCain in the White House. "You can't possibly let that happen," she said. And they came back to Donilon's point, and the central role civil rights had played throughout Biden's political career. How could he refuse to help the first viable African American candidate?

So Biden called Obama back the next day and agreed to be vetted. "But here's the condition," he said. "Even if you pick me, I'm not prepared to accept it unless you and I have some very long conversations."

Which is why months later, on August 6, when the list of prospective running mates had been whittled down to two or three, Biden flew to Minneapolis for a secret meeting with the Democratic nominee. A private jet picked him up at the small Wilmington airport. ("A Lear jet, or something like that," Biden said. "I sure would like to have had one of those when I was campaigning.") He was smuggled into the candidate's hotel through an underground garage. They talked for three hours.

The political logic in choosing Biden was plain. He was the picture of a traditional American elder statesman, a perfect balance to the newcomer at the top of the ticket with the dark skin and foreign-sounding name. His decades of experience would add heft to Obama's slender résumé. At the same time, Biden, with his persona as Joey Bye-Bye from Scranton, might be able to shore up Obama's weakness with white, blue-collar voters, a vulnerability Clinton had revealed and exploited.

But even if choosing Biden made sense for Obama, did it make sense for Biden?

According to an account of the conversation in Minnesota that Biden gave the *New Yorker*, the two men discussed everything from "foreign policy and possible appointments to the federal courts to the legislative strategy that would be needed to pass an Obama agenda." Obama questioned Biden about some of his successes in the legislature, and asked if Biden might be more interested in a cabinet post than a spot on the ticket. (He was not.) Discussing the job of vice president, Biden said that he would not want to be handed a sweeping open-ended task to go off and manage on his own, like Vice President Al Gore's assignment to reorganize the federal government. He wanted, first, to be in the inner decision-making circle for all major issues, the last person in the room to have Obama's ear. If he was to tackle any specific assignments, he wanted them to be limited ones with an end date.

Not long after that session, Obama picked Biden. Axelrod said that in addition to satisfying the obvious considerations—Is he qualified to be president if it comes to that? Does he balance the ticket politically?—Obama believed Biden's long experience in Congress would shore up the ticket and help him govern. Beyond those factors, Obama was swayed by one more practical consideration.

"Senator Obama felt strongly that Joe understood the challenges and rigor of a national campaign," Axelrod told me. "[Obama] had learned from his own experience. He felt that it had taken him four to six months of campaigning to get comfortable with the demands." The other candidates on Obama's short list, reputed to be Governor Tim Kaine of Virginia and Senator Evan Bayh of Indiana, would have been as new to a national campaign as Obama had been a year earlier. Biden, who had impressed Obama during their primary debates, would not need months to hit full stride.

"At the last meeting . . . there were all these high-powered lawyers in my Capitol office's so-called hideaway," Biden told me. "And so they're all sitting there, eight, nine of these lawyers, and at the end Jim Hamilton"—a Washington lawyer who assisted with the vetting of potential VPs—"Jim says, 'Well, just one last question, Mr. Chairman.' He said, 'Why do you want to be vice president?'"

"I don't," said Biden.

"And he looked at me. You can ask him. He looked at me and he said, 'No? Why?'"

"Guys," said Biden, "I'm not asking to be vice president, OK? If the president wants me to be vice president—our nominee wants me to be vice president, needs the help—obviously I'm not going to be able to say no. But if you're asking me why do I want to be, I don't want to be vice president."

"Is that really your final word, like, you know, your final answer?" Hamilton asked.

"Yeah, that's my final answer," said Biden.

"But I had decided by then if he were to ask me, obviously I'd do it," Biden told me. "Donilon was right. If, in fact, they could show me, that, *A*, I could actually help him win in places like Pennsylvania and Ohio, et cetera. And if, *B*, in fact he really did want me to help him govern, what the hell do you say? But I never—swear to God—I never ever, ever, ever thought that I'd be asked, and I never contemplated being vice president."

Donilon's argument had prevailed and, at least as much, so had Marttila's. Obama's skills were evident, but beyond them was a narrative that reached back to the founding of America. Here was an African American candidate poised to write, not an ending, but a triumphant new chapter in one of the central and most troubling threads of the American story.

"And it was driven home to me on the seventeenth of January," Biden told me. "I'm standing on a platform [at the train station] in Wilmington, Delaware. If you looked to the northwest and the southeast, it was no-man's-land back in 1968. That's the part of the city that got burned down . . . that got burned to the ground when Dr. King was assassinated. . . . And here I am forty years later. And it hit me like a ton of bricks. I'm standing there on a cold day, waiting, and all of a sudden I'm looking out . . . and I thought to myself, Son of a bitch. I'm standing here waiting for the first black man in the history of America to pick me up to ride 127 miles to be sworn in as vice president of the United States with the first African American."

He recalled seeing enormous crowds of cheering black citizens along the route as the train moved slowly south. One man in particular—"I knew him," Biden said—held up a child so close to the train that Biden worried for his safety. "I came back five days later, I'm home, and I run into him at a thing they did for me," he said. "And I said, 'What the hell were you doing holding the baby up like that?' And he said, 'Joe, I wanted my grandson to be able to say, I saw it. I saw it. It's real. It's real.' So that's what I mean. The two things I cared about most in my career were the civil rights movement and foreign policy and these wars, and here I am with a guy who in one fell swoop"—Biden clapped his hands—"changes everything."

A Big Fucking Deal

In March, the vice president gave an informal speech at an opulent home in northwest Dallas, standing behind a lectern in a large room decorated with modern art. The subject was Barack Obama.

"I didn't know how good he was until I joined the outfit," Biden said. "And then I realized why it was I did not win. So for those of you who endorsed me first, you all made a mistake." It's not unusual for Biden to give several speeches a day, so most of the things he has to say he says more than once. This comment about the president, and variations on it, he repeats often.

Biden's unqualified respect was not always there. Like many of those who sought the Democratic nomination, Biden felt early on that the press was giving Obama a free pass, in part thanks to his race. But now that he has spent more than a year and a half in office, any doubts about Obama's talents have disappeared. Biden is not given to downplaying his own gifts, but it's clear that he regards Obama as phenomenal.

In part, this transcends the president's personal qualities. "Look, I ran for president" Biden told me, "because I honest to God believed that for the moment, given the cast of characters and the problems of the country, I thought I was clearly the best equipped to lead the country. . . . But here's what I underestimated: I had two elements that I focused on, which made me decide to run. One was American foreign policy, and the other was the middle class and what's happening to them economically. If Hillary were elected or I were elected, and assume I did as good a job as I could possibly get done, it would have taken me four years to do what he [Obama] did in four weeks, in terms of changing the perception of the world about the United States of America. Literally. It was overnight. It wasn't about him. It was about the American people. [I]t said, These guys really do mean what they say. All that stuff about the Constitution and all about equality, I guess it's right."

But Biden has been impressed by Obama the man as well. "He has a backbone like a ramrod," the vice president told me. "He sits there, he gets handed the toughest damn decisions anyone has since Roosevelt, and he sits there and he wants an opposing view. He wants to hear all of it, and he'll sit there and he'll listen. He'll ask really smart questions and he'll decide. And it's like he goes up, he goes to bed, he doesn't re-litigate it. I mean the guy's got some real strength. And the thing about him is—what I find impressive is—he really starts off almost everything from a moral and ideological construct, knowing exactly who he is. . . . He knows what he thinks. When he talks about Niebuhr [Reinhold Niebuhr, the theologian and political theorist] it's not because he's trying to impress. He really does think about the social contract. I mean, the guy's thought it through.

"He reminds me of [Bill] Clinton. I don't think he'd like it, and maybe Clinton wouldn't like it, but whenever you're with Clinton . . . he was never afraid to say to you, 'I don't understand that. Explain that to me.' Or, 'I didn't know that.' Because he knew you'd never walk out of the room thinking you were smarter than he was. Barack has the same internal confidence."

That said, it's clear that Biden feels he has the superior people skills—not that he puts it that way. He says the skill set he brings is "different," but it's a difference he values, and one that he sees as part of his contribution to the administration. "[Obama's] personality is more reserved," Biden said. "He has the ability to touch large audiences, but he is a little more buttoned-up. I'm a little more Irish. I'm more old school. What used to be normal. [Bill] Clinton and I are more similar, whereas [Obama] and probably some of the newer candidates are more similar in terms of the way they went through the system. And so I just think it's a difference in style—but it works. I think we complement each other."

There was some initial worry in the White House over Biden's looseness in front of cameras and microphones. Most of his slips have proved minor—such as the one that earned him a withering look and a nudge from the president on day one when Biden, standing beside Obama behind a lectern, poked fun at Chief Justice of the United States John Roberts for flubbing his recitation of the oath of office at the inauguration. But some have been more troubling. During the swine flu epidemic of 2009, when the administration was treading a delicate line between stressing caution and triggering a panic, Biden told a *Today Show* audience of millions, in a nutshell, to avoid air travel. "I would tell members of my family—and I have—I wouldn't go anywhere in confined places now," he said. "If you're in a confined aircraft and one person sneezes it goes all the way through the aircraft. That's me." The air travel and tourism industries reeled. A visibly annoyed Robert Gibbs found himself at the lectern in the White House pressroom trying to explain what Biden "meant to say."

But while Biden's batting average for such bloopers is unquestionably high, the administration has come to see it as a feature, not a bug. Gibbs explained, "It is true [Biden] has earned a reputation, and he definitely has a tendency, to say whatever is on his mind *when* it is on his mind, and that has been much, much more of a plus for us than a detriment. Not just in public. The president wants to know what people really think, what their opinions are, and he has benefited a lot by listening to the questions the vice president asks in meetings. His experience and his candor are valuable things for us. When you look at the two of them side by side, they share none of the same background or experience. In some ways they could not be more different. But they complement each other powerfully."

Judged strictly by appearances, the black, youthful Obama is without question the least likely man to ever occupy the Oval Office. Biden, on the other hand, is close to what you might get if you digitally blended the portraits of the forty-three white men who have been president. Whereas Obama is cerebral, Biden is emotional. Where the president is methodical, the vice president is steered more by his gut. And where Obama is famously disciplined both in public and in private, Biden is . . . well, you know.

On March 23, minutes after the signing of the national health reform bill, at which Biden famously greeted the president behind the lectern by saying, "Mr. President, this is a big fucking deal," alarmed White House aides showed the incriminating video to Gibbs. "The sound is not that good on my office computer," Gibbs told me, "and one of the guys said, hopefully, 'I think he might have said, "This is a big *freaking* deal."' I said, 'Have you ever actually heard the vice president use that word?' Later, when [Biden] talked to me about it, he said that he didn't think he could be heard. I said, 'You were standing in front of a lectern in the White House with a microphone and the whole world watching!" Still, in the end Gibbs couldn't deny that Biden had a point, tweeting, "Mr. Vice President, you're right, it is a big fucking deal."

If the White House is still worried about Biden's verbal blunders, there's little evidence of it. He is being encouraged to speak more in public, not less, and is regularly trotted out to the Sunday morning TV interview shows, where his loose oral style has long made him a favorite, and where he can mix it up with the administration's critics while allowing the president to remain above the fray. There are some weeks when the vice president is more the public face of the administration than his boss.

And Biden has grown accustomed to the constant ridicule. He is a regular target for the late-night talk show hosts—"Joe Biden is living proof that people can give up sensitive information without being tortured," quipped David Letterman. On *Saturday Night Live*, cast member Jason Sudeikas regularly portrays him as a cheerful, loud, fast-talking buffoon, wincingly tolerated by the more sober, judicious Obama. "It's always been that way," Biden said. "I think it's the nature of the office. [W]hen you come to be vice president, it is clear that all you are is an appendage of, you know, a part of—it's not a bad thing, it's just—by nature it's a diminishing office."

As I watched Biden on his visits to Warsaw, Prague, and Bucharest last fall, arriving with all of the pomp and circumstance of a head of state, the red carpets, the ceremonial bands, the squadrons of security . . . I wondered how it felt for him to have landed so close to his life's goal, and yet short of it.

"I crossed the Rubicon about not being president and being vice president when I decided to take this office," he told me. "The only power you have is totally, completely, thoroughly reflective. There is no inherent power. And so it depends totally on the relationship you have with the president."

Biden is pleased with that relationship, and seems to be enjoying the perks of the office. The biggest change, he says, is his mode of travel, which has both its pleasures and its drawbacks. On the one hand, he has helicopters, jets, and fleets of armored SUVs at his fingertips. He often brings members of his family along with him on state trips. He sat in the front cabin of Air Force Two on the long flight to Warsaw with his eleven-year-old granddaughter Finnegan poring over a map, imparting lessons in history and geography. He and his wife live at the vice president's official residence on the grounds of the U.S. Naval Observatory during the week, but travel back home to Wilmington most weekends. During his first year in office he insisted on taking the train home, which was troubling for his security detail.

"First time we get on, one of the conductors sees me and he goes, 'Joey!' and he grabs my cheek," he said, grabbing a thick pinch of flesh to illustrate. "He's an Italian kid from north Jersey. And, swear to God, Secret Service was going to take his arm off because he reached out for me and he grabbed my cheek. So it drives them crazy."

Security concerns have since prevailed: Biden now usually makes the commute on a small jet. But when he's home in Wilmington, he insists that his Secret Service detail maintain a very low profile. "It's so easy to get bubble-ized here," he said. "I told them, 'Guys, look, I'll do whatever you tell me I've got to do in Washington and in other states, but in Delaware, no limos, no police escort, and I don't want any goddamn ambulances following me.'"

One weekend, he and Jill decided they wanted to see a movie, so they went to their usual multiplex on Route 202, the Regal Brandywine Town Center 16. The vice president and his wife got in line to buy tickets, and when they got to the window, learned that the movie they wanted to see was sold out. Disappointed, they turned to leave.

"And the Secret Service says, 'What do you mean?'" said Biden, chuckling. His escort felt an exception should be made for the Second Couple of the United States. "I said, 'Look, no, no, no, no. Do not do this. They're sold out, they're sold out.'"

"In Delaware," Biden continued, "there's a semblance of reality. I still go to the drugstore. I still go to the hardware store. I still go to the haunts that I go to, and restaurants. Because after all these years in Delaware, I'm Joe."

The Inheritance

Vanity Fair, May 2009

I was in a taxi on a wet winter day in Manhattan five years ago when my phone rang, displaying "111111," the peculiar signature of an incoming call from the *New York Times*.

"Mark? It's Arthur Sulzberger."

For weeks I had been trying to talk with Arthur Ochs Sulzberger Jr., the publisher and chairman of the New York Times Company. We had met once before, on friendly terms, and sometime after that I had informed him I was writing a story about him. I hoped he was calling now to set something up. Instead he asked, "Have you seen the *New Yorker* piece?"

The article in question, just published, was bruising. It had surely been painful for him to read. Among other indignities, it featured a quotation from the celebrated former *Times*man Gay Talese, the author of one of the most popular histories of the institution, *The Kingdom and the Power*. Speaking of Arthur Sulzberger, the fifth member of the Sulzberger-Ochs dynasty to preside over the newspaper, Talese had said: "You get a bad king every once in a while." I told Arthur that I had not yet fully read the story. "Well, I'm getting out of the business," he said. Startled, I looked out the window at the cars and people shouldering through the cold rain, the headline already forming in my mind: *Publishing Scion Resigns!*

"Wait, Arthur," I said, "is this a major scoop, or are you just saying that you aren't talking to writers anymore?"

He laughed his high-pitched, zany laugh. "The latter," he said.

Now, I respect people who avoid the spotlight, and a reluctance to be publicly vivisected is a sure sign of intelligence, but ducking interviews is an awkward policy for the leader of the world's most celebrated newspaper, one that sends a small army of reporters—hundreds—into the field every day to seek answers. Still, I could understand Arthur's decision. After presiding or helping to preside over a decade of unprecedented prosperity, the publisher and chairman of the *Times* had recently begun to appear overmatched. Two of his star staffers were discovered to have violated basic rules of reporting practice; he had been bullied by the newsroom into firing his handpicked executive editor, Howell Raines; and he had spent much of the previous year in a confusing knot of difficulty surrounding one of his reporters and longtime friends, Judith Miller. For an earnest and well-meaning man, the hereditary publisher had begun to look dismayingly small.

He has been shrinking ever since. In 2001, the *New York Times* celebrated its 150th anniversary. In the years that have followed, Arthur Sulzberger has steered his inheritance into a ditch. As of this writing, New York Times Company stock is officially classified as junk. Arthur made a catastrophic decision in the 1990s to start aggressively buying back shares ($1.8 billion worth from 2000 to 2004 alone). This was considered a good investment at the time, and had the effect of increasing the stock's value. Shares were going for more than $50. Now they

are slipping below $4—less than the price of the Sunday *Times*.
Arthur's revenues are in free fall: the bottom has dropped out
of both newspaper and Internet advertising. He has done more
than anyone else in the business to showcase newspaper journalism online. It hasn't helped much. The content and page views
of the newspaper's website, nytimes.com, may be the envy of
the profession, but as a recent report from Citigroup explained,
"The Internet has taken away far more advertising than it has
given." Layoffs have occurred in the once sacrosanct newsroom.

Having squandered billions during the newspaper's fat
years—buying up all that stock, buying up failing newspapers,
building gleaming new headquarters—Arthur is scrambling to
keep up with interest payments on hundreds of millions in debt,
much of it falling due within the next year. To do so, he is ped-
dling assets on ruinous terms. Arthur recently borrowed $250
million from Carlos Slim Helú, the Mexican telecommunications
billionaire, who owns the fourth-largest stake in the Times Company. Controlling interest is held closely by the Sulzberger family,
which owns 89 percent of the company's Class B shares. These
shares, not traded publicly, are held by a family trust designed
to prevent individual heirs from selling out, and ultimately to
shelter editorial matters from strict concern for the bottom line.
The family owns about 20 percent of the Class A shares, which is
about the same percentage owned by the hedge funds Harbinger
and Firebrand. The third-largest Class A shareholder is T. Rowe
Price, with 10 percent. Slim comes next, with 7 percent. Given
the current state of the investment and credit markets, Slim would
appear to have the inside rail should the paper ever be sold, a
prospect once unthinkable. It is now *very* thinkable. Among the
other prospective buyers whose names have surfaced in the press
are Michael Bloomberg, the billionaire mayor of New York City;
Google; and even, perish the thought, the press baron Rupert
Murdoch, whose *Wall Street Journal* has emerged as journalistic

competition for the *Times* in a way it never was before. (Murdoch has publicly dismissed reports of his interest in the *Times* as "crap," but this has served only to heighten speculation.) This quarter, for the first time since Times Company stock went public, in 1969, the fourth- and fifth-generation Sulzbergers who hold shares (there are forty of them in all) received no dividends. As recently as last year they divvied up $25 million.

Beyond these professional trials, Arthur has personal ones. He has separated from his wife of more than three decades, the painter Gail Gregg, and embarrassing speculation about his sleeping partners has surfaced in tabloid columns. His son, Arthur Gregg Sulzberger, is now working as a reporter at the paper, as his father and grandfather once did, but for the first time in five generations the heir apparent's inheritance is in doubt.

While the crushing forces at work in the newspaper industry are certainly not Arthur's fault, and many other newspapers have already succumbed to them, the fate of the *New York Times* is of special importance: it is the flagship of serious newspaper journalism in America. The *Times* sailed into the economic storm that began in 2001 in good financial shape, bearing the most respected brand name in the profession. It was far better equipped than most newspapers to adapt and survive. What is increasingly clear is that the wrong person may be at the helm. Arthur Sulzberger's heart has always been in the right place, but he assumed leadership from his father uniquely ill-equipped for this crisis—not despite but *because of* his long apprenticeship. To their credit, the Sulzbergers have long treated the *Times* less as a business than as a public trust, and Arthur is steeped in that tradition, rooted in it, trained by it, captive to it. Ever the dutiful son, he has made it his life's mission to maintain the excellence he inherited—to duplicate his father's achievement. He is a careful steward, when what the *Times* needs today is some wild-eyed genius of an entrepreneur.

The Sulzbergers embody one of the newsroom's most cherished myths: *journalism sells*. Arthur says as much at every opportunity, and clearly believes this to his core. It encapsulates his understanding of his inheritance and of himself. But as a general principle, it simply isn't true. Rather: *advertising sells; journalism costs*. Good journalism costs more today than ever, while ads have plummeted, particularly in print media. This is killing the *Times*, and every other decent newspaper in America. Arthur has manfully tied himself to the wheel, doggedly investing in high-quality reporting and editing even as his company loses more and more money. Few investors or analysts consider this to be sound business practice.

Many people are rooting for Arthur Sulzberger, and many people like him. It can be hard to persuade those who know him to talk candidly on the record. For this story, Arthur stuck by his decision to get out of the business of being interviewed, and he also declined to permit his employees to talk to me. Nevertheless, many did. I interviewed dozens of current and former *Times* reporters, editors, and business managers, as well as industry analysts, academics, and editors and publishers at rival newspapers. Nearly every one of them hopes that Arthur will succeed. Few expect that he can.

Only two years ago the New York Times Company moved into a new skyscraper on Eighth Avenue designed by Renzo Piano. Its facade rises into the clouds like an Olympian column of gray type. Whether owing to hubris or sheer distraction, the erection of new headquarters often seems to spell trouble for corporations, and many had questioned the wisdom of this investment. The new Times building has now been sold, one more measure to relieve the company's mounting debt. Eyeing the handsome grove of birch trees planted in its soaring atrium, one reporter told me, "We used to joke about how many trees died for a story. Now we ask, How many stories died for those trees?"

1. The Sword and the Stone

America is not kind to the heir. He is a stock figure in our literature, and an unappealing one at that. He tends to be depicted as weak, pampered, flawed, and a fop, a diluted strain of the hardy founding stock. America celebrates the self-made. Unless an heir veers sharply from his father's path, he is not taken seriously. Even in middle age he seems costumed, a pretender draped in oversize clothes, a boy who has raided his father's closet.

Arthur Ochs Sulzberger Jr. is fair-skinned with small, deep-set, light brown eyes. He has a high forehead with a steepening widow's peak; his crown is topped with a buoyant crop of wavy hair, now graying. He is a slight man who keeps himself fit, working out early in the morning most days of the week. He has a wide mouth that curls up at the edges, and when he grins he is slightly bucktoothed—this adds to the impression, unfortunate for a man in his position, of puerility. He is a lifelong New Yorker, but there is no trace whatever of region or ethnicity in his speech. When he chooses to be, Arthur is a fluent, eager, even urgent talker, someone who listens impatiently and who impulsively interrupts, often with a stab at humor. He has delicate hands with long fingers, which he uses freely and expressively in conversation. He is long-winded and, in keeping with his tendency toward affectation, fussily articulate, like a bright freshman eager to impress, speaking in complex, carefully enunciated sentences sprinkled with expressions ordinarily found only on the page, like "that is" and "i.e." and "in large measure," or archaisms like "to a fare-thee-well." He exaggerates. He works hard, endearingly, to put others at ease, even those who in his presence are not even slightly intimidated or uncomfortable.

His witticisms are hit-or-miss, and can be awkward and inadvertently revealing. "Some character traits are too deep in the mold to alter," says one longtime associate. Arthur has the clever adolescent's habit of hiding behind a barb, a stinging comment hastily disavowed as a joke. Some find him genuinely funny, while others, particularly those outside his immediate circle, read arrogance—the witty king, after all, knows that his audience feels compelled to laugh. His humor can also be clubby. He will adopt, for instance, a pet expression, which becomes an in-joke and which he will repeat often. One of these expressions is "WSL." It stands for "We suck less," a self-deprecatory boast, which he will vent in discussions of the industry's woes as a reminder for those in the know that, for all their travails and failings, they remain, after all, the *New York Times*.

While clearly smart, Arthur is not especially intellectual. For what it's worth, he is a *Star Trek* fan. His mind wanders, particularly when he is pressed to concentrate on complicated business matters. Diane Baker, a blunt former investment banker who served for a time as the chief financial officer of the New York Times Company, has described him as having the personality of "a twenty-four-year-old geek." She did not long survive Arthur's ascent to the chairman's office. His thirty-year marriage has reportedly foundered over a relationship Arthur had with Helen Ward, from Aspen, Colorado, whom he met on a group excursion to Peru. Since separating from Gail, he has been living alone and has not been involved with Ward or anyone else. Perturbations on the home front are also a family tradition. (Arthur's grandfather Arthur Hays Sulzberger was always, as the saying goes, a tough hound to keep on the porch. His father, Arthur Ochs ("Punch") Sulzberger, paid child support for sixteen years to a newspaper staff member who bore a child she claimed was his—this according to Susan E. Tifft and Alex S. Jones in *The Trust*, a history of the *Times*.) Arthur is provincial. Asked once if he had seen a story on the front page of that day's *Post*, he looked confused until it was explained that the item had appeared in the *Washington Post*. He said, "I only read the *Times*, the *Wall Street Journal*, and the

New York Post." He sometimes takes the bus or subway to work, and for many years jogged in Central Park. Recently his knees have started to bother him, so he now prefers exercising on an elliptical trainer. He also takes Pilates classes and can be evangelical about them, telling friends the practice wards off arthritis, which has begun to worry him. But he is not a complete health nut. He still enjoys unwinding with a cigar and a martini. He still goes on motorcycle treks with his cousin Dan Cohen and other friends. His attraction to feats of personal daring, and to rock climbing, is a vestige of his enthusiasm for Outward Bound. He has little interest in sports, particularly team sports, and dismissed as silly the effort to lure the Olympic Games to New York City, which included plans for a sports stadium in Manhattan. In a presentation at the Times building, Arthur greeted the scheme's promoters with cutting sarcasm, even though the paper's editorial board supported it.

He has been publisher for seventeen years now and chairman of the board for twelve of those years, yet no weight seems to adhere to him. What Arthur's manner does suggest is a hyper self-awareness: he is one of those men who seem condemned to stand apart from themselves, watching. Arthur is theatrical. His theatricality shows in his public speeches, which can be impressive. He has a nice sense of comic timing, and enjoys attention and applause. This is a man who, after spending a few years living in London in his youth, returned home wearing suspenders and a top hat, and carrying a cane. He long ago abandoned that Carnaby Street affectation, although the suspenders lasted well into middle age, but the basic impulse for showmanship is still there, manifested by a very calculated ease. He prowls the Times building in his stocking feet, and will pounce on colleagues as they happen by his sixteenth-floor office, urging them to step in and visit, saying conspiratorially, "Let me show you something cool." His corner office in the new building is spare and sunny and much smaller and less imposing than his old one, the one his father had. The old office was musty and formal, with rich wooden bookcases and heavily sculptured furniture upholstered in leather. It was the *Citizen Kane* version of the publisher's lair. The new office has windows that stretch from floor to ceiling. On his desk is a crystal Steuben sculpture of a gold-handled Excalibur embedded in stone, a gift from his sisters when he was named publisher, the third Arthur in the line.

The plainer office is an expression of Arthur's desire to lessen the distance between himself and those he employs. He deliberately placed his office in the center of the floors inhabited by the *Times* in the new building. At his most romantically self-effacing, he speaks of the *Times* in the language of family. In an hour-long interview with Charlie Rose in 2001, to mark the newspaper's anniversary, he talked about how fortunate his own family was to have been "adopted" by the extraordinary talents who create the newspaper. He frets when people on his staff are unhappy, and he looks out, or tries to look out, for his friends. When one of his old reporter pals was transferred and asked the *Times* to cover the loss on the sale of a residence, Arthur wanted to do it. When his business managers balked, complaining about the precedent it would set, he backed down, annoyed, and sent them to inform the reporter—"You handle it," he said. To a degree some of his top staff consider unwise, he tends to base promotions not on a cold-eyed assessment of people's talent but on how comfortable he feels around them—on how much *fun* they are. As Arthur was deciding between Howell Raines and Bill Keller for the executive editorship of the newspaper, in 2001, the reserved Keller kept a professional distance. The gregarious Raines sought to sweep Arthur off his feet. "I remember seeing them at the 2000 Democratic convention, in Los Angeles," said an editor at another newspaper. "Joe Lelyveld [then the *Times*' executive editor] was there. He was running the paper. But what everyone noticed most was how Howell Raines seemed glued to Arthur. It was evident that Howell was seducing Arthur, insinuating himself. Howell is a brilliant journalist, and he exudes confidence. You could watch him making this big impression on Arthur." Raines became the executive editor.

2. "Dad, Can I Come See You?"

The single defining fact of Arthur Sulzberger's life is his birth. His father; his grandfather Arthur Hays Sulzberger; his uncle Orville Dryfoos; and his great-grandfather Adolph Ochs were publishers and chairmen of the *Times*. Arthur was the firstborn male heir in a line that stretched back to 1896, when Ochs bought the newspaper. In an era when merit generally counts for more than genes, Arthur is ill at ease about his archaic path to power, so he handles it the way he handles many things that make him uncomfortable: he jokes about it.

Near the end of his interview with Arthur, Charlie Rose scanned the long history of family ownership and success, and asked, "Does this make you believe in nepotism?" "To hell with nepotism!" said Arthur, smiling. "I'm a believer in primogeniture!" He was kidding . . . and he wasn't. He does in fact have three sisters with exactly the same genetic link to old Adolph, and while there is much discussion of his son eventually succeeding him, there is no such speculation about his daughter. On a stage before a big audience at the University of California, Berkeley, in 2002, Arthur was asked a similar question by his host, Orville Schell, then the dean of Berkeley's Graduate School of Journalism. Earlier, Arthur had joked with the dean about how he had achieved his position in the same way as Kim Jong Il, the North Korean dictator, who had succeeded his dictator father, Kim Il Sung.

Schell: "You said the difference was that in their family [the line of inheritance] was only two generations, whereas in your family it was four."

"I don't like where this is going one damn bit!" Arthur protested comically, to much laughter. "And if you don't be a little more careful, I may nuke you!"

"My question is," Schell persisted, "really, I mean, the *New York Times* is governed and held in a very unique way for corporate America. It decides who the successor will be in a way that is neither very corporate nor democratic. Tell us about that, and the effect you think it has on how this great paper comports itself in the world."

Arthur sighed.

"There's a lot behind that question," he said. "First of all, just to get it on the record, the family did go for talent." More laughter.

But Arthur wasn't just born to his position—the story is more complicated. He may have been the firstborn son in the line of succession, but he also staked his claim to the crown deliberately and dramatically, when he was only fourteen years old. His mother, Barbara Grant, and Punch Sulzberger divorced when Arthur was just five. He lived throughout his early childhood on the Upper East Side with his mother and her new husband, David Christy, a warm and supportive stepfather. Punch is nominally Jewish, although not at all religious, but his son was raised Episcopalian. Arthur senior and Arthur junior were not close: Punch was generally aloof, even when Arthur was around. Yet, understanding what his famous name meant, and who his distant father actually was in the world, he packed up his things and moved himself the half mile to his father's home on Fifth Avenue, to live with Punch and his stepmother and their daughters. He was not pulled by any strong emotional connection. It seemed more like a career move. His biological father and his stepmother were wealthy, socially connected, and powerful; his biological mother and his stepfather were not. Arthur opted for privilege and opportunity. That his stepmother, Carol Sulzberger, despised Arthur—she would stick out her tongue at pictures of him—did not seem to matter. He was Arthur Ochs Sulzberger *Jr.*, and showing up on his father's doorstep was a way of asserting, consciously or not, that when Punch changed wives he had not washed his hands of an obligation to his son. While the inheritance was his by birth, it was also very much Arthur's choice.

Some heirs flee the burdens and expectations of family, determined to make their own way. Arthur chose to be defined by his name, and his father. When he went off to summer camp in 1966, the year he moved in with Punch, Arthur took his father's old portable typewriter case with him. It was stamped, "A. O. Sulzberger, *The New York Times.*" This was at a moment when many members of Arthur's generation were questioning received wisdom in all its forms, turning their backs on conventional careers, disdaining not just their parents but the entire establishment. Arthur, too, would grow his bushy hair long, try drugs, demonstrate against the Vietnam war, and embrace the style and rhetoric of the 1960s. He has said that he worked on his high school newspaper but not his college paper, at Tufts, because "we had a war to stop." But even then Arthur, draped in Punch's old (and newly fashionable) marine corps fatigue jacket, was just acting out the editorial policy of the newspaper he planned someday to run. Notwithstanding appearances to the contrary, he was the exact opposite of a rebel.

Arthur has spent a lifetime faithfully placing his feet in his father's footsteps. Like Punch, he served a long apprenticeship during his inevitable rise. Perhaps *inevitable* is too strong a word. He began as a reporter for the the *Raleigh Times*, then moved on to the London bureau of the Associated Press. He was a hard worker and a cheerful colleague, and he produced competent if unspectacular work. His friend Steve Weisman, a former *Times* reporter (and now the editorial director for the Peterson Institute for International Economics), asked him once—when they were both in their late twenties and working as reporters in the *Times'* Washington bureau, where Arthur landed after the AP—if he was going to be publisher one day. "Well, there's always the fuckup factor," said Arthur, which Weisman took to mean that, barring a serious misstep, Arthur's path was assured.

In *The Kingdom and the Power*, Gay Talese described the similar path taken by Punch in his youth. Talese and Sulzberger were roughly contemporaries (Punch was six years older). They started working at the newspaper at about the same time, Punch having gone to college only after his stint in the marines. Talese, the son of a tailor, considered himself fortunate when he landed a job as copyboy at the *Times*, after distinguishing himself as a college journalist and a columnist for his hometown newspaper, the *Ocean City* (New Jersey) *Sentinel-Ledger*. He went on, one finely crafted story after another, to earn distinction as the best writer at the *Times*. What he wrote about Punch's apprenticeship could have been written about Arthur's:

> *He would learn a good deal during the next few years, but he would never become a top reporter, lacking the qualities that are essential and rarely cultivated by men such as himself, the properly-reared sons of the rich. Prying into other people's affairs, chasing after information, waiting outside the doors of private meetings for official statements is no life for the scion of a newspaper-owning family. It is undignified, too alien to a refined upbringing. The son of a newspaper owner may indulge in reporting for a while, regarding it as part of his management training, a brief fling with romanticism, but he is not naturally drawn to it.*

There is one other essential trait shared by ambitious reporters that the Sulzbergers, father and son, would never know: desperation. Reporting is a highly competitive craft where one's work is on display, sometimes on a daily basis. There is no faking it—not for long, anyway. When Arthur started working in Raleigh, the young men and women competing furiously for plum beats and a front-page showcase could only dream of someday working at the *New York Times*. For the ambitious, those early years at small newspapers were a scramble to get noticed, to shine brightly enough to catch the eye first of the local editors, then of those at bigger papers, and then of editors at the top newsrooms across the country. It was a fierce winnowing. Little wonder that his coworkers in those years found Arthur a man without an edge. He was charming, eager, cheerful, and ever willing to take on the most mundane assignments. He wore a leather jacket and roared to work on a motorcycle. He was having a ball. And why not? He wasn't competing; he was paying his dues. He didn't need front-page stories. He didn't need sources, a scoop, or any particular narrative flair to get ahead. It was easy to be Arthur. And it was smart to befriend Arthur.

His career progressed in prodigious and unearned leaps. He went from the Washington bureau, where he was close friends with Steve Rattner, Judith Miller, and a few other reporters, to New York, where he worked briefly as a very young assistant editor on the Metro desk, before moving on to stints in the advertising and production side of the paper, becoming deputy publisher in 1987. People liked Arthur everywhere he went, and he worked at being liked. But he was not deeply respected. Just as Arthur would never pass as an authentic reporter among those who have spent their lives in newsrooms, his brief apprenticeships in advertising, production, and various other departments were seen for exactly what they were: way stations on the road to publisher. The *Times'* business

managers do not enjoy the same status in their field as the paper's
top reporters and editors do among journalists. Newspapers do
not attract top-tier business and financial talent, because it would
be unseemly to pay those on the business side disproportionately
more than the most senior editors, and the salary scale for even the
highest-paid editors is a small fraction of that for high-level CEOs
and bankers. Yet even the mid-level talent around Arthur does not
regard him as a peer, much less a suitable leader. He is accepted, of
course. The family does own the newspaper, and there appears to
be a consensus that—as one veteran *Times*man, no longer at the
newspaper, told me—if a family member has to run the newspaper,
Arthur is "the Sulzberger you would want."

This is faint praise. There was an attempt by the business side
of the Times Company to thwart his final ascent. On January 22,
1996, a front-page article in the *Wall Street Journal* by Patrick
M. Reilly suggested that Arthur, then the *Times'* publisher, might
not succeed his father as the company's chairman, and that the
company was considering looking outside the family for the next
generation of leadership. One or another Sulzberger patriarch had
held both jobs for a century, but Reilly's story indicated that the
tradition could very well come to an end. It portrayed Arthur as
someone who "sees himself as both a journalist and a business-
man," but who in fact was fully neither. The story was based on
highly placed but anonymous sources inside the building, and it
quoted Arthur's aunt Judith Sulzberger, a member of the board
of directors, as saying that the job "might go to anyone."

Penny Muse Abernathy, who worked closely with Arthur
on the business side of the *Times* before leaving for Harvard, the
Wall Street Journal, and then a professorship at the University
of North Carolina, remembers walking into Arthur's office at
around 7:30 a.m. the day the article came out. He was crestfallen.
"What are you going to do about that story?" she asked him.
"I don't know," he said, and then made an attempt at gallows

humor, suggesting that he might need to try an entirely new line of work. As they were speaking, Punch called. "Dad, can I come see you?" Arthur asked. It was the first time Abernathy had ever heard Arthur call his father "Dad." Around the office, he always referred to Punch as "the chairman."

The effort to end-run the dynasty proved to be short-lived. Many at the paper saw the fingerprints of company president Lance Primus on the *Journal* story. It had identified Primus as "a top prospect" for the chairmanship, and the article was interpreted as the opening salvo in a putsch—a play by the company's professional managers to wrest control of the business side of the company from the amateurs. Family won. Arthur formed an alliance with Russ Lewis, who would be named company CEO when Punch retired, in 1997, and handed the top post to his son. Primus was invited to leave.

3. The Moose in the Room

Here, in a nutshell, in the words of a longtime staffer, is what is supposedly wrong with Arthur: "He has no rays"—rays, as in the lines cartoonists draw around a character to suggest shine, or power. In the comics trade these lines are called *emanata*. The emanata deficit is a standard lament by insiders about Arthur, although most *Times* people need a few more words to make the point.

No one can plumb another's depths. Arthur certainly seems clever enough, but try as he might, he fails to impress. He comes off as a lightweight, as someone slightly out of his depth, whose dogged sincerity elicits not admiration so much as pity. While no one blames him for what is clearly a crisis afflicting all newspapers, he has made a series of poor business moves that now follow him like the tail of a kite. He has doubled down on print over the last two decades, most notably with his own newspaper but also spending more than $1 billion to buy the *Boston Globe* and the *International Herald Tribune*. These purchases appear to have been historically mistimed, rather like sinking your life savings in hot-air balloons long after the first excited reports from Kitty Hawk. Back when he had the money to do it, Arthur failed to adequately diversify the Times Company's holdings, stranding it in an ocean of debt with no flotation device—unlike, say, the *Washington Post*, which is being buoyed through this industry-wide depression by the highly profitable Kaplan, an education services company that provides test-preparation classes and online instruction. (The *Post*'s diverse investments were made under a board that included Warren Buffett and like-minded business gurus.) Except for his admirable website, Arthur has failed to expand the *Times* effectively into other media. Back in 2000 he announced that television was "our next great frontier," but his one timid step in that direction, a partnership with the Discovery Channel to produce news-related documentaries, was halfhearted (and abbreviated). The *Times* still lacks a presence in television. Arthur has not missed the boat entirely with digital start-ups—his decision to buy the online information site About.com, which provides assisted Internet searching, has paid dividends—but he passed up (along with a lot of other people) early opportunities to invest in the great search engines, such as Google, which today is sucking ad revenue from the paper while at the same time giving away its content. Arthur's often repeated assertion that he is "platform agnostic"—that is, he doesn't care what medium delivers the *Times*, and is open to all media—is both misguided and revealing. It sounds fancy and daring and forward-thinking but betrays a deep misunderstanding of the forces at play.

There are other knocks on his leadership. His chosen executive editor, Howell Raines, played favorites in the newsroom, overlooked shoddy journalism, and so alienated his reporters and editors that they forced Arthur to dump him. So goes one version of the story. Not everyone thinks jettisoning Raines was the right thing to do. Raines was shaking things up, presumably with Arthur's blessing, and when you shake things up you upset the rank and file. As one former *Times*man puts it, "If the sheriff of Nottingham gets mugged on his way through Sherwood Forest, and can't do anything about it, then the thieves are running the forest." Whichever take on Raines you prefer, Arthur's reversal looks bad. It suggests either poor judgment or a lack of conviction.

He is, or was, big on managerial gimmickry. There is the now infamous moment, at the height of the in-house furor over the serial fabulist Jayson Blair, when Arthur tried to break the ice before a large audience of restive reporters and editors by pulling a toy stuffed moose out of a bag, a favorite device of his meant to facilitate candid discussion—the moose was supposed to represent the core issues that no one dared address. Newsmen, it should be noted, are rarely shy about expressing their opinions, and on this occasion the crowd was about as reserved as a lynch mob. The moose was so silly and so unnecessary, and reflected something so tone-deaf, that Arthur has yet to live it down. One reason is that it was of a piece with other behavior. *Times* veterans remember with pained expressions the "bonding games" Arthur forced them to play at company retreats in the late 1990s, and the time and effort he demanded they lavish on crafting "mission statements" for the newspaper and the company. "We have it written down and we carry it with us," Arthur told Charlie Rose in 2001. He handed over the mission statements on camera with a flourish, and when asked later about his proudest achievement came back to this "defining vision of what we are and where we have to go." The mission statements are now, in the words of one former editor, "stuffed in desk drawers throughout the building." In his eagerness to champion First Amendment rights he blundered into a losing and ultimately embarrassing fight over his old friend Judith Miller, who went to jail to protect a source, Cheney's former chief of staff Lewis "Scooter" Libby, before striking a deal with prosecutors. The fight was widely regarded as a poor one to make into a First Amendment test case, but that didn't stop Arthur from charging to Miller's defense. The "Free Judy" buttons he distributed made a ludicrous contrast to his father's storied battle over the Pentagon Papers. An explanatory mea culpa about the Miller case, written by the executive editor, Bill Keller, suggested that Miller had had an "entanglement" with Libby, which some read as a suggestion that she was sleeping with him. Keller, who had succeeded Raines after the Jayson Blair affair, quickly retreated from his retreat. The episode illustrated a broader perception: no adult was in charge. Whereas Arthur senior had been seen as solid and serious, Arthur junior appeared callow. One of those involved in the Miller episode describes Arthur's behavior throughout as "childish." Another word you hear is "goofy."

The conventional wisdom about Arthur can be turned on its head. His goofiness might more kindly be interpreted as a winning informality, a healthy antidote to the stuffy, hidebound ways during executive editor Abe Rosenthal's long reign. So, too, his efforts to unbend and humanize the newsroom's tyrants, and get them to see the company's business managers not as enemies but as partners. No wonder they grumbled! Arthur's fixation on newsprint is evidence of a devotion to quality journalism amid the growing din of propaganda and digital frivolity; after all, most of the real reporting done in America is still done by newspapers. His eagerness to defend reporters' freedoms stems from noble instincts, and demonstrates that, for Arthur, the paper's mission takes priority over its profits. His enthusiastic defense of Judith Miller may have backfired, but the same impulse led Arthur to defy a strongly worded request from the Bush administration— delivered in person at the White House—not to print stories that revealed legally dubious domestic spying, stories that would win a Pulitzer Prize in 2006. Arthur's "political correctness" shows an admirable sensitivity to the rights of women and minorities in an institution where both were long held down or shut out. And might his willingness to back down and fire Raines be seen as a sign not of pusillanimity but of humility and flexibility?

"Sure, Arthur has made his share of mistakes. But they get recycled all the time, and he rarely gets the credit he deserves for what he's done right," says his longtime friend Peter Osnos, a former *Washington Post* reporter and the founder of the publishing house PublicAffairs. "You can't judge him solely on the basis of success, because no one in the business can claim success in the current situation. You do have to give him credit for good judgment in anticipating the role of the Internet and his deep commitment to the values of the institution. Arthur was talking about the impact of the Internet on newspapers earlier than anyone else in our industry, and the records show that. So you have this strange kind of thing where you have the vision and you have insight, but you don't get the business side of it right—but literally, without exception, no one has. Arthur has, however, reinvented the newspaper on several levels and positioned it for the future."

Nine years ago, in an entirely different economic climate, the industry magazine *Editor and Publisher* named Arthur Sulzberger Jr. Publisher of the Year, and he was hailed as "brilliant" and "visionary." His investments in satellite printing had pushed the national edition of the *Times* to unprecedented success, "achieving a 20 percent advertising revenue growth . . . largely due to national and help-wanted business going gangbusters." The mistakes he has made with investments and in adapting to new technology are the same mistakes made by every newspaper in America. Most journalists consider Sam Zell, the billionaire who bought the Tribune Company, to be a Neanderthal for his wholesale trashing of the once proud *Chicago Tribune* and *Los Angeles Times*, and regard Gary Pruitt, chairman of the McClatchy chain, as a well-mannered and passionate defender of journalistic excellence. Yet both are staring at bankruptcy. "Who has gotten it right?" asks one industry analyst. "Arthur has made some bad decisions, but so has everyone else in the business. Nobody has figured out what to do." In short, you can choose whichever take on Arthur you prefer. As an old football coach once told me, "Write whatever you want: if I win, you can't hurt me, and if I lose, you can't help me." The publisher's reputation shifts with the wind, and today journalism is leaning into an exceedingly ill wind.

4. The Wrong Lesson

Arthur is still often referred to as "young Arthur," even though he is old enough to be a grandfather, or as "Pinch," a despised nickname that puns on his father's. Even as his locks gray and he nears almost two decades as publisher, he remains the prince-in-waiting who once haunted the newsroom in his socks, his trousers held up by colorful suspenders, peering in a harmless but nevertheless insufferably proprietary way over the shoulders of hard-boiled reporters on deadline. "I have heard him many times refer back to 'when I was a reporter,'" says one former *Times* executive, theatrically cringing. "He'll just do it as a throwaway— 'When I was a reporter.' I will say this to him one day: *Don't say that. You know what? You don't have to say that. Do you think it's giving you more credibility with journalists? It actually gives you less.*" On the business side, according to one former associate, he was viewed with contempt. "They saw him as insubstantial, as flighty, as glib, and as not caring about them as much as he cared about journalists."

But Arthur has one big thing going for him, particularly with the reporters and editors, who are the real stars in the Times building. Arthur is motivated, as he himself says, not by wealth but by *value*. He believes, to be sure, that wealth follows from value, but you can see, even as he says it, that wealth is not what drives him. Journalism drives him. The *Times'* reputation and influence drive him. He is not just a newspaper publisher and a chairman of the board. He is Arthur Ochs Sulzberger Jr., and the pride he takes in that name doesn't have anything to do with how much is in his bank account. No matter what moves he makes, no matter what errors he commits, Arthur will remain every journalist's dream publisher. He has long protected the newsroom from predatory managers with their bean-counting priorities, and today he represents its best hope, reporters and editors would like to believe, of weathering the crisis without the soul-killing budget cuts that turn great newspapers into little more than supermarket circulars. The same people who roll their eyes when they hear him wax nostalgic about his years in the newsroom pray for him daily, because, like them, he completely buys the myth: journalism sells.

"This is ridiculous," says a former business-side executive at the *Times*. "It flies in the face of logic and reason, this belief that if your news product is so good and so comprehensive the normal rules of business are suspended. Think about it. Think about the inanity of saying that you survived by putting in more news and cutting ads."

Arthur repeated this belief proudly in his interview with Rose, describing how Adolph Ochs responded to the lean years after he purchased the paper by expanding its news hole—"We're going to give our readers more! That's gutsy!"—and how his grandfather Arthur Hays Sulzberger did something similar during World War II, when newsprint was being rationed: "Major decision, major gutsy decision from him there. Perhaps the critical decision of his time . . . whether to continue to print ads—revenue, money, profit—or to say, No, we're going to add more news. He went to news, the *Herald Tribune* went to ads, and the rest was just a matter of time. By the time the war ended the *Times* had taken such a huge leadership that it was just a matter of time before the *Herald Tribune* was to fold."

This story is false. It is dismissed even in *The Trust*, a mostly glowing account of the newspaper and the family written with the full cooperation of the Sulzbergers, including Arthur, and published more than a year before he spoke those words to Rose. The authors, Susan E. Tifft and Alex S. Jones, thoroughly debunked the legend.

"One of the enduring myths about *The New York Times* is that it nobly sacrificed profits from revenue-generating ads during World War II in order to print more news," wrote Tifft and Jones. "But the truth is somewhat more complicated." It seems that the *Times* actually slashed its news hole in this period "far more severely than it cut the space devoted to ads." With newsprint rationed, and with more ads and news than he could fit in, Sulzberger increased space for ads and decreased space for news. In fact, he devoted the majority of the newspaper's space to ads, and earned more revenue than he had since 1931. Ad revenue "had actually increased during the period, from $13 million to $15 million, while the amount of money spent on news had slumped slightly from $3.9 million to $3.7 million," Tifft and Jones wrote.

Arthur's grandfather did make one important change during this period, but it was more of a shrewd business move than a principled stand for journalism. While the rival *Herald Tribune* sat on its swollen profits during the war, Sulzberger used his profits to print not more news but more newspapers, greatly expanding the *Times*' reach. That strategy left the *Times* with a larger circulation than the *Herald Tribune* after the war. The *Times* was better positioned to survive. The lesson of the story is not that investing in news pays but that a clever business strategy adapts to a changing market.

Arthur likes his own version of the story better. He once told interviewers that the *Times* was his "religion": "That's what I believe in, and it's a hell of a thing to hold on to." Reason has no purchase on belief. Nor does basic business theory.

5. The Editor as Algorithm

American journalism is in a period of terror. The invention of the Internet has caused a fundamental shift not just in the platform for information—screen as opposed to paper—but in the way people seek information. In evolutionary terms, it's a sudden drastic change of climate. One age passes and a new one begins. Species that survive the transition are generally not the kings of the old era. The world they fit so perfectly is no more. They are big and slow, wedded to the old ways, ripe for extinction.

When Arthur became chairman of the Times Company, in 1997, he dragged his top people to retreats in leafy locations, there to learn better cooperation and to think big thoughts. He was less worried about adapting the *Times* to a new era than about making his company and newsroom a happier place to work. The underlying assumption was that there was nothing ahead but smooth seas. Many of the newsroom's hard-bitten veterans found these events revealing. "We were having a retreat," David Jones, a former assistant managing editor, recalls. "It was a wonderful old inn, business-meeting place, in upstate New York. They were doing games as bonding experiences. One of the games they did was fly casting. And they put three big loops out on the lawn. One was close, one was farther out, and one was farthest. And the idea was to cast your lure and hit inside the loop. The farther away you cast, the more points you got." The risky way to play was to cast for the big scores; the safest way was to steadily accrue points by hitting the nearest loop.

"So we played this game," says Jones, "and when it was all over, I talked to the guy who worked there, who ran the game, and I said, What was your impression of us from the way we played? How do we compare with other groups? And he said—and they have business groups that come—he said, 'This is the most conservative group I have ever seen.' "

Arthur himself, despite his leftist politics and social liberalism, despite the lip service he pays to the need for change, is deeply conservative where the family business is concerned. This is not to say that he resists change. His nytimes.com is the most successful newspaper website in the country. It can claim an ever-rising number of hits and, until the general economic slump of 2008–2009, recorded steady growth in ad revenue. But none of this will save him, because at the core Arthur and the *Times* remain wedded to an archaic model of journalism.

For ten years or more, Arthur's signature phrase about this seismic change in the news business, the one he repeats to show that he *gets* it, has been *platform agnostic*. "I am platform agnostic," he proclaims proudly, meaning that it matters nothing to him where his customers go for *New York Times* content: the newspaper's print version, television, radio, computer, cell phone, Kindle—whatever. The phrase itself reveals limited understanding. When the motion-picture camera was invented, many early filmmakers simply recorded stage plays, as if the camera's value was just to preserve the theatrical performance and enlarge its audience. To be sure, this alone was a significant change. But the true pioneers realized that the camera was more revolutionary than that. It freed them from the confines of a theater. Audiences could be transported anywhere. To tell stories with pictures, and then with sound, directors developed a whole new language, using lighting and camera angles, close-ups and panoramas, to heighten drama and suspense. A director could make audiences laugh by speeding up the action, or make them cry or quake by slowing it down. In short, the motion-picture camera was an entirely new tool for storytelling. To be platform agnostic is the equivalent of recording stage plays.

"When I first heard Arthur talk about being platform agnostic, I knew he was trying to suggest that he was not stuck in a newspaper mind-set," says Tom Rosenstiel, director of the Pew Research Center's Project for Excellence in Journalism. "But I thought there were two problems with that language. One is, agnostics are people who don't—who aren't sure what they believe in. That's the first problem. And the second problem is, in practice, there is no such thing as being platform agnostic. You actually have to choose which platform you work on first, which one comes first. At the time that he was talking about this, what he really meant was, *Everything we put in the newspaper, we'll put online.* If you really want to move to the Internet in a serious way, you need to change the culture of a news organization and decide that the Internet is the primary new thing. Platform agnostic means that all the online companies are going to zoom past you, because they're going to exploit that technology while you're sitting there thinking: Well, we don't care which platform we put it on. You need to exploit the technology of each platform. You need to be, in fact, not platform agnostic but platform *orthodox.* So that expression, *platform agnostic,* always struck me as something he heard someplace, rather than something that he really grasps and understands."

Arthur's idea is to continue producing the *New York Times* the way it has always been produced, and then to offer a digital edition of the product, with video, images, interactive graphics, blogs, and so on. That's what nytimes.com does superbly. According to Nielsen, it attracts more than twenty million unique visitors a month. Imagine a newspaper that was picked up by twenty million readers every month! If only a tiny fraction of that number came back and became subscribers, circulation would explode. But those users are not "picking up" the newspaper; many of them are just picking up individual stories. Nearly half of those who access nytimes.com to read a story come in, as it were, through a side door. They begin by plugging search terms into an engine such as Google, which spits out a long list of links to related sites. And in any case, they're not spending a lot of time with the newspaper: the average amount, says Nielsen, is thirty-five minutes per month. (The figure is worse for other sites—only about sixteen minutes per month for washingtonpost.com.) One of Arthur's hopes is that, once on the site, readers will linger, sampling the *Times*' other superb offerings, but usage patterns suggest that this isn't happening.

Those who grew up using the Internet—they now include a full generation of Americans—are expert browsers. It's not that they have a short attention span. If anything, many of them are more sophisticated and better informed than their parents. They are certainly more independent. Instead of absorbing the news and opinion packaged expertly by professional journalists, they search out only the information they want; and they are less and less likely to devote themselves to one primary site, in part because it is less efficient, and in part because not doing so is liberating. The Internet has disaggregated the news. It eliminates the middleman—that is, it eliminates editors. At a newspaper, top editors meet several times a day to review the stories and photographs gathered from their own staff and wire services. These editors decide which are the most important or compelling, and then prioritize and package them. When you buy a newspaper you are buying a carefully prepared meal. Inevitably stories and artwork are left off the plate for a great variety of reasons, all of them subjective—they are deemed less significant, less credible, less tasteful, less useful. Or maybe there just isn't enough room. The Internet replaces editors with an algorithm. Google is a search engine. It makes no value judgment about information unless you instruct it to make one. All of the stories and photos in the world are there, including billions of items that the reader never imagined wanting to see. It is unmediated. There is no adult supervision. And the kicker is, it's free.

Much more is at work here than a change of platform. Whether you think more is lost or gained depends upon which side of this evolutionary divide you fall on. For me—someone who spent most of his adult life working in a newsroom; someone who reads three newspapers every day, including the *Times*—the loss will be far greater. Newspapers enable serious journalism. They provide for the care and feeding of career reporters and editors. They strive to be fair, accurate, and objective. They are independent sources of credible, well-researched information. They are watchdogs for the public interest, an important part of the communal mind and memory of the nation. When an editor is replaced by an algorithm, all information is equal. Propaganda shares the platform with honest reporting, and the slickest, most attractive websites and blogs will be those sponsored by corporations, the government, or special interests, which can afford to pay for professional work.

Arthur's argument, or his hope, is that the quality of the *Times*' brand will prevail, that high-quality independent journalism is so obviously valuable that serious readers will continue to seek it out. He has been offering the *Times* content free because experience has shown that subscriber-only stories leak—they are copied and e-mailed and rapidly proliferate free anyway—and because Internet users, accustomed to getting information free, are loath to pay for it. Do you remove yourself from the global conversation if you wall yourself off? Can you make enough money on subscriptions to survive? The *Wall Street Journal* has gone in this direction online, while offering some free content. The jury is still out. Arthur has continued to provide *Times* content free, but is considering reversing direction. His brand remains the best in the business, but that hasn't solved his revenue problems. *Journalism costs.* The revenue from Internet advertising is still only about a tenth of total revenue. Even if those millions of brief hits on nytimes.com continue to swell, the *Times* itself may be in bankruptcy court long before the website generates enough revenue to replace what Arthur has lost.

In fairness, no one has the answer for newspapers. Some—such as former *Time* managing editor Walter Isaacson; Alan D. Mutter, a former newspaperman and Silicon Valley CEO; and Peter Osnos of PublicAffairs, all of whom have experience as executives—are pushing some form of micropayment. If the *Times*, in partnership with the big search engine companies, got paid a few pennies for every person who clicked on a link to its content, it might replace the old business model for advertising. The price of accessing a single item would be so small that it would hardly be worth the trouble to hunt up a pirated version. Some have suggested that all of the major news providers should band together and withhold their content from the Internet until such a pricing agreement can be put in place. It seems clear that drastic action is required. One top editor at another newspaper put it this way: "Ask yourself this—if the Internet existed and newspapers didn't, would there be any reason to invent newspapers? No. That tells you all you need to know."

Some at the *Times* anticipated this tectonic shift years ago, but Arthur wasn't listening. Despite lip service about change, he presides over a slow-moving beast. Diane Baker, who was regarded as an energetic and forceful outsider, ran up against this in her years as CFO. When she took the job, in 1995, she was shocked to discover that the company was still doing all its accounting by hand. "They literally did not have the ability to produce spreadsheets," she says. "They had not invested in the software you need to analyze data. It is a company run by journalists. The Sulzbergers are journalists at their core, not businessmen."

Her biggest disappointment came when she crafted a potentially lucrative partnership with Amazon.com, already the biggest bookseller on the Internet. The *Times* would link all the titles reviewed in its own prestigious Sunday Book Review section, ordinarily a money drain, to the online bookseller and receive a percentage on every book sold. "We could have made the Book Review into a big source of revenue," she recalls. Baker knew that Amazon.com planned to eventually sell everything under the sun, to become the first digital supermarket. Not only would the deal have produced revenue from book sales; it would also have cemented a partnership with a tremendous future. She envisioned the newspaper as a virtual merchandising machine. Instead of the old carpet-bombing model of advertising, it would in effect target ads to readers of specific stories. "You know what they said?" Baker recalls. "They said, 'We can't do it, because Barnes and Noble is a big advertiser.'"

Toward the end of his tenure as executive editor, Max Frankel was asked to think about the impact of computers on the news business. This was back in the mid-1990s, when the *Times'* national edition was taking off and most Americans were embarking on their first hesitant drives on the "information superhighway." For the *Times* there was money to maneuver with, and to invest, and a chance to adapt to the new age. Frankel wrote two memos, which he no longer has, but whose content he remembers clearly. In the first memo he argued that, because computers were so good at generating and cross-referencing lists, classified ads in newspapers were doomed. He suggested that the *Times* set up a computer system to allow buyers and sellers to deal with each other directly online—"It was essentially Craigslist," Frankel jokes. "I should have started it up!" Craigslist was created in 1995 and today averages billions of page hits per month, with reported annual revenues in excess of $80 million. It is a major factor in the decline of newspaper ad revenue.

"The second idea was much more important, and came a little later," Frankel says. "I wrote that one big coming threat posed
by the computer was disaggregation: the Internet disaggregates
the hunt for information. The need for information would survive
the advent of the digital era, but the package offered by the *New
York Times* might not. So how do you protect the package? What
was so great about the *New York Times* was not that we offered
the best coverage in any particular field but that we were very
good in so many. It was the totality of the newspaper that was a
marvel, not any of its particulars. The Web threatened to break
that up. One way to weather this, which I suggested, was that we
needed to pick the fields in which to be preeminent. If you want
to have the best sports package, then start hiring the staff and
make yourself the best go-to place for sports information. If it is
business, or politics—whatever—pick one and make yourself the
best, or make a strategic alliance." This is the approach taken by
ESPN.com, Bloomberg.com, IMDB.com, Weather.com, and a
multitude of others. Any one of dozens of sites specializing in, say,
politics or the arts could have been taken over and built up around
the *Times*' expert staff. It could still happen. The *Washington Post*
is increasingly staking out the national government as its field,
but an even more immediate threat to the *Times* is coming from
downtown. Rupert Murdoch's *Wall Street Journal* already has a
larger national circulation than the *Times*, and its rapacious new
owner is vigorously competing on new fronts. Both newspapers
are losing revenue in the current downturn, but the *Journal* may
be in a better position for the long term. It has a smaller staff,
and a clearly specialized arena with deep importance and broad
appeal—business and finance. It has clearly dominated coverage
of the ongoing economic crisis, with perceptive stories that are
more knowingly reported, more analytical, and consistently better
written. Online, the *Journal*'s editorial matter is largely password-
protected, which means its readers are already paying for content,

and it has been steadily improving its coverage of culture, sports, and lifestyle, and in its weekend edition featuring original essays by acclaimed writers and thinkers. And while the *Times* is busy throwing assets overboard to stay afloat, the *Journal* is attached to Murdoch's international empire, News Corp. Arthur aspires to be the patron saint of journalism, but the smart money may be on the pirate. The kind of specialization Frankel forecast is also driving most smaller newspapers, which are aggressively focusing coverage on their own communities, where they have exclusive content. Many see this as the only strategy that will enable them to survive. The retired executive editor says that he sent both of his memos up the chain of command—as he puts it, "off into the ether." He did not hear a word from Arthur or anyone else about them.

6. "Never Give In"

Arthur Sulzberger can be a loyal and thoughtful friend, someone who will surprise a distant or old acquaintance with a small note of congratulation or commiseration, a gesture out of the blue that is felt and remembered. He is sincere and determined. He is, by all accounts, a doting and involved father. He did not have to work at all, yet he has always worked hard. "He is kind, decent, and good," says his longtime friend Steve Rattner. "In everything he does, he means well." His convictions about journalism are above reproach, and he cultivates his journalistic values in the ever-expanding Sulzberger clan. In speaking with many who know him well, I discovered a nearly universal desire to *protect* Arthur. "It's funny. There's something about him that makes you want to—it's almost like this maternal instinct kicks in," says Vivian Schiller, who was an executive at the *Times* before becoming president of NPR. Part of the desire to protect Arthur stems from his role at the head of a great newspaper in hard times. Part of it is loyalty to the Sulzberger family. But beyond all of this is fear—not just that Arthur will be hurt but that he will *fail*.

It is sometimes true that a man's greatest strength is also his greatest weakness. Soon after Robert J. Rosenthal was named managing editor of the *San Francisco Chronicle*, in 2002, he ran into Arthur at a conference on the West Coast. Arthur congratulated Rosenthal, who had started his career as a copyboy at the *Times*, and when they shared a car ride Arthur talked about how different their challenges were. "Yours is to turn the ship around," he said. "Mine is to keep the *Times* on course."

He still might—though in fact staying on course *means* turning the ship around. If he makes the right moves in the next few years, he may yet be able to ride his inheritance into the digital age. If he pulls that off, the achievement will outstrip those of his revered ancestors. It would be something more akin to the feats attributed to the original Arthur, the one who pulled Excalibur from the stone. But precisely because he is who he is, Arthur may be the last person in the world with the answers. The more likely outcome is that he will lose the *Times* to someone with deep enough pockets to carry the enterprise at a loss until circumstances sort themselves out—a rich individual, or a rich corporation, or a rich philanthropic institution. In recent years there have been persistent reports of Rupert Murdoch's interest in the *Times*, if only because he has historically lusted after prestige broadsheets. Michael Wolff, who wrote a biography of the Australian billionaire, reported in these pages last year that Murdoch had entertained the idea of a merger with his *Wall Street Journal*'s backroom operations and "fantasize[d] about the staff's quitting en masse as soon as he entered the sacred temple." (Given the recent layoffs at the *Journal*, and reports of the newspaper unit's drag on News Corp's bottom line, the acquisition of another sagging national newspaper might seem to be an irrational act—but that may be beside the point.) A business model to sustain a professional staff of reporters and editors could yet emerge in this new era, most likely a model devised by entrepreneurs with everything to gain and little to lose. This is a course that would save the institution, but would mean the end of the Sulzberger dynasty.

Arthur keeps a framed quotation by Winston Churchill in his office, a passage from a speech Churchill delivered during Britain's darkest hours: "Never never never give up." What Churchill actually said was "Never give in, never give in, never, never, never, never—in nothing, great or small, large or petty—never give in," and he added an important qualifier: "except to convictions of honour and good sense." The bulldog approach worked for Churchill. But for Arthur, as the prospect of success dims, good sense may dictate the very terms he resists. Serving the institution at some point may require selling it. Many of the newspaper's superb journalists have already left. Many others are actively cycing second careers. It is hard to imagine what a second career would be for Arthur.

The inheritance has shaped Arthur Sulzberger's life, but as he turns fifty-eight, this year, the age of the newspapers may be ending. For the *New York Times*, the greatest of them, it would mean the collapse of a dynasty and of a national treasure. No one would feel the loss more than Arthur. For him, more than anyone else, everything is at stake.

"What would he do?" asks Penny Abernathy. "What would he do? That's who he is."

The Bright Sun
of Juche

Published as "Understanding Kim Jong Un, the World's Most Enigmatic and Unpredictable Dictator," *Vanity Fair*, March 2015

Does anybody make an easier target than Kim Jong Un?

He's Fatboy Kim the Third, the tyrant with a Fred Flintstone haircut; the grinning, chain-smoking owner of his own small nuclear arsenal; brutal warden to about 120,000 political prisoners; and the last true hereditary monarch on the planet. He's the Supreme Leader, nay, *Great Leader* of the Democratic People's Republic of Korea (DPRK), Heaven-Sent Brilliant Commander—I am not making these titles up—and Marshal of its military (which includes the fourth largest standing army in the world), general secretary of the Workers Party of Korea (the only outfit in play north of the thirty-eighth Parallel) . . . a man who at age thirty-two owns the longest list of excessive honorifics anywhere, every one wholly unearned. He is the youngest head of state in the world, and probably the most spoiled. On the great grade-school playground of world affairs, he might as well be wearing across his broad bottom a big "Kick me" sign.

Kim is so easy to kick that even the United Nations, which famously agrees on nothing, voted overwhelmingly in November to recommend that he and the rest of North Korea's leadership be hauled before the International Criminal Court in The Hague and tried for crimes against humanity.

In the world press, Kim is a bloodthirsty madman and buffoon. He is said to be a drunk; to have become so obese gorging on Swiss cheese that his genitals have shrunk; and, having so far produced no male heir, to use bizarre remedies for impotence— like a distillation of snake venom. He is said to have had his uncle, Jang Song Thaek, and the entire Jang family mowed down with heavy machine guns (or possibly exterminated by mortar rounds, rocket-propelled grenades, or flamethrowers) and then fed to ravenous dogs. He is reported to have a yen for bondage porn and to have ordered all young men in his country to adopt his peculiar hairstyle. According a frenzy of global speculation after he had minor surgery on his ankle last summer, he was at death's door and had already been ousted by his younger sister, Kim Yo Jong, who is now secretly governing the country, or, no . . . by the Ministry of Information, which is actually governing and using her as a prop, or . . . maybe the real power is now the nation's defense minister, Hyon Yong Chol.

All in the preceding paragraph is untrue, or, perhaps safer to say, unfounded. It is a testimony to media's timeless talent for making things up. The story that Jang was fed to dogs was actually invented by a Chinese satirical magazine, as a joke, before it began racing around the world as a viral version of truth. In light of this, is it too much of a stretch to consider that our take on Kim is *all* wrong?

What if, despite the well-documented horrors of the Stalinist regime he inherited in 2011 while still in his twenties, a vast machine into which he was born and which has groomed him every day of his life, Kim is actually a capable young man who is even—within carefully defined limits—well-intentioned? What if he is actually trying to reverse the brutal sixty-eight-year-old regime's direction? What if, largely unrecognized in the rest of the world, he has already taken tangible domestic strides toward normalcy? What if he is trying hard, unartfully and against terrific odds, to alter North Korea's relationship with the rest of the world? We know that anyone in his rarefied position would face entrenched and dangerous enemies, perhaps the worst in his own extended family.

Kim is, in fact, playing a deadly game, says Andrei Lankov, a Russian expert on Korea who attended Kim Jung Il University in Pyongyang in 1985, and who now teaches at Seoul University. In his crowded office there, Lankov had this to say about Kim:

"He has had a spoiled, privileged childhood, not that different than the children of some western billionaires, for whom the worst thing that can happen is that they will be arrested while driving under the influence. For [him] the worst that can actually happen is to be tortured to death by a lynch mob. Easily. But he doesn't understand. . . . His parents understood it. They may not have had encounters with death, but they knew it was a deadly game. I'm not sure whether [he] fully understands it."

Kim faces a problem peculiar to dictators. His power is so great in North Korea than not only does no one dare criticize him; no one dares *advise* him. After all, if you are too closely associated with the king, your head might someday share the same chopping block. Safer to adopt a *Yes, Marshal* posture. That way, if the king stumbles, you are just one of the legion who were obliged to obey his orders. One way to read the confusing signals from Pyongyang in recent years is that they show Kim, isolated and inexperienced, clumsily pulling at the levers of state.

Whether he fully grasps it or not, Kim has a hard road ahead if he is trying to remake the world's most rigidly totalitarian regime. Many of the experts I interviewed feel that he deserves, at the very least, time. Many feel that a benevolent dictator in Pyongyang might be the best prospect for the short term—better than dramatic change—not just for North Korea but for the entire peninsula, and the world. Yet the Obama administration's posture toward North Korea, purposefully aloof and unresponsive, has not changed since Kim Jung Il was alive.

For years, North Korea has engaged in what experts in Washington have called a "provocation cycle." Its leaders under Kim Jung Il would periodically ramp up provocative rhetoric and behavior, like launching missiles or conducting nuclear tests, followed by charm offensives and offers to begin dialogue. Two steps forward and one step back. The end result was slow and steady progress toward their aims, at least in foreign policy.

"The centerpiece of the Obama administration's policy has been to try and deincentivize, as it were, that type of approach," explained Sydney Seiler, who served as the director for Korea on the National Security Council through most of Obama's terms. I spoke to him in the Old Executive Office Building months before he left the job to become U.S. special envoy to the Six-Party Talks, a diplomatic effort aimed at denuclearizing North Korea. "Traditionally, what North Korea was able to do, particularly in the advancement of this nuclear program, would be to go into this provocation cycle, which would raise tensions and convince all the parties that we just needed to rush back to the table and get quickly back to talks to, in essence, bribe North Korea to behave. And so what we try to do—and we have talked with North Korea, we do talk with North Korea—is to make it clear that we are not going to reward bad behavior. We are not going to run around with our hair on fire and go chasing after Kim Jung Un in a way that just reinforces the previous cycle."

So in the three years since Kim took over, the United States has not responded significantly to either provocation or charm.

The approach makes sense, but what if it ignores a major shift in the game?

There is no shortage of evidence to the contrary, that Kim is just a bad approximation of his canny father. He has continued his father's military-first policies. There are still the same shrill denunciations and saber rattling from Pyongyang, the same cyberattacks, the same emphasis on nukes and ICBMs, the same stark political oppression. But suppose, if only as a thought experiment, we consider those things about Kim that don't fit the mold. What if he is not a crackpot belligerent?

"We should realize that he is still in something of a formative period," said a former CIA analyst who still actively studies North Korea, and who asked not to be named. "He is learning lessons about the world, how it reacts, what is possible with it. And I sense that we are teaching him all of the wrong lessons. We are confirming for him the worst tendencies of the North Koreans to be paranoid *with reason*. Look, the United Nations is debating [whether] . . . to put him on trial for crimes against humanity. He's only been in power for three years!"

It's a theory worth exploring, especially if we consider how mysterious and dangerous North Korea is, and that its youthful leader is the least-known head of state on the planet.

1. The Known (A Short Section)

We're not even sure how old he is. Kim was born on January 8 in either 1982, 1983, or 1984.

To tidy up their historical narrative, Pyonyang's propagandists have placed his birthday in 1982. The original Kim, the current leader's grandfather and national founder, Kim Il Sung, for whom universal reverence is mandatory, was born in 1912. As the story goes, in 1942 his son and heir came along, Kim Il, Kim Jung Il, for whom a slightly lesser wattage of reverence is mandatory. Actually, Kim II was born in 1941, but in North Korea myth trumps fact to an even greater extent than elsewhere, and numeric symmetry hints at destiny, like a divine wink. This is why 1982 was such an auspicious year for the birth of Kim III. For reasons of their own, South Korean intelligence agencies, which have a long history of being wrong about their northern cousins and about Kim III in particular, have placed his birthday in the Orwellian year 1984, which is a dark horse but is the date I am rooting for. Kim himself, who occasionally shows magisterial disdain for the adulatory slaving of his underlings, has said that he was born in 1983—this according to that notable American statesman, former rebounder, and famous cross-dresser Dennis Rodman, who had been drinking heavily at the time, and shortly afterward reentered rehab.

But for now, 1983 has the edge, at least outside Pyongyang. Whichever date is correct, the Heaven-Sent Brilliant Commander has walked among us for three decades.

What do we know for sure about those years? About enough to fill one long paragraph: We know that Kim is the third and youngest son of his father, and the second-born son of Kim II's second mistress, Ko Young Hui, who died in 2004. There is a picture of Kim III as a boy, perhaps seven years old, seated alongside his youthful father, with a severe, purse-lipped expression on his distinctively wide round face, wearing a powder blue T-shirt and very large Mickey Mouse ears. In the last half of the 1990s he was sent to two different schools in Switzerland, where his mother was being secretly, and ultimately futilely, treated for breast cancer. The first of these was the International School of Berne, a private school in Gumligen; the second was an upper-level school nearby in Bern, the Leibefeld-Steinholzi School, where he was introduced to his teenage classmates as "Un Pak," the son of a North Korean diplomat. Kim and his younger sister were housed during these years among workers at the North Korean embassy, and were presented as children of a functionary there. His old classmates remember him on his first day of upper school, a skinny boy dressed in jeans, Nike trainers, and a Chicago Bulls sweatshirt. He understandably struggled in classes taught in German and English. He was shy, undistinguished academically, and apparently unbothered by it. He is remembered as having been fond of video games, soccer, basketball—in which despite his size he was able to hold his own on the court—skiing, and those Bulls. The Bulls were in the process of winning the last three of their six NBA championships behind Michael Jordan, who is reportedly one of Kim's personal heroes. In 2000 he returned to Pyongyang, where he attended the military academy that bears his grandfather's name. At some point around 2009 his father decided that his older brothers were unsuitable and selected Kim as his heir. At about this time young Kim began putting on weight—literally and figuratively. Some believe that in order to more closely resemble his grandfather, whom he resembles anyway, he was "encouraged" or ordered to do so—in the upper echelon of North Korea these amount to the same thing. An American intelligence profile of Kim produced that year noted that he was overweight already at 198 pounds—"probably due to lack of exercise." He assumed power when Kim II died in December 2011, around the same time he was wed, in an arranged marriage, to Ri Sol Ju, a former cheerleader and singer about ten years his junior. He is said to be genuinely in love with his wife. The Kims have a daughter, whose birth is believed to have been induced so that she would be born in 2012. Mrs. Kim is often seen with her husband in public—a clear departure from his father's practice. Kim II's women were usually kept offstage. (A notorious womanizer, he was officially married once and kept four known mistresses.) Kim stands five feet, nine inches, taller than most North Koreans, and his bulk is now estimated to be 210 pounds and ascending. He has already showed signs of the heart problems that plagued his father, and of diabetes, and seems to regard modern notions of healthy living as western nonsense. He openly chain-smokes North Korean cigarettes (manufactured at a special plant; his father preferred Marlboros), drinks a lot of beer and hard liquor, enjoys chocolates and cheeses, and evidently approaches mealtimes with gusto. There is no picture of him jogging.

2. A Chip off the Old Block's Block

And that's it. Nothing better defines Kim than how little we know about him. Even the most respected outside experts on North Korea in the United States and in South Korea, when asked, invariably refer back to Rodman and a Japanese sushi chef, Kenji Fujimoto, who was employed by the ruling family from 1988 to 2001 and who now peddles trivial details about them (such as how Kim II once sent him to Bejing to pick up some food at McDonald's). Fittingly, when *Time* named him one of the hundred most influential people in the world in 2012, to prepare a short bio of him the magazine hired a novelist to write it.

With so little to go on, it is hard to imagine what Kim is like, but here's a place to start: At age five, we are all the center of the universe. Everything—our parents, family, home, neighborhood, school, country . . . everything that came before, everything that might come after—revolves around us. For most of us what follows is a long process of dethronement, as his majesty the child confronts the ever more obvious and humbling truth.

Not so for Kim. His world at age five has turned out to be his world at age thirty, or very nearly so. Everyone around him *does* exist to serve him. The known world *really is* ordered with him at its center. At some point—perhaps when his family sent him off to Switzerland—he become aware that his kingdom had limits, but within those limits, millions hang on his every word and gesture. The most powerful men in his kingdom have power because he wills it, and they smile and bow and scribble notes on little pads whenever he deigns to speak. He is not just the one and only Kim Jong Un; he's officially the only *Jong Un*—all North Koreans with that given name have had to change it. His every word and thought is precious. Multitudes stand and cheer and furiously clap at the mere glimpse of him. Men and women and children weep for joy when he smiles and waves.

Which of us departs dramatically from the path prepared for us by parents, class, society, and culture? And when that path promises so much, which of us would not step boldly into it, and perhaps feel bound to perpetuate it? Which of us would not accept the need for vast gulags to confine those who threaten us, because any threat to us is a threat to . . . well, *everything*? And when it comes to that, you might not hesitate to have a rival uncle denounced and shot.

"People need to understand that the [North Korean] system cannot help but produce a person like Kim Jong Un," said Seiler. ". . . I think the first thing that we have to remember, as with any leader in any country, is that he is going to reflect the culture and values and worldview of North Koreans themselves."

And what is that worldview? It is certainly alien to our own. Kim is part—the *key* part—of a system that is brutal and archaic. In that sense, trying to understand North Korea by studying Kim III in particular may be the wrong way to proceed. To understand him, we need to understand the system that produced him. His role demands complete allegiance to that system, which despite its cruelty and well-documented failings, works for a sizable portion of North Korea's population. These are people whom the widespread famine of the late 1990s barely touched. In Pyongyang, where the most educated, most able, most attractive, most *deserving* North Koreans reside, some people are actually making money these days. Brian Myers, a professor at Dongseo University in South Korea, says that he routinely invites defectors from the north to his graduate school classes, and that in recent years his South Korean students, expecting familiar tales of starvation and woe, have been surprised to hear from some who describe North Korea as a "cool place," where they wish they could have remained. "My students are always a little disappointed to find this out," he says.

For the privileged few, things are actually looking up these days. Atop that rigid and hopeful hierarchy sits the Supreme Leader, on the perch he was born to occupy. With his exceptional status; total isolation from the general public or what most of us would consider normal life; the abject devotion (or fear, or both) of those entrusted to educate, nurture, and serve him—how could Kim not become what he is: arrogant, entitled, aggressive, confident, and also, on occasion, flamboyantly immature?

We *sort of* know other, interesting things about Kim's life, all of which are secondhand and ought to be regarded skeptically.

He has led an extraordinarily sheltered life . . . so much so that the word *sheltered* doesn't do it justice. *Imprisoned* is more like it. Even in his years in Switzerland his school was just a short distance from the North Korean embassy, where he spent most of his time, and outside those walls he was always accompanied by a bodyguard. Imagine a small Asian boy who is attending a European school where no one else speaks his language and who is accompanied by an adult who sternly eyeballs anyone who gets close, and you can guess how normal his social interactions were. All western influences came through the mediated world of pop culture—movies, TV, video games. Kim's tastes are said to remain rooted in the late 1980s and early 1990s—thus his fascination with the Bulls, and, reportedly, with the music of Michael Jackson and Madonna. Back in his home country he lived behind the walls of the ruling family's vast estates, in dwellings so opulent they wow even visiting dignitaries from the United Arab Emirates, according to the author of the blog "North Korea Leadership

Watch," Michael Madden. Kim's father once issued an edict that no one was allowed to approach any member of his family without his written permission. Playmates were imported for Kim and his siblings. That said, Kim is likely to have paid surreptitious visits to China, Japan, and possibly Europe. His German and French are thought to be fair, and Rodman reports that Kim made several remarks to him in English.

Madden would add Chinese to the list of languages that Kim probably speaks to some extent. From his home in Swampscott, Massachusetts, Madden writes his blog; contributes to "38 North," a respected website that closely monitors North Korea; and devours everything he can find about the Supreme Leader. Information comes from Korean publications, the DPRK's official pronouncements, defectors, and his own sources inside the country. The Kim he envisions is something of a physical wreck. He has bad knees and bad ankles, both problems aggravated by his obesity, and is still suffering from the aftereffects of one or more reputed car accidents—one particularly bad one "in 2007 or 2008" according to Madden (the vagueness about when gives you an idea how trustworthy the information is). He's not out racing through traffic in Pynonyang, but he is, or was, avid about driving expensive sports cars fast on his family's vast private estates.

"He's a rich guy," says Madden. "I mean Kim Jong Un might be in North Korea, but he is a rich guy. So . . . rich guy activities. Like the town where I grew up in in Massachusetts, they used to say you could tell a really, really, really, rich kid because he drove with bare feet. Kim Jong Un is the kind of kid that drives with bare feet."

Those thrilled by high speeds enjoy flirting with risk, an alarming trait in a man with a nuclear arsenal.

More than his reticent father, Kim seems to enjoy the meet-and-greets and photo ops with regular folks. In this he appears to be more like his mother, Ko Yong Hui, who in old videos can be seen avidly shaking hands, smiling, and chatting at official functions while her husband, Kim II, tended to hang back and exude an aura of menace. Kim is crazy about sports, particularly soccer, and also takes an avid interest in military studies. The military is something his father would have left to the generals, but young Kim is a student of strategy and tactics. He pays close attention to the international weapons market and stories about American military operations, and would be, Madden says, particularly keen on intelligence about the United States' current low-key offensive against ISIS inside Iraq and Syria. He is too young and inexperienced to be considered anything more than a dabbler, despite the generals who fervently scribble notes when he holds forth at photo shoots—they are always there with their giant hats and little notebooks behind him. But Kim's interest in such matters is the sort of trait that might have made him a more appealing choice for the succession.

Kim's elder half brother, Kim Jong Nam, reportedly fell out of favor in 2001 after an ill-fated effort to enter Japan on a fake passport to visit Tokyo Disneyland. Madden says there was no family problem with the visit itself, or the destination.

"He basically blew the cover off the fake passports that the Kim family used when they traveled abroad," says Madden.

His elder full brother, Kim Jong Chul, is said to have exhibited too many feminine characteristics to be considered Heaven-Sent. He has an older half sister, Kim Sul Song, who reportedly works for the propaganda department; and a younger sister, Kim Yo Jong, who was recently given a high position in the regime. Neither sister was considered eligible for the throne, presumably because both are female.

Whatever the whole story, it's clear that early on, Kim II's youngest son was anointed heir. Cheong Seong Chang of the Sejong Institute, a think tank in Seoul with links to South Korean intelligence, says Kim was being prepared to become Supreme

Leader while his ailing father was still alive. When Kim II died earlier than anticipated, in December 2011, his son was thrust into the leadership, but he was hardly unready. He would probably have assumed the role even if his father were still living. His rollout was well under way.

The unveiling of Kim III began as far back as 2008, when party cadres throughout the country began praising him as "the young four-star general," according to Myers, who has made North Korean propaganda a primary academic interest. He wrote a book, *The Cleanest Race*, debunking the conventional notion that the country's guiding philosophy was Marxism. Myers traced the origins of its ruling mythology to a long-standing belief in Korean racial superiority; according to this belief, the people who inhabit the peninsula are the purest race on the planet, and are thus purer in spirit and goodness than the rest of us. The Kim family story has been liberally retouched and grafted onto the legends of Korea's founding. Kim Il Sung, born into a line of Protestant Christian ministers, is said instead to have descended from the nation's ancestral leaders. His son, Kim II, was actually born in Russia, where his parents had gone to flee the Japanese occupation, but in the myth he was secretly born on Mount Paetku, a volcano on the border with China that is the highest peak on the peninsula, and the place where the father of Korea's mythical founder, Tangun, descended five thousand years ago from heaven. For Kim III, myth, his father and grandfather are hard acts to follow, but Pyongyang's propagandists have put their shoulders to the task. The younger Kim is said to have absorbed the mysteries of modern western technology by studying abroad, and to have demonstrated his genius for combat and military maneuvers commanding a "shock brigade" in the harsh mountains of the far northeast. The battle-hardened, albeit pudgy, North Korean prince began to make appearances as a minor but intriguing character in the standard-issue novels and poems praising his father. Young

Kim was portrayed as a precocious military genius who piloted helicopters, drove tanks, manned the most sophisticated weapons systems, and demonstrated an astonishingly intuitive grasp of weaponry and tactics. He was said to have disciplined himself to sleep only three or four hours at night in order to devote more time to his studies at the military academy. According to Brian Myers, children in North Korean schools were being taught to sing Kim's praises years before his existence was formally revealed to the rest of the world—at a time when Kim II's marriage and the existence of his children was still unknown even to most Koreans.

At his official coming-out in 2010, Kim III was presented as a four-star general and vice chairman of the nation's Central Military Commission, a relatively modest post. "The domestic public probably knew how to interpret [this]," wrote Myers in a 2014 study of Kim's rise: "That he was demonstrating humility by going through a kind of on-the-job training of which, being brilliant, he had no need." He began immediately being seen at his father's side in the state-controlled media. By late 2011, a few months before his father's death, Kim was appearing on TV news "not just as another member of his father's entourage," Myers wrote, "but as an object of affection and respect in his own right." Within weeks of Kim Jung Il's death, after a period of histrionic grieving, the country's propagandists were declaring that the country was in the "warm care" of Kim III. Since then, the emphasis has been not so much on glorifying his father as on stressing Kim's resemblance to his far more popular grandfather.

The descriptor most often applied to the DPRK is "Stalinist," and with its old-style communist imagery and propaganda, and with its political purges and frightening gulags, the state does resemble the Soviet Union's darkest age. But a closer analogy for the current North Korean state is a sixteenth- or seventeenth-century European monarchy, something that is hard for the western world to take seriously. After all, it has been more than two centuries since Thomas Paine was rallying American colonists to throw off King George III by denouncing monarchy as "a degradation and lessening of ourselves." Paine reserved special contempt for hereditary succession, which he called "an insult and an imposition on posterity." He wrote, "One of the strongest *natural* proofs of the folly of hereditary right in kings, is that *nature* disapproves it, otherwise she would not so frequently turn it into ridicule by giving mankind an *ass for a lion*." We have long since lost the ability to easily imagine a truly monarchical society, and that is one of the reasons North Korea seems so alien to us today.

But is it really so alien? Cheong points out that despite our inclination to disbelief and ridicule, hereditary succession is alive and well. Corporate power and even the leadership of major churches in South Korea are still typically passed from father to son. Hereditary succession and even primogeniture still dictate not just ownership but leadership of major business enterprises the world over, even in the presumably enlightened districts of the media, whether such an enterprise is the vast conservative empire of Rupert Murdoch or the esteemed liberal *New York Times*. Americans elected the son of President George H. W. Bush to serve for two terms, and may be casting votes for another Bush in 2016. There are still enthusiasts who long for another Kennedy to emerge from a new crop at Hyannis Port and pick up the torch. The current president of the Republic of Korea (South Korea), Park Geun Hye, is the eldest child of the nation's former dictatorial leader Park Chung Hee, who ruled from 1961 until his assassination in 1979, and who is still more highly regarded than any of the presidents who have followed. There is no doubt that his daughter's election in 2011 resulted in large part because of nostalgia for her father's rule.

North Korea has never known anything else. It has no experience with government by consent. Just before Korea's annexation by Japan in 1910, Koreans were still living under monarchy. And after that the rule was imperial Japan, so they bowed to the emperor. After the USSR freed North Korea from Japan in 1945, Kim Il Sung stepped into the role. The vague nationalist ideology the regime calls *juche* is nothing more than an effort to rationalize in pseudo-Marxist terms what Myers calls "radical ethno-nationalism." The myth of the Kims and of Korean racial superiority is not some strange invention being forced down the people's throats. It is the traditional way. It is who they are.

"North Koreans have never grasped the idea of freedom or democracy," says Cheong. "They just don't have that concept in their heads. Even many defectors, those who have fled North Korea—they still have respect and even reverence for Kim Il Sung."

It is worth remembering that during the early years of the original Kim's reign, North Korea actually surpassed South Korea in prosperity. It was only after his death in 1994, and the elevation of Kim II, that years of inept centralized planning caught up. The state was managed into catastrophic ruin. Industry collapsed. Millions starved. People boiled grass and stripped the bark off trees in their desperate search for sustenance. Many Koreans who enjoyed prosperity during the original Kim's reign saw a direct connection between his death and the famine and continuing disaster that followed under Kim II's reign. Since anger against the Supreme Leader cannot be expressed directly, it registered in mounting reverence for the good old days, and the good old ruler.

If special status, divine inspiration, is carried in a bloodline, then physical similarity counts for a great deal. Some believe that a big factor—perhaps the biggest—in Kim's ascendance may well have been how much he looks like his grandfather. In 2010, when pictures of Kim III were first made public by the family, everyone on the Korean peninsula was struck by the resemblance.

"He had the face of Kim Il Sung when he was young," says Cheong. "Naming him as the heir captured the nostalgia of the North Korean people."

Cheong is certain this is deliberate. There is a popular belief in Korea, *gyeok se yu jeon*, that inherited traits skip a generation. A grandson tends to be more like his father's father than his own. This predisposed North Koreans to see the designated heir as a reincarnation of the beloved founder. And where nature falls short, artifice steps in. Whether or not he was ordered to bulk up, there's no doubt that Kim's expansion has given him the patriarch's rotundity. There are even reports, Cheong says, that he was flown to Germany for plastic surgeons to tweak his facial features in order to enhance the resemblance. It seems more likely that the young man simply looks like his grandfather, but there is little doubt that Kim works at enhancing the visual connection. You see it in his his odd haircut, in his clothing, and in the way he walks and moves like a much older man in public appearances. In a steady stream of publicity stills, he adopts the stances, gestures, and facial expressions of his grandfather—or, rather, of the painted images of Kim Il Sung in generations of party propaganda.

What's he really like? A man in his position has few unguarded moments. Bill Richardson, formerly New Mexico's governor and a congressman from New Mexico, has served as U.S. ambassador to the UN and has negotiated with North Korean leaders in Pyongyang during visits there on several occasions. He has retained high-level contacts in North Korea and remains deeply interested in the country.

"So let me first give you what others in North Korea have told me about him," Richardson told me in a phone interview. He was kind enough to jot down some of his impressions before we spoke:

Number one—He frequently jokes with other officials about not knowing anything, that he is new, and young, and he has no experience. He actually thinks that is funny. So that is one. Number two, that he seems to be insecure. However, he hears no one, and he does not like to be briefed about issues. However, that does not mean he is not street smart nor he is not skillful. Surmising the way he has replaced the people, especially in the military, that he felt were not his people, he has actually done that quite effectively. And brought his own people in or people that he thinks are more loyal to him. But it strikes me that he feels, by his actions, by his bluster, and by his missile launchings, that he is trying to consolidate his power. Which, even after more than [three years], he feels, he still has a way to go.

Of course, none of this hesitancy or insecurity is displayed in public. No one in North Korea displays what he really thinks or feels in public.

3. Theater

Kang Mi Jin comes by her insights into North Korea the hard way. A small, very delicate woman whose polite and quiet demeanor masks steel, she fled the country twelve years ago with her then eleven-year-old daughter, crossing the Yalu River into China. Living in Changsong county in the mountainous North Korean border region, she was doing reasonably well as a single mother, working long hours for the People's Army Welfare Bureau and supplementing her income by selling produce from a booth in a neighborhood market. When she resisted payoff demands from the local police, she says, they began looking for ways to harass her and her family. A friend tipped her off that she was about to be arrested and sent to a prison camp, so Kang plotted her escape. In the winter of 2008, she and her daughter walked a two-hundred-yard strip along the river for a month, studying the shifts, habits, and patrols of border guards. They found a place where two guards routinely met patrolling from different directions, and then parted, walking away from each other. This happened every day between 6:30 and 6:40 p.m. After consulting with a fortune-teller, Kang and her daughter waited for the guards to part and then simply walked across the frozen Yalu into China near the Changbai Malugouzhen Protection Station. Another escaping woman they met on the other side was immediately seized by bandits and sold into slavery. They were more fortunate. A sympathetic woman helped Kang make contact with relatives in China, and she eventually made her way to Seoul, where she now writes stories for Daily NK, an activist website that reports on human rights abuses and agitates for democratic reforms.

In the years since her escape, Kang has maintained a string of confidential informants in North Korea, with whom she communicates by Chinese-registered cell phone, these days mostly through text messages. She doesn't tell them she is a defector or a journalist; more often she'll say she works for a bank or is a graduate student doing research. In this way she monitors daily life inside Kim's kingdom, where she says many are doing better financially while experiencing even greater political oppression. She watches DPRK propaganda videos with a practiced eye. I asked her if the mass displays of emotion one sees in videos from North Korea were genuine.

Kang smiled and shook her head no. She described one, showing the funeral ceremonies for Kim II. In it, a crowd of women, bundled against the cold and kneeling in the snow, wept hysterically as the funeral procession passed.

"They were all bending forward, reaching out with their arms and then lowering themselves to the snow," she says. "Only, when their hands came to close to the snow, they stopped. Their hands did not actually touch the snow."

She laughed.

"What did that tell you?"

"They didn't want to get their hands cold and wet."

It was all theater. The grief, the weeping, and the prostrating were not just expected, but *required*. Here is where our inability to imagine a true monarchy shows. Kingship requires display. It accounts public belief more important than private belief. Pretending in public is essential. We see the same thing in a theocracy like Iran, where the state's legitimacy rests on shared religious conviction. Strict piety is the rule in public, while in private you encounter the same variety of opinion in Tehran as you do anywhere. Official hypocrisy is known and largely accepted. Behind closed doors women wear western clothes, guests are served alcoholic drinks, conversation is candid and often irreverent and critical of the state—but never in public. It is the same in a royal state, where the prevailing myth is the monarch. Even in eighteenth-century England, accepting accident of birth as the determinant of power meant suspending reason and common sense. I doubt that Thomas Paine's scorn of hereditary succession was especially shocking to educated Englishmen, who were aware of King George III's occasional bouts of madness. One bows to the king not because he is in fact superior to other men, but because he is the king. He embodies the entire social and economic order—the status quo. One bows because if the throne is safe, so is the empire. Sober, rational men still have private opinions and beliefs, but in public they shower praise on, and indulge even the foolish whims of, a monarch in order to preserve their own well-being. Today in Pyongyang privileged millions enjoy a relatively good life because of the system that coddles them, and that system *is* Kim. The mass displays of loyalty and affection, which may seem ridiculous to us, make perfect sense there. They are reassuring, and mandatory.

Jean Lee, a former AP reporter who became the wire service's bureau chief in Pyongyang in 2012, is Korean American and has spent a lot more time in the "hermit kingdom" than most western journalists. The only outside reporters allowed to actually live in Pyongyang are Russian and Chinese. After setting up the bureau, Lee began "visiting" the capital for three- to five-week stints. She would fly out for a week back in the United States or Seoul, escaping the strain of constant surveillance, and then return to the kingdom for another stay. So—unlike most western reporters, who see the country only on media junkets, where everything is carefully choreographed, what Lee calls "the spectacle and the theater"—she saw North Koreans in their daily lives, offstage: "the in-between moments," she says. What she observed was not the slavish devotion required in public, but something close. She observed a very proud people determined to put their best foot forward for foreigners, a sturdy, complex, hardworking population, largely ignorant of the world outside their kingdom, and resigned to the difficulties of their own world. Humor ran deep. To convey their real feelings, many North Koreans employed wisecracks and facial expressions, a far richer resource than the official line. But Kim was the exception. No one jokes about the Supreme Leader.

Lee won't call such deference "reverence," she says, because, "it's a required behavior. . . . It's highly illegal to criticize or deface anything related to the leader. So, I'm not talking about how people feel. I'm talking about how they're required to behave. There are a lot of times where people—you can see those kinds of flickers in people's faces where they want you to know that they have to say certain things, but very few North Koreans would be unwise enough to say anything openly critical about the leadership. They're perfectly OK criticizing other elements of their society but not the leadership, so that's kind of a steadfast rule. I think those who feel they can't suppress that would be inclined to leave."

Lee was the first western journalist invited to attend a meeting of party leaders in Pyongyang in 2012. Kim had been in power for less than a year, and after seeing many propaganda images of him exuding youth and vitality (in sharp contrast to his late father) she was struck by the way he entered the hall.

"He was walking like an old man, so it was really odd," she said. "He can do things like bend down, and he obviously has the kind of flexibility of a young man, but [here] he was walking like an old man. It wasn't like he was walking like he had difficulty walking. It was more like he had adopted a certain gait that was kind of self-conscious, kind of like the gait of authority. It's striking because he is such a young man. So, that was one thing that really struck me. And of course you can't help but notice how big he is in a place where you don't see any obesity."

She was struck by another thing at this and other such meetings where she was given a chance to observe the country's leadership closer up than anyone before. At Kim's entrance, all those present leaped to their feet and began clapping vigorously—everyone except his uncle Jang Song Thaek. The brother of Kim Il's only sister, Jang was initially considered by many to be the real power in North Korea when the elder Kim died. This notion proved to be dramatically wrong, but from where Lee was sitting, it certainly appeared as though Jang had special status because he had the effrontery not to play along.

"His uncle kind of sat in his seat and didn't really get up," she said. "He was very slow to get up until the very last minute. And then, [he] didn't do the full clapping. He just kind of did a half clap. It was really striking because there was nobody else who would dare to do that."

This refusal to enthusiastically perform was interpreted by Lee, and by others, as a sign of Jang's special status, the assumption being that he alone among the ranks of the faithful could get away with it. Clearly Jang thought so. It was a fatal error. In December 2013, the supposed (or perhaps would-be) power behind the throne was arrested, vigorously denounced, and shot. It was such a sudden and unexpected move that many North Korea–watchers anticipated shock waves within the regime. Surely one that powerful and that closely allied with Kim II would have legions of loyal comrades. There was bound to be fallout. Some predicted at least an uptick in high-level defections. Victor Cha, former director for Asian affairs at the U.S. National Security Council, told NBC News, "When you take out Jang, you're not just taking out one person—you're taking out scores if not hundreds of other people in the system. It's got to have some ripple effect."

But there were no ripples. No whisper of internal dissent escaped Pyongyang. There were no high-level defectors.

"The regime continues to enjoy mainstream support, which derives largely from the appeal of official myth," writes Myers. "We have no reason to assume that the ruling elite does not subscribe to the same worldview as its citizens. Interinstitutional rivalries exist in Pyongyang as in every capital, but these do not derive from ideological disagreement."

Part of the national myth is that North Korea is in constant danger. The United States, Japan, and other world powers are poised to attack. In paintings and videos the nation is often symbolized by its rocky eastern shoreline, where great cliffs and boulders absorb blow after blow from a stormy sea. In the fanciful national story, Kim I single-handedly routed the Japanese and expelled them from the peninsula, and then fought off the invading armies of the United States. Kim II staved off the threatening enemy powers and steered the country through hard times. Kim III will someday steer it to a final victory, unifying all of Korea under his rule and asserting Korea's place at the pinnacle of all nation-states. The world press inadvertently plays into the narrative. It

THE BRIGHT SUN OF JUCHE

has been obsessed with Kim's every move ever since the young man inherited power three years ago. Virtually no information comes from the state, and, like nature, the media abhor a vacuum. Misinformation and manufactured stories generate headline after headline, TV specials, daily updates, and, most recently, even a goofy Hollywood movie starring James Franco and Seth Rogen. North Koreans who have access to international media—though not many do—cannot fail to appreciate the global obsession with their leader. The fact that Kim is cast as a villain, that he is reviled and lampooned, just confirms that the world is out to get them.

On July 8, clad in slimming black, Kim led a stiff phalanx of generals and admirals and lesser party powers into the vast ceremonial Kumsusan Palace for an annual salute to the dynasty. A mighty multitude had assembled, and rose as one when the heir entered, front and center of the power procession, strutting like . . . Hey, what's this? Kim was walking less like a deity than a man with a flaming bunion . . . or a sprained ankle . . . or whatever. The Marshal had a limp!

This was followed by a brief period of silence. Kim vanished from the public stage. By September, world punditocracy was febrile with speculation: It spun. It speculated . . . all to the effect that Kim was a goner. He had been dumped. Serious evidence came in the form of Jang Jin Sung, a former North Korean propagandist (surely a solid source there), now living in China. The other sources were . . . well, there were no other sources, but the thing now had enough Internet traction to justify front-page stories in the more respectable press. The *Washington Post*, Huffington Post, the *Daily Mail*, the *Washington Times*, and even the venerable *New York Times* all reported that, while nobody actually knew anything, it was probably worth noting that Kim had not been seen for a few months or so, and that everyone was saying. . . . It was enough to make one long for the serenity of Pyongyang's state-controlled press, which consistently reported what happened to be the truth. The Marshal, it seemed, had problem with his ankle.

Kim reappeared with a cane in early fall and things settled down. The official story is that he had undergone a procedure to remove a cyst. Unlike the reports in western media, it had the ring of truth.

4. A Great Dictator?

Talk show comedians and the tabloid press may delight in mocking Kim, but many of those who watch him professionally are impressed.

"I think he is a great dictator," said Daniel Pinkston, a project director for the International Crisis Group, who studies North Korea closely. We spoke at a coffee shop near his office in Seoul in early October. "I do not like dictatorships," he said, "but as far as being a dictator, what a dictator is supposed to do in that kind of system, given that system, and what type of person is needed to manage it, maintain it, and sustain it—he is a great dictator."

What are the things a dictator needs to be good at? You need to manage the system, the party structure, the military, the economy, and the security forces in such a way that your people feel empowered and remain loyal. This is done by adopting policies that bring prosperity not necessarily to all, but to *enough* people, by artfully elevating those most loyal and able, and by demoting the able but disloyal—sometimes radically. Threats to your power must be eliminated ruthlessly. A dictator needs to know how to present himself in public, and at this, Kim III already excels. He has a deep, rich voice which sounds commanding and reassuring.

"I have noticed in my viewing of him, that he moves well as a politician," said Richardson, who speaks from experience. "He is a lot better than his father. He smiles, goes and shakes people's hands. He gives a better speech, better photographs. His father was very conservative; he did not move much, possibly because of his height. He was just not the garrulous type. . . . This man, when you look at him, the photographs, the newsreels, he moves well. He gives a good speech. When I was in North Korea about a year and a half ago, I heard his speech. Of course I did not understand it but the diction was good. He aroused people, not exceedingly well but it was a lot better than his father."

Of course, a great dictator must project a lot more than impressive voice and posture. He must be decisive, and project fear. In his first three years, Kim has removed the two men who posed the most serious risk to his rule. It is not too much of a stretch to assume that given Kim III's youth, at least some of the senior leaders closest to Kim II might have expected an interregnum after his death, where one or more of them would be the de facto Supreme Leader. What is certainly true is that mere suspicion of such designs would have targeted them for elimination.

The first to go was Marshal Ri Yong Ho, chief of staff of North Korea's army and a member of the central presidium of the Workers Party. Ri had been close to Kim II. He had direct responsibility for protecting Pyongyang and, perhaps more important, the Kim family. He had been one of the stars of his generation. In July 2012, Kim III called an emergency meeting of the entire presidium and abruptly stripped Ri of his duties. It was the first sure sign that Kim planned to run the entire show himself, and would brook no challenge, even from the nation's most senior leaders. If Kim III were a more careful or wiser leader, he might have simply removed Ri from power, along with the other top generals he has purged. He could easily have retired them or placed them in rubber-stamp positions, where he could, if he chose, consult them, use them as a source of independent counsel, given that their careers were finished and the influence of ambition and faction was gone. Ri vanished. He was reportedly under house arrest and later that year he was charged with being a "counterrevolutionary." No one knows his ultimate fate for sure, but no one is expecting him back.

The second threat was Uncle Jang, who, being a family member and a far more powerful figure than even Ri, was more emphatically dumped. On December 3, 2013, after all those lackluster displays of devotion in public, Jang was dismissed from his posts and arrested during a politboro meeting. The humiliation could not have been more public in Pyongyang; the event was broadcast on state television. It was also a sign that Kim intended to act with more flair in such matters than his father, who was content to quietly retire crrant generals to rural estates. It reminded some of the old Soviet show trials or the flamboyant excesses of Saddam Hussein, who liked to get up onstage with a fat cigar before his assembled leadership and personally point out those who were to be taken from the hall and shot. Ten days later the regime announced that Jang had been "tried" by a special tribunal and promptly executed. While there have been rumors of Ri's execution, there is little doubt about Jang's. Kim was sending a message this time.

"I think [Kim] is fully in control . . . and he runs a tight ship," Pinkston said. "He is managing the structures [of state] very adeptly. . . . The actual micromanaging—going around seeing who is loyal, who is not, giving the orders, executing the orders, all of that stuff—the guy is, like, totally on top of it. And most people, I guess they are unwilling to accept that because this guy is, like, thirty-one years old. . . . Some people say that this thirty-year-old cannot do this, but you watch; he is doing it. People underestimate him at their own peril."

So, what exactly is Kim up to?

One of the first things he did was to clean house in the military, replacing older leaders, loyal to his father, with younger men. Not only did this ensure that the military commanders were beholden to him; it infused the old Cold War–era ranks with more modern thinking and made them less resistant to change.

He has initiated sweeping economic reforms. His father was leaning toward some of these in his later years, but the changes have been so aggressive it appears that the prime mover behind them is Kim himself. Most are designed to ground North Korea's economy on money. This may seem an almost silly thing to say, since an economy is by definition about money. Except in North Korea, that is. Until fairly recent years, the only path to prosperity was ideological purity. Promotion in even the best of circumstances was a combination of ability and party approval. Status was strictly determined by the state. If you lived in a better apartment, drove a nicer car, were permitted to live in the relatively affluent districts of Pyongyang, that meant you had the approval of the regime. Increasingly, North Koreans can better their lot by earning more money, as is the case throughout the world. Managers of factories and shops have been given financial incentives to do better. Success means they can pay their workers and themselves more. Kim has pushed for the development of special economic zones in every province of the country, setting up internal competition and rewards, so that the fruits of success in one area no longer must be fully returned to the state. It is part of a general effort to decentralize economic power.

This is in the industrial sector. Kim has also made agricultural reforms that have proved surprisingly effective.

"He decided to do what his father was deadly afraid of doing," said Lankov. "He allowed farmers . . . to keep part of the harvest. Farmers are not working now as, essentially, slaves on a plantation. They work for themselves, and they work much better. That was his policy. His father did not dare to do it. The policy was never made public. It's still classified. The next stage, I hope, will be allowing farmers to plant their own crops [completely]. They allowed farmers to work at the same part of the field. Technically, the field is still state property, but as a farming family you can register yourself as a 'production team.' And you will be working on the same field for a few years in a row. And you keep 30 percent of the harvest for yourself. And this year, according to unconfirmed reports, it will be between 40 and 60 percent that will go to the farmers. So they are not slaves anymore; they are sharecroppers."

Famine and disaster generate headlines, while steady improvement in a country's farm output generates yawns. With no dramatic announcement of the change in policy, few have noticed the turnaround, but in 2013, according to the UN, for the first time in twenty-five years North Korea harvested enough food to feed its population. In the spring of 2014, it had a drought, which produced the usual raft of alarmist predictions worldwide, but none of them have proved true. Initial reports are that the country's annual harvest will prove to be surprisingly good. Malnutrition remains a problem in the country, with an estimated 84 percent of households having "borderline or poor food consumption," according to the UN Food and Agricultural Organization, but most indicators show that the regime is gaining ground on hunger.

Even though the people have fuller bellies and money to spend, Kim has done nothing to interfere with North Korea's markets, all of them technically illegal. His father acquiesced in the existence of black marketeering when the population was starving in the 1990s, but oscillated as the famine eased, sometimes treating illicit merchants as criminals and sometimes tolerating them, as need dictated. It was a fairly reliable pattern. When hardships eased, the state cracked down. Kim has left the black markets alone even in these years of relative prosperity. At this point the markets represent a substantial part of the nation's economy, which has seen a boom in consumer goods, mostly imported from China. Visitors to Pyongyang report large numbers of cell phones in use, more cars and trucks moving on the streets, more colorful fashions worn by the women. Kim's wife has become something of a style leader, appearing in public wearing high heels and sleek dresses that reflect tastes in booming China. These are changes that just a few years ago would have been unthinkable, so it is reasonable to assume that they have not been universally welcomed among the state's elite.

In this respect, the remarkably colorful and detailed 2,700-word official denunciation of Jang Song Thaek, calling him "despicable human scum," was revealing. It begins theatrically: "Upon hearing the report on the enlarged meeting of the Political Bureau of the Central Committee of the Workers' Party of Korea, the service personnel and people throughout the country broke into angry shouts that a stern judgment of the revolution should be meted out to the antiparty, counterrevolutionary factional elements." It then proceeds in the same vein, describing Jang as "thrice-cursed" and a "traitor for all ages," and listing his sins against the regime and mankind. Jang had been plotting to overthrow "the peerlessly great men of Mount Paetku," the Kims, and neglecting to play his assigned role in the national pageant by "projecting himself internally and externally as a special being" on a par with Kim III. He is accused of accepting bribes and of preventing a tile factory from erecting a mosaic depicting Kim I and Kim II; and he "was so reckless as to instruct" that a granite monument engraved with a letter from Kim III to an internal security unit and destined for the front entrance of its headquarters instead "be erected in a shaded corner." He is accused of gambling, distributing pornography to his "confidants," and otherwise leading a "dissolute and decadent life." This was a bad person.

More significantly, Jang was accused of opposing Kim's economic reforms. This sent a stern message to the rest of North Korea's leadership. Internal debate over reform was ended. To oppose change was to oppose Kim. It is now treason.

"The entire party, whole army, and all people are dynamically advancing toward the final victory in the drive for the building of a thriving nation, meeting all challenges of history, and resolutely foiling the desperate moves of the enemies of the revolution under the leadership of Kim Jong Un. Such a situation urgently calls for consolidating as firm as a rock the single-minded unity of the party and the revolutionary ranks with its unitary center and more thoroughly establishing the monolithic leadership system of the party throughout the party and society. Jang seriously obstructed the nation's economic affairs and the improvement of the standard of people's living in violation of the 'pivot to the cabinet principle' and the 'cabinet responsibility' principle [a return of authority for steering the economy to Pyongyang's top executive body, which has been calling for reforms]."

The execution of Jang underscored how seriously Kim is betting on his economic reform policies. The early returns are good.

"The crude economic indicators that we get are of steady growth," said John Delury, who met with me in Seoul. "It's anemic relative to East Asia and relative to [its] huge development potential. North Korea should be in the ten-plus GDP growth range. So, it's like two. It's kind of trudging forward as opposed to getting worse and worse."

Delury estimates that trade with China is up threefold since Kim took office. On his most recent trip in Pyongyang in 2013, he was struck by the number of people he saw with cell phones. During past visits he could readily count the number of cars he saw; now he no longer could.

"You can see the emergence of a consumer like a public-consumer culture," he said. "It's like a leisure class. You can call it a middle class using a very loose definition of what a middle class is. Probably the best is that it's a consumer class. That's clearly an important sort of constituency for Kim Jong Un. So he's building stuff for those people. A lot of [the time] when he's appearing in public, he's doing stuff for those people. He's giving them stuff. He's feeding that. That's important because obviously that's the slippery slope into capitalism and into economic opening and all of those things. And so, he has very consciously and pretty aggressively associated himself as the leader of that constituency."

In acknowledging that a big thrust of Kim's leadership so far has been aimed at improving the lives of his citizens, we should not mistake it for leniency. At the same time that he has been freeing the economy, Kim has been cranking up the state's repressive machinery.

"Kim's father also wanted [the people's] lives to improve," said Lankov, "but his father was far more cautious. His father understood that . . . well, the masses are not always happier when you try make them happy. Alexis de Tocqueville identified the paradox: when a bad government tries to become better, it becomes more vulnerable. In this regard, Kim Jong Un's policy is very smart. He began to tighten ideological controls, which became very loose under his father because his father didn't care that much."

Under Kim II, the long border between North Korea and China was almost open—witness Kang Mi Jin's story of her relatively easy escape across the frozen Yalu. Today it has become much more difficult to cross. In the three years since Kim took power, the number of defectors to South Korea (most of whom, like Kang, arrive by way of China) has been nearly halved—from 3,000 annually to about 1,500. This is probably not because living conditions have improved in North Korea. Living conditions are far better in Mexico than in North Korea, and yet millions of Mexicans are still running to the United States to seek a better life. The slowdown is the result of tighter border controls. Those caught trying to cross illegally are beaten, tortured, or killed. Kim's regime means to do well by those who accept it, but it has, if anything, grown harsher toward those who do not.

Propaganda under Kim has become more pervasive and also more persuasive. Good propaganda is not about lies; it's about exaggeration. Years ago, when North Koreans defected to the south, they were denounced as fools. They had been deceived by the devious propaganda of the Americans. South Korea was so backward, went the party line, that defectors would starve to death. Most North Koreans, even with their limited access to outside information, knew this was a lie. Today the story is not that South Korea is destitute. The regime acknowledges that South Koreans are doing better than its own people. But it argues that defectors will not do better in the south than the north. The North Korean defector will be despised, discriminated against, and exploited. And there is at least some truth in this. The stories are exaggerated.

The most hopeful reading of Kim's rule so far is that he is on the path to becoming a relatively benevolent dictator—in comparison with his father and grandfather. This is what many North Korea–watchers consider the best-case scenario for Kim's prospects: that he will smoothly steer North Korea out of its dark age, and himself live to a ripe old age overseeing decades of moderate prosperity and maybe even cracking open the door to more domestic freedom and better relations with the west.

Except that nothing about the way Kim is proceding is smooth.

"Nothing about the things he is really doing is stupid," said Lankov. "The way he is doing it is stupid."

5. "Bottoms Up!"

One of the more recent signs of change in North Korea has been little noticed by the larger world, but it is sure to have caused a stir in Pyongyang. Mrs. Kim has begun frequently stepping out in public, usually beside her husband, without a badge.

Since 1972, according to Lankov, Korean adults in public have been required to wear on their lapel or chest a small red badge advertising their loyalty to the Kim dynasty. Initially the red badge showed the face of Kim Il Sung, but later a two-Kim version became popular, depicting both Kim I and Kim II. So far there is no Kim III badge. There are now a few dozen variations; someone will surely write a monograph on the subject eventually. Lankov said that "every" adult must wear the badge, but perhaps it is only members of the leadership. You will look hard to find anyone in a picture from North Korea who is not wearing one . . . except the fashionable Mrs. Kim. This may be intended as a fashion statement, but to those who have slavishly obeyed the requirement for decades it would hardly register as something that simple.

"She is the only person who appears in public without the badge," said Lankov. "It's a bit like, in a Catholic country, the wife of the most Christian king appearing in public without a cross. Or, worse still, in some strict Muslim country, the wife of a leader appearing without a veil. Not a good idea."

"Why do you think she does it?"

"Because they are spoiled, rich young people who don't understand how risky is the game they are playing."

Lankov may be reading too much into this. It may be a sign that Mrs. Kim and her husband are feeling more confident in their roles, and like every new generation, shedding vestiges of the old. Whether that confidence is warranted remains to be seen. One of the most unsettling things about Kim's rule so far is his tendency to act out unpredictably and even strangely, and in his enthusiasm, to overdo. From time to time he gets goofy. Call it his Dennis Rodman problem.

Consider the ski resort. Under his direction, the regime has built, in the Masik Pass in the southeast, a reportedly first-class facility billed as "the most exotic ski resort on Earth." It is certainly the most unusual. Built at enormous cost in a country where most people are more concerned about their next meal than the thickness of snow powder, the Masik Pass project can only be called a hopeful gesture. The idea is to attract foreign tourists, which seems unlikely, but also to attract newly prosperous citizens. That sufficient numbers of domestic customers who can afford such an expensive holiday will materialize may be even less likely than attracting tourists. What the resort most clearly reflects is Kim's whim. Skiing was one of his pastimes in Switzerland when he was a boy. There is a spectacular but ultimately sad state photo taken at the resort's opening in December 2013, showing Kim in a heavy black coat and a big black fur hat sitting on a ski lift ascending a snowy slope. The landscape is stunning, but Kim is sitting by himself on the lift. The dangling lift behind his is empty. The Heaven-Sent Brilliant Commander is alone at his multimillion-dollar playground, looking nothing so much as forlorn.

Some see this simply as a spectacularly bad investment, a sign of Kim's impulsiveness.

"Very often he is driven by his emotions," says Lankov, who calls the resort one of his "absolutely crazy business schemes."

"He wants to be popular," says Lankov, but he also wants success. He has reportedly ordered that his minions attract one million tourists to the resort annually. "They have no chance of getting that many people. They don't have the resources, they don't have the infrastructure, they don't have the climate. . . . It's a fantasy world, a world of dancing Mickey Mouses [Kim is fond of Disney characters]."

Lankov is not the only one who sees it that way.

"If the leadership says it, or decides, they just do it, regardless of how inefficient it might be," said Pinkston. "Kim has really focused on sports and recreation. [The ski resort] was really given high priority, and aquariums in Pyongyang or dolphinariums, whatever they call them, amusement parks, those types of things. There is a children's camp that has been upgraded, that is one of the projects this year that they have been working on. So this is what dictatorships do. You go back to the Roman times, right, so you provide circuses and gladiator bouts and these kinds of big public projects to the people or society to demonstrate that you are looking out for them, because you do have to maintain some critical mass of support. So that is what you do in a dictatorship."

Like monarchs everywhere, Kim does whatever he wants. It doesn't have to make sense. This is evident in his amateurish efforts to reach out. Those who believe that Kim, even if he wanted to do it, could simply halt his country's nuclear program and reverse a half century of implacable hostility are being unrealistic. Given who he is, it's unlikely he thinks this way. But he has shown a surprising desire to normalize relations with the rest of the world. He has sent goodwill delegations to China, Russia, South Korea, and Europe, and has made odd and sometimes startling gestures of friendship toward the United States—like releasing three American citizens under arrest in his country and asking nothing in return but a high-level state visit. He didn't get it, unless you count National Intelligence Director James Clapper, who retrieved the errant Americans without meeting with Kim or other top North Korean officials.

When I was visiting Seoul in October, during a time when Kim had not been seen for weeks and was presumably recovering from minor surgery on his ankle, the dictator shocked South Koreans by dispatching to the Asian Games, a regional Olympics-like sports contest, three of the regime's most powerful figures—Vice Marshal Hwong Pyong So, head of the North Korean army's General Political Bureau and Kim's presumed second in command; Choe Ryong Hae, secretary of the Workers Party; and Kim Yang Gon, a senior official responsible for South Korean affairs. All three men are known to be very close to Kim, and as such represented the highest-level delegation from the north to ever visit the south, and prompted widespread hopeful speculation that Kim was serious about inviting a substantive dialogue with his southern, democratic counterparts, with whom his country has been in a tense military standoff since before he was born. The three top North Koreans posed for pictures, waved, and expressed "heartfelt greetings," but apparently had little else to offer. Ordinarily a top-level delegation like that would arrive only if it had something important to say, or offer. Enthusiasm for the outsize gesture faded in a few days, when it became apparent that the smiles and waves and heartfelt greetings were the whole story.

"Again, [Kim] overdid it," said Lankov, just a few days after the visit had made an exciting splash in Seoul. "It was necessary to send somebody to South Korea, to send a feeler, and to check whether the South Koreans are ready, under some conditions, to lift . . . the ban on inter-Korean cooperation. It was necessary to send somebody. But instead of sending one senior diplomat, for some reason they decided essentially to send half of their entire movers and shakers here. A delegation which suddenly, with twenty-four hours' notice, arrived here. It was the highest delegation which ever visited South Korea. Ever. . . . Unbelievable! And they came essentially empty-handed! With no exact plans. I can easily imagine Kim Jong Un, lying in bed after recent surgery, taking the phone, and saying, 'We should do something. Let's impress them. Let's send them half of my government.'"

Kim has expressed a desire to meet personally with President Obama. In none of these outreaches has he offered anything substantial: no compromise on nukes; no promises to end provocative missile tests and the country's occasional acts of hostility toward South Korea. It is as though he wants the rest of the world to like North Korea just as it is, and believes his wanting it is enough to make it happen. And when you consider it, how else would a boy king think?

The most notoriously strange example of an overture by Kim to America was, of course, Kim's meetings with Rodman.

"I think just personally, Kim just likes basketball; he is a basketball fan and he likes the Bulls, right?" said Pinkston. "So many times, or I would say in general, sports will often transcend politics."

In this case, the real story is better, and more complicated. The meeting is certainly the most direct contact any Americans have had with the young dictator. It was fun. The trip to North Korea with Rodman was conceived as a TV stunt. Shane Smith is the bearded, tattooed cofounder and CEO of Vice Media, a highly successful offbeat news/entertainment company that has made a name for itself, in part, by visiting difficult spots on the map. Several years ago, Smith proposed to his staff that they figure out a way to get inside North Korea with their cameras. Various approaches were kicked around before it was decided to try to exploit Kim's reported fascination with Michael Jordan and the Bulls. Vice Media contacted Jordan's representatives, proposing to fly him to Pyongyang with its crew, and was met with a combination of profound disbelief and silence.

"We had thrown out the idea of Dennis Rodman as [laughter here] a gay, very crazy idea," said Jason Mojica, a Vice producer. "And then someone who kind of overheard it here just literally got in touch with his agent." The agent conveyed that his client was generally keen on anything to make a buck—he had recently appeared at dental convention—and so Rodman was enlisted. They had a Bull.

"He did great," said Mojica.

It was surreal. With his variously colored hair, piercings, and tattoos; with his flamboyantly ill-defined sexuality—he wore a wedding dress for the cover shot of his autobiography—and reputation of substance abuse, Rodman might be considered a poster child for individual liberty, for better or worse. A less likely ambassador to the world's most totalitarian state cannot be imagined. But his name opened doors magically. The concept Vice proposed was to visit North Korea with Rodman and to stage a basketball camp for kids. Rodman was to help recruit other pro basketball players—who wound up being members of the Harlem Globetrotters, adding to the bizarre character of the event. The highlight of the camp would be an exhibition basketball game between two teams made up of the campers and the pros.

"I guess we kind of expected that it would be held in a run-down gymnasium with like eighty to a hundred kids, and that the game would just be this little thing that we really did just for the cameras and the very few people in attendance," said Mojica. "And, of course, we did put in the app [application] that we would love to meet Kim Jong Un and so forth. Waves, hello, maybe we can shake his hand before he disappears. But we never expected it to actually happen."

Certainly not the way it did. The proposal was accepted, and Rodman flew to Pyongyang in January 2014 with the Globetrotters and the Vice crew. Along for the ride (and for his language skills) was Mark Barthelemy, an old friend of Mojica's—they both attended college in Chicago in the early 1990s and played in punk rock bands. Barthelemy went on to specialize in Korea and learn the language. He is an entrepreneur and stock analyst who lives in Seoul for half of the year. Mojica wanted someone along whom he could trust and who spoke fluent Korean.

"This whole thing was set up as an attempt to meet the guy [Kim]," said Barthelemy. The visiting Americans were given the full-on Potemkin village treatment, visiting new shopping malls, workout centers, supermarkets . . . all designed to dispel the somewhat dated notion that North Koreans stripped bark off trees to make soup. The group was shocked when, on the day of the basketball camp, instead of being led into a run-down gymnasium, they were escorted into an arena more like Madison Square

Garden, packed to the rafters with North Koreans. Barthelemy was on the floor shooting still pictures when . . .

"We were quickly setting up and all of a sudden, that roar happened, and that was our first indication that Kim Jong Un was there," said Mojica. "And it was incredibly shocking, I could not believe it."

The moment was captured in the film Vice made for HBO of the trip. The crowd of about ten thousand uniformly dressed spectators rises as one and begins thunderous cheering and clapping. Then the camera turns to view Mr. and Mrs Kim.

"I was just walking around the sideline of the court shooting pictures and then suddenly I see people just stand up and start screaming," said Barthelemy. "It was insane. It was like when . . . you can't imagine an American stadium . . . this was like the wave was going by everywhere in the stadium at the same time. Everyone was on their feet going crazy and showing whatever they need to show. The whole time that I was ever in the same area as him he seemed to be on Leg Three of the Kim Jong Un Shows Himself to the Country PR Tour. I get the sense that he was equal parts projecting cool, I get it, I have people from the NBA coming to hang out with me and we can sit around and have a good time and also . . . I can drop bombs if I want to and I can get to space so . . . fuck you, I'm Kim Jong Un. He seemed playful. It seemed like a bit of playfulness mixed in with the sort of visual body language that you would want to do to project authority . . . this weird combination of maybe compulsive glee . . . compulsive playfulness and fun or whatever and . . . *Oh my God! I can't believe this is happening to me!* That was maybe somewhat mitigated by . . . *OK, hang on a second. I'm leader here. I may have people around me that might murder me at any given moment so I'd better gesticulate wildly with my hands to show that I'm a tough guy in charge* . . . and that type of thing. He walked in and sat down and then Rodman went over to sit next to him and the atmosphere in the place was electric for a moment and then just very aware. . . . You could feel everyone watching and I got the sense of being aware of eyes on them as well."

Rodman sat and chatted with the Great Leader through translators throughout the event, forming his overall impression of Kim as a great and highly misunderstood guy.

"I realized at one point that Kim Jong Un was pointing to me and waving at me," said Barthelemy. "He was craning his neck forward a bit, waving at me like somebody would be waving at a little kid that they see getting off a plane at the airport like . . . *Hey buddy!* That kind of a thing. . . . I turned around to see if there was somebody behind me that he was waving at and there was nobody back there. Then I look again and he nudges his wife, gets her attention, points and me and then they both wave at me, smiling. I got a picture of that. That was really bizarre. That was definitely something I didn't expect in North Korea."

There was more to come. After the game, the Americans were invited to a reception.

"We were told we could not bring any cameras, we could bring no phones, no pens, no notebooks, nothing, like bring nothing," recalled Mojica. "Oh, and also, by the way, it is formal and we leave in thirty minutes. And so we had our crew running around, shop in the lobby. Jake, our cameraman bought like a child's sport jacket and squeezed into it. I happened to have a jacket with me so we did the best we could. So we jump into our vans and we are driving around. And by this point, we are starting to understand the layout of Pyongyang. You know, we were heading out by to the Kumsusan Palace, then we made this drop to another brick road, and then we were driving down another which we had never been on before. And it was very dark, and I asked my minder, 'So where are we going?' He is like, 'I do not know; I have never been here before.' And then we pull off to this kind of gray building, gray stone building. [There are] intense multilayers of security as they are checking us in. We walk into kind of like a white marble foyer type thing, and there is a bar."

Mojica said he asked for a glass of Scotch at the bar, and then he and the rest of the Vice entourage were escorted into a banquet hall.

"And we walk in, and there is kind of a receiving line, kind of like a wedding reception," he recalled. "And I look over to see, like, who the person at the end of the line is. And I saw kind of an old man and could not figure out who he was, and I was like, OK, interesting. So then, I turned, and immediately the very first person in the line is Kim Jong Un. Like right to my right, and I am like, Oh shit! So I put this glass of Scotch down, and I go over, and suddenly the cameras are flashing, and I have my kind of my Saddam-Rumsfeld moment. [Donald Rumsfeld was photographed shaking the dictator Saddam Hussein's hand in 1983, as an American envoy to Iraq. The shot became famous years later when Rumsfeld, as secretary of defense, directed the violent overthrow of Saddam.] So it was kind of like, here is my handshake photo with the evil dictator that will come back to haunt me years later."

When he took his seat at the assigned table a waiter brought his discarded drink back, and then set down a large tumbler and a full bottle of the Scotch brand he had ordered. Koreans were alternated with Americans around each table, and whenever an effort was made to converse, a translator would scurry up and lean in. The menu was elaborate, starting with caviar and ending with a terrific dessert. An attentive waiter kept Mojica's tumbler of Scotch full. Throughout the meal, there were well-lubricated toasts, and at one point Mojica was pushed forward to make his contribution. He was slightly ready for this. He had jotted down a few notes in anticipation when it became clear he would have to do it. So he stood with a microphone in one hand and his full tumbler of Scotch in the other, the notes back at his table. He was already feeling no pain.

He tried to remember his notes. He said the most difficult part of the trip was trying to get Rodman, the NBA's former bad boy, to get along with the Globetrotters, who were like Boy Scouts.

"And I think that we have done that, and therefore it proves that anything is possible, even world peace!"

There was laughter and cheering, first from the Americans, and then, moments later, from the Koreans as his words were translated. Jason lifted his glass to Kim at the head table, took a sip of the Scotch, and put the microphone down and started back to his seat. Then he heard a voice yelling at him from across the room. He turned to look, and realized that it was Kim, sitting on the edge of his chair, shouting and gesticulating with a raised left hand. Mojica was confused. Then Kim's translator shouted the Great Leader's words in English, "Bottoms up! You have to finish your drink!"

Mojica looked down at the giant glass of brown fluid. This was clearly a command performance.

"I am a guest so I am going to do it," he said. "So I finished— kind of guzzled this drink and [when] I finish, my head is kind of spinning."

He reached back for the microphone and spoke again, amazing himself as the words came out of his mouth, "If we keep it up at this rate, I will be naked by the end of the evening."

Some of the women in the audience looked aghast. There was silence as his challenge was relayed to Kim in translation.

"He is sitting there kind of like on the edge of his seat with his mouth open and eyes wide," said Mojica. "And he is like listening, listening, and nodding and nodding, and then he is like, *Oooh!* slapping the table, and everyone laughs with great relief."

Mojica said his memory grows foggy at that point. He recalled the all-girl band revving up the theme music from *Dallas*, and then *Rocky*. Things got a little out of hand. One of the group's translators got up onstage and played the saxophone. There was crazy dancing. One of Rodman's friends got into a drunken fight with someone in the Globetrotters' entourage and they were escorted from the hall. At one point one of their North Korean hosts came over to Mojica with a message from Rodman.

"He suggested that we may want to chill out a little bit," he said. It was alarming. Things had apparently drifted further out of hand than Jason had thought. Also . . . memorable. How many people can say that they were advised at a party by Dennis Rodman to tone things down?

At one point in the evening, before things got too hazy, Mojica remembered staring at Kim for a long time because . . . "he was, like, *right there*." Sitting just twelve feet away, he tried to drink in every detail, knowing how rare it was for an American to get such a close look at the young dictator. Kim seemed perfectly relaxed. Not at all drunk. Friendly. Smiley. Fat. Interacting with his guests in a very formal way.

It was hard for Mokica to believe that this young man was, in this place, completely, utterly, in a way most Americans cannot fully grasp, *in charge*.

Defending the Indefensible

Published as "Dzhokhar Tsarnaev Has the Most Ferocious Lawyer in America Defending Him," *Vanity Fair*, March 2015

We do not often think of a defense lawyer as someone who wars with her own client, but if it comes to that, Judy Clarke will go to war. Her latest client, Dzhokhar Tsarnaev, so far claims that he is not to blame for detonating a bomb among spectators at last year's Boston Marathon, killing three people and severely maiming dozens. It is doubtful that he will prevail on that point, but with Clarke in his corner, it is even more doubtful that he will ever be put to death for the crime, even if he gets it in his head that he wants to be, or that his cause demands martyrdom. Clarke is on a mission bigger than Tsarnaev alone. She is at war with the state—in particular, with the state's power to impose death. She calls the death penalty "legalized homicide."

Clarke has taken one notorious death-penalty case after another. Among others, there was Ted Kaczynski, the deadly Unabomber, now living out his days in a supermax prison in Colorado, and still furious with his onetime defense attorney ("Judy Clarke is a bitch on wheels and a sicko," he wrote to me); Susan Smith, who strapped her two small boys into car seats and then drove them into a lake and watched them drown; Eric Rudolph, the racist and Christian zealot who set off a bomb in Atlanta during the 1996 Summer Olympics as part of a spree that killed two people and injured 150 more; Zacarias Moussaoui, the Al Qaeda operative accused of helping to plan the September 11 attacks; and Jared Loughner, who opened fire in a parking lot near Tucson in 2011, shooting Representative Gabrielle Giffords through the head and killing six others. Clarke's client list is a catalog of the worst.

You might suspect a lawyer with a record like that to be a publicity seeker, but Clarke is the opposite. She shuns attention. She almost never gives interviews, and she does not stand before cameras and microphones on courthouse steps. She cultivates invisibility, right down to the muted way she dresses for court appearances. There is a deeper logic at work in her predilection to defend those who have achieved monstrous notoriety. In every instance cited above, there is little mystery about the crime itself—and in all the cases, her clients have been convicted. But while prosecutors have tried to invoke the death penalty, none of her clients have been executed, even when, as with Kaczynski and Rudolph, they are actually *proud* of what they have done. It's not unusual for clients like these to resist Judy Clarke's help. One, the white supremacist Buford O. Furrow Jr.—who in 1999 walked into a Jewish community center in Los Angeles and sprayed seventy shots, wounding five victims, before shooting and killing a mailman outside—has threatened to kill her. Clarke defends even people who do not wish to be defended, and who don't have a prayer—clients who are not just dream candidates for the death penalty but in some cases seem determined to embrace it. One case at a time, with whatever legal methods will work, she halts the march toward execution.

Clarke makes her point not with stirring courtroom rhetoric or brilliant legal reasoning but by a process of relentless accretion, case by case, win by win. This is her cause. Because if the state cannot put *these* defendants to death, then how can it put *anyone* to death? Thirty-nine executions took place in the United States in 2013 for crimes that form an inventory of human cruelty—and yet few of these crimes were as willful and egregious as those committed by Judy Clarke's clients. Meanwhile, Kaczynski is hard at work on his next book. Smith, from her cell, advertises for pen pals. And Rudolph writes essays defending the bombing of abortion clinics—essays that his followers post on the Internet.

We are more willing to impose death when the killer is painted in monochrome—if we can define him or her by the horror of the crime. Many think this is just: that is what blame and punishment are about. But in 1990, in rare public comments to the alumni magazine for Washington and Lee University, where she teaches law, Clarke has argued that no person should be defined "by the worst moment or worst day" of his life. She laboriously constructs a complex and sympathetic portrait of the accused, working with a far more varied palette; sketching out the good and the bad; unearthing the forces that drove a killer to the terrible moment; and insisting that judges, juries, and prosecutors see the larger picture, weighing not just the crime but the whole person. She seeks, not forgiveness, but understanding. It takes only a small spark of understanding to decide against sentencing someone to death.

Her record defending the indefensible speaks for itself. Among those who want capital punishment abolished in this country, Judy Clarke is the most effective champion in history.

David Kaczynski's estimation of Clarke can be encapsulated in a single wordless gesture as she stood beside his brother, Ted, in a Colorado courtroom on January 7, 1998. Ted was trying to fire Clarke.

He wasn't supposed to stand up or speak at that point in the hearing, but he jumped to his feet before Judge Garland Burrell Jr., and announced in his high-pitched voice, "Your honor, I have something very important to say!"

A bailiff shouted, "Sit down!"

Ted had been legally cornered. Defending him was never going to be easy. The evidence was overwhelming. From the strict isolation of his small cabin in Lincoln, Montana, he had painstakingly built and mailed bombs that had killed three people and injured twenty-three others. A once brilliant math student with advanced degrees, Kaczynski had become one of the most deliberate killers in history. He had drawn up a detailed manifesto with numbered paragraphs that he blackmailed the *Washington Post* and the *New York Times* into publishing by threatening to continue killing if they did not. The tract was a far cry from incoherent, though it was certainly turgid and extreme, arguing that the steady march of modern technology, of industry, and of socialization was profoundly dehumanizing and was destroying the possibility of happiness. Here was a man who had carefully thought through his reasons for murder, and then carried out his attacks with great deliberation over a period of years. His crimes fell well within at least two of the modern criteria for capital punishment—premeditation and multiple victims. His trial was almost certain to end in a sentence of death. He could avoid it by pleading guilty and accepting life in prison without hope of appeal, pardon, or parole, which he did not wish to do. Or he could proceed to trial and let Clarke and the other lawyers present the defense they had painstakingly prepared in the two years since his capture—an approach that he had just realized would portray him as mentally ill. Kaczynski would later accuse Clarke of having deceived him about this until shortly before the trial. For this murderously proud man, something more than personal humiliation was at stake. An insanity defense would forever color his theories as madness. And, for him, his ideas were the important thing. They were why he had killed. He was prepared to die for them.

None of this was made explicit in the courtroom, but from his seat in the front row Ted's brother had pieced it together. David had mixed feelings about the trial. He himself had led the FBI to Ted, and he was pleased that he had stopped his brother's violence, but he dreaded the prospect that his principled act of betrayal would lead to Ted's execution.

"It must have been the most awkward and difficult moment for Judy, as well as Ted, because at this point the real issue for him was that he didn't want the world to think he was crazy," David recalled. "He thought there was meaning in what he did, and to be described as a crazy person would have taken the meaning out of it. Of course, Judy as an attorney is trying to use her best influence with Ted to save his life, and here it was kind of falling apart at this critical moment. She could have been just really frustrated. She could have [felt], *My client is taking himself down despite all of my planning and best efforts to save his life.*"

There was a sidebar conference and then a further discussion inside the judge's chambers, at which point Clarke effectively torpedoed Ted's request to rid himself of his attorney. The judge did not want to further delay the trial, so he proposed a compromise: he would allow Ted to represent himself if his defense team would remain in the courtroom as his "advisers." Clarke rejected this proposal. Such a trial would be a charade, she said. She and her team would not take part. Her refusal forced the question, and she must have known that doing so would scuttle her client's wishes. Back in the courtroom, as Ted listened to Burrell deny his request, Clarke raised one hand and rested it gently on his shoulder. She knew, as David did, what a blow this was to him. Within hours he would attempt to hang himself in his cell. A few weeks later he grudgingly pleaded guilty—not to avoid the death penalty, but to avoid Clarke's insanity defense. He is still complaining about it—that was the point of his letter to me.

But it was Clarke's kind gesture that impressed David.

"Her instinct in that moment is not to turn a cold shoulder to him or express frustration or anger, all of which would have been understandable, but to put her hand on him. To touch him."

Compassion, the quality David Kaczynski saw in her, cannot by itself explain Judy Clarke. There is a steel in her that we don't ordinarily associate with kindness. In her interview with the alumni magazine, Clarke spoke of teaching students to act in the best interests of their client—and of "their cause." She said, "The idea is that we stand between the power of the state and the individual." If Clarke is compassionate and kind, she is also defiant and committed. This is no marshmallow.

Which may not be immediately apparent, to look at her. Says one old friend, "Her face has always reminded me of a sweet little forest animal," with small, pinched features and deep-set eyes. She is surprisingly tall and lean, a lifelong runner. She wears her straight brown hair short and flat. She eschews makeup and for court has always dressed in a perfectly sensible female version of standard lawyerly attire: a conventionally cut wool suit, a knee-length skirt, a jacket over a cotton shirt buttoned at the collar, and, for many years, a big floppy silk bow tie, which became her signature if only because most women stopped wearing them twenty years ago. Friends recently tried to talk her out of the bow ties, but she said she could not be bothered. Knowing exactly what to put on each morning saved her having to think about it, she explained, but in Boston during the early stages of the Tsarnaev trial the bow tie was gone, replaced by a black turtleneck or simply an open collar. Her manner, like her choice of clothing, is deliberately understated. In photos, she often looks pensive, even severe—eyes averted, mouth pursed—but her friends say she is the opposite in private: animated, with a warm sense of humor, someone who enjoys lifting a beer and telling a story, someone who laughs often. In court she is more earnest than clever. She impresses more with impeccable preparation and sincerity than with oratory. With judges and juries and before a classroom, her tone is conversational, genuine, and direct. She is, all in all, more inclined to listen than to speak.

And yet argument is a big part of her character. Judy Clarke grew up one of four children in Asheville, North Carolina, part of an extended family of Republicans fond of spirited disputation. Parents, grandparents, and siblings would gather for supper around a large custom-built oak table, where opinions kept easy pace with the corn bread and gravy. Her parents, Harry and Patsy, sometimes hosted John Birch Society meetings in their living room. They were strong supporters of the late North Carolina senator Jesse Helms until their youngest son, Mark, died of AIDS in 1994 and Helms, who was hateful on the subject of homosexuality, spurned an appeal from Patsy for more research funding to combat the disease, expressing sympathy for her in a return letter, but condemning Mark for having "played Russian roulette in his sexual activity." Patsy wasn't just hurt and angry. She cofounded an organization called "Mothers Against Jesse in Congress," which raised money and worked unsuccessfully to deny him reelection in 1997.

"We debated a lot in the family," Clarke told a reporter for the *Spokane* (Washington) *Spokesman-Review* in 1996. "We were very vocal, and we always took positions. . . . From about the sixth or seventh grade, I wanted to become either the chief justice of the Supreme Court or Perry Mason. One summer when I was young, my mother wanted to teach my sister [Candy] and me crocheting and the Constitution. She says that for my sister, the crocheting stuck, and for me, the Constitution stuck."

Judy and Candy had put the family's right-wing politics behind them before leaving home—they had both secretly voted for George McGovern in the 1972 presidential election. Judy migrated farther south to attend Furman University and then the University of South Carolina law school, and after graduating, in 1977, moved west to take a job with the public defender's office in San Diego, where she and her husband, Thomas H. "Speedy" Rice, also a lawyer and law professor, had decided they wanted to live. New lawyers were asked to sign a "blood letter" when they started, promising to work sixty-hour weeks, which for Clarke was apparently no stretch. Childless, she has earned a reputation through a long career for working heroically long hours and for pushing her staff with unrelenting, almost martial, discipline. She would eventually lead the public defender's office in San Diego, and later the one in Spokane, Washington, and as boss not only drove her staff hard at work but pushed them to adopt a regular fitness regimen away from it. Those so inclined were encouraged to join her at dawn for a daily four-mile run.

"I like to fight," she told the *Los Angeles Times* in 1990, when, as the San Diego public defender, she took a $50 fine for a misdemeanor related to smuggling aliens across the border all the way to the U.S. Supreme Court—*United States v. German Munoz-Flores*. In the end she lost the case, but she enjoyed the scrap. "I love the action," she said. "I like the antagonism. I like the adversarial nature of the business. I love all of that. I think that's the fun stuff. Especially when it's over an issue that I think is of significance to all of us, and that's our freedoms, our individual liberties."

To her, this devotion to civil liberties is deeply rooted in her conservative upbringing. She bristled, in that interview for the alumni magazine, at being characterized as a liberal. "I don't know but what my opinions have been the most conservative in the world," she said. "What does it take to be an absolute supporter of what the Constitution says? That's hardly liberal. I don't smoke dope. I don't snort cocaine. I'm not into drugs. You associate that with a liberal view of a lawyer. I'm not into that. . . . Yes, I am a defense lawyer but I think I have very conservative values."

Clarke first came to national attention in 1994, when she helped defend Susan Smith. After drowning her two small boys in a South Carolina lake, Smith made up a story for the police about having been carjacked by a "black man." She aggressively maintained the fiction for a week in television appearances, appealing for the boys' release.

Clarke and attorney Lesley "Lee" Coggiola met when Clarke showed up in Columbia to help with Smith's defense and needed a place to stay. Coggiola's daughter had just left for college, so she offered the vacated room. She also warned Clarke, "I have these teenage boys [four], and dogs [two] and cats [three]."

"Sounds great; I'll be there," said Clarke.

"So she moved in and lived with me off and on for that year," Coggiola recalled. "And the kids loved her and the dogs loved her and the cats loved her, and her husband, Speedy, came periodically and stayed there, and the trial consultant came and stayed there, and various law clerks came and stayed there. It was quite a year."

In the middle of it, a student from Cornell University showed up at the front door when Clarke was home alone. Coggiola had promised to provide housing, and then had forgotten about it. Clarke answered his knock.

"Well, come on in," she said. "We'll find a place."

During the months she spent with Coggiola, Clarke got up every morning for her run and then would be gone all day. Many evenings she didn't come back to the house until very late, as she and her team went about reconstructing their troubled client's past. This involved long hours of listening sympathetically to Smith in the county lockup, eliciting her story in excruciating detail, and then tracking down family members, old friends, first-grade teacher, second-grade teacher, Girl Scout troop leaders, and more. There was plenty to discover: Smith's biological father had committed suicide when she was six. She had been molested by her stepfather—an intimate relationship that had continued secretly into adult life and her marriage (a revelation that came as a terrible shock to Smith's mother). Smith had twice attempted suicide as a teenager. There had been multiple infidelities and splits with her husband. There was an ongoing affair with yet another man. There may have been no doubt, once the fiction of a black kidnapper was abandoned, that Smith had drowned her two small boys, but the story grew ever more complex. How could anyone, Clarke argued, fail to see reasons why Smith had so cruelly lost her bearings? In the months before trial, as Clarke lived upstairs in the busy Coggiola household with the teenagers and dogs and cats and law clerks, came selective leaks and interviews with sympathetic family members to the press, bits and pieces of Smith's troubled past, leaks that began to chip away at the image of Susan the monster and to reveal something more like Susan the victim.

Tommy Pope tracked all of this closely. He was the county prosecutor, solicitor for the Sixteenth Judicial Circuit (York and Union counties), no rube but a good old boy nevertheless, a man with a viscous local drawl serving the community where he had been born and raised, and where he now helped teach Sunday school and coach Little League. Clarke and her cocounsel, David Bruck, took Pope to school.

"I think I did an average job," Pope told me, looking back from the perspective of two decades. "I guess people expected dueling banjos and the redneck sheriff. . . . The bar was set so low that when Tommy here jumped over it they thought he was brilliant. But I am not a yin to their yang. I am not a death-penalty zealot. There are plenty of prosecutors that—I hate to say it is like a bloodlust, but you know what I mean: they've *got to get* the death penalty, *got to get* the death penalty. And I saw it as part of my job, almost like a soldier. Just because I have to go kill, does not mean I relish it. But again, I am not backing down from my duty either."

The way Pope saw it, if the Smith boys' father had drowned them, or if the story about a black carjacker had been true, then his community would have howled for the executioner. So was he supposed to go easy on Susan Smith because she was a pretty young white woman? How would that look? Besides, he saw Smith as a stone-cold killer, a promiscuous young wife who had betrayed her husband *and* her mother, who had sized up her children as obstacles to her future happiness with another man, and so she had killed them and then constructed an elaborate lie—acted out vividly in public—to cover her tracks.

He was not fully prepared for the complete focus and de-termination of Clarke and Bruck. In retrospect, he sees that he was outmaneuvered from the beginning, in ways large and small. "They really start way ahead of the courtroom," he said. "I was ready to try the case by January. In other words, three months after it happened, I was pretty much ready to go to trial. And they made some motions to say that they were not particularly ready, and we ended up trying it that summer." In retrospect, the delays proved critical for remaking the image of the accused. In the interim, Pope said, he felt honor-bound by his position not to comment on the case. Susan's defenders did not feel so bound. "I cannot answer publicly what Susan's mama says on *Dateline* the week before the trial," he said. He was surprised when Clarke did not ask the judge to move the trial from Union County; and he didn't seek a change of venue himself—only to realize later that nowhere had all of the leaked details of Smith's life story been more avidly consumed than at home, by the community that would deliver up her jury. He did not contest the defense request to bar cameras from the courtroom, fearing that if he argued for them he would be accused of grandstanding and trying to further his political career. (Pope has since been elected to the state legislature.) Looking back, he would love to have had cameras to catch how Smith giggled and played tic-tac-toe during the trial breaks, only to resume sniffling into a tissue when the jury was ushered back in. Once the trial began, there was no way for the death-seeking prosecutor to compete for geniality with Clarke's principled compassion, and she wasted no opportunity to make the contrast plain.

"I think she and David probably played a little good cop–bad cop kind of thing," Pope told me. "In other words, he was kind of softer-spoken; she was more aggressive. Like when she would make statements, she would come over and kind of bang on our table and look us in the eye, all for dramatic effect I am sure."

Coggiola remembers a moment in the trial when Pope, whose disdain for Smith was palpable, and who can be caustic, said or snorted something dismissive as a defense witness grew weepy on the stand. Clarke turned and glared at him "Shame on you," she said.

"I just remember us doing the glare down at each other," he recalled.

Clarke made an impassioned plea to the jury on Smith's behalf, according to the 1996 *Spokesman-Review* story, arguing, "This is not a case about evil. This is a case about despair and sadness." She conceded that Smith had made bad choices and bad decisions: "Her choices were irrational and her decisions were tragic. She made a horrible, horrible decision to be at that lake that night. She made that decision with a confused mind and a heart without hope. But confusion is not evil, and hopelessness is not malice."

In the end, Pope lost. And he is not surprised he lost. He respects Clarke's skills as a lawyer, but calls her what he says he is not, a "zealot." She brought a level of determination he could not match, and a willingness to do whatever it took to save her client. Smith was sentenced to life in prison, which, Pope is quick to point out, will not actually *mean* life in prison, because under South Carolina law she will be eligible for parole in 2024.

There were such hard feelings in South Carolina over the carpetbagger defender's success in this case, Clarke's Carolina roots notwithstanding, that some in the state legislature sought to ban payments to out-of-town lawyers in such cases. Clarke promptly returned her court-awarded fee—$82,944.

Judy Clarke spoke last April at a small legal symposium in Los Angeles. She declined to answer questions from the audience, and according to a news report, was "reticent" throughout. But she referred back to the Susan Smith case, noting that it was the reason she had been "sucked into the black hole, the vortex" of death-penalty cases.

"I got a dose of understanding human behavior and I learned what the death penalty does to us," she said. Clarke argued that most of those who commit heinous acts "have suffered from severe trauma, unbelievable trauma. We know that from brain research. Many suffer from severe cognitive development issues that affect the core of their being." In other words, "most" of those who commit these terrible crimes, the worst of the worst, are not evil; they are *sick*.

She is not alone in thinking this way. Dr. Dorothy Otnow Lewis, a professor of psychiatry at New York University, has been studying inmates on death row for years. In her 1998 book *Guilty by Reason of Insanity*, and in medical journals since, she argues that on death row a history of brain trauma and of mental illness is a constant. One study of fifteen death-row inmates that she conducted with Dr. Jonathan H. Pincus, chief of neurology at the Veterans Administration hospital in Washington, found that every one of them had suffered head injuries in childhood or had received brain injuries in violent assaults. Her work is not considered to inhabit an obscure or extreme scholarly fringe. It has been cited by the Supreme Court three times, most notably in a 1992 dissent by Justice Thurgood Marshall in a decision that allowed the execution of a brain-damaged killer, Ricky Ray Rector.

The insanity defense has been around for many centuries, and has long turned on whether the accused was capable of understanding what he was doing. A person who killed while sleep-walking, say, or in the grip of a profound hallucination, would not be guilty of having knowingly committed a crime. A mind lost to dementia or retardation may well be incapable of telling the difference between right and wrong, or realistically weighing the consequences of a decision. Over the centuries, criminal justice has embraced ever-wider reasons to avoid execution. The definition of "not guilty by reason of insanity" was broadened in the twentieth century to include crimes that grow out of mental illness—in other words, acts that would not have been committed were it not for the underlying pathology (a schizophrenic, say, goaded to kill by the voices in his head, or any deranged soul whose tormented truth somehow justifies the taking of a life). In her talk in Los Angeles, Clarke seemed to expand the definition further when she suggested that the most terrible killings are themselves an expression of deep mental damage—insanity is inherent in the crime, because only someone with "severe cognitive-development issues" would commit it. We cannot judge her clients, she argues, without fully inhabiting their heads. To comprehend the affliction is to understand the crime. So she had Kaczynski's tiny cabin disassembled and shipped to Colorado, and had he gone to trial, she planned to have it reassembled so that jurors could literally walk around inside her client's starkly isolated home, if not his mind.

The *New York Times* reported at the end of last year that the death penalty in the United States was in "broad decline," a pattern some believe reflects a growing societal rejection of the practice. Only nine states put one or more people to death last year, despite the fact that in polls a (declining) majority of Americans still favor execution for the most serious crimes. Gallup polls show that since the early 1990s there has been both a steady fall in support for execution and a steady rise in opposition to it. Thirty-two states still have capital punishment on their books, though the number is shrinking. Activist opponents of the death penalty, like Clarke, have raised the bar so high that many states are opting not to pursue the death penalty, for purely practical reasons: they cite the enormous and mounting expense of contesting seemingly endless appeals, and the difficulty in establishing a "humane" method of putting the condemned to death. But it's doubtful, even if we stop executing people in the United States, that we will settle the deeper question: Are those who kill sick, or are they simply evil?

If Judy Clarke has an opposite number, it would be Jacabed Rodriguez-Coss of the U.S. Justice Department's Capital Case Unit, which, among other things, provides help for U.S. attorneys who pursue the death penalty. When I suggested to Rodriguez-Coss that if Clarke was the angel of life, she might be considered the angel of death, she was justifiably horrified. She could not imagine the side of justice being so characterized. The prosecutor's job goes beyond the defense attorney's, she says: the prosecutor's responsibility is to the entire community, to see that justice is done.

The question of evil versus illness cleanly divides the legal community. It even divides the U.S. Justice Department, where today prosecutors like Rodriguez-Coss, who professionally supports the death penalty, may find themselves at odds with colleagues and supervisors who are ambivalent toward it, if not outright opposed. Those who support capital punishment are quick to acknowledge that some defendants *are* sick enough to lack the ability to appreciate the consequences of their actions. But that hardly includes a killer like Kaczynski, who brought exceptional intelligence and deliberation to his murders, and who was quite ready to step forward and take credit for them once he was caught. Here was a man who had freely chosen wrong over right, who had with great deliberation assigned greater importance to his own objectives than to the lives of those targeted by his mail bombs. Indeed, in his journals, Kaczynski gloated over the "success" of his murderous mailings, which he would read about in newspapers.

If the act itself were proof of insanity, then no one could be executed, which is, of course, Clarke's intent. It allows us to believe that all people are essentially good, and that they do very bad things only when their brains misfire. If this is true, then it directly contradicts our primary cultural traditions, if not common sense. Christianity and traditional Judaism teach that all men are born sinful and need redemption. Humanists regard civilization as the remedy for our savage nature. The impulse to regard horrible criminals as "crazy" is common enough, but from a prosecutor's perspective it's also a cop-out. If punishing crime is a solemn social responsibility, then the worst crimes deserve the worst penalty. If you believe perfectly sane men are capable of doing horrible things, then the problem isn't always illness. Sometimes it's evil.

Of course, accepting that there is evil in the hearts of men does not necessarily mean one endorses the death penalty. There are those who oppose it on moral grounds (the two-wrongs argument); on practical grounds (statistics do not show that executing killers deters murder); or on simple philosophical grounds (a flawed criminal justice system should not be empowered to carry out a final, irrevocable punishment—inevitably, mistakes will be made). I happen to agree with this last point. So does attorney general Eric Holder. Clarke may well agree with all of them. But she is less interested in winning any particular legal or philosophical argument than in actually staying the executioner's hand, whatever it takes.

The prosecutors I interviewed for this story respect her legal talent, which stands out even among the exceptionally talented and dedicated community of public defenders across the country who regard Clarke as a hero. Together they have played a huge role in slowing down capital punishment. But the lion's share of the credit, proponents of the death penalty say, goes to the courts. The Supreme Court had imposed a moratorium in 1970, ruling that the death penalty was being imposed in an arbitrary manner and in ways that violated the Eighth Amendment, which forbids "cruel and unusual punishments." For state courts, the moratorium was lifted in 1976, when the Court ruled that revised state death-penalty laws instituting more safeguards for defendants had remedied the constitutional issues. Gary Gilmore went before a firing squad in Utah a year later. Congress reinstated the federal death penalty in 1988, adopting many of the new state practices, notably the bifurcated trial system that considers guilt and punishment separately. Even so, the willingness of courts under the new regime to drag out the process, post-conviction, has turned litigation of the death penalty into such a thicket that few prosecutors, state or federal, are willing to enter. Since 1988, only three people have been put to death by federal authorities—Timothy McVeigh, who bombed the federal building in Oklahoma; Juan Raul Garza, a drug smuggler who was convicted of three killings; and Louis Jones Jr., convicted of sexually assaulting and then murdering a young woman.

Despite the attorney general's personal opposition, the Justice Department decided in January to seek the death penalty once more in the Tsarnaev case. If her past pattern holds, Clarke is already deep into developing a sympathetic relationship with the young man, and is diligently assembling his life story. She has already successfully petitioned the federal court in Boston to ease the conditions of his confinement, and has tried repeatedly (most recently without success), to change the trial venue and push back the date until later in 2015. There is no sign that Clarke or her defense team had anything to do with it, but a long, extraordinarily detailed, and sympathetic account of the younger Tsarnaev's life has appeared in *Rolling Stone* magazine, complete with a softly lit, romantic portrait of the big-eyed killer on the cover. By now Judy Clarke has no doubt become Dzhokhar Tsarnaev's best and perhaps only friend in the wide world.

But what if his fuller story contradicts her central premise? From what we know now, Tsarnaev does not appear to have been mentally unstable. He seems to have been a very ordinary, dope-smoking, cell-phone-toting American teenager. He was an especially beloved member of a financially troubled but hard-working and law-abiding immigrant family in Cambridge. Of them all, he had made the smoothest transition to American life, spoke nearly unaccented English, had a wide circle of friends, and had even become a naturalized citizen. He won a college scholarship and appeared to have a bright future. He apparently fell under the influence of his violent and powerful older brother, Tamerlan, his alleged associate in the bombing, who was killed in a shootout with Boston police; but there is plenty of evidence that the younger Tsarnaev's murderous choices were rational and deliberate, from his deepening identification with Islam and his growing anti-Americanism to his expressed approval of terrorism as an appropriate response to American military attacks on Muslims that he presumed unjust. Tsarnaev's choices were dark and increasingly extreme, but he is hardly the only young Muslim in these times to have made them. Are they all crazy?

Tsarnaev showed no hint of his state of mind during the jury selection portion of his trial. He sat at the defense side of the table scribbling notes that were passed to no one, fiddling with small scraps of paper, and gazing off into space. He looked like a bored teenager doing detention in the principal's office. But what if he does resist, as Kaczynski did, being portrayed in whatever light Clarke believes will afford his best defense? What if Tsarnaev really meant the bloody screed he drew on the inside of the boat on April 19, 2013, as he hid from police, the complete text of which has not been made public, but which reportedly justified the marathon bombing as retribution for the deaths of innocent Muslims—"When you attack one Muslim, you attack all Muslims"—included the phrase "Fuck America," and saluted his brother's martyrdom. What if the younger Tsarnaev now seeks the end?

At that point he will discover that Judy Clarke, his lawyer, his new best friend, while never leaving his side, never raising her voice or losing an ounce of compassion, may prove to be the most formidable obstacle in his path.

The Angriest Man in Television

Atlantic, January/February 2008

Behold the Hack, the veteran newsman, wise beyond his years, a man who's seen it all, twice. He's honest, knowing, cynical; his occasional bitterness is leavened with humor. He's a friend to the little scam, and a scourge of the big one. Experience has acquainted him with suffering and stupidity, venality and vice. His anger is softened by the sure knowledge of his own futility. And now behold David Simon, the mind behind the brilliant HBO series *The Wire*. A gruff fireplug of a man, balding and big-featured, he speaks with an earthy, almost theatrical bluntness, and his blue-collar crust belies his comfortable suburban upbringing. He's for all the world the quintessential Hack, down to his ink-stained fingertips—the kind of old newshound who will remind you that a "journalist" is a dead reporter. But Simon takes the cliché one step further; he's an old newsman who feels betrayed by newspapers themselves.

For all his success and accomplishment, he's an angry man, driven in part by lovingly nurtured grudges against those he feels have slighted him, underestimated him, or betrayed some public trust. High on this list is his old employer the *Baltimore Sun*—or more precisely, the editors and corporate owners who have (in his view) spent the past two decades eviscerating a great American newspaper. In a better world—one where papers still had owners and editors who were smart, socially committed, honest, and brave—Simon probably would never have left the *Sun* to pursue a Hollywood career. His father, a frustrated newsman, took him to see Ben Hecht and Charles MacArthur's classic newspaper farce, *The Front Page*, when he was a boy in Washington, D.C., and Simon was smitten. He landed a job as a *Sun* reporter just out of the University of Maryland in the early 1980s, and as he tells it, if the newspaper, the industry, and America had lived up to his expectations, he would probably still be documenting the underside of his adopted city one byline at a time. But the *Sun* let David Simon down.

So he has done something that many reporters only dream about. He has created his own Baltimore. With the help of his chief collaborator, Ed Burns, a former Baltimore cop and school-teacher; a stable of novelists and playwrights with a feel for urban drama (including George Pelecanos, Richard Price, and Dennis Lehane); a huge cast of master actors; and a small army of film professionals shooting on location—in the city's blighted row-house neighborhoods and housing projects, at city hall, at nightclubs, at police headquarters, in the suburbs, in the snazzy Inner Harbor, at the working docks—he has, over four seasons, conjured the city onscreen with a verisimilitude that's astonishing. Marylanders scrutinize the plot for its allusions to real people and real events. Parallels with recent local political history abound, and the details of life in housing projects and on street corners seem spookily authentic. (A New York City narcotics detective who loves the show told me a few years ago that street gangs in Brooklyn were watching it to learn tactics for avoiding cell-phone intercepts.)

Despite the show's dark portrait of "Bodymore, Murdaland," local officialdom has embraced *The Wire*, giving Simon and his cast and crew free rein, opening up municipal buildings, and cordoning off outdoor spaces. Many prominent citizens, including Baltimore's former mayor Kurt Schmoke and Maryland's former governor Robert Ehrlich, have made cameo appearances. The dress, manners, and colorful language of the show's cast, which is largely African American, are painstakingly authentic, down to the uniquely slurred consonants and nasal vowel sounds of the local dialect, Balmerese. *The Wire* seems so real that I find myself, a Baltimore native, looking for the show's characters when I pass through their familiar haunts.

The show hasn't been a big commercial success. It's never attracted a viewership to rival that of an HBO tent-pole series, like *The Sopranos* or even the short-lived *Deadwood*. It isn't seen as a template for future TV dramas, primarily because its form more or less demands that each season be watched from the beginning. Whereas each episode of *The Sopranos* advanced certain overarching plot points but was essentially self-contained, anyone who tries to plumb the complexities of *The Wire* by tuning in at mid-season is likely to be lost. If the standard Hollywood feature is the film equivalent of a short story, each season of Simon's show is a twelve- or thirteen-chapter novel.

Some years ago, Tom Wolfe called on novelists to abandon the cul-de-sac of modern "literary" fiction, which he saw as self-absorbed, thumb-sucking gamesmanship, and instead to revive social realism, to take up as a subject the colossal, astonishing, and terrible pageant of contemporary America. I doubt he imagined that one of the best responses to this call would be a TV program, but the boxed sets blend nicely on a bookshelf with the great novels of American history.

As *The Wire* unveiled its fourth season in 2006, Jacob Weisberg of Slate, in a much-cited column, called it "the best TV show ever broadcast in America." The *New York Times*, in an editorial (not a review, mind you) called the show Dickensian. I agree with both assessments. "*Wire*-world," as Simon calls it, does for turn-of-the-millennium Baltimore what Dickens's *Bleak House* does for mid-nineteenth-century London. Dickens takes the byzantine bureaucracy of the law and the petty corruptions of the legal profession; borrows from the neighborhoods, manners, dress, and language of the Chancery courts and the Holborn district; and builds from them a world that breathes. Similarly, *The Wire* creates a vision of official Baltimore as a heavy, self-justified bureaucracy, gripped by its own byzantine logic and criminally unconcerned about the lives of ordinary people, who enter it at their own risk. One of the clever early conceits of the show was to juxtapose the organizational problems of the city police department with those of the powerful drug gang controlling trafficking in the slums of the city's west side. The heads of both organizations, official and criminal, wrestle with similar management and personnel issues, and resolve them with similarly cold self-interest. In both the department and the gang, the powerful exploit the weak, and within the ranks those who exhibit dedication, talent, and loyalty are usually punished for their efforts.

There are heroes in *The Wire*, but they're flawed and battered. The show's most exceptional police officers, detectives Jimmy McNulty and Lester Freamon, find their initiative and talent punished at almost every turn. Their determination to do good, original work disturbs the department's upper echelons, where people are heavily invested in maintaining the status quo and in advancing their own careers. The clash repeatedly lands both of them in hot water—or cold water; at the end of the first season, the seasickness-prone McNulty is banished to the city's marine unit. What success the two attain against Baltimore's most powerful criminals is partial, compromised, and achieved despite stubborn and often creative official resistance.

One measure of the complexity of Simon's vision is that the powerful obstructionists in *The Wire* aren't simply evil people, the way they might have been in a standard Hollywood movie. While some are just inept or corrupt, most are smart and ambitious, sometimes even interested in doing good, but concerned first and foremost with their next promotion or a bigger paycheck. They are fiercely territorial, to a degree that interferes with real police work. In the premiere episode, the very idea of a separate squad to target the leadership of the city's powerful drug gangs—which one would assume to be a high lawenforcement priority—is opposed by the police department. It's imposed on the commissioner by order of a local judge, who's outraged when a witness at a murder trial in his courtroom fearfully recants her testimony on the stand. To spite the judge, the commissioner staffs the unit with castoffs from various police divisions. Some of the castoffs are so alcoholic or corrupt they're useless, but some—like the lesbian detective Shakima Greggs; or the patient, wise Freamon; or the ballsy, streetwise McNulty—are castoffs precisely because of their ability. In Simon's world, excellence is a ticket out the door.

In one of the show's most interesting set pieces, a remarkable police major, "Bunny" Colvin, frustrated by the absurdity of the city's useless drug war, conducts a novel experiment. Without the knowledge of his superiors, he effectively legalizes drugs in West Baltimore, creating a mini-Amsterdam, dubbed "Hamsterdam," where all of the corner dealers are allowed to set up shop. By consolidating drug dealing, which he knows he cannot stop anyway, Colvin eliminates the daily turf battles that drive up the murder rates and dramatically improves life in most of his district. Calm returns to terrorized neighborhoods, and his patrolmen, freed from their cars and the endless pursuit of drug-dealing corner boys, return to real police work, walking beats, getting to know the people they serve. The sharp drop in his district crime stats shocks the department's leadership and makes Colvin's peers jealous—and suspicious. They assume he's cooking the books.

Again, it's a tribute to the depth of Simon's imagination that this experiment isn't presented as a cure-all. He doesn't minimize the moral compromise inherent in Hamsterdam. Many addicts see their severe health problems worsen, and the drug-dealing zone becomes a haven for vice of all kinds. Decent people in the community are horrified by the officially sanctioned criminality and the tolerance of destructive addiction. The unauthorized experiment ends ignobly when news of it reaches the ears of a *Sun* reporter. City Hall reacts to the story with predictable horror, scurrying and spinning to escape blame. Colvin loses his job, and the city goes back to the old war, which is useless but politically acceptable.

Story lines like these reflect the truth about Baltimore; Mayor Schmoke's own promising political career crashed and burned some years ago when he had the temerity to suggest a less punitive approach to the city's drug problem. But they don't reflect the complete truth: like Dickens's London, Simon's Baltimore is a richly imagined caricature of its real-life counterpart, not a carbon copy. And precisely because the Baltimore in *The Wire* seems so real, down to the finest details, the show constitutes an interesting study in the difference between journalism and fiction. Simon's first book, *Homicide*, was a critically acclaimed work of nonfiction, from which some of the themes, characters, and even stories of *The Wire* are drawn. (It was also the basis for the 1990s NBC show *Homicide: Life on the Street*.) Which raises the question—if your subject is the real world, why deal in fiction?

The answer has something to do with Simon's own passions and his deeply held political beliefs. "I *am* someone who's very angry with the political structure," he said in a long 2006 interview with Slate. "The show is written in a twenty-first-century city-state that is incredibly bureaucratic, and in which a legal pursuit of an unenforceable prohibition [the war on drugs] has created great absurdity." To Simon, *The Wire* is about "the very simple idea that, in this postmodern world of ours, human beings—all of us—are worth less. We're worth less every day, despite the fact that some of us are achieving more and more. It's the triumph of capitalism. Whether you're a corner boy in West Baltimore, or a cop who knows his beat, or an eastern European brought here for sex, your life is worth less. It's the triumph of capitalism over human value. This country has embraced the idea that this is a viable domestic policy. It is. It's viable for the few. But I don't live in Westwood, LA, or on the Upper West Side of New York. I live in Baltimore."

This is a message—a searing attack on the excesses of Big Capitalism—that rarely finds its way into prime-time entertainment on national TV. It's audacious. But it's also relentlessly . . . well, *bleak*. "I am struck by how dark the show is," says Elijah Anderson, the Yale sociologist whose classic works *Code of the Street*, *Streetwise*, and *A Place on the Corner* document black inner-city life with notable clarity and sympathy. Anderson would be the last person to gloss over the severe problems of the urban poor, but in *The Wire* he sees "a bottom-line cynicism" that is at odds with his own perception of real life. "The show is very good," he says. "It resonates. It is powerful in its depiction of the codes of the streets, but it is an exaggeration. I get frustrated watching it, because it gives such a powerful appearance of reality, but it always seems to leave something important out. What they have left out are the decent people. Even in the worst drug-infested projects, there are many, many God-fearing, churchgoing, brave people who set themselves against the gangs and the addicts, often with remarkable heroism."

This bleakness is Simon's stamp on the show, and it suggests that his political passions ultimately trump his commitment to accuracy or evenhandedness. The imagination, values, and convictions of a writer play a big part in even the most accurate nonfiction, of course. Telling a true story well demands that the reporter achieve his own understanding of the events and people described, and arriving at that point can mean shading reality, even if only unconsciously. We view the world from where we sit. Truman Capote, in his nonfiction classic, *In Cold Blood*, finds a clue to the motives of the murderers, Perry Smith and Dick Hickock, in unrequited or unconscious homosexual desire. Norman Mailer's preoccupation with mystical themes gives the senseless killer Gary Gilmore a romantic aura in *The Executioner's Song*. In *The Right Stuff*, Tom Wolfe's fascination with masculinity and social status allows him to cast the early space program as a prolonged reprise of ancient single-combat rituals. In each case, the author's unique perspective gives a "true" story a starkly original shape.

But the more passionate your convictions, the harder it is to resist tampering with the contradictions and stubborn messiness of real life. Every reporter knows the sensation of having a story "ruined" by some new and surprising piece of information. Just when you think you have the thing figured out, you learn something that shatters your carefully wrought vision. Being surprised is the essence of good reporting. But it's also the moment when a dishonest writer is tempted to fudge, for the sake of commercial success—and a more honest writer like Simon, whose passion is political and personal, is tempted to shift his energies to fiction.

Which is precisely what he's done. Simon is the reporter who knows enough about Baltimore to have his story all figured out, but instead of risking the coherence of that vision by doing what reporters do—heading back out day after day to observe, to ask more questions, to take more notes—he has stopped reporting and started inventing. He says, *I have figured this thing out*. He offers up his undisturbed vision, leaving out the things that don't fit, adding things that emphasize its fundamentals, and then using the trappings of realism to dress it up and bring it to life onscreen.

The essential difference between writing nonfiction and writing fiction is that the artist owns his vision, while the journalist can never really claim one, or at least cannot claim a complete one—because the real world is infinitely complex and ever changing. Art frees you from the infuriating unfinishedness of the real world. For this reason, the very clarity of well-wrought fiction can sometimes make it *feel* more real than reality. As a film producer once told me, "It's important not to let the facts get in the way of the truth."

Fiction can explain things that journalism cannot. It allows you to enter the lives and motivations of characters with far more intimacy than is typically possible in nonfiction. In the case of *The Wire*, fiction allows you to wander around inside a violent, criminal subculture, and inside an entrenched official bureaucracy, in a way that most reporters can only dream about. And it frees you from concerns about libel and cruelty. It frees you to be unfair.

In a session before a live audience in Baltimore last April, for a local storytelling series called The Stoop, Simon was asked to speak on the topic "My Nemesis." He began by reciting, by name, some of the people he holds grudges against, going all the way back to grade school. He was being humorous, and the audience was laughing, but anyone who knows him knows that his monologue was, like his fiction, slightly overstated for effect, but basically the truth.

"I keep these names, I treasure them," he said. "I will confess to you now that anything I have ever accomplished as a writer, as somebody doing TV, as anything I have ever done in life down to, like, cleaning up my room, has been accomplished because I was going to show people that they were fucked up and wrong and that I was the fucking center of the universe, and the sooner they got hip to that, the happier they would all be. . . . That's what's going on in my head."

This vindictive streak, this desire to show people how wrong they are, is tempered somewhat by Simon's sense of humor and his appreciation for complexity, and by the vision of his many skillful collaborators. But in the show's final season, which debuts in January, Simon will revisit the part of Baltimore that's closest to his heart, the *Sun*. The season, more than any other before it, will reflect his personal experience. Given his long memory and his inclination to settle old scores, the difference between fiction and fact will be of particular interest to his former colleagues.

The newspaper's management rightly viewed Simon's intentions with trepidation, but given that city hall and the governor's mansion embraced his jaundiced vision, how could the fourth estate refuse to open its doors? So the *Sun* has allowed the show to use its name and even to build an exact replica of its newsroom so that Simon and his company can flesh out their story line with greater authenticity. It isn't going to be a comfortable ride, because Simon is apparently set to exorcise some personal demons. His vision of Baltimore was shaped largely by his work as a crime reporter, and it seems likely that his anger about capitalism and the devaluation of human life is rooted in his unhappy experience at the *Sun*.

A famous quote from the great Sun Papers columnist H. L. Mencken is reprinted in large type on the wall of the spacious lobby in the newspaper's building on Calvert Street: "As I look back over a misspent life, I find myself more and more convinced that I had more fun doing news reporting than in any other enterprise. It is really the life of kings."

It was this promise, this "life of kings," that animated Simon and many other reporters who started in the business twenty years ago.

"I love this place," Simon told the audience at The Stoop last April, speaking of his frame of mind at age twenty-two, when he was starting his career as a *Sun* reporter:

This is the place of H. L. Mencken, of Frank Kent, of William Manchester. It's like you can touch things that you can be proud of. I just have to do good work for its own sake. . . . I'm basically happy, and it's like the least ambitious I am in my life. Until . . . it gets sold out of town. And these guys come in from Philly. The white guys from Philly. And I say that with all the contempt you can muster for the phrase white guys. *Soulless motherfuckers. Everything that Malcolm X said in that book before he got converted back to humanity—no, no, he was right in the first place. These guys were so without humanity. And it was the kind of journalism—how do I describe bad journalism? It's not that it's lazy, it's that whenever they hear the word Pulitzer, they become tumescent. They become engorged. . . . All they wanted to do was win prizes. . . . I watched them single-handedly destroy the* Sun.

The "white guys" Simon so viciously abused in this talk (and not for the first time) were William Marimow and John Carroll, notable newspapermen who are my friends; Marimow was a longtime colleague of mine at the *Philadelphia Inquirer.* He eventually left the *Sun* in conflict over newsroom cutbacks with its corporate owners (originally the Times-Mirror Corporation, which was absorbed by the Tribune Company in 2000) and went on to head the news division of National Public Radio. Last year, Marimow returned to helm the *Inquirer,* a newspaper where he had earlier won two Pulitzer Prizes for reporting. Carroll became editor in chief of the *Los Angeles Times,* resigned defending the newsroom there, and is now at Harvard University. Both have impeccable reputations in their field, and I hold them both in high esteem. Simon hates them.

He hates them in part because they were agents of change at the *Sun,* the institution he loved, initiating a process familiar in newsrooms all over the country. Just as the efforts of great detectives like McNulty and Freamon are neither valued nor supported by their bosses, many superb reporters and editors at the *Sun*, and with them the paper's higher mission, were betrayed by the corporate pursuit of profit margins. Marimow and Carroll were for a time agents of that process, an unpleasant role that many fine newspaper editors have found themselves in during the past decade. Yet to Simon they are all the more culpable because they didn't publicly object to a talent drain that he felt devastated the newsroom. There's nothing unique about the situation. The sad story is familiar to newspaper people all over the country. (I watched it happen at the *Inquirer*, where Knight-Ridder threw just about everyone and everything of value overboard before bailing out of journalism altogether.)

Some of us chalk up this trend to market forces, to the evolution of information technology, to television, radio, and the Internet. At the long-since-departed *Baltimore News-American*, where I worked before being hired at the *Inquirer*, we used to joke that people didn't read our newspaper; they *played* it. The paper was full of number and word games, along with sports scores, racetrack results, TV listings, comics, want ads, and advertisements with clippable coupons. One by one, these multifarious reasons why people used to buy newspapers have been cherry-picked by newer media; that includes the paper's most basic offering— breaking news, whose headlines are now available on most cell phones. Declining circulation means declining advertising, which means declining revenues, so corporate managers face a tougher and tougher challenge maintaining the high profit margins that attracted investors thirty years ago. These are just facts, and different people and organizations have handled them with different measures of grace and understanding.

But to Simon, this complex process became personal, boiling down to corporate greed and the "soullessness" of Marimow and Carroll. It's an honest opinion, but arguably unfair, flavored by personal bitterness and animosity. (Simon told a writer from *American Journalism Review* that he was angered by the paper's unwillingness to grant him a raise after he returned from a leave of absence in 1995—he was writing *The Corner*—and he took a buyout six months later.) Given his vindictive strain, his talent for character and drama, and the national TV show at his disposal, such an opinion is also a combustible one.

I should note here that it isn't hard to join Simon's enemies list; I did it myself while writing this essay. I first contacted Simon several years ago, as a fan of his show and as a screenwriter and aspiring producer interested in learning more about him and how he'd created it. He was friendly and helpful, and I remain grateful. Then in 2006, after the fourth season of *The Wire*, I decided to write a tribute to Simon and his show. I contacted him by e-mail to see about renewing our conversation on different terms, and he consented. He asked me to avoid writing about his personal life, and I agreed. I was determined, as well, to avoid discussing his dispute with Marimow and Carroll, since I liked and admired both parties, and was disinclined to choose sides.

When I discovered, after my last conversation with Simon, that the final season of the show would be based on his experiences at the *Sun*, I felt compelled to describe the dispute, but I resolved to characterize it without *entering* it. To avoid exploiting anything that had passed informally between us on the subject, I relied on Simon's ample public commentary to explain his feelings, and then, realizing that the essay had strayed in an unanticipated direction, showed him an early draft to solicit corrections and criticism. I got it. The draft provoked a series of angry, long-winded accusations, which would have remained private had he not taken his complaints to the *Atlantic*'s editor, in an angry letter impugning my motives in contacting him originally, and characterizing all our interactions as my attempt to win his confidence in order to skewer him on behalf of my friends. I could see myself morphing into a character in his show.

Simon has already given Marimow's name to a character in *The Wire*, a repellent police department toady who, in the hilarious words of the show's Sergeant Jay Landsman, "doesn't cast off talent lightly, he heaves it away with great force." But this was just a minor swipe; the final season of *The Wire* will offer Simon the chance to take on his old enemies from the *Sun* directly. An article that appeared in the October 2000 issue of *Brill's Content* hinted at the tack he may take and went to the core of what he says are his objections to the pair. It featured Simon, then five years removed from the paper and well into his enormously successful second career, making the case that a widely respected *Sun* reporter, protected by Carroll and Marimow, was making up stories and distorting the truth in a hell-bent effort to turn a series on lead-paint poisoning into a competitive Pulitzer submission. Simon felt the editors, in an effort to bolster their new star, purposefully ignored the misgivings of some of the newspaper's veteran reporters. To the editors, it was a case of an aggressive reporter who had made a few mistakes in pursuit of an important story. To Simon, it was an example of all that was wrong with the remade newspaper, and a reminder of the clash over journalistic values that had led him to quit in the first place. In his mind, the *Sun* had also abandoned its mission to really cover Baltimore, and was now fiddling while the city burned. Instead of exploring the root causes of the city's intractable problems—drug abuse and the government's unenforceable "war" against it; racism; poverty; rampant Big Capitalism—the newspaper was engaged in a largely self-congratulatory crusade to right a minor wrong.

Sure enough, in the upcoming season one story line deals with a newspaper's muckraking campaign on homelessness. It's probably been crafted to represent Simon's take on a typical Carroll-Marimow project: motivated less by a sincere desire for social reform than by a zeal for Pulitzer Prizes. (The paper did, incidentally, win three Pulitzers under the editors' guidance. Normally, in the newspaper world, this is considered a triumph, but for Simon it just adds bitter spice to an already bad dish.) And whereas the *Brill's* reporter who wrote the story was painstakingly evenhanded, Simon's fictional version of events will carry no such journalistic burden.

Apart from the distress it causes the real people behind his sometimes thinly veiled depictions, there's nothing necessarily wrong with this. It's how an artist shapes a fictional drama out of his own experience. Simon is entitled to his take on things, entitled to exploit his memory and experience, his anger and sense of betrayal, just as he exploited his cynicism and political outrage about official Baltimore in the show's first four seasons. Indeed, given the richness and power of his vision in *The Wire*, we ought to be grateful for his unforgiving nature. The kind of reporting he felt could no longer be done at the *Sun* he has brought to the screen. But his fiction shouldn't be mistaken for fact. It reflects, as much as anything, Simon's own prejudices.

In my decades in newsrooms, I encountered my share of hard-core skeptics like Simon, but those resembling the stereotypical Hack were the exceptions. The more true stories you tell, the more acquainted you are with suffering, stupidity, venality, and vice. But you're also more acquainted with selflessness, courage, and decency. Old reporters and editors are softened by knowledge and experience. If anything, they become less inclined to suspect or condemn. They encounter incompetence more often than evil, and they see that very few people who screw up do so in ways that are indefensible. After years of drumming up the other side of the story, old reporters are likely to grow less angry and opinionated, not more.

In that sense only, David Simon may be truer to the stereotype than the stereotype is true.

The Measured Man

Atlantic, July/August 2012

Like many people who are careful about their weight, Larry Smarr once spent two weeks measuring everything he put in his mouth. He charted each serving of food in grams or teaspoons, and broke it down into these categories: protein, carbohydrates, fat, sodium, sugar, and fiber.

Larry used the data to fine-tune his diet. With input nailed down, he turned to output. He started charting the calories he burns, in workouts on an elliptical trainer and in the steps he takes each day. If the number on his pedometer falls short of his prescribed daily seven thousand, he will find an excuse to go for a walk. Picture a tall, slender man with the supple, slightly deflated look of someone who has lost a lot of weight, plodding purposefully in soft shoes along the sunny sidewalks of La Jolla, California.

Of course, where outputs are concerned, calories are only part of the story, and it is here that Larry begins to differ from your typical health nut. Because human beings also produce waste products, foremost among them . . . well, poop. Larry collects his and has it analyzed. He is deep into the biochemistry of his feces, keeping detailed charts of their microbial contents. Larry has even been known to haul carefully boxed samples out of his kitchen refrigerator to show incautious visitors. He is eloquent on the subject. He could *sell* the stuff.

"Have you ever figured how information-rich your stool is?" Larry asks me with a wide smile, his gray-green eyes intent behind rimless glasses. "There are about 100 billion bacteria per gram. Each bacterium has DNA whose length is typically one to ten megabases—call it 1 million bytes of information. This means human stool has a data capacity of 100,000 terabytes of information stored per gram. That's many orders of magnitude more information density than, say, in a chip in your smartphone or your personal computer. So your stool is far more interesting than a computer."

Larry's fascination is less with feces themselves than with the data they yield. He is not a doctor or a biochemist; he's a computer scientist—one of the early architects of the Internet, in fact. Today he directs a world-class research center on two University of California campuses—San Diego and Irvine—called the California Institute for Telecommunications and Information Technology, or Calit2 (the 2 represents the repeated initial *I* and *T*). The future is arriving faster at Calit2 than it is in most places. Larry says his eyes are focused "ten years ahead," which in computer terms is more like a century or two, given how rapidly the machines are transforming modern life. Intent on that technological horizon, Larry envisions a coming revolution in medicine, and he is bringing his intellect and his institute to bear on it.

At sixty-three, he is engaged in a computer-aided study of the human body—specifically, *his* body. It's the start of a process that he believes will help lead, within ten years, to the development of "a distributed planetary computer of enormous power," one that is composed of a billion processors and will enable scientists to create, among many other things, a working computational model of your body. Your particular body, mind you, not just some generalized atlas of the human frame, but a working model of your unique corpus, grounded in your own genome, and—using data collected by nanosensors and transmitted by smartphone—refreshed continually with measurements from your body's insides. This information stream will be collated with similar readings from millions of other similarly monitored bodies all over the planet. Mining this enormous database, software will produce detailed guidance about diet, supplements, exercise, medication, or treatment—guidance based not on the current practice of lumping symptoms together into broad categories of disorders, but on a precise reading of your own body's peculiarities and its status in real time.

"And at that point," says Larry, in a typically bold pronouncement that would startle generations of white-coated researchers, "you now have, for the first time in history, a scientific basis for medicine."

When those who consulted the Delphic Oracle saw the inscription, "Know thyself," they could not have imagined an acolyte so avid, or so literal, as Larry. You've heard of people who check their pulse every few minutes? Amateurs. When Larry works out, an armband records skin temperature, heat flux, galvanic skin response, and acceleration in three dimensions. When he sleeps, a headband monitors the patterns of his sleep every thirty seconds. He has his blood drawn as many as eight times a year, and regularly tracks a hundred separate markers. He is on a first-name basis with his ultrasound and MRI technicians, who provide him with 3-D images of his body, head to toe. Regular colonoscopies record the texture and color of his innards. And then there are the stool samples—last year Larry sent specimens to a lab for analysis nine times.

Larry is a mild, gentle soul, someone generally more interested in talking about you than about himself. He does not go out of his way to get your attention, and nothing about him is even remotely annoying or evangelical. But if you show an interest in his project and start asking questions—look out. Beneath the calm and the deference, Larry is an intellectual pitchman of the first order. In his quest to know, he burns with the pure intellectual passion of a precocious ten-year-old. He visibly shudders with pleasure at a good, hard question; his shoulders subtly rise and square, and his forehead leans into the task. Because Larry is on a mission. He's out to change the world and, along the way, defeat at least one incurable disease: his own. (More on this in a moment.)

Larry is in the vanguard of what some call the "quantified life," which envisions replacing the guesswork and supposition presently guiding individual health decisions with specific guidance tailored to the particular details of each person's body. Because of his accomplishments and stature in his field, Larry cannot easily be dismissed as a kook. He believes in immersing himself in his work. Years ago, at the University of Illinois, when he was taking part in an experiment to unravel complex environmental systems with supercomputers, Larry installed a coral-reef aquarium in his home, complete with shrimp and sixteen phyla of other small marine critters. It was maddeningly fragile. The coral kept peeling off the rocks and dying. He eventually discovered that just five drops of molybdenum, a metallic element, in a 250-gallon tank once a week solved the problem. That such a tiny factor played so decisive a role helped him better grasp the complexity of the situation. And as he fought to sustain the delicate ecosystem in his tank, he developed a personal feel for the larger problem his team was trying to solve.

Today, he is preoccupied with his own ecosystem. The way a computer scientist tends to see it, a genome is a given individual's basic program. Mapping one used to cost billions of dollars. Today it can be done for thousands, and soon the price will drop below $1,000. Once people know their genetic codes, and begin thoroughly monitoring their bodily systems, they will theoretically approach the point where computers can "know" a lot more about them than any doctor ever could. In such a world, people will spot disease long before they feel sick—as Larry did. They will regard the doctor as more consultant than oracle.

Not everyone sees this potential revolution as a good one. Do people really want or need to know this much about themselves? Is such a preoccupation with health even *healthy?* What if swimming in oceans of bio-data causes more harm than good?

"Frankly, I'd rather go river rafting," says Dr. H. Gilbert Welch, a professor of medicine at the Dartmouth Institute for Health Policy and Clinical Practice, and the author of *Overdiagnosed: Making People Sick in the Pursuit of Health.* "Data are not information. Information is not knowledge. And knowledge is certainly not wisdom." Welch believes that individuals who monitor themselves as closely as Larry does are pretty much guaranteed to find something "wrong." Contradictory as it sounds, he says abnormality is *normal.*

"It brings to mind the fad a few years ago with getting full-body CT scans," Welch says. "Something like 80 percent of those who did it found something abnormal about themselves. The essence of life is variability. Constant monitoring is a recipe for all of us to be judged 'sick.' Judging ourselves sick, we seek intervention." And intervention, usually with drugs or surgery, he warns, is never risk-free. Humbler medical practitioners, aware of the sordid history of some medical practices (see bloodletting, lobotomy, trepanning), weigh the consequences of intervention carefully. Doing no harm often demands doing nothing. The human body is, after all, remarkably sturdy and self-healing. As Welch sees it, "Arming ourselves with more data is guaranteed to unleash a lot of intervention" on people who are basically healthy.

Not to mention creating an epidemic of anxiety. In other words, the "quantified life" might itself belong to the catalog of affliction, filed under *Looking too closely, hazards of.*

In that sense, the story of Larry Smarr might be less a pioneering saga than a cautionary tale.

Larry's journey started with that most American of preoccupations, losing weight. Larry doesn't update the photo each time he renews his California driver's license, preferring to keep, as a reminder, the one taken soon after his arrival at UCSD twelve years ago, with his wife, Janet. It shows a fifty-one-year-old Larry, with more and longer hair, a wide round face, and an ample second chin. Call him Jolly Larry. He had just arrived from Illinois, a place he now refers to as "the epicenter of the obesity epidemic," and he had a girth to match his oversize professional reputation. (Deep-fried, sugarcoated pastries were a particular favorite of his back then.) Arriving in La Jolla, Jolly Larry found himself surrounded by jogging, hiking, biking, surfing, organic vegetable-eating superhumans. It was enough to shame him into action. If he was going to fit in on this sunny new campus, he would have to shape up.

So Jolly Larry started working out, reading diet books, and stepping on the scale every day. At first, his charts were disappointing. Like countless strivers before him, he dropped some weight, but not much, and it kept wanting to come back. Three or four popular books on weight loss left him mostly confused, but they did convey a central truth: losing weight was only 20 percent about exercise. The other 80 percent was about what he put in his mouth. What led to his breakthrough was the advice of Barry Sears, the biochemist who created the Zone Diet, which pressed Larry's buttons precisely. Sears proposed that to diet more effectively, one needed to *know* more. Larry decided to study his body chemistry.

Few people in history have been better positioned to act on such advice. Larry had begun his professional life as an astrophysicist, trying to unravel the core puzzles of the universe. In 1975, when he was working toward his doctorate at the University of Texas, one of his advisers suggested that he get a top-secret government security clearance: behind the walls of America's nuclear weapons program were not only some of the nation's premier physicists, but also the world's first supercomputers, hundreds of times faster than anything available on any college campus. Larry got his clearance, and in the following years, while working as a fellow at Princeton and at Harvard, he would disappear during summers behind the classified walls of the Lawrence Livermore National Laboratory, in the San Francisco Bay Area. There he would work sixteen-hour shifts on some of the most difficult problems in his field—but with a crucial difference. Working with a computer at one of his universities, Larry might set it a task to do overnight. He would go home, and when he returned the next morning, the task would be nearing completion. Working with the new Cray supercomputer at Livermore, he could get the same result in a minute and a half.

When he'd return to his university posts in the fall, and rejoin his colleagues working at a comparative snail's pace, he'd tell them, "You know, guys, we could be using supercomputers to solve the laws of physics, instead of trying to do these closed-form static solutions that you do." They would look at him as if he were crazy. "What are you talking about?" they'd ask. "That can't be done." To them, it seemed impossible. The supercomputer enabled not just faster work, but a different style and language of experimentation. But when he tried to explain this to his colleagues, who were still working mostly with pencil and paper, they scratched their heads. "It was like I was living in two different worlds," Larry says.

When one of the first Cray computers outside secret nuclear programs was set up in Munich, Larry started spending his summers there. "And in about 1982, we were at a beer garden and it was probably my second glass of beer, and I was being hosted by a German astrophysicist, world-class," Larry recalls. "He asks, 'Tell me something. My father helped build the trains Germany relied on during the war. And here in our occupied country, you guys, you Americans, come over here and mooch off our supercomputers because you don't have the wit to put them in your universities where people can get access to them. Have I got that right?' And I said, 'Pretty much.' And he asks, 'How did you guys win the war?'"

Larry brought that question home with him to his perch at the University of Illinois. There, in 1983, he helped draft the "Black Proposal," an unusually concise recommendation (in a black cover) for a $55 million National Science Foundation supercomputer center. When it was funded, along with four other NSF centers, Larry and others argued for using the protocols of the military's ARPANET (the precursor of the Internet) to link the centers, so that civilian researchers across the nation could use the fastest computers in America for basic research. The proposed linking was controversial not only because it took on the cult of secrecy surrounding the most-advanced computers in America, but because it specifically recommended that the NSF include only computer networks using TCP/IP, a universal computer protocol designed to facilitate not secrecy, but collaboration. TCP/IP allowed different kinds of computers to exchange data seamlessly. At the time, the large computer companies— DEC, IBM, General Electric, etc.—preferred a market model where manufacturers competed to create large fiefdoms, networks that used only their own machines. By adopting Larry's proposal, the NSF enabled computer networks to plug into the system, a critical step toward today's Internet.

By the time, years later, that Larry heeded Barry Sears's suggestion to learn more about his body chemistry, Larry had at his disposal at UCSD a supercomputer with a capacity many times greater than that of any he'd worked on at Livermore. His research interests had shifted from astrophysics to the impact computers were having on many fields, including medicine. Calit2 already had numerous grants to study "digitally enabled genomic medicine," so in 2010 Larry signed himself up as a test subject. As his personal quest to lose weight evolved into an effort to understand human biochemistry, his own body became the equivalent of the coral-reef tank he'd once kept in his living room.

Larry had already radically changed his diet, breaking his intake into subcategories, aiming for a caloric split of 40 percent low-glycemic carbohydrates, 30 percent lean protein, and 30 percent omega-3–enriched fat. His meal portions were about half of ordinary restaurant portions. Following what was essentially Barry Sears's Zone Diet, Larry had lost a pound every ten weeks, dropping twenty pounds in four years.

Most people would have been happy with that. But his dieting taught Larry something. If he wanted good health, he could not simply trust how he felt and wing it. If he wanted to understand what was happening in his body, he had to examine the data. And despite his weight loss, the data were now telling him something that didn't seem to make sense. By his calculations, the pounds should still have been falling off, but they weren't.

According to his measurements, he had doubled his strength and tripled the number of steps he took each day. His REM periods, the most valuable periods of sleep, accounted for more than half the time he spent in the sack—twice the typical proportion for a man of his age. His weight was steady. But Larry wanted to know more. He had been getting blood tests once or twice a year as part of his normal health maintenance, but by the end of 2010 he was sending off blood samples more often and graphing dozens of markers, which enabled him to at least better define the mystery. The Zone Diet is designed to reduce inflammation, and because he followed it faithfully, Larry expected his inflammation score on the blood test to be low. But the C-reactive protein (CRP), which rises in response to inflammation, was high.

"I had discovered that my body is chronically inflamed—just the opposite of what I expected!" he wrote in an account of his project published last year in a special issue of *Strategic News Service*, a computer/telecommunications newsletter. (The article was prefaced by an enthusiastic note from the publisher, Mark R. Anderson, who said that it "may be the most important Special Letter we have ever published. For many of you reading it, it may also save your lives, or extend them.") Larry wrote:

> Even more intriguing: after I had been tracking my CRP for two years, I noticed that it had suddenly more than doubled in less than a year. Troubled, I showed my graphs to my doctors and suggested that something bad was about to happen.

Here you should try to imagine the average physician's reaction when a patient, outwardly healthy, arrives with detailed graphs of his body chemistry, concerned that something evil is stalking his insides.

"Do you have a symptom?" Larry was asked.

"No," he answered. "I feel fine."

He was assured that charts like his were "academic," and not useful for clinical practice. The doctors told him to come back if and when he found something actually wrong with him, as opposed to finding anomalies in his charts.

I ask Larry a question his doctors might have been too polite to ask: "Are you a hypochondriac?"

"A hypochondriac is someone who imagines that he has things that are wrong with him and worries about that," he says.

"I am the opposite of a hypochondriac. I don't make any assumptions about what might be right or wrong with me, and I don't imagine it. I measure it."

Larry was beginning to have serious doubts about the way medicine is practiced in this country. "Here's the way I look at it; the average American has something like two twenty-minute visits a year with a doctor," he explains. "So you have forty minutes a year that that doctor is going to help you make good decisions. You have 500,000 minutes a year on your own, and every one of those, you are making decisions. So we're already in a situation where you are in charge of your ship—your body—and you are making a lot of pretty horrible decisions, or else two-thirds of the United States' citizens wouldn't be overweight or obese. You wouldn't have the CDC saying that 42 percent of Americans may be obese by 2030, and a third of all Americans may develop diabetes by 2050. That's the result of a lot of bad decisions that people are individually making on their own."

A few weeks after his doctors dismissed his graphs as "academic," Larry felt a severe pain in the left side of his abdomen. At his doctor's office, he was diagnosed with acute diverticulitis, an intestinal disease caused by inflammation. He was put on a ten-day antibiotic program to treat the ailment. To Larry, this perfectly illustrated the problem. Doctors were ready, eager, and well-equipped to address a clinical symptom, but unwilling to wade with him into his charts, which, although undeniably abstract, had foretold the problem! It was at this point that Larry decided to take over his own health care.

He asked to see the written report from his last colonoscopy, and underwent another. He began testing his stool, recognizing that all of us are, in fact, "superorganisms," that our gastrointestinal, or GI, tracts are a collaboration between human digestive cells and the trillions of bacteria that line our intestines. The stool samples provided detailed charts of the workings of these microorganisms, which is what Larry means when he calls his poop "data-rich." He was learning more about the biochemistry of his own body than any patient had ever known, and the numbers continued to add up in an alarming way. They suggested that he was suffering not from diverticulitis, but from some kind of inflamed-bowel disease. He then went looking for an expert to help him interpret the data. He didn't have to look far: Dr. William J. Sandborn had recently left the Mayo Clinic to take over the GI division of UCSD's School of Medicine.

"I think he felt he wasn't really being taken seriously," says Sandborn. "So he came over and we looked, and we ended up finding some degree of inflammation that was pointing in the direction of Crohn's disease, but he wasn't really having many symptoms. So the questions then became: Is this some kind of early subclinical Crohn's disease? Should we even go as far as treating it, or just wait?"

Larry's impressive quest to fine-tune his body had led him to this: an early diagnosis of Crohn's disease, an incurable condition. It isn't fatal, but it has a long list of uncomfortable and sometimes painful symptoms that tend to flare up from time to time; they center on the GI tract, but may include eye inflammation, swollen joints, fever, fatigue, and others. Apart from that one episode of abdominal pain, Larry was still feeling fine. But the graphs showed, and his new doctor more or less confirmed, that he was sick.

And that part about its being incurable? Let's just say that in Larry, Crohn's disease has encountered a very dedicated adversary.

If past thinkers leaned heavily on the steam engine as an all-purpose analogy—e.g., contents under pressure will explode (think of Marx's ideas on revolution or Freud's about repressed desire)—today we prefer our metaphors to be electronic. We talk about neural "circuitry," about "processing" information, or about how genes "encode" our physical essence. In this worldview, our bodies are computers, and DNA functions as our basic program, our "operating system."

This is certainly how Larry, the computer scientist, talks about the human body. In this context, all of human history can be seen as a progression from a world that was data-poor to one that is data-rich. Starting with those early summers working in secrecy at Livermore, Larry has witnessed firsthand the exponential progress of computing power posited by Moore's law, which states that processing power should double roughly every eighteen months. So when Larry talks about the potential for computers to help us understand our bodies, he isn't talking about their showing us more isolated details about an unfathomably complex system; he's talking about knowing *everything*.

"We are going to know—once you know each of your cells' six billion genome bases, with all the imaging down to the micron level, and when you know every damn gene and every bacterium—at a certain point, there are no more data to know," he says. "So certainly by 2030, there is not going to be that much more to learn. . . . I mean, you are going to get the wiring diagram, basically." Once they are armed with the wiring diagram, Larry sees no reason why individuals cannot maintain their health the way modern car owners maintain their automobiles.

Larry actually concedes the point made by Dartmouth's Welch—that presented with enough data, pretty much everyone is going to find something wrong with himself or herself. He just disputes that this would be a bad thing. "All of us do have something beginning to go wrong, but then, so do our automobiles," Larry says. "In today's world of automobile preventive maintenance, we don't wait for our cars to break down and then go to the 'car doctor.' Every ten thousand or twenty thousand miles, we go in and get an exhaustive look at all the key variables since the last check. If they find something wrong with my car—which will be different from what they find about yours—then they take appropriate action and I go back to driving a 'healthy' car. Occasionally, something is discovered that indicates a bunch of cars need to be called in and get a certain item replaced. I can imagine that occasionally, as a new DNA segment is related to some disease, people with that DNA signature will be called in for 'preventive maintenance.'"

If Larry is right, then our descendants may view early-twenty-first-century medical practices, which we consider a triumph of reason over superstition, in the same way we now view eighteenth- and nineteenth-century folk remedies. A particularly likely candidate for scorn in an age of "quantified" health care is our one-pill-fits-all approach to prescription drugs. In his book *The Creative Destruction of Medicine*, the physician-author Eric Topol cites such dosing as an example of medicine that is "population-based," rather than "patient-centered." He notes the widespread use of statins to lower LDL cholesterol, a factor in heart disease. Topol doesn't deny the cholesterol-lowering effect of these drugs, but he argues that double-blind testing also shows that this effect benefits only a tiny fraction of those treated. One of the most effective statins, Crestor, has been found to reduce the incidence of stroke, heart attack, or death from 4 percent of patients in the placebo group to 2 percent of the group taking the statin. And yet these drugs are widely administered to patients considered at risk. Topol writes:

> Instead of identifying the 1 person or 2 people out of every 100 who would benefit, the whole population with the criteria that were tested is deemed treatable. . . . What constitutes evidence-based medicine today is what is good for a large population, not for any particular individual.

Pharmaceutical companies don't mind. And as long as the harmful side effects are within acceptable limits, the Food and

Drug Administration doesn't mind, either. Some patients will be helped. All of them will be buying the pills, and all will be subjected to follow-up tests, some of them uncomfortable and most of them unnecessary. What if there were a way, Topol asks, of knowing, before prescribing the drug, which 2 percent would be most likely to benefit from it? In an observation that Larry wholeheartedly endorses, Topol writes:

> Fortunately, our ability to get just that information is rapidly emerging, [and we are] beginning an era characterized by the right drug, the right dose, and the right screen for the right patients, with the right doctor, at the right cost.

Getting there will mean essentially dismantling the health care industry as we know it. (Thus the *creative destruction* of Topol's title.) Or, as Larry puts it: "A lot of enormously wealthy, established, powerful institutions in our society are going to be destroyed." And why not? Over the past twenty years, computers have been toppling and rebuilding industries one by one, from retail sales (Walmart and Amazon) to banking (ATMs and online services) to finance (high-speed online investing) to entertainment (Web streaming, downloads, YouTube, etc.) to publishing (e-books and news aggregators). We're just babes in this new digital era, and it will eventually upend almost every field of human endeavor.

Larry sees medicine as a stubborn holdout. Current efforts to reform the system—for instance, the Obama administration's initiative to digitize all health records by 2014—are just toes in the water. Medicine has barely begun to take advantage of the millionfold increase in the amount of data available for the diagnosis and treatment of disease. Take the standard annual physical, with its weigh-in, blood-pressure check, and handful of numbers gleaned from select tests performed on a blood sample. To Larry, these data points give your doctor little more than a "cartoon" image of your body. Now imagine peering at the same image drawn from a galaxy of *billions* of data points. The cartoon becomes a high-definition, 3-D picture, with every system and organ in the body measured and mapped in real time.

Indeed, a very early prototype of this kind of high-definition image already exists at Calit2. It is, of course, of Larry.

Inside a "cave" fashioned from large HD screens (each with dual rear projectors) and linked to eighteen gaming PCs to create a graphics supercomputer, Larry and I step *into* a stunning image assembled from an MRI scan of his torso. The room, the size of a walk-in closet, is lined with giant screens, front, sides, and back. More screens angle from these walls toward a floor that is illuminated from above. Two curved, waist-high metal railings offer support, because viewers at the center of this visual world can easily lose their balance. A sensor strapped to your forehead tells the computer where you are looking, so as you turn your head it smoothly blends the images on the screens to create a seamless 360-degree alternative world. (This is clearly the future of video games and cinema.) I had to lean on the metal bars to remind myself I was not someplace else. Once we were in position, Jürgen P. Schulze, a Calit2 research scientist, punched up a display of Larry's own coiled, sixty-three-year-old entrails. I felt as if I could reach out and touch the wrinkled contours of his intestines and arteries.

Larry's inner ten-year-old rejoices. "Look!" he says, lifting and opening his hands. "This is me!"

He points to the source of his health concerns, the precise six-inch stretch of his sigmoid colon that is visibly distorted and inflamed. This is Larry's discovery, and his enemy.

I note that the display breaks new ground in the annals of self-disclosure: Larry is literally turning himself inside out for a journalist. He does worry a little about making public such intimate details, but this openness is part of how he believes medicine ought to be—and ultimately *will* be—practiced. The current consensus that medical records should be strictly private, subject to the scrutiny of only doctor and patient, will be yet another casualty if Larry's health care vision comes to pass. "A different way to organize society is to say it is human-focused, human-centered, and patient-centered, and that there are no legal or financial repercussions from sharing data," he says. "There is a huge societal benefit from sharing the data, getting data out from the firewalls, letting software look across millions of these things."

The way the system works now, when a technician examines the MRI of a patient's abdomen, in two dimensions, on a single screen, she compares and contrasts it with perhaps thousands or even tens of thousands of other images she has seen. She then writes a report to the physician explaining, on the basis of her memory and experience, what is normal or abnormal in what she sees.

But "software can go in, volumetrically, over, say, a *million* different abdomens," says Larry, gesturing at the image of his own innards, "and come up with exquisite distribution functions of how things are arranged, what is abnormal or normal, on every little thing in there. In my case, what I have found is inflammation. Unaddressed, it may lead to structural damage and maybe eventually surgery, cutting that part out. So I am going to have another MRI in three months, and that will tell me whether the things I am doing have made it better, or if it is the same, or has gotten worse."

It's that sense of control that appeals to Larry as much as anything.

"The way we do things now," he says, "the technician will examine it and write up a report, which goes to my doctor, and then he explains it all to me. So I am *disembodied*. Patients are completely severed from having any relationship with their body. You are helpless."

Shedding that sense of disembodiment and helplessness is, in theory, one of the most attractive features of Larry Smarr's quantified self. Individuals will understand their own bodies and take care of themselves; doctors will merely assist with the maintenance and fine-tuning. With that sense of personal ownership established, Larry believes, the average American won't continue to drink five hundred cans of soda a year, or ingest some sixty pounds of high-fructose corn syrup. After all, educational campaigns about cigarettes have helped lower the proportion of smokers in America to below 20 percent. If we made such inroads into the obesity epidemic, Larry says, "we would have a national celebration."

For his part, Larry is no longer disembodied. He has had key snippets of his DNA sequenced, and will have the whole thing completely sequenced by the end of this year. In just what he has seen so far, he has discovered telltale markers linked with late-onset Crohn's disease. He has developed his own theory of the disease, based on his reading of the most recent medical literature and his growing perception of himself as a superorganism. In a nutshell, he suspects that some of the essential bacteria that should line the walls of his intestine at the point where it is inflamed have been killed off, probably by some antibiotic regimen he underwent years ago. So he has begun charting, through stool samples, the bewilderingly complex microbial ecology of his intestines.

He showed me a detailed analysis of one such sample on his computer, drawing my attention to the word *firmicute*. "So, what the hell is a *firmicute*?" he asks rhetorically. "And in particular, it is in these two groups, *Clostridium leptum* and *Clostridium coccoides*. So I go back, and I go, '*Clostri-Clostri-Clostri*, that rings a bell. I had it in my last stool measurement.'" He pulls up an older chart on his screen. "Here is my stool measurement from January 1, 2012. And here are my bacteria. *Lactobacillus* and *Bifidobacteria*: that is what you get in, like, a yogurt and stuff like that, right? *Clostridia*: you can have them from zero to four-plus. Four-plus is what they should be. And you can see I am deficient here on a number of them," he says, pointing to low numbers on the chart. "So then I went back over time and got them plotted, and they never were above two, and now they are collapsed down to one. So it looks like I am losing. So what do *Clostridia* do? Because I am missing them—I am missing that service."

You may note the *Alice in Wonderland* quality of all this. Every question Larry seeks to answer raises new questions, every door he opens leads to a deeper level of bewildering complexity. One could easily conclude that these levels never bottom out, that the intricacy of the human body, composed of its trillions of cells—each dancing to the tune of a genetic program but also subject to random intersections with outside forces such as radiation, chemicals, and physical accidents—is for all practical purposes infinite, and hence permanently beyond our full comprehension. But Larry, with his astrophysics background, is utterly undaunted by complexity. This is the gift of the computer age: things once considered too numerous to count can now be counted. And Larry believes that questions about how the human body functions are ultimately finite.

In his own case, Larry has zeroed in on what he believes is the specific missing bacterial component behind the immune-system malfunction causing his bowel inflammation. He's begun a regimen of supplements to replace that component. If it doesn't work, he'll devise a new plan. He isn't aiming for immortality—not yet, although, as far as he is concerned, it's not out of the question. As we develop our ability to replace broken-down body parts with bioengineered organs, and as we work toward a complete understanding of human systems and biochemistry . . . why not?

Reflecting on Larry's vision of a patient-centric, computer-assisted world of medical care, Dr. Welch allows: "I can conceive of this happening. But is this the model we want for good health?

What does it mean to be healthy? Is it something we learn from a machine? Is it the absence of abnormality? Health is a state of mind. I don't think constantly monitoring yourself is the right path to that state of mind. Data alone are not the answer. We went through all of this with the Human Genome Project. You heard it then: if we could just get all of the data, all of our problems would be solved. It turned out that the predictive power of mapping the genome wasn't all that great, because there are other factors at play: the environment, behavior, and chance. Randomness has a lot to do with it."

And these are not the only reasons to be skeptical of Larry's vision. Researchers will certainly continue to map the human body in ever-greater detail, enabling doctors to spot emerging illness earlier and to design drug treatments with far more precision. But in the end, how many people will want to track their bodily functions the way Larry does, even if software greatly simplifies the task? Larry says the amount of time he has spent monitoring and studying himself has grown a lot, but that it still adds up to less time each day than most Americans spend watching television. But even if that time is radically reduced by software, how many of us, understanding that our decrypted genome may reveal terrible news about our future—Alzheimer's disease, crippling neuromuscular diseases, schizophrenia, and so on—will even want to know?

When I ask Larry this question, he frowns and says, "I can't understand that." The very idea stumps him. To him, *not wanting to know something*—even bad news—just doesn't compute. His whole life is about finding out. He's a scientist to his core.

"I hear it a lot, but I don't understand it. Because whatever it is, if you suspect that you are going to have, say, Alzheimer's disease within five years or ten years, then that should focus your mind on what it is you want to accomplish in the days that you have left." Then, after a moment for more thought, he adds, "And if you don't know, those days are going to just slide by, in which you could have done something that you always meant to do."

He knows that the way he lives and works might seem eccentric or even a little crazy to others. "Most of my life, people have thought I was crazy at any given point," he says. "Maybe being crazy simply means you are clear-sighted and you are looking at the fact that you are in a period of rapid change. I see the world as it will be, and of course, that is a different world from the one we live in now."

Larry is in a hurry to get there. He sees himself ten years down the road as someone healthy and active and strong, instead of someone struggling to manage the increasingly uncomfortable and debilitating effects of Crohn's disease. As he makes his way down the supplements aisle at his Whole Foods Market, looking for a very specific assortment of probiotics with which to mix his remedial cocktail, he's not just trying to save himself. He's trying to save you.

SPORTS

The Silent Treatment

Sports Illustrated, September 2013

You might not expect a long-retired, much-dinged, memory-impaired NFL quarterback to recall the details of a single play from twenty-seven years ago, but when I began describing the one that interested me to former Browns play-caller Bernie Kosar, he interrupted me. "Unfortunately, I can finish this story, but go ahead," he said. "I'll be nice and pretend I don't know. I could claim, 'Hey, I've had concussions; I don't know what you're talking about.' But . . . go ahead."

Kosar is a boisterously cheerful man who has had a rocky time in retirement. He has weathered a widely publicized bankruptcy and struggled with memory loss, a consequence of the many concussions he suffered in more than 130 pro games. He starred in easily half a hundred more as a Pennsylvania high schooler and then as quarterback of the Miami Hurricanes. That means he took thousands of snaps. Some went well; some went badly. Most were unmemorable. The one I was asking about was a cock-up.

It came in the final, futile series of the Browns' 1986 division playoff loss to the Dolphins. It happened in the Orange Bowl, where Kosar had led the Hurricanes to a national championship two Januaries before. The Browns were a big surprise that season. Under Kosar, then a rookie, they squeaked into the playoffs and on this day stunned the heavily favored Dolphins by jumping out to a 21–3 lead. Miami's defense stiffened, however, and its offense scored three unanswered second-half touchdowns. With less than two minutes to play, the Dolphins led by three points.

Kosar had one last chance. Seventy-five thousand Miami fans, whipped to a frenzy by the Dolphins' second-half heroics, were doing their best to flatten the Browns' offense with sound, and they seemed to be succeeding. Then, when every down and every second mattered, the Browns squandered a play. It wasn't a game loser; it wasn't even the critical play in the drive. But it hurt. Inside that cauldron of noise, Cleveland's deafened offense was trying something new, a silent snap count, the brainstorm of the Browns' offensive line coach, Howard Mudd. Kosar didn't have much choice. He could not make himself heard even when he lined up over the center and barked the snap count at the top of his voice. So he was back in the shotgun formation, ten feet behind the center, orchestrating the play with his feet. He lifted his right foot to signal wide receiver Glen Young to go in motion, but as Young trotted across the backfield, center Mike Baab prematurely snapped the ball. Maybe Kosar had gotten his footwork wrong, or maybe Baab, peering back through his legs at the world upside down, with a hulking, ferocious defender poised to run him over, had misread his cue. The ball hit Kosar and fell to the turf. The Browns came up with it, but they had lost a big chunk of precious time, several yards, and one critical down. Cleveland managed several more plays, even made a big first down, but the clock ran out before the team could get into position for a field goal.

"I still remember it like it was yesterday," says Kosar. "I was sick over it. I'm still sick over it."

Baab and Kosar still don't agree over who was at fault, and all these years later they still jocularly point fingers at each other, but both know that the overriding reason, one that no self-respecting NFL player would dare float as an excuse, was noise. The old "twelfth man."

The first use of this term or the form "12th Man" in football came in 1912, in an alumni publication of the University of Iowa, and referred to the intangible contribution of fans to the school's team. Texas A&M has formally trademarked the term. But in the NFL, around the time of Kosar's disaster in Miami, crowd noise had become something more than emotional support. It had started messing with outcomes.

Howard Mudd played guard for the 49ers and the Bears from 1964 through 1970, when the league was really taking off, and he doesn't remember ever having any trouble with noise. But during the 1970s the volume grew and grew and grew, in step with the league's skyrocketing popularity. By 1985 the sound level in stadiums routinely topped a hundred decibels, about what you hear sitting astride a revving Harley-Davidson or operating a table saw. In other words offensive linemen, who must brace to meet the mad charge of locomotive pass rushers, could no longer hear the quarterback calling for the snap of the ball.

This might seem a small thing to someone who has never experienced it, but it was a nightmare for blockers. Why not, you might ask (and coaches implored), just watch the football? When it moves, you move! Isn't that what defenders have to do? But this advice was of little help to offensive tackles. Pigeons may be able to see separate things independently out of each eye, but human beings cannot. An offensive tackle, at the far end of the interior line, cannot watch both the ball and the pass rusher who is preparing to flatten him. When he can't hear, he has to watch the ball, which means he has to turn his head, which means he's doomed.

Jeff Saturday, the Colts' two-time All-Pro center, says that crowd noise was an occasional problem for him in certain stadiums during his college career at North Carolina, but it became a constant problem when he turned pro in 1999. "In the pros the game is so much more advanced, with all the calls and checks and changes at the line of scrimmage, that verbal communication is at a premium," Saturday says. "If linemen can't hear, they don't have a fighting chance."

"When we would go to Seattle, in that dome, it was a tremendous problem," says John Alt, an offensive tackle for the Chiefs from 1984 through 1996. "It took away a lot of your offense. You couldn't audible the way you normally would. And for those of us playing tackle, well, you've got a defensive end running forward [at a ridiculous speed] while you're trying to block him a half second late running backward. The line coach would be yelling, 'Watch the ball! Watch the ball!' But you just couldn't do it."

Alt was not alone. Tackles failed a lot in their mission starting in the mid-1980s, which meant quarterbacks were getting creamed in the backfield with regularity. Kosar jokes about it, but his memory loss bears witness. Over two decades, from 1980 to 2000, it was open season on NFL quarterbacks; the average number of sacks per team spiked as high as 46.9 in the mid-1980s. Everyone knew where the point of weakness was. Stranded in the din at either end of the interior line, tackles struggled to do the impossible. Those years produced seven of the league's top ten all-time sack leaders: Bruce Smith (1985–2003), Reggie White ('85–00), Kevin Greene ('85–99), Chris Doleman ('85–99), Richard Dent ('83–97), Lawrence Taylor ('81–93), and Leslie O'Neal ('86–99). The three others in the top ten—Michael Strahan ('93–07), John Randle ('90–03), and

Jason Taylor ('97–11)—overlapped that period. The most likely reason for the great blossoming of pass-rushing skills in the last two decades of the twentieth century was crowd noise.

Players, coaches, and NFL officials tried all sorts of remedies—to no avail. Rules permitted only the quarterback to communicate by radio with the sideline, but the league tried outfitting offensive guards with speakers in their shoulder pads to broadcast the snap count to the tackles. Didn't work. They tried fitting tackles with hearing aids designed to filter out background noise. Didn't work. They tried having the center bark out the count. Didn't work. They tried amplifying the snap count with speakers at the thirty-yard lines on both sides of the field. Didn't work. They tried having the linemen hold hands. Didn't work.

Players experimented with their own approaches. I was covering a game in Buffalo's Rich Stadium in 1990 between the Bills and the Eagles. In a scene recounted in my 1994 book, *Bringing the Heat*, the Eagles' giant right tackle, Ron Heller, a brick wall on most occasions, was getting scorched by Bills defensive end Bruce Smith, and midway through the game Philadelphia coach Buddy Ryan benched him. The exasperated Heller confronted his quarterback, Randall Cunningham, on the sideline. "Look, Randall, I can't hear you out there," he said.

To Heller's amazement, Cunningham explained that despite the din, he was deliberately not raising his voice on the snap count. Someone had told him that was the way to capture another person's attention. "I'm using my soft voice," he said. The infuriated tackle had a few choice words for that theory, delivered loudly enough to be heard over the din. In short: didn't work.

Then, around 1998–1999, something made the problem go away. That something was the silent snap count. Its first master practitioners were Peyton Manning, Jeff Saturday, and the Colts. Its architect? The man who had experimented with it during that

ill-fated Browns game in 1986, the man Manning calls "a phi-
losopher of football, an honest-to-God guru": Howard Mudd.

He coached for eight NFL teams over five decades after he
stopped playing. When he retired in 2009 from the Colts, with
whom he had his greatest success, Mudd was feted as an NFL
great. Manning pulled out all the stops. He had a commemorative
video made, gathering old footage from NFL films and testimo-
nials from Mudd's former playing and coaching colleagues and
setting it all to some of Mudd's favorite Simon and Garfunkel
music. Manning mounted and framed three jerseys signed by
some of the game's greatest names. It was all presented to the
coach at a private dinner attended only by Manning and the Colts'
offensive line. "It was like attending his own funeral!" Manning
says. A few weeks later Mudd came out of retirement to coach
for the Eagles.

Manning called him. "I want all that stuff back!" he said.
"Hell, Howard, when you retire you're supposed to stay retired!"

Mudd coached for two seasons in Philadelphia. He recently
retired for the second time—"for good," he tells me. To see him
today, at seventy-one, with hips and knees so battered that he
walks hunched over a cane, you would never guess that in his
prime he was a giant. He was six foot six, weighed more than 250
pounds, and made three trips to the Pro Bowl. He is a member
of the NFL's All-Decade Team of the 1960s. But as the body
fades, it reveals mind; Mudd aged from Yeti to Yoda.

"Coach Howard is a true student of the game," says Saturday, who worked with Mudd during most of the center's thirteen
years in Indianapolis, "and he is one of those guys who played at
a high level, so he respects the athleticism on both sides of the
ball. For example, if you were beat on a play not because you did
something wrong but because the guy opposite you just beat you,
Coach Howard rarely had an issue with that. He knew how good
the guy on defense was. But he also believed the mental aspect

of the game wasn't just some abstraction. He preached that the better prepared and focused you were, the more you could 'slow the game down,' as he put it. I found that to be true."

When the Eagles coaxed Mudd back, they gave him an electric cart so he could maneuver around their practice fields. He looked hobbled, but he was still as tough as jerky. His wide, round face was rimmed with a full white beard, and his thick brow could still clench his whole face into a fist, but the look was deceptive. Mudd is less tough than clever. He has a hair-trigger sense of humor and a quick and playful mind. He is also startlingly blunt and utterly without pretense. He is at work on an instruction book for blockers with the terrific working title, "Shit That I Know Works." Kosar recalls, "Coach Howard wasn't just stubborn and physical like many football coaches are, banging their heads against the wall all the time. He tried to be creative. And this silent count, it was one of the things he really believed in."

As Mudd remembers it, the league brought the noise problem on itself. He noticed it while coaching for the Seahawks in the late 1970s and early 1980s. The team played in the Kingdome, which, because of its concrete structure, seemed to retain sound even more than other roofed stadiums. When the home fans' deafening cheers sowed confusion in enemy offenses, the team did things to encourage the crowd: it broadcast chants over the loudspeakers and promoted the antics of a beer-vending unofficial cheerleader, Bill Scott, who became famous as Bill the Beerman. Opposing teams began preparing for the Kingdome by blasting noise from loudspeakers on the sidelines during practice.

Soon teams throughout the league were imitating the Seahawks. Bill the Beerman went pro. He toured other stadiums, teaching new crowds the finer points of pumping up the volume. And fans loved it. When they forced the visiting team to waste time-outs and botch offensive plays, they realized the fantasy of every fan who has ever donned a team jersey. They were in the game. They were the 12th Man! The league loved it too. It was fun, and it created a nice incentive to buy tickets and actually attend the games, which were increasingly available on TV.

Offensive coaches hated the noise. In 1981, in what can be described only as an act of deep hypocrisy, Seahawks coach Jack Patera did something about it. Seattle was scheduled to play Green Bay at Lambeau Field, where the Packers had enthusiastically embraced crowd noise as a weapon. Mudd was Patera's offensive line coach and at that point had no solution to the noise problem. So Patera dusted off his NFL rule book and found a 1956 stricture that no one ever recalled using. It said the referee had the power to stop the game if the quarterback could not make himself heard over the crowd. "Well, piss on it," Patera told his young quarterback, Jim Zorn. "What we are going to do is, I do not want you to snap the ball if you can't hear."

On game day the crowd was predictably deafening, so Zorn did as instructed. "I stood there while the twenty-five-second [play] clock was ticking," he recalls. "If the crowd was loud, what I had to do was turn around and look at the referee. And the referee would judge whether or not it was loud enough. I turned around, and the ref stopped the game. He came and stood over the ball and tried to quiet the crowd down."

This had a predictable effect. "The crowd got louder," says Zorn. The ref waited for the fans to tire out and then signaled for play to resume, but every time Zorn approached the center, the noise kicked up once more. This happened over and over, until the delay stretched to twenty-seven minutes. A scandal. It messed with the most sacrosanct feature of Sunday-afternoon football: the network programming schedule. In short order the ref was feeling a lot of heat. He turned it on Zorn.

"Eventually Mr. Official, he's saying, 'Hey, you've got to help me out here,'" the quarterback says. "And the players want to play, you know what I mean?" Zorn found himself very much alone at the center of the field. "I guess if I had been a little bolder or more devious," he says, "I might have said, 'Let's try and take this thing to the max.'" He folded.

"I just tried to be as loud as I could be," Zorn continues. "And I've got a pretty big voice. But with some of these crowds, the linemen just couldn't hear."

Clearly, the crowds were not going to back down. When Mudd left Seattle to help coach the Browns in 1983, he noticed that Cleveland Municipal Stadium had a large decibel meter on its scoreboard, which only encouraged the crowd to yell louder. By 1989 the noise problem was so out of hand—quarterbacks kept getting injured, and offenses had had enough—that the league at last stepped in. NFL Rule 4, Section 3, Article 7, Paragraph 13 ("Obvious inability of the offense to hear team signals due to crowd noise") was amended, installing a nine-step procedure so complex that it would have done UN arms negotiators proud. The new instructions said, in essence, that the ref could stop the game if the stadium was too loud, and after a series of warnings he could penalize the home team one of its time-outs. When all the time-outs were gone, he could assess five-yard penalties until the crowd backed off.

And it worked—except it didn't. Bengals coach Sam Wyche thought the rule was absurd, and he had his quarterback, Boomer Esiason, put it to the test in an exhibition game that year in the New Orleans Superdome. The crowd noise wasn't even that bad, but at Wyche's direction, Esiason complained, the ref stopped play, and when the warning went out over the public-address system, according to *Sports Illustrated* pro football guru Paul Zimmerman, "the decibel level [went] up by about 200 percent." So the ref threw the flag and subtracted a Saints time-out. The crowd roared all the louder. When New Orleans's timeouts were gone, the ref assessed a five-yard penalty, and finally the disgruntled crowd obeyed. Play resumed.

It proved to be a Pyrrhic victory. Football fans around the country erupted in protest. "Next day everyone who ever wrote a high school editorial was at his typewriter," Zimmerman wrote, "firing away about the high-handed NFL dictating to the fans, who spent their hard-earned money on a ticket, about when they could or could not make noise. There were cries of fascism from the left wing press." The league backed down.

"The rule was too complicated," says Joel Bussert, the NFL's vice president of player personnel and football operations. But that wasn't really it. The rule was universally unpopular. "We saw in that exhibition game that the crowd didn't care if the Saints kept their time-outs or not," says Bussert. "They lost all three time-outs! It was good sport. Everyone was having a good time. So the rule just disappeared by acclamation at the league meeting." Didn't work.

So linemen continued to flounder, and defensive ends continued to chalk up Hall of Fame sack totals. Various teams began experimenting with a silent count in the shotgun formation, but it was very limiting. Quarterbacks didn't like using it; they couldn't change the play once the team broke its huddle, and there was confusion when they signaled for receivers or running backs to go into motion. Mudd, who left Cleveland to coach in Kansas City and then went back for a second stretch with Seattle before joining the Colts in 1998, was convinced that the silent count could work. He was haunted by a conversation he'd had with a fellow Seattle coach, the late Andy MacDonald, who said he had spent some time early in his career coaching at a school for the deaf in Michigan.

"Wait," Mudd said, "they had a football team?"

Assured that they did, Mudd asked, "How do they coordinate the offensive line for the snap?" If a deaf team could launch a play in silence, why couldn't an NFL team?

After years of trial and error, of ill-conceived high-tech solutions and rules changes, here was the elegant answer: timing. Instead of calling out the count, the quarterback handed the responsibility to the center. He simply tapped the center on the butt when he was ready to receive the ball. The center then lifted his head to look squarely at the defensive player in front of him, signaling to the line that the silent snap count had started. He and the linemen would then count to themselves, "One-one-thousand," and the center would snap the ball.

It was so simple, it was beautiful. As soon as the center lifted his head, the other linemen could turn their heads toward the defenders, count one-one-thousand and go. To mix things up, the rhythm of the silent count was varied. In the huddle, the center was instructed to snap either one count after the signal or two. Football being the ultimate macho sport, the code became cock for one and balls for two.

Mudd had been around the NFL long enough to know that a new idea, even a great one, would be a hard sell. Football is a conservative sport. "It was like suggesting a different route home to someone who has been commuting the same way for years," Mudd says. "They'll say, 'I don't want to go that way.'"

At first Mudd's teams practiced the silent snap count reluctantly and used it sparingly, so the timing of the offensive linemen was off as much as it was on. But by the time Mudd started working with Colts linemen in 1998, charged with protecting Manning, the league's number one draft pick, he believed the silent count was more than just expedient. It was actually a better way to snap the ball.

What convinced him was left tackle Tarik Glenn.

A coach with a great idea is nothing without a great player. Glenn was the genius Mudd had been waiting for. "He was the best," Mudd says. "The best ever."

A first-round draft pick in 1997, Glenn spent his first year discovering that blocking NFL defensive ends was hard under ordinary circumstances, and when he couldn't hear, it was nearly impossible. Manning arrived the following year and was understandably frustrated when defensive ends kept hitting him like freight trains from his blind side. Mudd remembers hearing the quarterback chew out Glenn on the sideline during one game and stepping up to defend his tackle. "Tarik can't hear you," Mudd told Manning.

"Well, he should be able to hear," Manning complained. "It's not that loud."

"That's bullshit," Mudd said.

"Well, [tackle Adam] Meadows can hear!"

"You are not in charge of deciding what Tarik can hear and what he can't hear!" Mudd told him.

Mudd prevailed on his skeptical coach, Jim Mora, to let him drill the players on the silent count at every practice. If deaf kids could do it, Mudd told the players, pros could too. And he was right. In time Manning became a fervent convert.

"I was wrong, and Howard was right," Manning says. "It was my responsibility to make sure all the linemen could hear me, and it was especially difficult for us because we were using a no-huddle offense most of the time. The silent count solved a lot of problems for us."

The Colts got good at it. Glenn got very good at it. He learned to time the count to the swivel of his head. It was like a dance move. "It made a huge difference," he says. "It gave me time to face the task at hand. It's all about timing, and pretty quick I could just feel it." In fact Glenn started getting off the snap so fast that refs flagged him, claiming he had jumped too early. Mudd defended him. "He would send a man to the league office and have them review it," says Glenn. "After a while they started to see that I wasn't offside. Coach Howard didn't just come up with the silent count; he sold it, to the team and then to the league."

Soon Manning and Saturday were using the silent count for every snap on the road, and they even used it in their own domed stadium when things got too loud. Manning by then was famous for gesticulating and shouting instructions from the backfield before the snap of the ball. With the silent count he didn't have to worry about inadvertently triggering—à la Baab—the snap. Once he had things set the way he wanted, he would tap or signal Saturday, and the silent count would take over. "He could also do more to manipulate the defense with his leg, given that they had to anticipate the snap so much more intensely," the retired center recalls.

Manning noticed another advantage. "Our timing got so good with it," he says, "we were getting fewer offensive penalties on the road than at home." The silent count was not just a remedy for the noise problem; it was also a secret weapon. During Mudd's twelve years in Indianapolis, his offensive line allowed fewer sacks than any other in the NFL, even though Manning's offense relied on passing. The Colts won the Super Bowl in 2007.

In the highly competitive world of the NFL, anything that works is quickly adopted leaguewide. As Mudd recalls, the first team to pick up the silent snap count after Indianapolis was New England. Then came Pittsburgh. Coaches would call Mudd to ask about the count. That put him in a tough spot, because the Colts had come to regard it as a prized secret.

George Sefcik, the Falcons' offensive coordinator, called after Indianapolis gave his team trouble in the Georgia Dome in 1998. "Are you guys using a silent count?" he asked.

"Yeah," said Mudd.

"Well, how do you do that?"

Mudd was torn between his loyalty to the Colts and the kinship he felt with other longtime pro coaches—and he was damn proud of what he had done. "OK, there's a rhythm that the center has after the quarterback taps him on the ass," he told Sefcik. "You guys will have to figure out the rest. I don't feel comfortable telling you every little part of it."

The Falcons figured out enough to use the count against the Vikings in the cacophonous Metrodome in the 1999 NFC title game. "My gosh," Sefcik told Mudd afterward, "that is the most incredible thing."

Some found it hard to believe how often the Colts used the snap. Mudd got a phone call one day from Juan Castillo, who was then coaching the offensive line in Philadelphia. "I know you do the silent count on every snap, right?" he said. Mudd confirmed it.

"Well, Brad Childress [the Eagles' offensive coordinator, Castillo's boss] doesn't believe you do it every snap."

"You have that son of a bitch call me," said Mudd, "and I'll tell him."

Today every team in the NFL uses the silent snap count. Many centers signal its start by turning their heads to the side once or twice, but the basics are still the ones Mudd put in place in 1998 with the Colts.

Moments of true vindication in a man's life are rare, but Mudd's came at a 2006 meeting of the NFL Competition Committee. He had been asked to attend as a consultant on a proposed rule change having nothing to do with the silent snap count, but during the session Jeff Fisher—who was then the Titans' head coach, and whose entire career as an NFL defensive coach (1985–1994) had been square in the sack-happy era—launched a sustained objection to the growing use of the silent count. Fisher complained that the count was giving offensive linemen—here it came—an unfair advantage! When the center lifted or turned his head to signal that the silent count had begun, Fisher argued, he violated the rule against linemen moving before the snap of the ball.

"The rule says that the center has to come to a complete stop for a full second before the ball is snapped," said Fisher. He went on about it for some time, making the same point: it wasn't fair!

Eventually Seahawks coach Mike Holmgren, an old offensive coordinator, started chuckling. "Jeff, when are you supposed to go on defense anyway?" he asked.

"Well, they are drawing us offside, and they are not supposed to," argued Fisher.

"Jeff, when are you supposed to go on defense?" Holmgren repeated.

"They are not coming to a full stop!"

"Jeff, when are you supposed to go?"

Finally Fisher conceded, "When the ball goes."

Howard Mudd's revolution was complete.

Complaints like Fisher's didn't go away immediately. The next year the NFL circulated a memo instructing centers to stop moving their heads a full second before snapping the ball. Otherwise refs would flag them for illegal motion. It sounded like a small thing, but the Colts had perfected the rhythm of the silent count and did not want to mess with it. So they ignored the memo. Refs found the new rule too difficult to enforce, and it went the way of flags for excessive crowd noise.

It disappeared by acclamation.

The Hardest Job
in Football

Atlantic, January/February 2009

If you were one of the millions of Americans watching NFL football on Sunday afternoon, September 21, 2008, you might have caught the humdinger of a finish in the New York Giants–Cincinnati Bengals game. At the two-minute warning, the winless Bengals were up by four points, but the Giants were threatening: they had the ball inside the Bengals' ten, poised to score what looked like the winning touchdown.

Most of the people who witnessed this seesaw battle were watching it on CBS. The capacity crowd in Giants Stadium was 79,276 that afternoon, but was less than 1 percent of the game's total audience. More than any other professional sport, football is primarily a television show. Many die-hard fans have never even attended a contest in person. For them, a football game is something that unfolds on their screen in a smooth and familiar way, so commonplace that few give it a second thought. The broadcast arrives in their living room, packaged in stereo sound and in full-color high definition, shown from continually shifting angles, from stadium-embracing wide shots to intimate close-ups, all of it smoothly orchestrated and narrated, and delivered up as though from the all-seeing eye of the supreme NFL fan, God Almighty.

But let's give it a second thought. Consider for a moment the complexity of a mere snippet of what you might have seen on the tube that Sunday afternoon:

In the seconds between the return from the two-minute-warning commercial break and the snap of the ball to Giants quarterback Eli Manning, as play-by-play man Greg Gumbel quickly oriented the audience—*It has been a dandy here at Giants Stadium. Two minutes to play. Bengals by four. Giants at the six-yard line. Second and goal. The Giants have one time-out remaining*—the following scene-setting images flashed past in rapid succession:

- A high, wide shot of the stadium and the walls of cheering fans.
- Bengals quarterback Carson Palmer watching anxiously from the sidelines.
- Bengals coach Marvin Lewis looking perplexed on the sidelines.
- Giants coach Tom Coughlin, head down, talking intently into his headset microphone.
- On the field, a close-up of Bengals middle linebacker Dhani Jones pointing urgently to his teammates and shouting, positioning them for the snap.
- Manning shouting and gesturing behind center.
- Giants wide receiver Plaxico Burress lined up in the slot, poised, looking back toward Manning.
- A wide shot showing the complete line of scrimmage as the ball is snapped and the play begins.

Roll back to the beginning of this brief sequence, and here is how it sounded inside the windowless production trailer parked outside the stadium, where two rows of technicians sat beneath the glow of a hundred TV monitors, twenty screens across stacked five deep. Staring at this wall were three men: producer Mark Wolff on the left; technical director Dennis Stone on the right; and between them the show's impresario, its director, Bob Fishman, known as "Fish."

Just before coming back on the air after the commercial, the crew counted down in unison:

"Five!"

"Four!"

"Three!"

Wolff shouted, "Fish is going to cut some shots!"

"Two!"

"One!"

"Aaaand go!" shouted Fish, a wiry man wearing faded blue jeans, a loose-fitting long-sleeved cotton shirt, and a headset clamped over a baseball cap. He was leaning up and out of his swivel chair, choosing shots and barking orders, arms elevated, snapping his long fingers loudly with each new command. "Go fan shot! Ready four. Take four! Ready eight. Take eight! Ready one. Take one! Ready twelve. Take twelve! Ready five. Take five! Ready three—ready two. Take two! Ready three. Take three!"

Camera three, which Fish returned to just before the snap of the ball, offers a wide angle from above that's used to frame the play. In this case, with one eye on the play clock, Fish sneaked in one last scene-setting image—Burress lined up and looking back toward his quarterback—before returning to the wide angle as the ball was snapped.

This was just thirty seconds. The entire broadcast would last more than three and a half hours.

If the production crew of a televised football game is like a symphony orchestra, Bob Fishman is its conductor. He sits front and center in the dark trailer, insulated from the sunshine and the roar of the crowd, taking the fragments of sounds and moving images and assembling the broadcast on the fly, mediating the real event into the digital one. He scans the dizzying bank of screens to select the next shot, and the next, and the next, layering in replays, graphics, and sound, barking his orders via headset to his crew, plugging into a rhythm that echoes the pulse of the game.

Every bit as much as the athletic contest on the field, this is a performance, an improvisation, a largely unheralded art form peculiar to the modern age. Wolff is in charge of the broadcast; Gumbel and analyst Dan Dierdorf are its voices and faces, but their work exists to complement the show Fish orchestrates on screen. Having once seen him in action, having peeked behind the curtain in the Palace of Oz, I can hardly watch any other sporting event on TV without picturing this frantic, sinewy fifty-nine-year-old calling shot after shot after shot, half sitting and half standing, the dervish behind the professional program smoothly unspooling in your living room and in your brain.

Recently, some cable and satellite companies began offering viewers a chance to, in effect, direct their own experience of a game by selecting camera angles, isolated shots, and replays as they wish. This may satisfy a few eccentric fans who prefer, say, to watch a middle linebacker's–eye view for an entire game, but it suggests a failure to grasp the level of difficulty involved in what happens in that production trailer every Sunday. The television crews don't just broadcast a game; they inhabit it. They know the players, the teams, the stats, and the strategies. They interview players and coaches the day before the game. They brainstorm, anticipate, plot likely story lines, prepare graphic packages of important stats, and bundle replays from previous contests to bring a sense of history and context to the event. They are not just pointing cameras and broadcasting the feed; they are telling the story of the game as it happens.

And at the center of their effort is the director, Fish, who seems a more agreeable version of the finicky, exasperated comedian Larry David, whom he resembles, right down to the *Curb Your Enthusiasm* logo on the baseball cap he wears pulled down to his eyebrows. He peers out at the world through wire-rimmed glasses; plays guitar in a group of aging rockers; and loves to talk music, film, politics, journalism . . . but mostly, he loves to talk sports. He has won eleven Emmys, and justly so: for those who regard Sunday afternoons in football season as sacred, Fish is nothing less than a high priest.

His camera operators revere him. Out of Fish's earshot they have nothing but praise for him—and this from men (and one woman) with the blue-collar workers' hearty, time-honored disdain for the boss.

"Most of them are assholes," said one, sitting at a round table with four fellow operators, who all nodded in agreement.

"Fish is the best," the same cameraman explained.

"He appreciates what you bring to the job," said another.

"Suppose a defensive back makes an interception," said the first. "At some point, I know, they are going to want to come back to a close-up of him. So when I know they are on another shot, I'll use those seconds to start panning up and down the sidelines, looking for him. Fish knows what I'm doing. Another director might say, 'We don't need that now,' and they wouldn't say it nice, either. I'm thinking, *No shit, but you're going to ask for the shot in forty-five seconds, and you're going to get pissed off if I spend fifteen seconds panning around looking for the guy.*"

"He never gets excited," says another, "and he has this ability to see *everything*. If you have a good shot, he not only notices it; he uses it. Other directors might say, 'Wow, that's really nice,' and never work it into the broadcast. Fish pulls the trigger."

The first major event Bob Fishman directed was the Apollo 17 moon launch on December 7, 1972, when the assigned director fell ill and Fish was the only CBS employee in the NASA press grandstand with a Directors Guild membership card. People noticed that he was good at it. He shifted from news to sports in 1976, and since then he has conducted basketball, football, baseball, auto racing, and Olympics events, as one of a small corps of specialists who assemble and deliver the programs for which the networks pay billions.

Fish grew up in the Virgin Islands, part of a Jewish family that owned a big vacation hotel, a sports-crazy kid with no local teams to follow. For him, pro sports have always been synonymous with television, and like any sincere professional, he cares a great deal about the medium's aesthetics and standards. Nothing annoys him more these days than broadcasts—he mentions the name of one rival network (Fox) with particular disdain—that exhibit a faddish desire to neglect on-the-field action for reaction shots from the crowd. He cites with particular horror one NCAA playoff game on ESPN when the director routinely cut away from the court after a basket was scored to show fans' reactions, and thus missed a historically well-executed full-court press.

"There were seven steals!" he says. "Seven! Five of them resulted in baskets!" The team repeatedly stealing the ball was Kentucky, "and *everybody* knew that they always applied a full-court press after a basket! The steals were critical to their success in the game, and the audience didn't even see them!"

It was love at first sight when television met football for the first time, in 1939, in a game between Fordham University and Waynesburg College. Even though there was only one camera, mounted on a platform on the sidelines, the magic was apparent. Fans at home enjoyed a view comparable to that of a coach on the sidelines, and potential sponsors quickly realized that just as baseball came with built-in commercial breaks between innings, football afforded commercial opportunities between quarters and during time-outs.

Nineteen years later, when almost fifty million people, the largest crowd ever to witness a football game, watched the Baltimore Colts beat the Giants in overtime for the 1958 NFL championship, NBC had four cameras trained on the field, and a fifth pointed at an easel with cards reading "First Quarter," "Second Quarter," etc. Slow-motion replays and isolated shots were still in the future, but by then the sport and the medium were effectively engaged.

By the time Fish moved from news to sports in the mid-1970s, the union was complete. Since then, broadcast dollars have helped turn players into multimillionaires and owners into billionaires. The medium has infiltrated the game itself—as with TV time-outs, when players mill around aimlessly on the field waiting for commercials to end; and coaches' challenges that rely on footage from network cameras to revisit referees' questionable decisions. On the sidelines, coaches and players scrutinize shots from overhead cameras to study tactics and plot countermoves. Viewers at home see virtual bands drawn across the field denoting the lines of scrimmage and the first-down marker, and they can refer anytime to a floating graphic in an upper corner of the screen that displays the score, time remaining, and down and distance.

It's become so hard to imagine NFL football without television that when a power failure shut down all of CBS's cameras at a packed Ralph Wilson Stadium in Buffalo earlier this season, just minutes before kickoff, the first reaction from Mark Wolff, the stunned producer in the trailer, was, "There's *no way* they are playing this game."

"Mark, there are more than seventy thousand paying customers waiting for kickoff in there," I said. "They have two teams, officials, whistles . . . Why wouldn't they play the game?"

"It's just like a weather delay," insisted Wolff. "They'll wait until we have the power back, and then they'll play."

That day, Wolff was wrong; they kicked off on time in Buffalo and played much of the game without power, no doubt because CBS had several other regional games to offer its viewers. But if the same thing had happened on a Sunday night or Monday night, or on a playoff weekend, or, God forbid, before the Super Bowl, when the whole world is waiting with its bowls of popcorn, kicking off without the cameras might well have provoked worldwide rioting.

Up to twenty cameras and forty replay machines are employed in the broadcast of big games, offering views and replays of the action from every conceivable angle. Even with all this, the networks constantly strain to find newfangled gadgets to distinguish their coverage. Cameras have been suspended from cables over the field or, in one silly innovation, mounted on the players themselves—the short-lived XFL's "helmet-cam"—which on a running back typically delivered a violently jerky, incoherent swirl of bodies culminating in a close-up of the turf. In the Giants-Bengals game, CBS was experimenting with something called "flow motion," which employs GPS and replay technology to track the movements of players. Fish had used it the previous month while broadcasting U.S. Open tennis, where it charted the labyrinthine path traced by, say, Roger Federer during a long, hard-played point. But the system turns out to have little application to the gridiron, where the only distances that matter are measured by hash marks in the grass.

Cutbacks at CBS have reduced what Fish has to work with in regular-season games. There are the three primary cameras, positioned on platforms at the mezzanine level, peering down over the sideline. These are set thirty yards apart, with camera two in the middle over the fifty-yard line. Before each snap of the ball, Fish designates which camera operator will cover the action—generally the one closest to the ball—and the other two operators move their cameras to specific assignments. (One may focus on the defense, for instance, while the other isolates the far receiver.) Camera four is high behind the eastern end zone, and on each play, it frames the middle of the offensive line and then follows the ball, providing another high angle on the action for replay purposes. Camera five sits on a rolling platform behind the visiting bench and moves on a track from one end of the field to the other, giving a field-level view of the action. It is usually positioned about five yards ahead of the line of scrimmage, but when the offense is in the "red zone" (that is, inside the opposing team's twenty-yard line), it sits even with the goal line to provide a clear look at whether the ball crosses over for a touchdown.

These are the basics, cameras one through five, that are used to cover every televised football game, college or pro. The rest are specialty cameras. Six and eight are mounted on three-foot-high platforms behind each end zone, to one side of the goalposts. Camera six is equipped with "super slo-mo," which during baseball broadcasts can capture the spinning seams of a slider approaching home plate at nearly ninety miles per hour. Fish will sometimes instruct these cameras' operators to focus on specific players—in this game they were Justin Tuck, the Giants' gifted pass-rushing end; and Bengals receiver Chad Johnson—in order to put together a video package that summarizes those players' ups and downs during the game.

Camera seven is roving and handheld, good for close-ups of players and coaches on the sidelines, or of fans in the lower seats, or just to find the eye candy Fish uses to segue into and out of commercial breaks. High at one corner of the end zone is camera twelve, the "slash" camera (since this was just a regular-season game, there was no camera nine, ten, or eleven), which on most plays isolates the slot receiver or, if there is none, the middle linebacker. With the slash camera, camera five, and two of the primary cameras all focusing on individual receivers, it's pretty much guaranteed that on every passing play, the broadcast will have an isolated shot of the quarterback's target. On these shots, the camera operators know they should frame the receiver from head to toe, and keep the defender in the picture, so that on replay it's clear whether the pass catcher's feet were in-bounds, or whether there was pass interference. (The cameras are operated by a core crew that travels each week with the CBS technicians, and by a handful of local pros who sign on for single games.)

There are other cameras: one called "all twenty-two," which shoots the whole field from a fixed position high above; one in the booth for when Gumbel and Dierdorf are onscreen; and for this game, one, providing stunning September-afternoon vistas of Manhattan and northern New Jersey, from the blimp hovering over the stadium. And there's footage that doesn't come directly from the cameras—graphics packages, replays, preprepared features about specific players or situations, and so forth—all of which is supervised by Wolff.

But the cameras are all, of course, just tools. The goal is to tell stories with them. The game itself is the primary story, but within it are dozens of subplots. Hence the importance of the pregame sit-downs with players and coaches, which are essentially fishing expeditions for the CBS team—chances to pick up on potential story lines and revealing details that can be worked into the broadcast.

The ideal interviewee is someone like Bengals wide receiver Johnson, a ruthlessly candid player who began his session with Dierdorf, Gumbel, Fish, and Wolff by dramatically asking the Bengals' PR rep to leave the room. The Giants came into that Sunday riding high—counting their march to the Super Bowl victory the previous winter, they had won six straight games—but Johnson's Bengals were desperate for a win. They were coming off a losing season, and they'd dropped their first two games. In his conversation with the CBS team the day before the Giants game, Johnson quickly served up a dire prediction: "If we lose tomorrow, we have a chance of going zero and eight. It don't get any easier." (Dire and prescient: not until the ninth week of the season would the Bengals win their first game, over the Jacksonville Jaguars.)

Johnson has a genius for drawing attention to himself. The previous week, he had stirred things up by suggesting publicly that his team's offense was struggling because of poor pass-blocking by the offensive line.

In the pregame conversation, Dierdorf, a Hall of Fame offensive lineman with deep knowledge of the game, who knew that such comments drive the big men crazy, asked if the Bengals blockers had "gotten their noses out of joint."

"They better not. Get mad at what?" Johnson asked. "This ain't no fucking time to be sensitive! It's time to play. If they ain't blocking, my ass is gonna look bad."

Johnson, who had yet to catch a touchdown pass in 2008, had also engineered a stunt guaranteed to keep him on the flapping lips of every sports-talk radio and TV host in the country. He had legally changed his name to a Spanish version of the number on his jersey, "85." He was now officially "Ocho-Cinco," although the NFL marketing division had ruled that the name on his uniform would have to remain "C. Johnson" unless he wanted to reimburse Reebok for its stock of unsold jerseys with that name stitched on the back.

Dierdorf and Gumbel pounced on the name change.

"What do you do when somebody goes, 'Oh, there's Chad Johnson!' How do you respond to that?" Dierdorf asked.

Johnson just shrugged and smiled.

"Do you say, 'No, that's not my name anymore'?"

"No," Johnson said, shaking his head in disbelief. "I'm not that serious about it, man."

"What do you want us to call you tomorrow?" Dierdorf asked.

"It's on you."

"It's your life," Dierdorf said. "Your name."

"Hey, it's not that serious!" Johnson protested, dismayed at having to explain the joke. "Call me Chad."

"Did you have your credit cards and driver's license changed?" Gumbel asked.

Johnson looked pained—a wit trapped in a world with no sense of humor. "No, man, I did it to have the name changed on my jersey, that's it. And they messed it up. I'm not sure what they're doing, I just know that they boosted sales of my jersey back to number one. It's a money issue."

Then Ocho-Cinco, or Johnson, or Chad, ever the showman, left, with a tantalizing tip for the broadcast.

"Here's a hint," he said. "The first play of the game. I'll leave it at that. Don't tell anybody."

The next morning, Fish passed this bit of inside dope along to his camera crew.

"I will tell you this," he said. "Whoever is doing far receiver or near receiver, Chad Johnson, whether we can believe him or not, whether it's the typical player bullshit they give the press, watch for a deep pattern, a deep pass, on the first play from scrimmage. . . . I think they are going to go deep. Johnson says, 'Just make sure you cover me on the first play.' That may have just been blah-blah-blah-blah, but actually, some guys tell you the truth and that actually happens."

When the Bengals took possession for the first time in the game, the TV crew was poised. Moments before coming back from a commercial, Fish reminded his camera operators, "OK, guys, let's watch Chad Johnson on this first play."

In unison, the voices in the trailer counted down the seconds to the return from the commercial: "Six. Five. Four."

"Stand by," said Fish. "Slow push in."

"Three. Two. One."

"Ready five [a close-up of Carson Palmer breaking the offensive huddle]," said Fish. "Aaaaand take five!"

The music started, and as the Bengals quarterback positioned himself over center, Gumbel intoned, *Carson Palmer looking for a breakout game today. He has been very un–Carson Palmerlike so far. No TDs, three picks.*

"Ready three [the play-by-play camera]. Take three!" said Fish, and then, noting the Bengals' formation, added, "Two wides! Two wides, that's all."

Let's see if the Bengals try to jump on the Giants in a hurry, said Gumbel, like a man who knew something his viewers did not know.

The ball was snapped.

Fish: "Pass! Here it is!"

Only, here it wasn't. Johnson was racing deep, but the Giants defensive line swamped the quarterback immediately, dropping him for a six-yard loss.

Palmer under pressure, trying to get away, and can't! Gumbel said.

Fish: "Ready eight [a close-up of Palmer with his face in the turf]. Take eight! Ready two [standing Giants fans clapping and cheering]. Take two! Ready five [a close-up of Palmer getting to his feet]. Take five! Ready four [Giants tackle Fred Robbins, who got the sack]. Take four!"

Chad Johnson was flying up the left side, Gumbel said. *Palmer couldn't get it away.*

There was no chance of completing a pass, Dierdorf said. *He was fighting just to stay up.*

Fish: "Hold four [Robbins lining up for the next play]. Hold four."

The Bengals would end this first offensive series backed up against their own goal line, twenty yards behind where they started—victims of a sack, a penalty (on the offensive line), and a second Giants rush that forced Palmer to fumble the ball, which Cincinnati recovered. The frustration and disappointment on the field were mirrored in the broadcast booth and in the trailer, where Cincinnati's failure to execute had cost them the chance to show how on top of a big play they were.

The whole thing seemed like the Bengals' sorry season in a nutshell, underlining the truth of Johnson's impolitic insight: no blocking meant no throws, which meant no big plays. As the punt team lined up, Fish called for a shot of the Cincinnati receiver and quarterback walking off the field together.

The biggest fear of any broadcast team is a blowout. The audience changes the channel, and even the camera operators have trouble keeping their heads in the game. "You just want to get the hell out of there and move on to next week, because the game sucks," says Fish.

But in spite of the inauspicious start, the Giants-Bengals game turned out to be a terrific matchup, all the more so for being unexpected. "On any given Sunday . . . ," the adage goes, and in this one the winless Bengals found themselves four points up on the champs, 20–16, with less than two minutes to play. As the Giants conferred during a Cincinnati time-out, with Eli Manning preparing to attempt a go-ahead touchdown, the trailer was humming. Amid overlapping conversations, sound effects, and shouted instructions from the rows of technicians, Wolff primed his broadcasters and replay operators, and Fish, standing now, barked instructions and waved his hands to some rapid internal rhythm:

"Ready two [Bengals coach Marvin Lewis talking into his headset microphone]. Take two! Ready one [Carson Palmer craning his neck to see the field]. Take one! Ready twelve [Eli Manning walking toward the sidelines to confer with Giants offensive coordinator Kevin Gilbride]. Take twelve!"

He's pretty cool for someone so young, Gumbel said.

Well, it's in his DNA, Dierdorf replied. (Manning, as most NFL fans know, is the son of former New Orleans Saints quarterback Archie, and the kid brother of Indianapolis Colts star quarterback Peyton.) *I don't think we should be surprised. This is a regular-season game. They are two and zero.*

Fish: "Ready eight [Lewis from a fresh angle]. Take eight! Ready four [Manning trotting back out to the field]. Take four! Ready five [a field shot from ground level]. Take five! Ready . . . aaah . . . eight [Manning from another angle]. Take eight! . . . Ready four—five [another shot of Lewis]. Take five! Ready three [play-by-play camera]. Take three. Nice shot, Pat!"

As the Giants lined up over the ball, Wolff wanted attention paid to wide receiver Plaxico Burress, a likely target. "Cover seventeen! Iso [isolate] seventeen!"

Fish: "Where's seventeen?"

Wolff: "Far-side receiver."

Fish: "Far receiver on camera two!"

But the pass wasn't to Burress; it was to tight end Kevin Boss, who caught it in the end zone. From outside the trailer came the roar of jubilant Giants fans. Inside, the touchdown ignited a frenzy as well. Fish machine-gunned a mosaic of the scene, leaning toward his array of monitors as the cameras swung violently, finding one telling visual after another, his high-pitched voice squeaking at the upper reaches of its register:

"Ready five [close-up of Manning jumping for joy]. Take five! Ready two [close-up of Boss, still carrying the ball, mobbed by joyful teammates in the end zone]. Take two! Ready three [rejoicing New York fans]. Take three! Ready four [beaten Bengals strong safety Chinedum Ndukwe trotting off the field]. Take four! Ready eight [Marvin Lewis looking forlornly up at the scoreboard]. Take eight! Ready twelve [a pan of cheering Giants fans in the upper deck]. Take twelve! Ready two [another close-up of Boss]. Take two! Ready five [a close-up of Manning leaving the field]. Take five! Ready eight [close-up of the shell-shocked Chad Johnson]. Take eight! Ready three [another crowd shot]. Take three! Ready two [a close-up of Boss, reaching the sidelines, still carrying his touchdown catch]. Take two! Ready twelve [Bengals huddling on the field before the extra point]. Take twelve! Ready six [close-up of Manning accepting a pat on the helmet from Gilbride]. Take six! Ready four [close-up of Lewis, shaking his head with disgust]. Take four! Ready five [more high fives for Manning on the sidelines]. Take five! Break! Extra point! Ready four [a high shot in the end zone behind the goalposts as the Giants line up to kick]."

Wolff: "Fish, I'm going X, Y, Silver, Moe!"—the lineup of upcoming replay shots of the touchdown. (The replay machines are given letters, to differentiate them from the numbered cameras.)

Fish: "Ready two [Boss on one knee on the sidelines, having been mildly shaken up on his touchdown play, trainers crowded around him]. Take two! Ready four, aaaand take four!" The extra point was booted.

Wolff: "Are you listening?"

Fish: "Yes! X, Y, Silver, Moe!"

Wolff: "I'll talk you through it."

Fish: "Ready two [another shot of Boss on the sideline]. Take two! Ready X. Aaaand take X! Here it is!"

The replays of the touchdown followed, each from a different angle, the last an isolated shot from an end-zone camera showing Manning celebrating after the play. Then it was time for another blizzard of calls from Fish.

This frenzied movement after the Giants touchdown seemed to mark the conclusion of the symphony, a game-ending flourish. But the game was far from over. "I want to see Carson Palmer's career comebacks!" Wolff shouted to his graphics technicians, who summoned up a graphic showing that the Bengals QB had an impressive record of bringing his team back from late-game deficits. And sure enough, the scrappy Bengals mounted a last-second drive and kicked a tying field goal in the closing seconds, forcing the game into overtime, in which the Giants marched into field-goal range and won it, finally, 26–23, with a well-directed twenty-two-yard boot.

By the end, Fish was hoarse. A police escort waited to whisk him and the CBS crew to the airport ahead of the thousands of fans exiting the stadium. On the plane home, he would review a hastily assembled DVD of the broadcast, which he—unlike his millions of viewers—would be seeing for the first time. Like any other artist, when he watches the program, he mostly sees the things he might have done better.

When I last saw Fish, he was leaving the trailer, getting ready to figure out where he and his crew would be going next week. But I already knew the answer. Whether his windowless production trailer was in the parking lot outside Lambeau Field or Dolphin Stadium, he would be in the same place he is every week of the season for millions of football fans all across America: behind the curtain, lodged deep inside our brains.

The Man Who Broke Atlantic City

Atlantic, April 2012

Don Johnson finds it hard to remember the exact cards. Who could? At the height of his twelve-hour blitz of the Tropicana casino in Atlantic City, New Jersey, last April, he was playing a hand of blackjack nearly every minute.

Dozens of spectators pressed against the glass of the high-roller pit. Inside, playing at a green felt table opposite a black-vested dealer, a burly middle-aged man in a red cap and black Oregon State hoodie was wagering $100,000 a hand. Word spreads when the betting is that big. Johnson was on an amazing streak. The towers of chips stacked in front of him formed a colorful miniature skyline. His winning run had been picked up by the casino's watchful overhead cameras and drawn the close scrutiny of the pit bosses. In just one hand, he remembers, he won $800,000. In a three-hand sequence, he took $1.2 million.

The basics of blackjack are simple. Almost everyone knows them. You play against the house. Two cards are placed faceup before the player, and two more cards, one down, one up, before the dealer. A card's suit doesn't matter; only its numerical value matters—each face card is worth ten, and an ace can be either one or eleven. The goal is to get to twenty-one, or as close to it as possible without going over. Scanning the cards on the table before him, the player can either stand or keep taking cards in an effort to approach twenty-one. Since the house's hand has one card facedown, the player can't know exactly what the hand is, which is what makes this a game.

As Johnson remembers it, the $800,000 hand started with him betting $100,000 and being dealt two eights. If a player is dealt two of a kind, he can choose to "split" the hand, which means he can play each of the cards as a separate hand and ask for two more cards, in effect doubling his bet. That's what Johnson did. His next two cards, surprisingly, were also both eights, so he split each again. Getting four cards in a row of the same number doesn't happen often, but it does happen. Johnson says he was once dealt six consecutive aces at the Mohegan Sun casino in Connecticut. He was now playing four hands, each consisting of a single eight card, with $400,000 in the balance.

He was neither nervous nor excited. Johnson plays a long game, so the ups and downs of individual hands, even big swings like this one, don't matter that much to him. He is a veteran player. Little interferes with his concentration. He doesn't get rattled. With him, it's all about the math, and he knows it cold. Whenever the racily clad cocktail waitress wandered in with a fresh whiskey and Diet Coke, he took it from the tray.

The house's hand showed an upturned five. Arrayed on the table before him were the four eights. He was allowed to double down—to double his bet—on any hand, so when he was dealt a three on the first of his hands, he doubled his bet on that one, to $200,000. When his second hand was dealt a two, he doubled down on that, too. When he was dealt a three and a two on the next two hands, he says, he doubled down on those, for a total wager of $800,000.

It was the dealer's turn. He drew a ten, so the two cards he was showing totaled fifteen. Johnson called the game—in essence, betting that the dealer's down card was seven or higher, which would push his hand over twenty-one. This was a good bet: since all face cards are worth ten, the deck holds more high cards than low. When the dealer turned over the house's down card, it was a ten, busting him. Johnson won all four hands.

Johnson didn't celebrate. He didn't even pause. As another skyscraper of chips was pushed into his skyline, he signaled for the next hand. He was just getting started.

The headline in the *Press of Atlantic City* was enough to gladden the heart of anyone who has ever made a wager or rooted for the underdog:

> Blackjack Player Takes Tropicana
> for Nearly $6 Million,
> Single-Handedly Ruins Casino's Month

But the story was even bigger than that. Johnson's assault on the Tropicana was merely the latest in a series of blitzes he'd made on Atlantic City's gambling establishments. In the four previous months, he'd taken $5 million from the Borgata casino and another $4 million from Caesars. Caesars had cut him off, he says, and then effectively banned him from its casinos worldwide.

Fifteen million dollars in winnings from three different casinos? Nobody gets that lucky. How did he do it?

The first and most obvious suspicion was card counting. Card counters seek to gain a strong advantage by keeping a mental tally of every card dealt, and then adjusting the wager according to the value of the cards that remain in the deck. (The tactic requires both great memory and superior math skills.) Made famous in books and movies, card counting is considered cheating, at least by casinos. In most states (but not New Jersey), known practitioners are banned. The wagering of card counters assumes a clearly recognizable pattern over time, and Johnson was being watched very carefully. The verdict: card counting was not Don Johnson's game. He had beaten the casinos fair and square.

It hurt. Largely as a result of Johnson's streak, the Trop's table-game revenues for April 2011 were second-lowest among the eleven casinos in Atlantic City. Mark Giannantonio, the president and CEO of the Trop, who had authorized the limit of $100,000 a hand for Johnson, was given the boot weeks later. Johnson's winnings had administered a similar jolt to the Borgata and to Caesars. All of these gambling houses were already hurting, what with the spread of legalized gambling in surrounding states. By April, combined monthly gaming revenue had been declining on a year-over-year basis for thirty-two months.

For most people, though, the newspaper headline told a happy story. An ordinary guy in a red cap and black hoodie had struck it rich, had beaten the casinos black-and-blue. It seemed a fantasy come true, the very dream that draws suckers to the gaming tables.

But that's not the whole story either.

Despite his pedestrian attire, Don Johnson is no average Joe. For one thing, he is an extraordinarily skilled blackjack player. Tony Rodio, who succeeded Giannantonio as the Trop's CEO, says, "He plays *perfect* cards." In every blackjack scenario, Johnson knows the right decision to make. But that's true of plenty of good players. What gives Johnson his edge is his knowledge of the gaming industry. As good as he is at playing cards, he turns out to be even better at playing the casinos.

Hard times do not favor the house. The signs of a five-year slump are evident all over Atlantic City, in run-down facades, empty parking lots, and the faded glitz of its casinos' garish interiors. Pennsylvania is likely to supplant New Jersey this year as the second-largest gaming state in the nation. The new Parx racetrack and casino in Bensalem, Pennsylvania, a gigantic gambling complex, is less than eighty miles away from the Atlantic City boardwalk. Revenue from Atlantic City's eleven casinos fell from a high of $5.2 billion in 2006 to just $3.3 billion last year. The local gaming industry hopes the opening of a twelfth casino, Revel, this spring may finally reverse that downward trend, but that's unlikely.

"It doesn't matter how many casinos there are," Israel Posner, a gaming-industry expert at nearby Stockton College, told me. When you add gaming tables or slots at a fancy new venue like the Revel, or like the Borgata, which opened in 2003, the novelty may initially draw crowds, but adding gaming supply without enlarging the number of customers ultimately hurts everyone.

When revenues slump, casinos must rely more heavily on their most prized customers, the high rollers who wager huge amounts—tens of thousands or even hundreds of thousands of dollars a hand. Hooking and reeling in these "whales," as they are known in the industry, can become essential. High rollers are lured with free meals and drinks, free luxury suites, free rides on private jets, and . . . more. (There's a reason most casino ads feature beautiful, scantily clad young women.) The marketers present casinos as glamorous playgrounds where workaday worries and values like morality, sobriety, and prudence are on vacation. *When you're rich, normal rules don't apply!* The idea, like pickpockets' oldest tricks, is to distract the mark with such frolic that he doesn't notice he's losing far more than his free amenities actually cost. For what doth it profit a man to gain a $20,000 ride on a private jet if he drops $200,000 playing poker? The right "elite player" can lose enough in a weekend to balance a casino's books for a month.

Of course, high rollers "are not all created equally," says Rodio, the Tropicana's CEO. (He was the only Atlantic City casino executive who agreed to talk to me about Johnson.) "When someone makes all the right decisions, the house advantage is relatively small; maybe we will win, on average, one or two hands more than him for every hundred decisions. There are other blackjack players, or craps players, who don't use perfect strategy, and with them there is a big swing in the house advantage. So there is more competition among casinos for players who aren't as skilled."

For the casino, the art is in telling the skilled whales from the unskilled ones, then discouraging the former and seducing the latter. The industry pays close attention to high-level players; once a player earns a reputation for winning, the courtship ends. The last thing a skilled player wants is a big reputation. Some wear disguises when they play.

But even though he has been around the gambling industry for all of his forty-nine years, Johnson sneaked up on Atlantic City. To look at him, over six feet tall and thickly built, you would never guess that he was once a jockey. He grew up tending his uncle's racehorses in Salem, Oregon, and began riding them competitively at age fifteen. In his best years as a professional jockey, he was practically skeletal. He stood six foot one and weighed only 108 pounds. He worked with a physician to keep weight off, fighting his natural growth rate with thyroid medication that amped up his metabolism and subsisting on vitamin supplements. The regimen was so demanding that he eventually had to give it up. His body quickly assumed more normal proportions, and he went to work helping manage racetracks, a career that brought him to Philadelphia when he was about thirty. He was hired to manage Philadelphia Park, the track that evolved into the Parx casino, in Bensalem, where he lives today. Johnson was in charge of day-to-day operations, including the betting operation. He started to learn a lot about gambling.

It was a growth industry. Today, according to the American Gaming Association, commercial casino gambling—not including Native American casinos or the hundreds of racetracks and government-sponsored lotteries—is a $34 billion business in America, with commercial casinos in twenty-two states, employing about 340,000 people. Pari-mutuel betting (on horse racing, dog racing, and jai alai) is now legal in forty-three states, and online gaming netted more than $4 billion from U.S. bettors in 2010. Over the past twenty years, Johnson's career has moved from managing racetracks to helping regulate this burgeoning industry. He has served as a state regulator in Oregon, Idaho, Texas, and Wyoming. About a decade ago, he founded a business that does computer-assisted wagering on horses. The software his company employs analyzes more data than an ordinary handicapper could see in a thousand lifetimes, and defines risk to a degree that was impossible just five years ago.

Johnson is not, as he puts it, "naive in math."

He began playing cards seriously about ten years ago, calculating his odds versus the house's.

Compared with horse racing, the odds in blackjack are fairly straightforward to calculate. Many casinos sell, in their guest shops, laminated charts that reveal the optimal strategy for any situation the game presents. But these odds are calculated by simulating millions of hands, and as Johnson says, "I will never see 400 million hands."

More useful, for his purposes, is running a smaller number of hands and paying attention to variation. The way averages work, the larger the sample, the narrower the range of variation. A session of, say, six hundred hands will display wider swings, with steeper winning and losing streaks, than the standard casino charts. That insight becomes important when the betting terms and special ground rules for the game are set—and Don Johnson's skill at establishing these terms is what sets him apart from your average casino visitor.

Johnson is very good at gambling, mainly because he's less willing to gamble than most. He does not just walk into a casino and start playing, which is what roughly 99 percent of customers do. This is, in his words, tantamount to "blindly throwing away money." The rules of the game are set to give the house a significant advantage. That doesn't mean you can't win playing by the standard house rules; people do win on occasion. But the vast majority of players lose, and the longer they play, the more they lose.

Sophisticated gamblers won't play by the standard rules. They negotiate. Because the casino values high rollers more than the average customer, it is willing to lessen its edge for them. It does this primarily by offering discounts, or "loss rebates." When a casino offers a discount of, say, 10 percent, this means that if the player loses $100,000 at the blackjack table, he has to pay only $90,000. Beyond the usual high-roller perks, the casino might also sweeten the deal by staking the player a significant amount up front, offering thousands of dollars in free chips, just to get the ball rolling. But even with that scenario, Johnson won't play. By his reckoning, a few thousand in free chips plus a standard 10 percent discount just means that the casino is going to end up with slightly less of the player's money after a few hours of play. The player still loses.

But two years ago, Johnson says, the casinos started getting desperate. With their table-game revenues tanking and the number of whales diminishing, casino marketers began to compete more aggressively for the big spenders. After all, one high roller who has a bad night can determine whether a casino's table games finish a month in the red or in the black. Inside the casinos, this heightened the natural tension between the marketers, who are always pushing to sweeten the discounts, and the gaming managers, who want to maximize the house's statistical edge. But month after month of declining revenues strengthened the marketers' position. By late 2010, the discounts at some of the strapped Atlantic City casinos began creeping upward, as high as 20 percent.

"The casinos started accepting more risk, looking for a possible larger return," says Posner, the gaming-industry expert. "They tended to start swinging for the fences."

Johnson noticed.

"They began offering deals that nobody's ever seen in New Jersey history," he told me. "I'd never heard of anything like it in the world, not even for a player like [the late Australian media tycoon] Kerry Packer, who came in with a $20 million bank and was worth billions and billions."

When casinos started getting desperate, Johnson was perfectly poised to take advantage of them. He had the money to wager big, he had the skill to win, and he did not have enough of a reputation for the casinos to be wary of him. He was also, as the Trop's Tony Rodio puts it, "a cheap date." He wasn't interested in the high-end perks; he was interested in maximizing his odds of winning. For Johnson, the game began before he ever set foot in the casino.

Atlantic City did know who Johnson was. The casinos' own research told them he was a skilled player capable of betting large amounts. But he was not considered good enough to discourage or avoid.

In fact, in late 2010, he says, they called him.

Johnson had not played a game at the Borgata in more than a year. He had been trying to figure out its blackjack game for years but had never been able to win big. At one point, he accepted a "lifetime discount," but when he had a winning trip he effectively lost the benefit of the discount. The way any discount works is that you have to lose a certain amount to capitalize on it. If you had a lifetime discount of, say, 20 percent on $500,000, you would have to lose whatever money you'd made on previous trips plus another $500,000 before the discount kicked in. When this happened to Johnson, he knew the ground rules had been skewed against him. So it was no longer worth his while to play at the Borgata.

He explained this when the Borgata tried to entice him back.

"Well, what if we change that?" he recalls a casino executive saying. "What if we put you on a trip-to-trip discount basis?"

Johnson started negotiating.

Once the Borgata closed the deal, he says, Caesars and the Trop, competing for Johnson's business, offered similar terms. That's what enabled him to systematically beat them, one by one.

In theory, this shouldn't happen. The casinos use computer models that calculate the odds down to the last penny so they can craft terms to entice high rollers without forfeiting the house advantage. "We have a very elaborate model," Rodio says. "Once customers come in, regardless of the game they may play, we plug them into the model so that we know what the house advantage is, based on the game that they are playing and the way they play the game. And then from that, we can make a determination of what is the appropriate [discount] we can make for them, based on their skill level. I can't speak for how other properties do it, but that is how we do it."

So how did all these casinos end up giving Johnson what he himself describes as a "huge edge"? "I just think somebody missed the math when they did the numbers on it," he told an interviewer.

Johnson did not miss the math. For example, at the Trop, he was willing to play with a 20 percent discount after his losses hit $500,000, but only if the casino structured the rules of the game to shave away some of the house advantage. Johnson could calculate exactly how much of an advantage he would gain with each small adjustment in the rules of play. He won't say what all the adjustments were in the final e-mailed agreement with the Trop, but they included playing with a hand-shuffled six-deck shoe; the right to split and double down on up to four hands at once; and a "soft seventeen" (the player can draw another card on a hand totaling six plus an ace, counting the ace as either one or eleven, while the dealer must stand, counting the ace as eleven). When Johnson and the Trop finally agreed, he had whittled the house edge down to one-fourth of 1 percent, by his figuring. In effect, he was playing a fifty-fifty game against the house, and with the discount, he was risking only eighty cents of every dollar he played. He had to pony up $1 million of his own money to start, but, as he would say later, "You'd never lose the million. If you got to [$500,000 in losses], you would stop and take your 20 percent discount. You'd owe them only $400,000."

In a fifty-fifty game, you're taking basically the same risk as the house, but if you get lucky and start out winning, you have little incentive to stop.

So when Johnson got far enough ahead in his winning sprees, he reasoned that he might as well keep playing. "I was already ahead of the property," he says. "So my philosophy at that point was that I can afford to take an additional risk here, because I'm battling with their money, using their discount against them."

According to Johnson, the Trop pulled the deal after he won a total of $5.8 million, the Borgata cut him off at $5 million, and the dealer at Caesars refused to fill the chip tray once his earnings topped $4 million.

"I was ready to play on," Johnson said. "And I looked around, and I said, 'Are you going to do a fill?' I've got every chip in the tray. I think I even had the $100 chips. 'Are you guys going to do a fill?' And they just said, 'No, we're out.'"

He says he learned later that someone at the casino had called the manager, who was in London, and told him that Don Johnson was ahead of them "by four."

"Four hundred thousand?" the manager asked.

"No, four *million*."

So Caesars, too, pulled the plug. When Johnson insisted that he wanted to keep playing, he says, the pit boss pointed out of the high-roller pit to the general betting floor, where the game was governed by normal house rules.

"You can go out there and play," he said.

Johnson went upstairs and fell asleep.

These winning streaks have made Johnson one of the best-known gamblers in the world. He was shocked when his story made the front page of the *Press of Atlantic City*. Donald Witt-kowski, a reporter at the newspaper, landed the story when the casinos filed their monthly revenue reports.

"I guess for the first time in thirty years, a group of casinos actually had a huge setback on account of one player," Johnson told me. "Somebody connected all the dots and said it must be one guy."

The Trop has embraced Johnson, inviting him back to host a tournament—but its management isn't about to offer him the same terms again. (Even so—playing by the same rules he had ne-gotiated earlier, according to Johnson, but without a discount— he managed to win another $2 million from the Tropicana in October.)

"Most properties in Atlantic City at this point won't even deal to him," Rodio says. "The Tropicana will continue to deal to him, we will continue to give aggressive limits, take care of his rooms and his accounts when he is here. But because he is so far in front of us, we have modified his discounts."

Johnson says his life hasn't really changed all that much. He hasn't bought himself anything big, and still lives in the same house in Bensalem. But in the past year, he has hung out with Jon Bon Jovi and Charlie Sheen, sprayed the world's most expensive bottle of champagne on a crowd of clubgoers in London, and hosted a Las Vegas birthday bash for Pamela Anderson. He is enjoying his fame in gambling circles, and has gotten used to flying around the world on comped jets. Everybody wants to play against the most famous blackjack player in the world.

But from now on, the casinos will make sure the deck remains comfortably against him.

Attila's Headset

New Yorker, November 2002

In his debut performance as head coach of the Washington Red-skins—a home victory over the Arizona Cardinals on September 8—Steve Spurrier was among the injured. It was hardly surprising, given his flea-on-a-griddle exertions on the sidelines. He paced, he fidgeted, he shouted, he pleaded, he writhed, he leaped, he threw his handwritten laminated play sheets on the ground in anger or waved them impatiently to demand someone's atten-tion. When his offense left the field, he dropped to one knee and bore into his play sheets, scratching his head and grimacing; and when the offense took the field again, he was back in motion, leaning into passes and kicks as if he'd launched the ball himself. Sometimes, in a game, he will peer up at his assistant coaches in their boxes high in the mezzanine and throw his arms open wide, as if to say, "Help me out here, will ya!" He is a virtuoso of facial expression, with features that twist, flex, bend, stretch, slacken, and knot like putty, reflecting every nuance of mood during a game. In the opener, a bulky headset sat astride his sun visor, a trademark accessory that he had flung from his head many times during twelve seasons with the University of Florida Gators. He fiddled with the headset constantly. When one of his successful plays was nullified by a holding penalty, Spurrier tore it off and sliced his middle finger.

"The earphones had that little sponge padding on them and the edge went right through it—cut me pretty good," he said after the game, displaying the bandaged finger to a room crowded with reporters and cameras.

In addition to the usual pack of Washington sportswriters, a number of scruffy writers from the Florida swamplands had shown up to see how their ol' Gator "ballcoach" would fare in the big leagues. He did well this first time out, putting up thirty-one points (to Arizona's twenty-three), dispelling predictions that his "collegiate system" would collapse in the face of a genuine pro defense. Spurrier faced the room with cheerful resignation, his usual pose in the spotlight. He is a lean, loose-limbed man with a mop of chestnut-colored hair and a quarterback's physique. (He retired from the field twenty-five years ago, when he was thirty-two, and shows hardly a wrinkle or patch of gray hair.) After the hours he spent in the sun, his face was burned pink up to a distinct curving line under his eyes; above that, where the shadow of the visor had fallen, the skin was pale. His hair was tousled and matted with sweat, and his black cotton shirt—he has not worn the Redskins' team colors, burgundy and gold, presumably because they resemble too closely the colors of his old rival FSU (Florida State University)—hung limp on his sloping shoulders. He looked pleased and weary, as if he had just finished playing in the game himself.

In Washington, a city that straddles north and south, Spurrier's down-home style has tilted the axis toward Dixie. For many years, the Redskins were the capital's only big sports franchise, and pro football is followed there with a passion that unites its widely disparate social classes like nothing else. Fans now speak of their "ballcoach," and the "ballplays" with which he plans to "pitch and catch" the Skins back to the Super Bowl. "Spurrier Dazzles in Debut" was the headline on the *Washington Post* columnist Thomas Boswell's account of the Arizona Cardinals game.

Spurrier built his career in a league that is made of raw talent and youthful exuberance. He says that there are only two ways to be successful. One is to work harder than everyone else; the other is to do things differently. He long ago chose the second path, refusing to work long hours. When practice breaks, he often runs on a treadmill and lifts weights for about an hour, and then he drives home.

"He's the opposite of a workaholic," his wife, Jerri, says. "He doesn't overwork himself emotionally, mentally, or physically, and he doesn't want those working for him to, either. If he sees them working late, he'll kick them out. Some of them sneak back, but, eventually, when you work with Steve you get into that mode. You don't have to grind, not in anything."

Normally, college coaches who reach the NFL spend years as relatively low-paid, overworked assistants. Pro coaches like to think they play a more sophisticated brand of football, so Spurrier's sudden ascent was seen as an insult, and there has been some grumbling about the folly of bringing a collegiate system to the pros. The hard feelings were aggravated by Spurrier's salary. Under the five-year contract he signed with the Redskins' pugnacious young owner, Dan Snyder, he will earn almost $5 million a season—making him one of the highest-paid coaches in NFL history. Also, Spurrier is what even Jerri calls a "brat." His zeal for winning extends well beyond the football field. His family avoids playing games with him. On the golf course he insists that his partners keep strict count of their strokes, and is known to needle them at the tee. In speeches and at press conferences, he sometimes teases or belittles his opponents. When he's ahead, he tends to run up the score. He ridicules other coaches' punishing work habits, tangles spiritedly with reporters, and has an unassailable confidence in his own eventual success. Judging by his season so far, he will need that confidence.

After the opening win, the Redskins lost four of their next five games. This wasn't surprising. It usually takes a head coach at least two years to rebuild a team in his own image. Spurrier has been successful wherever he has coached—at Florida, where he took over as head coach in 1990, he compiled a record-setting 122 wins (to just twenty-seven losses and one tie), won seven Southeastern Conference championships, and captured the national championship in 1996 by defeating his rival FSU—so his owner and his fans are likely to be patient with him. If he should do well—and many expect he will—he may change the definition of the job. "Steve Spurrier is the future," Snyder told me. "I believe he will be very influential in the NFL, just as he has been in college ball."

Forty years ago, the exemplar for a football coach was Vince ("St. Vince") Lombardi, the avuncular head of the Green Bay Packers. He was blunt and unassuming, intensely competitive, and unfailingly sportsmanlike, and he experienced victory only vicariously. Lombardi's ethos of humility began to erode in the 1970s, when personalities like Don Shula, with the Miami Dolphins, and Tom Landry, with the Dallas Cowboys, assumed a status like that of CEOs in the increasingly corporate NFL. As the value of its franchises surged with television profits, and as the price for season tickets approached that of a small car, the teams' front offices tripled or quadrupled in size and their coaching staffs expanded and specialized. Teams moved from cramped, dirty locker rooms in the basements of drafty stadiums to state-of-the-art, multimillion-dollar campuses, with sprawling air-conditioned offices, three or four training fields (each with a different style of turf), and NASA-style weight rooms and physical-therapy

facilities. The head coach became a paragon of corporate leadership and public-relations savvy, working eighteen-hour days and
seeking to control aspects of the team that had traditionally been
the owner's prerogatives—scouting and drafting players, negotiating contracts, managing the team's salary cap. The mark of
true status in today's NFL is not just to be head coach but to run
the whole show, to be general manager or president of football
operations. Such ambitions sometimes get coaches into trouble.
Marty Schottenheimer, Spurrier's predecessor in Washington, was
fired because, Snyder said, he wanted "power I wasn't willing to
give up." Schottenheimer now coaches in San Diego.

Spurrier wants less responsibility, not more. He shuns many
of the traditional roles: he doesn't mentor his players or get over-
involved in scouting and recruiting talent. He has little or nothing
to do with the team's defense—for that, Snyder hired Marvin
Lewis away from the Baltimore Ravens. The result so far has
been disastrous—the Redskins defense has given up more points
than all but a handful of teams. Spurrier delegates to assistants
responsibility for coaching blockers, tacklers, kickers, and receivers, whom he calls "catchers." He works primarily with his quarterbacks, his "pitchers."

And for that the NFL affords him a tool he never had in all
his years of winning at the University of Florida. Eight seasons
ago, the league decided to allow head coaches to talk by one-
way radio directly to quarterbacks on the field between plays.
Once the ball is officially replaced on the field after a play, the
offense has forty seconds to plan before the next snap. For the
first twenty-five of those seconds, the coach is allowed to talk to
his quarterback, who has a transmitter in his helmet. It's as close
as Spurrier will ever get to being back on the field.

In his debut game against the Cardinals, Spurrier rode the
transmission button on his radio so heavily that his quarterback,
Shane Matthews, complained afterward that on top of the general

din of eighty-five thousand screaming fans he had to contend with the coach's breathing, sideline conversations, and the relooped roar of the crowd piped into his helmet. Matthews was voted offensive Player of the Week in the National Football Conference for his performance. At that moment, the future looked bright for both the new coach and the quarterback. Matthews encountered Spurrier in a hallway underneath the field after the game, held out his hand, and congratulated his coach.

"Some of it was you, some of it was me," Spurrier told him. "We'll sort it out when we look at the film."

Long after the rest of the team headed for the showers on the sunny campus of Redskins Park, in Ashburn, Virginia, this September, Spurrier stayed on the field with his three quarterbacks: Danny Wuerffel, Shane Matthews, and the rookie Patrick Ramsey. Wearing shorts and a white polo shirt with the collar turned up, Spurrier took snaps from center and, moving in slow motion, demonstrated again and again the proper execution of the three-step drop: head level, eyes downfield, ball poised under his right ear, arm cocked for a quick release. He was working with young men who have been playing quarterback—in high school, college, and the pros—for years, and still no detail of the mechanics was too minor for Spurrier's further instruction.

When he finished, he jogged off the field with the careful, slightly mincing steps of a middle-aged athlete whose knees are tender. He greeted the assembled local reporters who monitor the team daily—"Boys and girls, are you still here . . . I was trying to outlast you. I don't want y'all to write that we stayed out here and practiced."

A few minutes later, I followed him into the air-conditioned Redskins building, where he has a big office with windows that look out over the practice fields. Framed photographs of Spurrier romping with his various championship teams—sweaty, bloodied, and gleeful, in the heady glory of victory—fill one wall. Another group of pictures features his family: Jerri and their four children and seven grandchildren, including a set of triplet boys. The desk was piled with paperwork. At one end was a well-thumbed, highlighted, underlined copy of *The Art of War*, by Sun Tzu, and on top of it the Wess Roberts bestseller, *Leadership Secrets of Attila the Hun*. He picked it up.

"I gave Dan Snyder this book," he said. "There's some good advice in there, the way Attila there used to treat his Huns, or the generals under him. It's the same thing, Attila and his Huns, me and my players. There was one story in there. Attila lanced the boil on one of his soldiers and sucked out the pus and blood himself, and spit it away. The soldier's mother cried when she heard the story. She was asked why it made her cry, and she said because Attila had done the same thing for her husband, the boy's father, and afterward he had been so loyal he'd marched gladly off to his death in the front ranks of Attila's armies. 'Now my son will do the same,' she said."

Spurrier is less likely to find this kind of selfless player in the pros than at the college level. NFL locker rooms are filled with cynical, hard-bitten athletes, most of whom have already tasted a measure of glory elsewhere, some of whom are in the game solely for the money, and some of whom know that their worth to the team—and their paycheck—easily outweighs the coach's.

Spurrier compiles and memorizes lists of coaching maxims. There are thirty on his "Guidelines for a Good Ball Coach." Number one reads: "Treat all players fairly; the way they deserve to be treated." Number eighteen: "Make the game fun for your players." Number twenty: "Don't ever use foul language in front of your players." But Spurrier's magic lies not primarily in planning and motivating—the traditional skills of the head coach— or even in devising the complex plays in his thick book, which sportswriters consider the key to his success. His talent is for calling plays. Among the thirty-two head coaches in the pros, he is unusual in having been a celebrated football player himself. He has a gift for thinking on his feet, for understanding game situations and reading defensive formations. In the seconds between plays, he chooses from the subtle variations in his playbook or invents minor adjustments on the spot in order to surprise and snare his opponent.

For most coaches, victory is something carefully plotted in the film room, where the game's mysteries are dissected. Unless you have the luxury of studying game film, slowing it down and isolating different portions of the field, and unless you know exactly what was supposed to happen on a given play, you can't know for certain why most plays succeed or fail. The coach's painstaking strategies for the next game are kept deliberately obscure. They are printed out by computer in long coded patterns on the laminated play cards that the coaches take to the sidelines. Spurrier is more improvisational. His handwritten play cards look like something he threw together over breakfast. His offensive style has been called the "fun 'n' gun," because he disdains the slow, laborious methods that many NFL coaches consider basic for success in the pros. The traditional road to victory in football is to wear your opponents down. Spurrier prefers to fool them.

"Some people use tricks more often than others, and some people do it better than others," Bobby Bowden, Spurrier's rival coach at FSU, said. "He will do anything to move the ball forward, and he'll sometimes come up with things that make you ask, 'Where'd he get that thing?' or 'How'd he think that one up?' Especially in the passing game. It wasn't so much that he came up with plays or formations I hadn't seen before—it was his timing. Timing and execution. His timing was so good that unless you were really on your toes and at the top of your game he was going to get you."

Steven Orr Spurrier was born in Florida in 1945 to Marjorie and John Graham Spurrier. He was the youngest of three children. His father, a Presbyterian minister, took sports nearly as seriously as he took God. He coached his two sons in Little League, where he was known to lecture against the old saw about winning being less important than how you play the game. The point of playing the game, he informed his players (and his sons absorbed the lesson), was to win.

In basketball, Spurrier averaged almost two thirds of the points scored by his high school team, led them to their local championship twice, and was selected for the All-State team in 1963, his senior year. That same year, he also played shortstop and pitched his team to a second state baseball championship, an accomplishment that Spurrier says is "the most fun I ever had as a player in any sport." As quarterback, he gave his football team a comeback victory in their final game—the Exchange Bowl— overcoming a 21–0 halftime deficit with four touchdown passes. He was famous for drawing up plays in the huddle, a skill that his coaches at first didn't appreciate. Ken Lyon, one of his old teammates, told two reporters who were writing a story about Spurrier for the *Lakeland* (Florida) *Ledger* that Spurrier got into trouble once at practice for fiddling with a play:

> One of our coaches, Snake Evans, called everything to a halt and asked him, "What was that?" Steve said he thought it would be better if we did it this way. Coach Evans said, "You know, we've got a problem here. I thought I was the coach. Do you agree with me that I'm the coach? Well, if you can agree to that, then go back and run it my way. Otherwise, go get you a shower."

When Spurrier did the same thing in a game, however, and scored a touchdown, no one complained.

"He'd just draw it out on the ground," another teammate said.

Spurrier's success in high school led him to the University of Florida, where, after three years of quarterbacking for the Gators, he won the Heisman Trophy. In Gainesville, they called him by his initials, SOS, because he led the team to so many come-from-behind victories in the fourth quarter. His other nickname was Steve Superior.

"Steve just had that drive," said John Higbe, who snapped the ball to Spurrier in some of those games. "He seemed aloof even then—some people thought he was arrogant—but when you were with him in the huddle, no matter how bad things looked, you never felt like you were going to lose."

In 1967, the San Francisco 49ers took Spurrier in the draft, but they already had a quarterback, John Brodie, who was the highest-paid football player of his time. For the next five seasons, Spurrier did a lot of watching, enjoyed a lot of golf, and saw playing time mostly as the team's punter. He did well when he got the chance. In 1972, when Brodie was injured, Spurrier led the 49ers to a third consecutive Western Division championship, winning five of the team's last six games. When Brodie retired and Spurrier finally took over, he separated his shoulder in a preseason game and sat out the whole season. After yet another disappointing season, he was taken by one of the league's expansion teams, the Tampa Bay Buccaneers.

The Buccaneers consisted of rookies, washouts, has-beens, and might-have-beens, and they lost every game. "Hey, we set a record that year," Spurrier said with mock pride. "The only oh-and-fourteen record in NFL history! I remember a speech our coach, John McKay, was giving us at one point during that season. He was emphasizing that games were lost in the trenches, by failing to block and tackle on the front lines. And as he was talking he noticed a lineman asleep in the back. He called his

name, woke him up, and asked, 'Where are most games lost?'
And the lineman says, 'Right here in Tampa, sir.'"

"John McKay was the most caustic individual I ever met
in my life," Spurrier's former teammate the wide receiver Barry
Smith recalled. McKay was particularly tough on Spurrier, the
biggest star on the roster. "I tell you this," Smith said. "If there
was one man in this world who was totally shocked by Steve's
later success as a coach it's John McKay."

Spurrier was released by McKay after one season. He was
picked up by the Denver Broncos, who cut him, and then he
landed with Don Shula's Miami Dolphins just before the 1977
season was about to start. He and Jerri had three small children.
The situation in Miami looked stable. They rented a house and
sent the children off to school. Days after settling in, Spurrier
phoned his wife with bad news. Shula had cut him.

They returned to Gainesville, where they had always kept
a home for the off-season. Spurrier's whole career had been in
football, and at that point he didn't have his college degree. He
was offered work selling insurance and selling cars, prospects that
he and Jerri found deeply unappealing. Their financial situation
was deteriorating.

"I did not make much money as a pro football player—a
little bit, not a lot," Spurrier said. "I watched the Gators play
and thought I needed to get a job. Coaching was something that
seemed like fun and not a lot of work."

Spurrier went on, "I'm not very good at working. We all
need to do as a profession something that we find fun. I'd been
around a lot of good coaches and sorry coaches in my career . . . or
average coaches, I should say, not sorry . . . and I thought: By
God, if he can do this for a living, so can I."

Unfortunately, nobody was hiring. Just to break in, Spurrier
agreed to help out with the Gator quarterbacks. Nearly twenty
years later, in 1990, after coaching at Georgia Tech, at Duke, and

for the Tampa Bay Bandits, of the ill-fated United States Football League, he returned to the University of Florida as head coach. He led the Gators to their first national championship, in 1996, and in his twelve-year tenure there Spurrier compiled one of the most successful records of any major college coach in history. He recently told Pat Summitt, the University of Tennessee's celebrated women's basketball coach, "You and I both know why we do this. We do it so we can play games our whole lives. This way, we don't ever have to grow up."

It isn't easy playing for Spurrier. He does not always live up to the rules in his "Guidelines." Number two reads: "After chewing out a player, say something positive to bring him back tomorrow." Number four reads: "If you must criticize, do it to a player's face, not downtown or to the media. End all criticism with something positive."

"Sometimes he's as biting with his players as McKay was to us," his former teammate Lee McGriff said. "I know how much he hated it when McKay did it to him, but now he does it to players himself."

Since quarterbacks are the focus of Spurrier's attention, they feel his perfectionism the most. Bobby Sabelhaus, an All-American who set records as a high school quarterback in Maryland, and who was actively courted by many university football programs in 1995, says he still has nightmares about Coach Spurrier. He chose Florida not because Spurrier went out of his way to recruit him—"Of all the coaches who made pitches to me, he was the least appealing"—but because he knew Spurrier was a winner. His experience with Florida was a disaster that ultimately drove him out of football.

"Everything I did was wrong," Sabelhaus said. "I was used to coaches yelling at me, but they would also sometimes pat you on the back. Not Spurrier. Even when I threw a touchdown pass in practice once, he said to me, 'Are you just stupid or is it a lack of talent?' I hadn't run the play the exact way he wanted me to. I had an odd, sidearm throwing motion that had served me pretty well"—Sabelhaus had broken all records as a high school passer—"and Spurrier wanted me to change it to the way he threw the ball. I tried, but it threw me off so badly that I couldn't throw accurately anymore. He was constantly berating me. I would wake up in the morning and spend the entire day dreading the afternoon meeting. The other quarterbacks went through the same thing. Danny Wuerffel"—who would win the Heisman Trophy leading Florida to the national championship in 1996—"tried to help me. He encouraged me, and told me Spurrier had treated him the same way as a freshman. Wuerffel was the kind of guy who could take it. Not me."

To those willing to endure Spurrier's treatment, the payoff is the coach's undying loyalty. When he joined the Redskins this year, Spurrier didn't recruit the top names among available quarterback free agents; he signed Wuerffel and Matthews, neither of whom had translated his success at the University of Florida into a stellar NFL career. Both have been given a rare second chance with the Redskins, in part because of Spurrier's loyalty to them, in part because he knows they have learned to run his plays the way he wants them run.

Spurrier is impatient with the tact that his position demands. By tradition, the head coach does not boast, speak ill of opponents, or complain. In the NFL, whatever he says is amplified a hundred thousand times, especially if he loses his cool or breaches the unwritten code. The more outrageous a comment can be made to seem—whatever its original intent—the more widely it is broadcast, dissected, criticized, and gleefully commented on by the sports media. A person in this position would be wise not to speak at all, but head coaches are constantly called on to give speeches and interviews, and to answer the goading questions of the press. Most head coaches talk a lot but say little. Spurrier is incautious and irreverent, and the media love him for it.

As head coach in Florida, he gave speeches all over the state to Gator booster clubs. They roared when he described his rival FSU as "Free Shoes University," after a local shoestore gave FSU players free cleats, and when he lamented the destruction of books in a fire at Auburn University, because some of them "hadn't even been colored yet."

"Where I come from, talking a little smack is part of the game," he said. "You dish it out, but you got to be able to take it, too. It's all in the spirit of fun. A lot of it comes about because what I say gets misrepresented. Like taking over this job. Folks ask me how I expect us to do. Well, I expect to win my division. I didn't predict that I would, but that's what I expect of my football team. We may make it or we may not, but what am I supposed to expect? That we'll lose?"

Spurrier reads everything that's written about him, and says he remembers every word. "And if I don't like it I call them and let them know about it," he said. "They can criticize me, that's fair, but when they start saying things that I didn't say, that gets me going."

A number of Florida writers have been the recipients of insulting notes from Spurrier. He called Gerald Ensley, of the *Tallahassee Democrat*, an "a-hole," and said that Mark Bradley, of the *Atlanta Journal-Constitution*, was "chickenshit." In 1996, one of the big games on the Gators' schedule was against the University of Tennessee Volunteers. The *Knoxville News-Sentinel* phoned the *Orlando Sentinel*'s Gator-beat reporter, Chris Harry, before the season started and asked if he would file four stories for them in advance of the big game, offering analysis from the Gainesville perspective. It's a common practice on sports pages.

Harry filed the stories. Without his knowledge, the *News-Sentinel* was running them under the rubric "From the Enemy Camp," illustrated with a pair of binoculars.

One morning, Harry's phone rang, and he picked it up to hear Spurrier, his voice almost a whisper. "How much are they paying you?" the coach asked.

"What?"

"How much are they paying you, Chris Harry, to be a spy?"

"Everything I saw at the scrimmages was seen by thousands of other people!" Harry protested.

"Yeah, but they didn't have to send their own people down here, did they? Because they had you."

Spurrier said he was going to bar reporters from all future practices and scrimmages. The shutdown prompted a story in a Gainesville newspaper, which quoted Spurrier naming Harry as the culprit. According to Harry, the story, and Spurrier's remarks, resulted in phoned death threats at his Gainesville home.

The Gators won the game easily. The next week, Spurrier reopened practices, and he slapped Harry on the back when he saw him.

"Hey, Chrissie, how you doin'?" the coach asked.

Harry felt less forgiving. He explained about the death threats, how alarmed he and his wife had been.

The coach was unapologetic.

"Well, you shouldn't have done that story," he said.

Spurrier's contract with the Redskins will expire after the 2007 season, when he's sixty-two. According to his longtime friend Norm Carlson, who is an assistant athletic director at the University of Florida, Spurrier has said for years that he plans to retire in his early sixties. When he announced his decision to step down as Florida coach earlier this year, he said he wanted to see "if my ballplays will work in the pros." So far, his record is mediocre.

The Redskins were crushed in their second game, on September 16. In front of eighty-five thousand Washington fans and a national ABC *Monday Night Football* audience, the Philadelphia Eagles beat them, 37–7. Spurrier's offense looked as lame and collegiate as his detractors had predicted. It scored no points (the touchdown came on a punt return) and managed to move the ball into the Eagles' half of the field only once during the entire game—after an Eagles penalty handed the Redskins fifteen yards.

On the sidelines, Spurrier, wearing a white shirt, was in agony, head in hands, his face a mask of disappointment and frustration. After one blunder, he flapped his lips in such a genuine and original display of disgust that it made the TV program's highlights reel, and was replayed over and over in slow motion the rest of the week.

The next two weeks weren't much better. Midway through a third-week loss to the San Francisco 49ers, Spurrier benched Matthews for Wuerffel, but still the team failed to score more than one touchdown. Spurrier replaced Wuerffel the following week, against the Tennessee Titans, with the rookie Patrick Ramsey, and got a win and a surprising performance out of the young quarterback. Afterward, Spurrier expressed delight in the rookie's play—Ramsey threw two touchdown passes and completed twenty of his thirty-four passes for 268 yards—and pronounced him the team's new starting quarterback. The next week, though, Ramsey threw three interceptions, and the Redskins lost, 43–27. Spurrier said, "It's a little frustrating. You think you have things set, and it doesn't always work out." He replaced Ramsey with Matthews for the team's seventh game, against the Indianapolis Colts, and won with a meat-and-potatoes game plan that bore little resemblance to his usual trickery.

The team's performance has been so ugly that Spurrier has started coming to work early and showing up on weekends. The season still has a long way to go, and the other three teams in the NFC East (the division Spurrier expects to win) have also struggled. The Eagles had opened up a two-game lead on them when this story went to press. The Redskins might surprise everybody, but it's looking more and more doubtful.

Spurrier is patient, for now. His various lists of coaching maxims all include reminders that the journey is its own reward. Number sixteen: "The road is better than the end. The game, the competition, is more fun than the trophies." But note that the road ends with a trophy. One of the reasons Spurrier "talks smack," runs up the score when his team is winning, and taunts his opponents—whether over a chessboard, on the golf course, or before a football game—is to raise the stakes. Having something personal on the line enlivens the joust and sweetens the victory. Of course, when you play this way losing is more humiliating, too, but Spurrier accepts the bargain.

He was bewildered, and insulted, when, in the final minutes of the Monday-night Eagles blowout, Philadelphia's head coach, Andy Reid, chose not to kick an easy field goal to add three more points. Earlier in the game, pepper spray from a fracas with police had drifted out of the stands, sending Reid and his team sprinting from the sidelines, gasping for air. After the Eagles gallantly declined to run up the score, Spurrier caught a whiff of something else from across the field.

It smelled like pity.

"I still don't know why he did that," Spurrier said.

ESSAYS

The Story
Behind the Story

Atlantic, October 2009

If you happened to be watching a television news channel on May 26, the day President Obama nominated U.S. Circuit Court Judge Sonia Sotomayor to the Supreme Court, you might have been struck, as I was, by what seemed like a nifty investigative report.

First came the happy announcement ceremony at the White House, with Sotomayor sweetly saluting her elderly mother, who as a single parent had raised the prospective justice and her brother in a Bronx housing project. Obama had chosen a woman whose life journey mirrored his own: an obscure, disadvantaged beginning followed by blazing academic excellence, an Ivy League law degree, and a swift rise to power. It was a moving TV moment, well orchestrated and in perfect harmony with the central narrative of the new Obama presidency.

But then, just minutes later, journalism rose to perform its time-honored pie-throwing role. Having been placed by the president on a pedestal, Sotomayor was now a clear target. I

happened to be watching Fox News. I was slated to appear that
night on one of its programs, *Hannity*, to serve as a willing
foil to the show's cheerfully pugnacious host, Sean Hannity, a
man who can deliver a deeply held conservative conviction on
any topic faster than the speed of thought. Since the host knew
what the subject matter of that night's show would be and I
did not, I'd thought it best to check in and see what Fox was
preoccupied with that afternoon.

With Sotomayor, of course—and the network's producers
seemed amazingly well prepared. They showed a clip from remarks she had made on an obscure panel at Duke University in
2005, and then, reaching back still further, they showed snippets
from a speech she had made at Berkeley Law School in 2001.
Here was this purportedly moderate Latina judge, appointed to
the federal bench by a Republican president and now tapped
for the Supreme Court by a Democratic one, unmasked as a
race woman with an agenda. In one clip she announced herself
as someone who believed her identity as a "Latina woman" (a
redundancy, but that's what she said) made her judgment superior
to that of a "white male," and in the other she all but unmasked
herself as a card-carrying member of the left-wing conspiracy to
use America's courts not just to apply and interpret the law but,
in her own words, to *make policy*, to perform an end run around
the other two branches of government and impose liberal social
policies by fiat on an unsuspecting American public.

In the clip from Duke, she not only stated that appellate
judges make policy; she did so in a disdainful mock disavowal
before a chuckling audience of apparently like-minded conspira-
tors. "I know this is on tape and I should never say that, because
we don't make law, I know," she said before being interrupted by
laughter. "OK, I know. I'm not promoting it, I'm not advocat-
ing it, I'm . . . you know," flipping her hands dismissively. More
laughter.

Holy cow! I'm an old reporter, and I know legwork when I see it. Those crack journalists at Fox, better known for coloring and commenting endlessly on the news than for actually breaking it, had unearthed not one but two explosive gems, and had been primed to expose Sotomayor's darker purpose *within minutes of her nomination*! Leaving aside for the moment any question about the context of these seemingly damaging remarks—none was offered—I was impressed. In my newspaper years, I prepared my share of advance profiles of public figures, and I know the scut work that goes into sifting through a decades-long career. In the old days it meant digging through packets of yellowed clippings in the morgue, interviewing widely, searching for those moments of controversy or surprise that revealed something interesting about the subject. How many rulings, opinions, articles, legal arguments, panel discussions, and speeches had there been in the judge's long years of service? What bloodhound producer at Fox News had waded into this haystack to find these two choice needles?

Then I flipped to MSNBC, and lo! . . . it had exactly the same two clips. I flipped to CNN . . . same clips. CBS . . . same clips. ABC . . . same clips. Parsing Sotomayor's thirty years of public legal work, somehow every TV network had come up with precisely the same moments! None bothered to say who had dug them up; none offered a smidgen of context. They all just accepted the apparent import of the clips, the substance of which was sure to trouble any fair-minded viewer. By the end of the day just about every American with a TV set had heard the comments: "make policy" and "Latina woman." By the end of the nightly news summaries, millions who had never heard of Sonia Sotomayor knew her not only as Obama's pick, but as a judge who felt superior by reason of her gender and ethnicity, and as a liberal activist determined to "make policy" from the federal bench. And wasn't it an extraordinary coincidence that all these great news organizations, functioning independently—because this, after all, is the advantage of having multiple news-gathering sources in a democracy—had come up with exactly the same material in advance?

They hadn't, of course. The reporting we saw on TV and on the Internet that day was the work not of journalists, but of political hit men. The snippets about Sotomayor had been circulating on conservative websites and shown on some TV channels for weeks. They were new only to the vast majority of us who have better things to do than vet the record of every person on Obama's list. But this is precisely what activists and bloggers on both sides of the political spectrum do, and what a conservative organization like the Judicial Confirmation Network (JCN) exists to promote. The JCN had gathered an attack dossier on each of the prospective Supreme Court nominees, and had fed all the dossiers to the networks in advance.

This process—political activists supplying material for TV news broadcasts—is not new, of course. It has largely replaced the work of on-the-scene reporters during political campaigns, which have become, in a sense, perpetual. The once quadrennial clashes between parties over the White House are now simply the way our national business is conducted. In our exhausting 24/7 news cycle, demand for timely information and analysis is greater than ever. With journalists being laid off in droves, savvy political operatives have stepped eagerly into the breach. What's most troubling is not that TV news producers mistake their work for journalism, which is bad enough, but that young people drawn to journalism increasingly see no distinction between disinterested reporting and hit jobs. The very smart and capable young men (more on them in a moment) who actually dug up and initially posted the Sotomayor clips both originally described themselves to me as part-time, or aspiring, journalists.

The attack that political operatives fashioned from their work was neither unusual nor particularly effective. It succeeded in shaping the national debate over her nomination for weeks, but more serious assessments of her record would demolish the caricature soon enough, and besides, the Democrats have a large majority in the Senate; her nomination was approved, 68–31. The incident does, however, illustrate one consequence of the collapse of professional journalism. Work formerly done by reporters and producers is now routinely performed by political operatives and amateur ideologues of one stripe or another, whose goal is not to educate the public but to *win*. This is a trend not likely to change.

Writing in 1960, the great press critic A. J. Liebling, noting the squeeze on his profession, fretted about the emergence of the one-newspaper town:

> The worst of it is that each newspaper disappearing below the horizon carries with it, if not a point of view, at least a potential emplacement for one. A city with one newspaper, or with a morning and an evening paper under one ownership, is like a man with one eye, and often the eye is glass.

Liebling, who died in 1963, was spared the looming prospect of the no-newspaper town. There is, of course, the Internet, which he could not have imagined. Its enthusiasts rightly point out that digital media are in nearly every way superior to paper and ink, and represent, in essence, an upgrade in technology. But those giant presses and barrels of ink and fleets of delivery trucks were never what made newspapers invaluable. What gave newspapers their value was the mission and promise of journalism—the hope that someone was getting paid to wade into the daily tide of manure, sort through its deliberate lies and cunning half-truths, and tell a story straight. There is a reason why newspaper reporters, despite polls that show consistently low public regard for journalists, are the heroes of so many films. The reporter of lore was not some blue blood or Ivy League egghead, beholden to society's powerful interests, be they corporate, financial, or political. We liked our newsmen to be Everymen—shoe-leather intellectuals, cynical, suspicious, and streetwise like Humphrey Bogart in *Deadline— U.S.A.* or Jimmy Stewart in *The Philadelphia Story* or Robert Redford and Dustin Hoffman in *All the President's Men*. The Internet is now replacing Everyman with *every man*. Anyone with a keyboard or cell phone can report, analyze, and pull a chair up to the national debate. If freedom of the press belongs to those who own one, today that is everyone. The city with one eye (glass or no) has been replaced by the city with a million eyes. This is wonderful on many levels, and is why the tyrants of the world are struggling, with only partial success, to control the new medium. But while the Internet may be the ultimate democratic tool, it is also demolishing the business model that long sustained newspapers and TV's network news organizations. Unless someone quickly finds a way to make disinterested reporting pay, to compensate the modern equivalent of the ink-stained wretch (the carpal-tunnel curmudgeon?), the Web may yet bury Liebling's cherished profession.

Who, after all, is willing to work for nothing?

Morgen Richmond, for one—the man who actually found the snippets used to attack Sotomayor. He is a partner in a computer-consulting business in Orange County, California, a father of two, and a native of Canada, who defines himself, in part, as a political conservative. He spends some of his time most nights in a second-floor bedroom/office in his home, after his children and wife have gone to bed, cruising the Internet looking for ideas and information for his blogging. "It's more of a hobby than anything

else," he says. His primary outlet is a website called VerumSerum.
com, which was cofounded by his friend John Sexton. Sexton
is a Christian conservative who was working at the time for an
organization called Reasons to Believe, which strives, in part, to
reconcile scientific discovery and theory with the apparent whop-
pers told in the Bible. Sexton is, like Richmond, a young father,
living in Huntington Beach. He is working toward a master's
degree at Biola University (formerly the Bible Institute of Los
Angeles), and is a man of opinion. He says that even as a youth,
long before the Internet, he would corner his friends and make
them listen to his most recent essay. For both Sexton and Richmond, Verum Serum is a labor of love, a chance for them to flex
their desire to report and comment, to add their two cents to the
national debate. Both see themselves as somewhat unacclaimed
conservative thinkers in a world captive to misguided liberalism
and prey to overwhelmingly leftist mainstream media, or MSM,
composed of journalists who, like myself, write for print publications or work for big broadcast networks and are actually paid
for their work.

Richmond started researching Sotomayor after ABC News
Washington correspondent George Stephanopoulos named her
as the likely pick back on March 13. The work involved was far
less than I'd imagined, in part because the Internet is such an
amazing research tool, but mostly because Richmond's goal was
substantially easier to achieve than a journalist's. For a newspaper
reporter, the goal in researching any profile is to arrive at a deeper
understanding of the subject. My own motivation, when I did it,
was to present not just a smart and original picture of the person,
but a fair picture. In the quaint protocols of my ancient newsroom
career, the editors I worked for would have accepted nothing less;
if they felt a story needed more detail or balance, they'd brusquely
hand it back and demand more effort. Richmond's purpose was
fundamentally different. He figured, rightly, that anyone Obama

picked who had not publicly burned an American flag was likely to be confirmed, and that she would be cheered all the way down this lubricated chute by the Obama-loving MSM. To his credit, Richmond is not what we in the old days called a "thumbsucker," a lazy columnist who rarely stirs from behind his desk, who for material just reacts to the items that cross it. (This defines the vast majority of bloggers.) Richmond is actually determined to add something new to the debate.

"The goal is to develop original stories that attract attention," he told me. "I was consciously looking for something that would resonate."

But not just anything resonant. Richmond's overarching purpose was to damage Sotomayor, or at least to raise questions about her that would trouble his readers, who are mostly other conservative bloggers. On most days, he says, his stuff on Verum Serum is read by only twenty to thirty people. If any of them like what they see, they link to it or post the video on their own, larger websites.

Richmond began his reporting by looking at university websites. He had learned that many have little-seen recordings and transcripts of speeches made by public figures, since schools regularly sponsor lectures and panel discussions with prominent citizens, such as federal judges. Many of the events are informal and unscripted, and can afford glimpses of public figures talking unguardedly about their ideas, their life, and their convictions. Many are recorded and archived. Using Google, Richmond quickly found a list of such appearances by Sotomayor, and the first one he clicked on was the video of the 2005 panel discussion at Duke University Law School. Sotomayor and two other judges, along with two Duke faculty members, sat behind a table before a classroom filled with students interested in applying for judicial clerkships. The video is fifty-one minutes long and is far from riveting. About forty minutes into it, Richmond says, he was only half-listening, multitasking on his home computer, when laughter from the sound track caught his ear. He rolled back the video and heard Sotomayor utter the line about making policy, and then jokingly disavow the expression.

"What I found most offensive about it was the laughter," he says. "What was the joke? . . . Here was a sitting appellate judge in a room full of law students, treating the idea that she was making policy or law from the bench as laughable." He recognized it as a telling in-joke that his readers would not find funny.

Richmond posted the video snippet on YouTube on May 2, and then put it up with a short commentary on Verum Serum the following day, questioning whether Sotomayor deserved to be considered moderate or bipartisan, as she had been character-ized. "I'm not so sure this is going to fly," he wrote, and then invited readers to view the video. He concluded with sarcasm: "So she's a judicial activist. . . . I'm sure she is a moderate one though! Unbelievable. With a comment like this I only hope that conservatives have the last laugh if she gets the nomination."

A number of larger conservative websites, notably Volokh.com (the Volokh Conspiracy, published by UCLA law professor Eugene Volokh) and HotAir.com (published by conservative commentator Michelle Malkin), picked up the video, and on May 4 it was aired on television for the first time, by Sean Hannity.

On Malkin's website, Richmond had come across a short, critical reference to a speech Sotomayor had given at Berkeley Law School. In that speech, according to Malkin, the prospective Supreme Court nominee said "she believes it is appropriate for a judge to consider their 'experiences as women and people of color' in their decision making, which she believes should 'affect our decisions.'"

Malkin told me that her "conservative source" for the tidbit was privileged. She used the item without checking out the actual

speech, which is what Richmond set out to find. He had some
trouble because Malkin had placed the speech in 2002 instead
of 2001, but he found it—the Honorable Mario G. Olmos Law
and Cultural Diversity Memorial Lecture—in the Berkeley Law
School's *La Raza Law Journal*; bought it; and on May 5 posted
the first detailed account of it on his blog. He ran large excerpts
from it, and highlighted in bold the now infamous lines: "I would
hope that a wise Latina woman with the richness of her experiences would more often than not reach a better conclusion than
a white male who hasn't lived that life."

Richmond then commented:

> To be fair, I do want to note that the statement she made
> . . . is outrageous enough that it may have in fact been a
> joke. Although since it's published "as-is" in a law journal
> I'm not sure she is entitled to the benefit of the doubt
> on this. The text certainly does not indicate that it was
> said in jest. I have only a layperson's understanding of
> law and judicial history, but I suspect the judicial philoso-
> phy implied by these statements is probably pretty typical
> amongst liberal judges. Personally, I wish it seemed that
> she was actually really trying to meet the judicial ideal of
> impartiality, and her comments about making a difference
> are a concern as this does not seem to be an appropriate
> focus for a member of the judiciary. I look forward to hope-
> fully seeing some additional dissection and analysis of these
> statements by others in the conservative legal community.

The crucial piece of Richmond's post, Sotomayor's comment
about a "wise Latina woman," was then picked up again by other
sites, and was soon being packaged with the Duke video as exhib-
its A and B in the case against Sonia Sotomayor. Richmond told
me that he was shocked by the immediate, widespread attention

given to his work, and a little startled by the levels of outrage it provoked. "I found her comments more annoying than outrageous, to be honest," he said.

In both instances, Richmond's political bias made him tone-deaf to the context and import of Sotomayor's remarks. Bear in mind that he was looking not simply to understand the judge, but to expose her supposed hidden agenda.

Take the Duke panel first: most of the video, for obvious reasons, held little interest for Richmond. My guess is that you could fit the number of people who have actually watched the whole thing into a Motel Six bathtub. Most of the talk concerned how to make your application for a highly competitive clerkship stand out. Late in the discussion, a student asked the panel to compare clerking at the district court (or trial court) level and clerking at the appellate level. Sotomayor replied that clerks serving trial judges are often asked to rapidly research legal questions that develop during a trial, and to assist the judge in applying the law to the facts of that particular case. The appellate courts, on the other hand, are in the business of making rulings that are "precedential," she said, in that rulings at the appellate level serve as examples, reasons, or justifications for future proceedings in lower courts. She went on to make the ostensibly controversial remark that students who planned careers in academia or public-interest law ought to seek a clerkship at the appellate level, because that's where "policy is made."

This is absolutely true, in the sense she intended: precedential decisions, by definition, make *judicial* policy. They provide the basic principles that guide future rulings. But both Sotomayor and her audience were acutely aware of how charged the word *policy* has become in matters concerning the judiciary—conservatives, not without truth, accuse liberal judges of trying to set *national* policy from the bench. This accusation has become a rallying cry for those who believe that the Supreme Court justices should adhere strictly to the actual language and original intent of the Constitution, instead of coloring the law with their own modish theories to produce such social experiments as school desegregation, *Miranda* warnings, abortions on demand, and so forth. The polite laughter that caught Richmond's ear was recognition by the law students that the judge had inadvertently stepped in a verbal cow pie. She immediately recognized what she had done, expressed mock horror at being caught doing so on tape, and then pronounced a jocular and exaggerated mea culpa, like a scoring runner in a baseball game tiptoeing back out onto the diamond to touch a base that he might have missed. Sotomayor went on to explain in very precise terms how and why decisions at the appellate level have broader intellectual implications than those at the lower level. It is where, she said, "the law is percolating."

Seen in their proper context, these comments would probably not strike anyone as noteworthy. If anything, they showed how sensitive Sotomayor and everyone else in the room had become to fears of an "activist court."

A look at the full "Latina woman" speech at Berkeley reveals another crucial misinterpretation.

To his credit, Richmond posted as much of the speech as copyright law allows, attempting to present the most important sentence in context. But he still missed the point. Sotomayor's argument was not that she sought to use her position to further minority interests, or that her gender and background made her superior to a white male. Her central argument was that the sexual, racial, and ethnic makeup of the legal profession has in fact historically informed the application of law, despite the efforts of individual lawyers and judges to rise above their personal stories—as

Sotomayor noted she labors to do. Her comment about a "wise Latina woman" making a better judgment than a "white male who hasn't lived that life" referred specifically to cases involving racial and sexual discrimination. "Whether born from experience or inherent physiological or cultural differences . . . our gender and national origins may and will make a difference in our judging," she said. This is not a remarkable insight, nor is it even in dispute. Consider, say, how an African American Supreme Court justice might have viewed the *Dred Scott* case, or how a female judge—Sotomayor cited this in the speech—might have looked on the argument, advanced to oppose women's suffrage, that females are "not capable of reasoning or thinking logically." The presence of blacks and women in the room inherently changes judicial deliberation. She said that although white male judges have been admirably able on occasion to rise above cultural prejudices, the progress of racial minorities and women in the legal profession has directly coincided with greater judicial recognition of their rights. Once again, her point was not that this progress was the result of deliberate judicial activism, but that it was a natural consequence of fuller minority and female participation.

One of her central points was that all judges are, to an extent, defined by their identity and experience, whether they like it or not.

"I can and do aspire to be greater than the sum total of my experiences," she said, "but I accept my limitations."

Richmond seems a bright and fair-minded fellow, but he makes no bones about his political convictions or the purpose of his research and blogging. He has some of the skills and instincts of a reporter but not the motivation or ethics. Any news organization that simply trusted and aired his editing of Sotomayor's remarks, as every one of them did, was abdicating its responsibility to do its own reporting. It was airing propaganda. There is nothing wrong with reporting propaganda, per se, so long as it is labeled as such. None of the TV reports I saw on May 26 cited VerumSerum.com as the source of the material; this disappointed but did not surprise Richmond and Sexton.

Both found the impact of their volunteer effort exciting. They experienced the heady feeling of every reporter who discovers that the number of people who actually seek out new information themselves, even people in the news profession, is vanishingly small. Show the world something it hasn't seen, surprise it with something new, and you fundamentally alter its understanding of things. I have experienced this throughout my career, in ways large and small. I remember the first time I did, very early on, when I wrote a magazine profile of a promising Baltimore County politician, Ted Venetoulis, who was preparing a run for governor of Maryland. I wrote a long story about him, examining his record as county executive and offering a view that included both praise and criticism. I was twenty-five years old and had never written a word about Maryland politics. I was not especially knowledgeable about the state or the candidates, and the story was amateurish at best. Yet in the months of campaigning that followed, I found snippets from that article repeatedly quoted in the literature put out by Venetoulis and by his opponents. My story was used both to promote him and to attack him. To a large and slightly appalling extent, the points I made framed the public's perception of the candidate, who, as it happened, lost.

Several hours of Internet snooping by Richmond at his upstairs computer wound up shaping the public's perception of Sonia Sotomayor, at least for the first few weeks following her nomination. Conservative critics used the snippets to portray her as a racist and liberal activist, a picture even Richmond now admits is inaccurate. "She's really fairly moderate, compared to some of the other candidates on Obama's list," he says. "Given that conservatives are not going to like any Obama pick, she really wasn't all that bad." He felt many of the websites and TV commentators who used his work inflated its significance well beyond his own intent. But he was not displeased.

"I was amazed," he told me.

For his part, Sexton says: "It is a beautiful thing to live in this country. It's overwhelming and fantastic, really, that an ordinary citizen, with just a little bit of work, can help shape the national debate. Once you get a taste of it, it's hard to resist."

I would describe their approach as post-journalistic. It sees democracy, by definition, as perpetual political battle. The blogger's role is to help his side. Distortions and inaccuracies, lapses of judgment, the absence of context—all of these things matter only a little, because they are committed by both sides, and tend to come out a wash. Nobody is actually right about anything, no matter how certain people pretend to be. The truth is something that emerges from the cauldron of debate. No, not the truth: *victory*, because winning is way more important than being right. Power is the highest achievement. There is nothing new about this. But we never used to mistake it for journalism. Today it is rapidly replacing journalism, leading us toward a world where all information is spun, and where all "news" is unapologetically propaganda.

In this post-journalistic world, the model for all national debate becomes the trial, where adversaries face off, representing opposing points of view. We accept the harshness of this process because the consequences in a courtroom are so stark; trials are about assigning guilt or responsibility for harm. There is very little wiggle room in such a confrontation, very little room for compromise—there is only acquittal or some degree of guilt or responsibility. But isn't this model unduly harsh for political debate? Isn't there, in fact, middle ground in most public disputes? Isn't the art of politics finding that middle ground, weighing the public good against factional priorities? Without journalism, the public good is viewed only through a partisan lens, and politics becomes a blood sport.

Television loves this, because it is dramatic. Confrontation is all. And given the fragmentation of news on the Internet and on cable television, Americans increasingly choose to listen only to their own side of the argument, to bloggers and commentators who reinforce their convictions and paint the world only in acceptable, comfortable colors. Bloggers like Richmond and Sexton, and TV hosts like Hannity, preach only to the choir. Consumers of such "news" become all the more entrenched in their prejudices, and ever more hostile to those who disagree. The other side is no longer the honorable opposition, maybe partly right; but rather always wrong, stupid, criminal, even downright evil. Yet even in criminal courts, before assigning punishment, judges routinely order presentencing reports, which attempt to go beyond the clash of extremes in the courtroom to a more nuanced, disinterested assessment of a case. Usually someone who is neither prosecution nor defense is assigned to investigate. In a post-journalistic society, there is no disinterested voice. There are only the winning side and the losing side.

There's more here than just an old journalist's lament over his dying profession, or over the social cost of losing great newspapers and great TV news operations. And there's more than an argument for the ethical superiority of honest, disinterested reporting over advocacy. Even an eager and ambitious political blogger like Richmond, because he is drawn to the work primarily out of political conviction, not curiosity, is less likely to experience the pleasure of finding something new, or of arriving at a completely original, unexpected insight, one that surprises even himself. He is missing out on the great fun of speaking wholly for himself, without fear or favor. This is what gives reporters the power to stir up trouble wherever they go. They can shake preconceptions and poke holes in presumption. They can celebrate the unnoticed and puncture the hyped. They can, as the old saying goes, afflict the comfortable and comfort the afflicted. A reporter who thinks and speaks for himself, whose preeminent goal is providing deeper understanding, aspires even in political argument to persuade, which requires at the very least being seen as fair-minded and trustworthy by those—and this is the key—who are inclined to *disagree* with him. The honest, disinterested voice of a true journalist carries an authority that no self-branded liberal or conservative can have. "For a country to have a great writer is like having another government," Aleksandr Solzhenitsyn wrote. Journalism, done right, is enormously powerful precisely because it does not seek power. It seeks truth. Those who forsake it to shill for a product or a candidate or a party or an ideology diminish their own power. They are missing the most joyful part of the job.

This is what H. L. Mencken was getting at when he famously described his early years as a *Baltimore Sun* reporter. He called it "the life of kings."

The Great Guinea Hen Massacre

Atlantic, December 2009

I live on a small farm in Oxford, Pennsylvania, and this summer my wife, Gail, and I decided to install on our modest acreage a flock of guinea fowl.

Birds are colorful and entertaining, worthy of cultivating for their own sake, but we had a darker purpose. Guineas eat deer ticks. Like every unpaved acre in this part of the world, our property harbors an ever-growing herd of white-tailed deer, and is thus infested with the little Lyme disease–carrying arachnids. In the world of ticks, we were assured, guinea hens are feathered hell.

They arrived as chicks, twenty-five of them, small enough to fit quivering in the palm of our hands; quickly grew into rambunctious and noisy keets; and by the end of August were about the size and shape of rugby footballs, wandering around our property in a chattering flock. There were whites, royal purples, pearls, and lavenders. All sorts of grotesque wattles and growths popped out of their heads, above and below their orange beaks, but they had lovely plumage. The pearls, in particular, are so named because their dark gray coloring shows off an even spray of white specks.

One stood out. From birth, this bird was fearless. Whenever Gail and I would appear to change their water or clean their box, the flock would form a writhing, screaming mass trying desperately to merge itself into the far corner, or become invisible. This one, a pearl, whom we named Luke, after Cool Hand Luke, would sit alone on the top perch and eye us up and down, as if to say, "You again?" He would sometimes fly out of the box and strut around the bathroom, and when we stooped to pick him up, he didn't even try to get away. We figured he was either the world's smartest or stupidest guinea fowl—the latter distinction being highly competitive.

When they became too raucous, and started tearing apart their jury-rigged cardboard nest, we built a coop. Actually, less of a coop than a poultry condo, complete with a fourteen-foot ceiling and five roosting levels. The coop was roughly twenty times more expensive than the birds, but once you have hand-raised a flock, it is harder to abide the idea of a fox, dog, raccoon, or feral cat digging its way into their lair and turning them into a poultry smorgasbord. We have plenty of wild predators on our farm, and even if we didn't, we have a Jack Russell named Duey who, beneath his deceptive puppylike cuteness, is a ruthless serial killer with a particularly fowl appetite.

Put it this way: Duey once saw a chicken. Seconds later the bird was no more. Duey 1, Chickens 0.

Make that, Duey 2, Poultry 0, since he nailed one guinea when Gail left the door to the coop open behind her for an ill-advised split second. The Jack Russell has ever since been biding his time in close confinement, nose pressed to the screen. Mind you, dogs are especially good at biding their time.

Guineas have four modes: eating, sleeping, chattering, and screaming in terror. Chicken Little had some guinea in her. Here's what you need to know about a flock: they have no idea what is happening, they are scared of everything, they make noise constantly, and their long-term memory is about five seconds. You may note a resemblance here to the way news disseminates on the Internet and cable TV.

Their communications are very simple. In English, it would go something like this.

"I'm OK."

"Me, too."

"Good over here."

"I'm OK, too."

"Wait!"

"What was that?"

"Oh, my God!"

"Oh, my God!"

"Oh, my God!"

"Look out!"

"Look out!

"Run!"

"Run!"

At which point they are all fleeing and fluttering pell-mell. The unbridled terror lasts for just a few seconds, which is as long as it takes for them to forget whatever it was that prompted the stampede. The behavior repeats.

We let them out of the coop for the first time when they were about three months old, well past the recommended age. At first they sensibly refused to step out, all except for Luke, that is, who promptly hopped into one of the pastures and started chasing around our Andalusian mare as if he owned the place. It took the others a few hours to more timidly venture forth.

And then . . . they ran off. Contrary to encouraging advice about the breed, gathered mostly from books and the Internet, which assured us that they would not stray far from their coop, they took off like unleashed teenagers, the whole flock of twenty-three (another, alas, had expired in the coop on the hottest day of August, prompting the installation of a fan). They bore southwest and just kept on going, as if drawn by some poultry siren over the horizon, making their way across several broad Thorough-bred horse pastures, then across Route 472, and so on toward the setting sun. After it became clear they were not planning to turn around we made a heroic effort to herd them back, leaping tall fences; crossing the road; and, with curious Thoroughbreds peering over our shoulders, driving them before us with long sticks. The guineas were having none of it.

We gave up, and the guineas vanished.

Gail took it harder than I did. She is of the Bambi school, while I am more of a "nature red in tooth and claw" person. I was more resigned than saddened. We had given it our best shot, I figured, and had succeeded only in serving our neighborhood foxes, dogs, and hawks a movable feast. Neither of us ever ex-pected to see the guinea fowl again.

But, lo! Three days later they were back, chattering away in our middle pasture, minus two. One of the missing was Luke. We admire fearlessness, but it is a poor survival strategy. I thought, not bad, all in all, only one fatality per night in the wild. The flock seemed chastened, and had temporarily lost its appetite for wandering.

Temporarily.

Then came the great guinea hen massacre.

We have a fairly large property, so the flock has many safe acres in which to roam, chatter, panic, and vacuum ticks. But some madness weeks later propelled them once more to alien pastures. You would think that aeons of evolution would have clued the guinea to Labradors. But, no. Amber, the chocolate

Lab in question, is an especially obedient and friendly dog. She never saw a human hand she wasn't eager to lick, and never strays from her own farm.

"She just tore into them," said our neighbor Chuck, Amber's owner, who witnessed the slaughter and came away shocked by the flock's stupidity. "I kept thinking they would try to get away," he said.

Chuck found four carcasses, and five others just vanished, either down Amber's gullet or felled by sheer terror in the high weeds.

The rest returned, an even dozen, less than half of those we raised. Duey is still biding his time. Gail is afraid to let the guinea fowl out of the coop. At night, mixed in with the usual racket of tree frogs and katydids, I swear I can hear deer ticks out there laughing at us.

Rebirth of the Guineas

Published as "Rebirth of the Guinea Hens,"
Atlantic, March 2011

Animal husbandry is not for sissies. It has now been more than a year and a half since my wife, Gail, and I first brought a box of chirping, week-old guinea fowl home to our small Pennsylvania farm, and began diligently rearing them. We built them a luxurious coop and provided them with warmth, food, drink, and sixteen acres to roam.

Deer ticks were infesting our acreage, thanks to a Malthusian proliferation of their white-tailed hosts, and we were assured that the guineas would make short work of the little bloodsuckers. An organic solution! We never got a chance to see if it worked, because when our rambunctious flock of two dozen was turned loose, the birds proceeded to defy all predictions of guinea-fowl behavior—that they would not wander far from the coop; that they would establish a predictable daily routine; that they would return to the safety and warmth of the coop every evening; that they would fly up to a tree branch to avoid danger . . .

Ours made haste to their own demise. They showed no ability or even inclination to avoid the onslaught of neighborhood
carnivores, and were thus dispatched, one by one, by foxes, hawks,
and that most deadly scourge of local poultry, Amber, the ever-
cheerful chocolate Lab who lives next door—a course of events
that I documented earlier in this magazine.

By winter our hand-reared flock had been cruelly whittled
down to just two: one white and the other gray (the latter is called
a "pearl"). We decided to keep our two survivors safely cooped
up, and then give them away come spring, hopefully to someone
in a more peaceable spot.

It turns out to be hard to give grown guineas away. When
the weather grew warm, the two survivors clamored ever louder
each day to be turned out. They are insistent birds, and they
can make themselves *very* loud, as in scare the horses and annoy
the neighbors. We relented one morning, and against our better
judgment opened the coop door and bade them adieu.

Then an amazing thing happened. They came back! Not
just the first evening, but the next, and the next, and the next.
They stayed right on our hilltop property, just as all the books
and websites promised they would, and just as all their more
headstrong feathered brethren had not.

Intelligent behavior in guineas, it seems, is an inverse func-
tion of their number, a truth long known about human beings.
The large flock was good at only one thing: panic. Confronted
with a threat, its members acted out a perfectly choreographed
charade of a nervous breakdown, full of fluttering feathers and
high-decibel clatter, and then succumbed to whatever had alarmed
them.

Our survivors still panicked, but they also *evaded*. When
one of our dogs took off after them, they would squawk with
annoyance and fly to the nearest roof or high branch, hurling
fowl invective down at their tormentor. Conscious of danger

from above, they would move swiftly when crossing a pasture or yard, and mostly keep to tree lines, tall grasses, or brush. These two—the white and the pearl, almost a year old—seemed to have figured things out.

We still refused to name them, anticipating their certain extinction, but despite ourselves by early summer we had grown quite attached. I loved to see their wattled, bobbing heads pop up unexpectedly from our gardens, or watch them flee in loud panic when the lawn mower scared them from a thicket. There is something innately comical about them. Sure, two birds weren't enough to be useful for tick control, but they were a charming and (in their own way) beautiful addition to our farm.

Then the pearl stopped coming back. One night it was just the big white waiting outside the coop, and we assumed the worst. It was a sad but unsurprising turn. But, the next day, the pearl reappeared, frantically racing around with the white, as if feeding in double time. That evening, again only the white waited outside the coop. The answer was apparent. The previous summer's massacre had by chance left us with a male and a female. Our pearl was a girl. She had built a nest somewhere in the woods, had filled it with eggs, and was now sitting on them.

Every scrap of intelligence about guineas, who are native to much of Africa, assures you that their offspring are not likely to survive in the wilds of Pennsylvania. Eggs and newly hatched keets need a steady dry temperature of at least ninety-five degrees, the experts say. Besides, the hen, exposed outdoors overnight for weeks on end, is, to borrow an expression, a sitting duck.

So we stalked the pearl one afternoon, crawling through underbrush and lurking behind trees, following her to the hidden nest. This task was ironic, in that we had purchased the guinea flock to help rid our farm of deer ticks. We were now crawling through tick-rich habitat, inviting far greater exposure to the tiny bastards than ever. The nest was on the ground in a deep thicket of grass and brush, so cunningly placed that had we not watched the hen wriggle into the spot, we might have stood right over it without seeing it. In her nest were twenty-two eggs.

I shooed her off with a broom, which she pecked at valiantly, while Gail collected all the eggs. The pearl was vocally unhappy about the theft for about thirty seconds, and then promptly went off in search of her mate. They went right back to their old routines. We went to the local grain and feed store and bought an incubator.

The pearl built and filled four nests last summer. She laid upwards of eighty brown-speckled eggs. We incubated three of the batches, enthusiastically but inexpertly. I had ambitions for replacing the entire original lost flock, but we ended the season with fourteen new birds. The coop was once again a noisy, lively place.

It wasn't easy. Some of the keets popped right out of the egg after twenty-eight days, as though arriving on time at a train station. Once out, most were hardy and fast-growing. But nature is neither clean nor perfect. Some got stuck in their eggs and didn't make it, so we listened to them chirp plaintively for days, trapped and dying. We learned the hard way that helping them out is ill-advised—if they can't make it out of the egg, they are usually doomed.

A few of our hatchlings arrived damaged. One keet chick could not stand. It could move only one leg, enough for it to scoot itself around well enough to reach foot and water, but not enough to protect it from being viciously pecked by its siblings. I watched it waste away day by day until I couldn't take it anymore. It took longer than anyone would wish to drown it in a tennis-ball can, and while I still believe it was the merciful thing to do, I can't shake the feeling that I will be punished for it. Another of my interventions ended more happily, at least at first. One white chick was born with a more common deformity: the long orange toes of one foot were curled. Taking instructions from a website, I straightened the toes and taped them firmly to a small square of cardboard. The keet stomped around unhappily on the makeshift flapper for about five hours, and—voilà! Straight toes! But even after the foot was fully restored, he remained suspect, for some reason, to his fellow hatchlings, a fact that was not immediately apparent.

We now had three groups of birds. There were the older two, the parents. Then came the first batch of offspring, hatched in early July, whom we now considered teenagers. And we had a batch of toddlers, hatched in early September. As with all the other issues we faced in this saga, we turned to our not-so-trusted adviser, the Internet, for how best to integrate younger birds with older ones in the coop.

Some websites stated flatly that it was best to introduce the younger birds when they were still small, because they would naturally submit to the authority of the teenagers and adults. If you waited until they were more mature, the new birds would be more likely to fight back, and that could get ugly.

Others argued that the right way was to place the smaller birds in the coop inside their own cage, so that the flock could get used to them over time without being able to attack them.

We initially opted for the first approach, which went fine for all except the one white keet whose foot I had straightened. There was nothing different about him anymore to my eyes, but the teenage birds attacked the little guy mercilessly. I found him one afternoon jammed into a corner of the coop with his head hidden in a narrow opening between a pipe and the wall, where the other birds could not get at him. I rescued him and nursed him back to health.

I then attempted, with him, the second approach. I put him back inside the coop in his own cage. He was in with the rest of the flock, but they couldn't attack him. This apparently just built resentment, because when, after a few weeks, I decided to let him back out, the teenagers waited until I left and then pecked the poor little guy nearly to death. I found him bloody and unconscious, with what looked to be a hole pounded into the top of his head.

He survived, and I ended up giving him away with the one bird that hatched out of the third batch of eggs we recovered. The newly hatched sibling seemed to think his older brother was hunky-dory, and they got on famously. Both are reported thriving.

As for the dozen new guineas we kept, we don't plan to let them leave the coop until the spring, when they will be about the same age their parents were when they demonstrated a knack for survival. We are hoping they will follow the example set by their elders—the eternal hope of parents everywhere.

The two adult guineas—the male white and female pearl—have names now. Our son Ben dubbed them Adam and Eve, although we prefer the more pedestrian Mr. and Mrs. They are inseparable. Next summer, when we turn their offspring loose, we do not plan to hunt down every last nest and egg, nor do we plan to go through the sordid business of incubating and integrating another batch.

We are instead going to test the theory that guineas cannot successfully breed in the wild in these parts. Internet advice has been iffy about everything else. My money is on the birds.

Last words on the guinea fowl (2015):

I lost my bet on the birds, who are no more. It was a failed experiment. We replaced them with three chickens—two Barred Rock and a Buff Orpington—who have done wonderfully. My granddaughters Clara and Audrey named them Flotsam, Jetsam, and Buttercup, respectively.

As farm birds go they are superior to guinea fowl. They don't run off. They don't flap around and kill themselves. They get along. They have sweet dispositions and are not annoyingly loud. They lay delicious eggs like clockwork. Before Gail and I ever started with the guinea hen experiment, my friend Walt Leis, a man with far more experience in such matters, said, "Don't do it. Guineas are nuts. Get chickens." As usual, Walt was right. When we sold the farm last year, Walt took the three chickens to live with him. He sometimes brings us fresh eggs, for old times' sake.

Cry Wolfe

In Defense of the Last Writer in the World Who Needs Defending

Atlantic, April 2006

In one of many deft set pieces in Tom Wolfe's *I Am Charlotte Simmons*, a group of student journalists at his fictional Dupont University hold a meeting in the "lumpen-bohemian clutter" of their campus newsroom. The editor wants a firm story list for the next issue's fast-approaching deadline, but the discussion bogs down over an item that might just be important breaking news—they're not sure.

It seems that the campus custodial staff cleaned from the quad sidewalks crude chalk depictions of homosexual acts. Camille Deng, a feisty archfeminist and civil libertarian, is outraged by such heedless destruction of gay art. The campus administration has countered the charge, not by asserting its obligation to erase obscene graffiti, but by an alert piece of politically correct one-upmanship—it claims the drawings were "homophobic," meant as a slur on campus gays. Deng isn't buying it.

"Do you think it's just a coincidence that Parents Weekend is coming up?" she argues; ". . . you think they might just possibly not want the parents to see descriptions of how Dupont guys make love written in chalk all over the sidewalks? 'We're Queer and We're Here'—you think Dupont Hall wants to let that big cat out of the bag? Because *they are* here."

Then another staffer, who is gay, turns on Deng's use of the word "they."

"You sure you don't have an issue yourself?" he accuses her. "Like maybe a little covert pariah-ism? Like maybe a little self-loathing lesbianism?"

Their argument forms a perfect uroboros, illustrating that the game of impugning motives (even subconscious ones) forms a self-destructive loop. It's a neat insight, and *I Am Charlotte Simmons* is full of such little gems, stabs at the rich variety of pseudo-intellectualism that flourishes on a college campus. It is above all a novel of ideas, a point perhaps obscured by the entertainment value of Wolfe's prose. In addition to being one of the most original stylists to ever write in the English language, Wolfe has long been America's most skillful satirist, and in *Charlotte Simmons* he struck a nerve. In his first two novels, *The Bonfire of the Vanities* and *A Man in Full*, Wolfe lampooned the excesses of the nouveau riche, the criminal justice system, and other generally urban white-collar targets, all of which were widely considered fair game. In *I Am Charlotte Simmons*, he took aim at youth culture—at the children! Many young critics resented being made fun of by a septuagenarian in a fusty suit, and some dismissed Wolfe as a scold, arguing that binge drinking, social cliques, and rampant screwing have always been part of the undergrad journey . . . right? Reviewers with children or students (or both) the same age as those in the novel reacted defensively. They stuck up for the modern student, and for the quality of thought at modern universities, and found Wolfe's take on campus life to be shallow, prudish, inaccurate, and unfair. "In the course of a very long 676 pages [Wolfe] serves up the revelation—yikes!—that students crave sex and beer, love to party, wear casual clothes and use four-letter words," wrote Michiko Kakutani, whose reviews in the *New York Times* are routinely parroted by critics throughout the land. Daniel Mendelsohn in the *New York Review of Books* faulted Wolfe for losing his cool, for letting the fine contempt that fuels satire degrade into mere outrage, which, the critic wrote, is "flaccid as social satire."

The book became a best seller, as all Wolfe's books do, but fell somewhat short of the blockbuster status achieved by his first two novels and unmatched journalism. There may have been other factors involved in the slight drop-off in sales, but no doubt it resulted in part from the sour reviews. The assault this time out owes something, I suspect, to the contemptuous treatment Wolfe received a few years ago from several of his esteemed contemporaries in the modern literary pantheon—notably John Updike, Norman Mailer, and John Irving. Their attacks are best summed up in one deliciously bitchy sentence from Updike's otherwise flattering *New Yorker* review of *A Man in Full*, in which the celebrated author and critic assessed Wolfe as a writer of "entertainment, not literature, even literature in a modest aspirant form." Thus did a high priest of the novel brand Wolfe a pretender, and grant dispensation to the herd to have at him.

Charlotte Simmons is a fat gray-and-green paperback now, and despite the assertion by Slate critic Jacob Weisberg, who wrote in the *New York Times* that Wolfe is fun but that no one ever rereads him, I recommend a second look. The book is brilliant, wicked, true, and like everything Wolfe writes, thematically coherent, cunningly well plotted, and delightfully told. It should firmly establish him as not just one of the most popular of serious American writers, but one of the most accomplished. Writing that sentence means aligning myself with the proles in an ongoing dustup, but, hey, if you're going to get into a fight, make it a literary one. Ever since Mailer's hips gave out there isn't much chance of anyone throwing a real punch.

Certainly one factor that elevates fiction from mere "entertainment" to even "moderately aspirant literature" is substance. Is the book about something important? Does it reward study? Is the author saying anything new? Is the work carefully crafted around a theme?

In *Charlotte Simmons* Wolfe is attacking a pet insight of the emerging science of the brain: that consciousness itself is nothing but an illusion, that inside us all there is no "I," just a theoretically predictable pattern of firing synapses. This is behaviorism taken to the furthest extreme, and a fairly startling premise, one that precludes not just free will but presumably the very notion of morality. The novel's assertive title takes issue with that notion and its consequences, echoing Descartes's famous declaration, "I think, therefore I am." It is about the testing and ultimate triumph of Charlotte's selfhood.

Wolfe opens the book by describing the experiment that earned Dupont psychologist Victor Starling a Nobel Prize: when a critical portion of a cat's brain was removed in the lab, it triggered a "hypermanic" state of sexual arousal, which was then imitated by "control" cats who had not undergone the operation. "Starling," writes Wolfe, "had discovered that a strong social or 'cultural atmosphere,' even one as abnormal as this one, could in time overwhelm the genetically-determined responses of perfectly normal, healthy animals." The experiment is, of course, an analogy for Dupont University, where the school's national champion basketball team is revered, and its players, all genetic freaks with, in effect, the thinking portion of their brains removed (they are discouraged from taking real courses), enjoy a "hypermanic" sex life with the eager coeds who line their paths. They are the equivalent of Starling's surgically altered lab cats. Normal students are the "control" group, who observe the players on the court, on ESPN, and on campus, and imitate them. Dupont, which Wolfe depicts as the nation's premier seat of higher learning, is in thrall

to jock values—sex, booze, drugs, and pursuit of the big postcol-
lege payday. One of Wolfe's early triumphs, *The Electric Kool-Aid
Acid Test*, ridiculed the pretensions of the hippie movement, and
here, nearly two generations later, is the legacy of the "summer
of love," not an egalitarian free love utopia but a repellent pit of
sexual predation, where status is conferred by fucking.

Into this rampant promiscuity wanders beautiful, innocent,
idealistic, painfully traditional Charlotte Simmons, a Candide-like
scholarship student from the deep backwoods town of Sparta,
North Carolina, in search of the "life of the mind." Some of
the novel's critics complained that anyone so naive as Charlotte
in this day and age is implausible, but these are people who are
apparently unfamiliar with rural America, where for better or
worse traditional values thrive in places cable television doesn't
yet reach, and where evangelical preachers are building mall-sized
churches. But whether someone like Charlotte actually exists is
irrelevant. She is a construction, a device, one of a long and celebrated series of satirical vehicles in English literature, all the way
back to Henry Fielding's Joseph Andrews. On the surface she is
fragile, but underneath she is a warrior, a "Spartan." Charlotte
is, by degrees, sucked into the campus culture. She is lured into
the self-abnegating realm of Starling's neuroscience lab, ravished
and discarded by the novel's premier predator, and plunged into
a profound period of depression and confusion, only to rally and
establish herself (and her jock boyfriend, Jojo Johanssen) on her
own terms, mind and body. She doesn't just triumph over the
tawdry reality of Dupont; she transcends it. Mendelsohn completely misses the point when he describes Charlotte at the end
of the book as having been "reduced by her own craving for
'acceptance' to being arm-candy for a famous college jock." Far
from it: she has beaten back the hedonistic tide of peer pressure,
escaped the soul-deadening pull of Starling's lab, and reasserted
her selfhood and her moral bearings. She is said jock's girlfriend,

a fact that marks her ascension to the top rung of social status on campus—always a prime Wolfean preoccupation—and she holds that distinction strictly on her own terms; she has restored the missing piece of Jojo's brain (turned him into a real student), and is, as Wolfe makes abundantly clear, the dominant partner in the relationship. In the distorted context of campus life, she rules. All this in her freshman year, no less.

Vladimir Nabokov wrote that the ultimate task of the novelist was to create an imaginary world that seems real to the reader, but which, of course, is not. Elaine Showalter in the *Chronicle of Higher Education*, along with Mendelsohn and a few others, made the mistake of taking Wolfe's description of Dupont Univeristy too literally, and so felt the need to argue that real-life elite schools are better than that. But Wolfe is not Upton Sinclair, exposing the horrors of a meatpacking plant. The novel's university, like Charlotte, is an exaggeration (the very idea of an Ivy League college having a national championship basketball team is a dizzying leap). Despite all his bluster about Émile Zola and the importance of social realism, at heart Wolfe is not a realist. The New York of Sherman McCoy, the Atlanta of Charlie Croker, and the Dupont University of Charlotte Simmons are caricatures, not faithful portraits. With Dupont University Wolfe projects the nightmarish—take his "rutrutrutrutrut," for instance—moral consequences of a philosophy that won't admit the existence of self, much less soul, and imagines one pure, intellectually honest character thrust into that distopia. Poorly executed, a work of extended analogy like this usually comes off as stiff and contrived; *I Am Charlotte Simmons* is so intricately imagined and carefully reported that it's no wonder the book is mistaken for social realism. It is indeed scary how close this story comes to the real world.

There are so many delicious moments: the socially ambitious nerd Adam tripping over his own cleverness trying to impress Charlotte with a long riff about "Bad-Ass Rhodies"; Jojo, the

MARK BOWDEN

jock boyfriend, struggling to explain to a scornful history professor why there are words in his term paper (written for him
by Adam) that he cannot define; Wolfe's precise delineation of
the subtle gradations of sarcasm and the now universal Shit and
Fuck patois; the uneasy alliance between black and white players
on the basketball team, and the role of "Swimmies," marginally
talented players with good grades who help maintain the team's
all-important academic standing. The supposed villain of this
imagined world is Buster Roth, the basketball coach, who turns
out to be the university's only admirable grown-up.

Of all the writers in the world, Tom Wolfe is the last to
need defending. I imagine him as a schoolboy in immaculate old-
fashioned knee pants picking fights on the playground with all the
bigger, tougher boys. Beneath that skinny, pale, dandified exterior
is a two-fisted brawler and committed self-promoter. In his long
career he has rhetorically stuck his thumb in the eye of the *New
Yorker* (a history that lends Updike's appraisal a tincture of tit for
tat), the New Left, hippies, Black Panthers, astronauts, architects,
and artists, among many others, but his longest-running battle has
been with the fashionable notion of the "serious" literary novel.

His first broadside against it was his famous 1973 essay "New
Journalism," in which he lamented the "otherworldy precious-
ness" of most modern novels. More and more, he wrote, they
seemed to be written not for a general reading public but for other
writers. The writers of such books, in their preoccupation with
characters' internal lives, had turned their backs on the real story
of their times, Wolfe argued, abandoning the kind of reporting
and observation that had distinguished the great novels of the
past and effectively ceding the turf to journalists like . . . him!
He didn't actually place the crown on his own head; the essay
was an introduction to the collected works of other "literary"
journalists, but Wolfe was already (as he well knew) the bright
eminence of that pack, whose work, he proclaimed, had become

the "main event" in the literary arts. Then, having planted his own flag on literature's peak, he abandoned the very form he had championed to start writing novels himself. In a celebrated 1989 essay, he anointed himself point man for "a battalion, a brigade of Zolas" who would sally forth, notebooks and tape recorders in hand, to rescue fiction from its cul-de-sac of self-obsession and restore it to its central role in American life, chronicling the "lurid carnival" of modern existence.

It matters a great deal to someone, I suppose, what kind of fiction commands the peak of Mount Literature. History teaches us that such preferences change only slightly more slowly than hemlines, and many an author celebrated in his lifetime is barely remembered a decade after his last book. Much critical prestige today is accorded writers of "experimental," or "post-modern," fiction, who play clever games with language and traditional storytelling forms, and whose works are dazzlingly hard to follow. If simple readability matters, these authors are the most likely candidates for obscurity, even giants like Thomas Pynchon and William Gaddis, to name just two National Book Award winners whose erudite, dense, fat, recondite works are considered by some to be the towering literary achievements of the late twentieth century. There is a certain rarefied pleasure in tracking the desperate flight of Tyrone Slothrop through the wild triple-canopy jungle of Pynchon's imagination, but it is work very few readers are ready to perform. A recent essay in *Harper's* in defense of such writing, by the author Ben Marcus, set out to describe such an ideal reader:

> [*His or her*] *Wernicke's area* [*the portion of the brain presumed to process language*] *is staffed by an army of jump-suited code-breakers, working a barn-sized space that is strung about the rafters with a mathematically-intricate lattice of rope and steel, and maybe gusseted by a synthetic*

coil that is stronger and more sensitive than either, like guitar
strings made from an unraveled spinal cord, each strand
tuned to different tensions.

It goes on. Marcus lost me at code breakers, although I was struck by his momentary indecision—the "maybe"—over whether or not to embellish this bizarre metaphor with his "synthetic coil." He concludes the long paragraph thus:

My ideal reader would cough up a thimble of fine gray pow-
der at the end of the reading session, and she could use this
mineral-rich substance to compost her garden.

This is just silly. There will always be readers who enjoy "code breaking," but I suspect great fiction is and will always be about language, story, characters, and serious ideas, and will remain stubbornly coherent.

Wolfe scores for me in every category, most notably language. My own Wernicke's area has long thrilled to the surprising and inventive turns of Wolfe's narration. It is a voice so distinctive that it has launched a thousand bad imitations, and is the vibrant core of everything Wolfe writes. His exuberant experiments in punctuation are easy to ridicule, but they are not just pointless pyrotechnics; they are an effort to harness on the page the velocity of his rhetoric, which runs at full throttle in a continual state of intellectual astonishment. He began his career as a social scientist, and he has remained, first and foremost, a man the opposite of dumbstruck by the hilarious pageant of American life, whether revealing the vapid meanderings that pass for serious thought on a bus full of tripping hippies or demonstrating how the U.S. space program faithfully reenacted—in modern times, on a massive scale—the ancient tribal ritual of single combat. One cannot imagine a Wolfe story without that voice, any more than one can convey the humor in *Tom Jones* without the voice of Fielding, or *Tristram Shandy* without that of Laurence Sterne.

In his *Harper's* essay, Marcus describes the visceral pleasure—Nabokov called it a "tingle" in his spine—of language that stretches normal constraints and combines in a new and interesting way. Complex prose need not be obtuse. At its best, it takes us to startling new places, whether inside the head of operatively conditioned chimpanzee number sixty-one hurtling into orbit in *The Right Stuff*:

> *He didn't panic for a moment. He had been through this same sensation many times on the centrifuge. As long as he just took it and didn't struggle, they wouldn't zap all those goddamned blue volts into the soles of his feet. There were a lot worse things in this world than g-forces. . . . The usual shit was flowing. The main thing was to keep ahead of those blue volts to the feet. . . . He started pushing the buttons and throwing the switched like the greatest electric Wurlitzer organist who ever lived, never missing a signal.*

or describing basketball star Jojo coughing up something a bit more substantial than a "fine gray powder" (and much better compost material):

> *Jojo swelled up his chest, lifted his head upward as high as it would go, and snuffed, scouring his sinuses, nasal pathways, and lungs so furiously it was as if he wanted to suck the bench, the girl, the entire Buster Bowl and half of southeastern Pennsylvania up into his nostrils. He grimaced until his neck widened, striated by muscles, tendons, and veins, swelled up his chest to the last milliliter of its capacity—and spat. The girl stared at the edge of the court where it landed, a prodigious, runny, yellowy pus-laced gob of phlegm.*

So what makes fiction great? What is the standard? Is time a fair judge of quality? Are all the books that have endured for a long time great, and those forgotten less so, or is the process more random? In his put-down of Wolfe, Updike didn't explain the difference between "entertainment" and "literature," other than to suggest that the dapper former journalist's writing was not "exquisite." The word means "carefully done or elaborately made," "very beautiful or lovely in a carefully wrought way," "highly sensitive; keenly discriminating; fastidious." To me, books that are merely entertaining would be like those of, say, Michael Crichton, Elmore Leonard, and J. K. Rowling, which are an absolute delight, but which melt in the mouth like cotton candy. I don't mean that as a put-down; I love cotton candy, and it's hard to write an entertaining book, and it's worth noting that Fielding himself described his masterpiece, *Tom Jones*, as an "entertainment."

So how does one judge? The put-down invites a comparison between Wolfe's writing and Updike's own. I admire Updike's books, although I have read only a small portion of his prodigious output. Among those I have, the *Rabbit* series in particular, *Couples*, and *Villages* are intensely realistic, and capture better than anyone the texture of American suburban life and the subtle transactions of emotional and sexual need in modern relationships. But his books run together in my mind. They all have a similar feel, and as engrossing and exquisitely written as they are, I find I have a hard time remembering them afterward. In the long run, fiction that endures is, by definition, memorable.

By that standard, my money is on Wolfe.

Abraham Lincoln Is an Idiot

Published as "'Idiot,' 'Yahoo,' 'Original Gorilla':
How Lincoln Was Dissed in His Day," *Atlantic*, June 2013

By nearly any measure—personal, political, even literary—Abraham Lincoln set a standard of success that few in history can match. Did anyone notice?

Sure, we revere Lincoln today, but in his lifetime the bile poured on him from every quarter makes today's Internet vitriol seem dainty. His ancestry was routinely impugned, his lack of formal learning ridiculed, his appearance maligned, and his morality assailed. We take for granted, of course, the scornful outpouring from Confederate states; no action Lincoln took short of capitulation would ever quiet his southern critics. But vituperation wasn't limited to enemies of the Union. The north was ever at his heels. No matter what Lincoln did, it was never enough for one political faction, and too much for another. Yes, his sure-footed leadership during this country's most difficult days was accompanied by a fair measure of praise, but also by a steady stream of abuse—in editorials, speeches, journals, and private letters—from those *on his own side*, those dedicated to the very causes he so ably championed. George Templeton Strong, a prominent New York lawyer and diarist, wrote that Lincoln was "a barbarian, Scythian, yahoo, or gorilla." Henry Ward Beecher, the Connecticut preacher and abolitionist, often ridiculed Lincoln in his Congregational newspaper, the *Independent,* rebuking him for his lack of refinement and calling him "an unshapely man." Other northern newspapers openly called for his assassination long before John Wilkes Booth actually pulled the trigger. He was called a coward, "an idiot," and "the original gorilla" by none other than the commanding general of his armies, George McClellan.

One of Lincoln's lasting achievements was to end American slavery. Yet here's how he was seen by Elizabeth Cady Stanton, the famous abolitionist, in a letter she wrote to Wendell Phillips in 1864, a year after Lincoln had freed the slaves in rebel states and only months before he would engineer the Thirteenth Amendment: calling Lincoln "Dishonest Abe," she "deplored the 'incapacity and rottenness' of his administration, and pledged that if he 'is reelected I shall immediately leave the country for the Fijee Islands.'" Stanton eventually had a change of heart, and lamented her work against Lincoln, but not all prominent abolitionists did—even after victory over slavery was complete, and even after he was killed. In the days after Lincoln's assassination, William Lloyd Garrison called the murder "providential," because it meant Vice President Andrew Johnson would assume leadership.

Lincoln masterfully led the north through the Civil War. He held firm in his refusal to acknowledge secession; maneuvered the Confederate president Jefferson Davis into starting the war; played a delicate political game to keep border states from joining the rebellion; and drew up a grand military strategy that, when he found the right generals, won the war. Yet he was denounced for his leadership throughout. In a monumental and meticulous two-volume study of the sixteenth president, *Lincoln: A Life* (2008), Michael Burlingame, a professor of Lincoln studies at the University of Illinois, presents Lincoln's actions and speeches not as they have come to be remembered, through the fine lens of our gratitude and admiration, but as they were received in his day. (All of the examples in this essay are drawn from Burlingame's book, which should be required reading for anyone seriously interested in Lincoln.) Early on, after a series of setbacks for Union troops and the mulish inaction of General McClellan, members of Lincoln's own Republican Party reviled him as, in the words of Michigan senator Zachariah Chandler, "timid, vacillating, & inefficient." A Republican newspaper editor in Wisconsin wrote, "The president and the cabinet, *as a whole, are not equal to the occasion.*" Ohio Republican William M. Dickson wrote in 1862 that Lincoln "is universally admitted a failure, has no will, no courage, no executive capacity . . . and his spirit necessarily infuses itself downwards through all departments."

Charles Sumner, a Republican senator from Massachusetts to whom Lincoln often turned for advice, opposed his renomination in 1864. "There is a strong feeling among those who have seen Mr. Lincoln, in the way of business, that he lacks practical talent for his important place. It is thought there should be more readiness, and more capacity, for government." William P. Fessenden, the Maine Republican, called Lincoln "weak as water."

As anyone struggles to do well; to be honest, wise, eloquent, and kind; to be dignified without being aloof; to be humble without being a pushover, who affords a better example than Lincoln? And yet as he looked and listened to the way his efforts were received, how could he not despair?

His wife said that the constant attacks on him caused him "great pain." At one point, after reading one of Henry Ward Beecher's salvos, Lincoln reportedly exclaimed, "I would rather be dead than, as President, thus abused in the house of my friends." Lincoln would often respond to the flood of naysayers with a weary wave of his hand, and say, "Let us speak no more of these things."

Democracy is rowdy, and political abuse its currency, so perhaps the ill-treatment of even Lincoln's unerring judgment is to be expected. But how do we explain the scorn for his prose?

No American president has uttered more immortal words than Lincoln. We are moved by the power and lyricism of his speeches a century and a half later—not just by their hard, clear reasoning, but by their beauty. It is hard to imagine anyone hearing without admiration, for instance, this sublime passage from the first Inaugural Address: *"I am loth to close. We are not enemies, but friends. We must not be enemies. Though passion may have strained, it must not break, our bonds of affection. The mystic chords of memory, stretching from every battlefield, and patriot grave to every living heart and hearthstone all over this broad land, will yet swell the chorus of the Union when again touched, as surely they will be, by the better angels of our nature."* Yet this speech was characterized by an editorial writer in the *Jersey City American Standard* as, "involved, coarse, colloquial, devoid of ease and grace, and bristling with obscurities and outrages against the simplest rules of syntax."

As for the Gettysburg Address—one of the most powerful speeches in human history, one that many American schoolchildren can now recite by heart (*Fourscore and seven years ago our fathers brought forth . . .*), and a statement of national purpose that for some rivals the importance of the Declaration of Independence—the local newspaper in Gettysburg reported, "We pass over the silly remarks of the President. For the credit of the nation we are willing that the veil of oblivion shall be dropped over them, and they shall be no more repeated or thought of." The *London Times* correspondent wrote, "Anything more dull and commonplace it wouldn't be easy to produce."

And the Second Inaugural Address—*With malice toward none, with charity for all*—the third pillar in Lincoln's now un-disputed reputation for eloquence, inscribed in limestone at the Lincoln Memorial in Washington? A. B. Bradford, who was a pas-tor in Pennsylvania and a member of one of the oldest European families in America, wrote, "One of the most awkwardly expressed documents I ever read . . . When he knew it would be read by millions of people all over the world, why under the heavens did he not make it a little more creditable to American scholarship?" The *New York Herald* described it as "a little speech of glittering generalities used only to fill the program." The *Chicago Times*, a powerful voice in Lincoln's home state: "We did not conceive it possible that even Mr. Lincoln could produce a paper so slip-shod, so loose-jointed, so puerile, not alone in literary construction, but in its ideas, sentiment, and grasp."

Poor Lincoln. By all accounts he appears to have been the gentlest and most honorable of husbands and fathers, and yet he found little solace even at home. Burlingame records the constant duplicity and groundless suspicion, the nagging criticism and jealous rants of Mary Lincoln, who—coming home on a steam-boat from Lincoln's triumphant entry into a fallen Richmond—reportedly flew into such a rage that she slapped her husband in the face.

"It is surprising how widespread [the criticism] was," said Burlingame. "And also how thin-skinned he could be. But that was the nature of partisanship in those days; you never could say a kind word about your opponent."

As if things have changed.

Many appreciated Lincoln's greatness and goodness while he lived, of course. He was elected twice to the presidency, after all, and was revered by millions. History records more grief and mourning on his death than for any other American president. But as a consensus forms about historical events and people over time, the past is simplified in our memory, in our textbooks, and in our popular culture. Lincoln's excellence has been distilled from the rough-and-tumble of his times. We best remember the most generous of contemporary assessments, whether the magnanimous letter sent by his fellow speaker on the stage at Gettysburg, Edward Everett, who wrote to him, "I should be glad, if I could flatter myself that I came as near to the central idea of the occasion in two hours, as you did in two minutes"; or Edwin Stanton's "Now he belongs to the ages," at the moment of his death; or Frederick Douglass's moving tribute in 1876 to "a great and good man."

This process of distillation obscures the difficulty of Lincoln's journey, and it makes, by comparison, our own age seem diminished. Where is the political giant of our era? Where is the timeless oratory? Where is the bold resolve, the moral courage, the vision?

Imagine all of those critical voices from the nineteenth century as talking heads on cable television. Imagine the snap judgments, the slurs, and the put-downs that beset Lincoln magnified a millon times in social media. How many of us in that din would hear him clearly? How many of us would have noticed him doing well? His story illustrates how even immortality—let alone humbler things like skill, decency, good judgment, and courage—is rarely even recognized, and never goes unpunished.

Dumb Kids' Class

Atlantic, June 2012

Catholic school was not the ordeal for me that it apparently was for many other children of my generation. I attended Catholic grade schools; served as an altar boy; and, astonishingly, was never struck by a nun or molested by a priest. All in all I was treated with kindness, which often was more than I deserved. My education has withstood the test of time, including both the lessons my teachers instilled and the ones they never intended.

In the mid-twentieth century, when I was in grade school, a child's self-esteem was not a matter for concern. Shame was considered a spur to better behavior and accomplishment. If you flunked a test, you were singled out, and the offending sheet of paper, bloodied with red marks, was waved before the entire class as a warning, much the way our catechisms depicted a boy with black splotches on his soul.

Fear was also considered useful. In the fourth grade, right around the time of the Cuban missile crisis, one of the nuns at St. Petronille's, in Glen Ellyn, Illinois, told us that the Vatican had received a secret warning that the world would soon be consumed by a fatal nuclear exchange. The fact that the warning had purportedly been delivered by Our Lady of Fátima lent the prediction divine authority. (Any last sliver of doubt was removed by our viewing of the 1952 movie *The Miracle of Our Lady of Fatima*, wherein the Virgin Mary herself appeared on a luminous cloud.) We were surely cooked. I remember pondering the futility of existence, to say nothing of the futility of safety drills that involved huddling under desks. When the fateful sirens sounded, I resolved, I would be out of there. Down the front steps, across Hillside Avenue, over fences, and through backyards, I would take the shortest possible route home, where I planned to crawl under my father's workbench in the basement. It was the sturdiest thing I had ever seen. I didn't believe it would save me, but after weighing the alternatives carefully, I decided it was my preferred spot to face oblivion.

At the schools I attended, each grade level was divided in two. Teachers observed their charges' performance, and sorted them accordingly. Even in that euphemism-deprived period, no adult ever labeled the two academic tiers explicitly, but we children saw the truth. There was the smart kids' class, and there was the dumb kids' class.

It was the same in all three of the parochial schools I attended. My family moved twice: from Glen Ellyn, where I attended St. Petronille's through sixth grade; to Port Washington, Long Island, where I attended St. Peter of Alcantara for seventh grade. After a year, we left Long Island for Maryland, where I attended eighth grade at St. Joseph's, in Cockeysville. These were formative years, from ages eleven to fourteen, from boyhood to adolescence. And both times we moved, I began the school year in the dumb kids' class. Judging by my yellowed report cards, it's safe to say that the nuns at St. Petronille's had been merely whelmed by my potential. Since the nuns at the new schools had never met me, they decided to start me in the class where expectations might be more easily met.

Children are exquisitely attuned to the way adults size them up, so there was never any mystery about where anyone stood. Those of us in the dumb kids' class took it as a badge of honor. Smart kids were pampered kiss-asses, overly concerned with pleasing teachers and parents. Dumb kids took no shit. With the burden of expectation lifted, we were unafraid, boisterous, occasionally defiant, and generally up to all manner of mischief. Dumb kids were *fun*. My bet is that when a comprehensive inventory is made of my generation, it will be found that not one person from a smart kids' class was ever expelled from a Catholic elementary school. If there was trouble to be had—stealing wine from the sacristy, sneaking into the basement to smoke cigarettes, peering up the stairwells at girls' underpants—the dumb kids got there first.

Dumb kids were also tougher than smart kids, as a rule. You didn't last long on the playground with the dumb kids if you were unwilling to take a swing at somebody, or were too afraid of getting hit. I was not particularly brave, or tough, but I had fallen off my bike at a young age and, to my mother's horror, broken one of my front teeth. Thankfully, this was before the age of universal cosmetic dentistry in America. Throughout grade school, my broken tooth gave me a degree of rough-and-tumble cred that was as invaluable as it was false. I had also observed—and moving from school to school gives a kid a broad sample—that you usually had to hit somebody only once to be considered dangerous enough to be left alone. Drawing blood guaranteed actual respect. At St. Joseph's, a popular activity was humiliating the weak kids by dropping them into the "spit pit," an outdoor stairwell that led down to the school's basement. Victims would be spat upon as they tried to escape up the steps. I bloodied the mouth of the first bully who suggested such a fate for me, immediately claiming the status of legendary playground thug.

Such were the invaluable lessons of the dumb kids' class. So when the nuns promoted me to the smart kids' class midway through the school year, I had the best of both worlds. Overnight, I was anointed with academic potential, a designation all the more meaningful because I had earned it. Arriving with my broken tooth and dumb-kid rep, I instantly became the most feared and respected student in my new classroom. It was too much success for a twelve-year-old to handle. Soon after my first elevation, I remember my new seventh-grade teacher roughly pulling me aside on the playground and announcing that my head was so big, she wished she could "just pop it with a pin!" This was a disturbing concept, and still occasionally visits my dreams: a towering, wrathful nun, pink face wrapped and pinched in starched white linen, wielding a huge pin pulled from some obscure corner of her habit. This was the closest any of the good sisters ever came to abusing me, if you don't count the Fátima message. Still, given my swaggering self-importance, she showed saintly restraint.

I relished my role as the bad boy among the goody-goodies. Once, in the second half of eighth grade, our nun, a kindly old soul, fell asleep at her desk while I was reading aloud the answers to the previous night's homework from her teachers' edition of our math book. She would award this privilege to a student who had performed especially well on a test, so what I did next was abject betrayal. Before nudging her back to awareness, I read out the answers to the next few homework assignments. This was the kind of thing a dumb kid did without thinking, but among the smart kids, it was considered daring and ingenious.

The combined efforts of saints Petronille, Peter, and Joseph failed to make me a religious man, but my Catholic-school years shaped me in many ways. The nuns taught us to think about big things, about the whole sweep of life and death and right and wrong. Such thoughts could be disturbing, but they were valuable. The nuns taught us that the capacity for evil is real and present in this world, especially inside ourselves. They taught us to at least consider the moral implications of our actions and ideas, and they showed us that real goodness is in giving up something not when doing so is easy, but when it is hard.

Nevertheless, some of the best lessons came from my "dumb" classmates, and those two mid-semester promotions. It's well and good to enjoy the world's esteem, I learned, but better still to be underestimated.

Saddam on Saddam

Philadelphia Inquirer, July 2009

Saddam Hussein was perfect. From first to last, perfect in every way. So perfect—and here I hope you can grasp the subtlety of the man's self-image—that he could see and even admit to some personal flaws. How can a man who admits his own flaws be perfect? Because to be perfect he must!

After all, only Allah is completely free from error, and for a man to claim he is the equal of God would be prideful and impious; it would of all possible errors be the worst.

The Iraqi tyrant believed the world would begin to understand his true greatness only after five or perhaps even ten centuries had passed. And even though he was only imperfectly understood in his lifetime, he told his American interrogator, 100 percent of the Iraqi people had voted for him in his last presidential election. His pride in this was understandable. One hundred percent! Out of love, each and every one.

These glimpses into Saddam Hussein's character emerge from twenty-five interviews and "conversations" with the captured dictator by FBI special agent George Piro, a young Lebanese American who was chosen for the job, in part, because of his fluent Arabic. Piro was interviewed on *60 Minutes* earlier this year and most of the revelations from the sessions have been widely reported, but what particularly interested me in the agent's detailed notes was Saddam's personality.

Years ago I made a study of Saddam for the *Atlantic*. My request to interview him received no response so I pieced together a portrait of him from his speeches and published interviews, and from people who had known or interacted with him personally.

What emerged was a portrait of unfathomable, murderous vanity.

"Repetition of his image in heroic or paternal poses; repetition of his name, his slogans, his virtues, his accomplishments seeks to make his power seem inevitable, unchallengeable," I wrote. "Finally he is praised not out of affection or admiration but out of obligation. One must praise him."

What that story sought was to show how Saddam, at the peak of his power, saw himself. Having never met him, I could only speculate about his inner life. Piro's interviews with him in the months after his capture in December 2003, before he was turned over to Iraqi authorities, offer an invaluable glimpse inside Saddam's head, and to some extent into the heads of such strongmen everywhere—think of Kim Jong Il or Robert Mugabe.

Saddam was, at least in his own mind, a multifaceted genius. His boundless intellect displayed wisdom, courage, insight, leadership, military expertise, historical analysis, literary gifts . . . the list goes on and on. Part of that greatness was his generosity, which— and this says all you need to know about the man—he was even willing to extend to his enemy interrogator. In their fourteenth interview, on March 3, 2004, Saddam offered to instruct Piro in how to be a more effective questioner.

Piro asked Saddam what he meant, and the tyrant played coy.

"A doctor does not chase people asking them what is wrong," the tyrant said. "They come to him."

Piro chose not to ask for Saddam's help, but he did make a point of playing along with the sixty-six-year-old prisoner's illusions, treating him, within limits, with respect.

The agent listened to Saddam's poetry and praised it and cleverly used his supposed appreciation of the tyrant's speechwriting talents to pry open a discussion of Iraq's weapons programs—Iraq had destroyed its most dangerous weapons but continued to bluff about having them to ward off invasion or attack from Iran or the United States. Saddam said he fully intended to resume building such weapons as soon as pressure from the United Nations eased.

Piro listened to Saddam's decidedly self-aggrandizing take on some of the more notorious episodes in his career, such as the purge of 1979. Saddam filled an auditorium with top Baath Party officials, had the doors locked, and then unmasked a supposed plot to overthrow him. Chief plotters rounded up in advance were made to confess onstage, and then Saddam began fingering alleged coconspirators in the audience one by one—they were led off to be summarily tried and executed. He conducted this nightmare like theater, pacing the stage, smoking a cigar, visibly enjoying himself, alternately lecturing the terrified underlings and weeping—or pretending to weep—over their alleged betrayal. The session was videotaped, and copies were widely distributed.

Piro asked him whether such displays were orchestrated to spread fear rather than the "love" he insisted the Iraqi people felt for him, and from the tyrant's response you get the sense that he really did not much differentiate between the two concepts. Both were aspects of something more important: respect. As for the theatrics, Saddam said that he tended to smoke cigars in time of stress; that fear was only one of many emotions present at the event, which he likened to a "family gathering"; and that the video was primarily informational—made and distributed "to present information to Iraqis living outside the country concerning events occurring within Iraq."

As the discussions proceeded it became clear that Saddam was the star in the truly epic tale of his own life, and that everyone else was just a bit player. He was the all-wise, all-loving center of the world's oldest and greatest nation, the true center of human civilization, albeit a bit down on its luck in recent centuries, but certain to prevail ultimately.

Any evidence of disparity between the brutal way his regime conducted business and his own flowery and benign conception of it was either a lie, a forgery, a consequence of some "simpleton" down the chain of command, or, in cases like the wholesale displacement of the Marsh Arabs in southern Iraq (Saddam had the marshes drained) or the gassing of the Kurds, a matter of majestic imperative. There was no place in his worldview for sympathy or regret.

Shown a video of a woman from the Marsh Arab culture complaining pitifully that because of Saddam's actions she and her family had lost everything, the tyrant laughed and scoffed, "What did she have before? Reeds?"

It also seems Saddam was not wedded to any normal concept of cause and effect, at least where he was concerned. When he was asked why he invaded Kuwait, for instance, his answer would differ from one day to another: because Kuwaitis were draining Iraq's economy dry by stealing oil or because a Kuwaiti official had met a peace initiative with an insult. On another day it was because the United States and Kuwait were secretly conspiring to attack Iraq; on another because the Kuwaiti people, whom he considered historically Iraqi, had "invited him" to invade. When you are all-powerful, it seems, you don't need any one reason, or any reason, for that matter. You act because you wish to act, because fate moves through your fingertips.

When you are all-powerful you are unconstrained by logic and fairness, which are principles for lesser mortals. When Piro asked Saddam about mistreatment of prisoners during the first Gulf war, Saddam "did not deny that others may have 'behaved in a bad manner,'" but said he had not been informed of it. "He stated that he subscribes to a document much older than the Geneva Convention, the Quran. The Quran and Arab tradition believe that it is 'noble' to treat a prisoner well."

This piety is, of course, laughable coming from one of the most brutal dictators in modern times, whose prisons were notorious for routine torture and summary execution. "We assigned responsibility to who was going to handle the situation," he said in explaining his innocence of widespread executions when his regime crushed the Shiite uprising in 1991, and he grew indignant when Piro suggested that in some cases he might not have known of atrocities because he did not want to be informed of his underlings' methods. "Who says that I did not want to know?" Saddam asked. Piro informed him that he had.

The bottom line is that Saddam was not terribly concerned about consistency, moral or otherwise. He loved platitudes and saw himself as a model leader, but there was nothing he would not do to retain power. If ruling meant being brutal on occasion, so be it: "The sins of a government are not few," he said.

"He must know that it will end badly for him," I wrote in 2002. He certainly knew it two years later, when the United States had invaded Iraq; overthrown him; hunted him down; and, after gently questioning him for months, handed him back to his countrymen. He was executed on December 30, 2006.

His American imprisonment must have been a brief and bittersweet sojourn for Saddam on his road to retribution. After his capture he was cleaned up, fingerprinted, fed, and housed like an important prisoner. All his adult life he was used to people doing things for him, and here, when he was confined alone in the Baghdad Operations Center, his basic needs were all covered. He grew plants. He wrote. He ate regular meals and received good medical care. Piro listened to him and complimented his verses. After eight months of hiding in a hole, it must have been a pleasant respite.

At least compared with his own harsh world, where his many local enemies waited. His death was a horror, but a fitting final scene for the saga that was his life, and an end he had foreseen. He once predicted that his enemies, if they ever got hold of him, would tear him apart. As Saddam stood brave and defiant on the scaffold, exchanging insults and taunts with those who had come to see him hang, his final moments would have merely confirmed what he already knew. He was leaving a world ruled by brute force, by cruelty and cunning and vengeance, where, for a time, he had prevailed.

Zero Dark Thirty Is Not Pro-Torture

The Atlantic, January 2013

In the opening minutes of *Zero Dark Thirty* there are two ugly interrogation scenes, which haunt the rest of the experience and which have come to haunt critical reception of the film itself.

After we hear, against a black screen, the terrified voices of Americans trapped on the upper floors of the doomed, burning towers on 9/11, the movie opens on a character named Ammar, suspended from the ceiling by chains attached to both wrists. It is two years later. Ammar is bloody, filthy, and exhausted. We learn quickly that he is an Al Qaeda middleman, and a nephew of Khalid Sheikh Mohammed, architect of the 9/11 attacks. Ammar is believed to know details of a pending attack in Saudi Arabia, and he is uncooperative.

His questioning by CIA officer Daniel is uncomfortable to watch. It is brutal and ultimately futile. As his tormenters fold him into a small punishment box, demanding the day of the attack, Ammar murmurs "Saturday," then "Sunday," then "Monday," then "Thursday," then "Friday."

In the script, referring to the frustrated Daniel, the scene closes with the words, "Once again, he's learned nothing."

The subsequent Saudi attacks occur. Daniel accepts responsibility for the failure, along with his new associate, the film's heroine, Maya. This is all in the first minutes of the movie. Torture has been tried, and it has failed. It is Maya then who then proposes something different. Why not trick him?

"He doesn't know we failed," says Maya. "We can tell him anything."

And it is cleverness, coated with kindness, that produces something useful. The Saudi attack can no longer be prevented, but Ammar offers them a name. More correctly, a pseudonym, what in Arabic is called a *kunya*, a nom de guerre: Abu Ahmad al-Kuwait, the father of Ahmed from Kuwait. Maya doesn't know it yet—indeed, she won't find out for years—but this is the first small clue on the long trail to Abbottabad.

Zero Dark Thirty, or *ZD30*, by director Kathryn Bigelow and screenwriter Mark Boal, is an extraordinarily impressive dramatization of the ten-year hunt for Osama bin Laden, which I wrote about in far more detail in my book *The Finish*. Warmly praised by many film critics and a box office hit, *ZD30* is sure to be in the running for major recognition during the coming awards season. But it has also been attacked by some as a false version of the story that effectively advocates the use of torture. To put it simply, they argue that the film, while brilliant, shows torture to have played an important role in finding Osama, which they say is not true. It is reminiscent of the late movie critic Pauline Kael's memorable put-down of director Sam Peckinpah as a virtuoso of "fascistic" art.

This no doubt has come as a shock to Bigelow, whom I have never met, but who has been described to me as "someone who will stop to lift a snail off the sidewalk." The criticism is unfair, and its reading of both the film and the actual story is mistaken.

A screenplay is more like a sonnet than a novel. Action onscreen unfolds with visceral immediacy, but any story with sweep—this one unfolds over nearly a decade—can be told only with broad impressionistic strokes. The challenge is greater in trying to tell a true story. It is easy to see how the interrogation scenes in the beginning color the entire tale, but they are necessary. They are part of the story. Without them, I suspect some of the same critics now accusing it of being pro-torture would instead be calling *ZD30* a whitewash.

First, let's consider whether the film is pro-torture. This is the easiest charge to debunk. I have already noted the dramatic failure depicted in the opening scenes with Ammar. The futility of the approach is part of the more general organizational failure depicted in the movie's first half, culminating in a dramatization of the tragic 2009 bombing of Camp Chapman, in Khowst, Afghanistan, where an Al Qaeda infiltrator wiped out an entire CIA field office. The agency is shown to be not only failing to find bin Laden and dismantle Al Qaeda, but on the losing end of the fight. In case the point hasn't been made clearly enough, a visit from an angry CIA chief to the U.S. embassy in Pakistan in the next scene underlines it:

"There's nobody else, hidden away on some other floor," he says. "This is just us. And we are failing. We're spending billions of dollars. People are dying. We're still no closer to defeating our enemy."

The work that leads to Abbottabad in the second half of the film unfolds as dramatic detective work in the office and the field, and ends with a faithful and detailed reenactment of the raid on the Abbottabad compound. Through it all, Maya is playing a long game, in dogged pursuit of a lead, battling those in command more preoccupied with short-term goals—finding and killing Al Qaeda operational figures. Torture is presented as part of this story, something Maya accepts as necessary, but to the extent it is portrayed it is shown to be, at best, only marginally useful and both politically and morally toxic.

So, how true is it? I think it was a mistake for those involved in the film to suggest that *ZD30* is "journalistic," and to have touted their access to SEAL team members and CIA field officers. No matter how remarkable their research and access, the film spills no state secrets, and no feature film can tell a story like this without aggressively condensing characters and events, fictionalizing dialogue, etc. Boal's script is just 102 pages, not even ten thousand words, the length of a longish magazine article.

Within these limits the film is remarkably accurate, certainly well within what we all understand by the Hollywood label "based on a true story," which works as both a boast and a disclaimer. There apparently was a female CIA field officer who performed heroic service in the ten-year hunt for Osama, and whose fixation on "Ahmed from Kuwait" helped steer the effort to success. In the film she is seen butting heads with an intelligence bureaucracy that regards her fixation on Ahmed as wishful thinking. This makes for some dramatic scenes, and gives Jessica Chastain a great many chances to brood with ethereal intensity. The real-life "Maya" may be even more beautiful than Chastain, but she was just one of many officers and analysts fixated on "Ahmed," in an agency that never stopped regarding him as an important lead. The Saudi attacks in the beginning of the film, identified as the "Khobar Towers" incident, actually occurred in 1996, six years prior to the action in the film. The raid itself involved four helicopters—two Chinooks and two Black Hawks—not the three Black Hawks shown. Key planning sessions that occurred in the White House Situation Room, chaired by President Obama, are depicted as having happened at Langley with CIA director Leon Panetta—indeed, those who have accused the current administration of rolling out the red carpet for Bigelow and Boal in the hope of hyping its role may be surprised to find that the president, whose participation was central throughout, has been almost completed edited out. The list could go on. The same is true of any film "based on a true story," whether it's the Jerry Bruckheimer/Ridley Scott version of my book *Black Hawk Down*, or Stephen Spielberg's *Lincoln*.

Everyone understands the rules of this game. Theater is theater. It is a show, not a scrupulous presentation of fact. We ought to feel betrayed only when a filmmaker departs egregiously and deliberately from the record, the kind of thing Oliver Stone has made his trademark, substituting what he thinks *might* be true, or perhaps would prefer to believe, for what is known. One of the attractions of a true story is, after all, that it be at least . . . sort of . . . *true*. But filmic truth will always stumble over the sheer complexity of reality, which is messy, often contradictory and confusing, and which only rarely lines up neatly enough for a two-hour script. Hollywood's "true story" aims only to color safely inside the lines of history.

In this broader sense, *ZD30* is remarkably true. The hunt for Osama bin Laden and other Al Qaeda leaders began with efforts that were clumsy, costly, and cruel. We wrongly invaded Iraq, for instance. We stupidly embraced a regime of torture in our military prisons. Some of the steps we took were tragic and are likely to be enduring national embarrassments. But over the years, tactics, priorities, personnel, even administrations changed. The nation learned how to fight this new enemy intelligently. Through it all, the search for Osama proceeded with bureaucracy's unique talent for obduracy. This isn't as sexy or dramatic as watching Jessica Chastain paling before the stink and blood of rough interrogation, a red-tressed Ahab pursuing her lead through bullets, bombs, and boneheaded bosses . . . but it stays within the lines. For two hours or so I'm willing to munch my popcorn and enjoy.

As for the real story, the question of what role torture played is more difficult. Torture, or coercive interrogation, is a subject I wrote about at length in this magazine—"The Dark Art of Interrogation," in October 2003. I argued then, before the revelations of Abu Ghraib and other scandals, that the use of such morally repugnant tactics may yield important information, and may even be morally compelling in certain rare circumstances, but that it ought to be banned, and that interrogators who practiced it should do so only at risk of being disciplined or prosecuted. The word itself, *torture*, is pejorative, in that it equates keeping a prisoner awake with the most sordid practices of the Inquisition. But even mild pressure does tend to lead rapidly to severe mistreatment, as we saw during the Bush administration, which made the mistake of authorizing it—a step that predictably led to tragic and widespread abuses. These have been ably documented by, for one, Alex Gibney (a prominent critic of *ZD30*) in his stirring "Taxi to the Dark Side"; by tenacious journalists like Seymour Hersh; and by the candid snapshots of depraved American military jailers. Former vice president Dick Cheney and others have argued that this coercive regimen produced vital information, which prevented terror attacks; but so far we have only their word for it, and plenty of other informed voices that contradict it. I do not know the answer, although the reluctance of the current professedly anti-torture administration to explore and punish past abuses may suggest that such practices were not altogether useless. The one certain thing is that they happened, and on a large scale. They became such a scandal that the practices were halted by the Bush administration itself in 2004. But by then the early interrogations that put "Ahmed from Kuwait" on the CIA's radar had all happened, and nearly all had involved torture.

These are facts, most of which were unearthed by reporters seeking to expose the abuses. Critics of these practices, and of the film, now find themselves in the curious position of arguing that torture played no role in the intelligence-gathering that led to Abbottabad. This is presumably because if the opposite were true, then the hunt's successful outcome might lead weak minds to conclude that torture has been proved effective.

Their logic has become, forgive the word, *tortured.* The key interrogation that focused the CIA's attention on "Ahmed" concerned Mohammed al-Qhatani, whose relentless months-long ordeal was detailed in a particularly gruesome Wikileaks disclosure, a case that prompted the Department of Defense to rewrite its guidelines for interrogation—part of that overall course correction in 2004. Qhatani said "Ahmed" was a key player in Al Qaeda, and one of Osama bin Laden's prime couriers, a fact that elevated him to prime importance in the search. Those who now say that torture played no role in Qhatani's revelations argue that he offered the information *before* the rough stuff started. I don't know if this is true, but I'll accept it for argument's sake. It hardly removes torture from the mix. The essential ingredient in any coercive interrogation is not the actual infliction of pain or discomfort, but *fear.* There can be little doubt that well before Qhatani was actually tortured, he knew damn well that he was in trouble. In the film *ZD30,* Ammar, who is a fictional amalgam, gives up the name *after* his torture sessions. Does this mean that the prior pain and discomfort played no role? In either case, real or fictional, torture creates a context. It creates fear. The only way to know if Qhatani would have been cooperative without being pressured is to have conducted a torture-free interrogation, which did not happen.

Fear was a part of the climate of American interrogations in those years. I detailed for this magazine in May 2007, in a story entitled "The Ploy," the clever and essentially nonviolent inter-rogation of a detainee in Iraq that led to the successful targeting of Al Qaeda's leader in Mesopotamia, Abu Musab al-Zarqawi. The story was later told in even greater detail in a book, *How to Break a Terrorist,* by the interrogator himself, who wrote under the pseudonym Matthew Alexander; he has offered the story as proof that an artful interrogator need not employ coercion. Yet the detainee in his own story voluntarily submitted to questioning in part to avoid being sent to Abu Ghraib, which by then had a fearful reputation.

The most prominent among those who now insist torture played no part in the hunt for Osama bin Laden are senators Dianne Feinstein, Carl Levin, and John McCain. All three serve on congressional committees with access to classified material, and are in a position to know what they are talking about. Indeed, in a letter protesting *ZD30* to Sony's chairman Michael Lynton earlier this month, they claim to have reviewed "six million pages" of intelligence records, which may help explain why Congress has such a hard time getting anything done.

But there is lawyerly subtlety here. In the letter, they raise the rather fine point about the timing of Qhatani's mention of "Ahmed" as proof that torture was not involved, and write that the CIA "did not first learn" of the courier's existence "from CIA detainees subjected to coercive interrogation techniques." True. The CIA first heard the name from Mohamedou Ould Slahi, a Mauritanian who was arrested in 2001 at the behest of American authorities and questioned in Mauritania and in Jordan. He says he was tortured. I believe him. Acting CIA director Michael Morrell, another critic of the film's veracity, has been more careful. He does not deny that torture is part of the story, although he uses different words to describe it:

"Some [information leading to Osama bin Laden] came from detainees subjected to enhanced techniques, but there were many other sources as well," he wrote. "And, importantly, whether enhanced interrogation techniques were the only timely and effective way to obtain information from those detainees, as the film suggests, is a matter of debate that cannot and never will be definitively resolved."

I'm with Morrell on this. Torture is part of the story, but not a key part of it, just as the film depicts. The story of finding and killing Osama bin Laden makes a good case neither for nor against torture. It makes a poor case for torture because neither of the original sources—neither Slahi nor Qhatani—necessarily realized he was giving up something terribly important by naming "Ahmed from Kuwait." Probably, neither even knew who "Ahmed" really was. Neither Slahi and Qhatani nor their questioners could have imagined that "Ahmed" would end up sheltering Osama in Abbottabad. Khalid Sheikh Mohammed could not have known this either, but he certainly realized the man's importance. Despite repeated waterboarding he lied about "Ahmed." So much for torture producing a breakthrough. Ironically, Mohammed's mendacity—his claim contradicted everyone else's—further piqued the agency's interest. Under torture he lied, but his lies *helped*.

We don't know much about the key breakthrough that led to Osama bin Laden. That came years later, when the CIA was finally able to connect the pseudonym "Ahmed from Kuwait" with a real person, Ibrahim Saeed Ahmed. In the film this moment is handled perfunctorily. A young CIA officer simply hands the information to Maya and says, "It's him," explaining that she happened across the nugget while "painstakingly" reviewing "old files." My sources at the CIA refused to say how the connection was actually made, saying only that it involved sources from "a third country." One high-level agency official told me, "You could write a book about how we [did it]." The agency says torture was not involved, and there's no evidence to suggest it was.

If you start the story of finding Osama bin Laden from there, and only from there, then the hunt was torture-free. It's almost a passable argument. Until then, after all, "Ahmed from Kuwait" was just one insubstantial lead among many, just a semi-fact in an ocean of facts. But torture was in the room when that semi-fact was delivered up, and belongs in any truthful telling of it.

Gibney, an especially influential critic given his standing as a filmmaker and as a principled opponent of such methods, agrees that it was right for Bigelow and Boal to show the torture, but argues that they ought to have used these scenes to more clearly demonstrate how futile and "ridiculous" such tactics were. He sees torture as "one of the great moral issues of our times," and views this story as one that could have made a strong argument *against* the use of torture. This is something that Bigelow and Boal might well have intended. If the film leans in any direction on the subject, it is in this one. Gibney doesn't see it that way. He is a passionate artist, and makes films that are shaped by his convictions. That is a fine thing to do. But pure storytelling is not always about making an argument, no matter how worthy. It can be about, simply, telling the truth. Because torture was in the mix during all of the early interrogations, it would be wrong to ignore it, and impossible to say it had no effect.

The truth about torture itself is not clear-cut. Those who argue that it simply does not work go well beyond saying that it is wrong. They do not even consider it a moral question. After all, if threatening or mistreating a detainee will *always* fail to produce useful intelligence, who other than a sadist would bother? I am not convinced. I think the moral question arises precisely because torture, or more precisely, *fear*, can be an effective tool in interrogation. If we as a nation ban it, we do so despite that fact. We forgo the advantages of torture to claim higher moral ground. In order for that be to a virtuous choice, as opposed to a purely practical one, it means we must give up something of value—in this case intelligence that might forestall tragedy.

That is not the choice our nation made back in 2001, when this story begins. The fear that contaminated our military prisons in subsequent years became a scandal. It would be very tidy to conclude that because it was wrong, it was also useless, that it yielded nothing of value. *ZD30* doesn't do that, nor should you.

Acknowledgments

I would like to thank all of the editors and copy editors who have saved me from a great many errors and grammatical atrocities in these stories. I am particularly indebted to Cullen Murphy and Graydon Carter at *Vanity Fair*, and to Scott Stossel, James Bennet, and Yvonne Rolzhausen at the *Atlantic*.